Housework and Housewives in Modern American Advertising

Previous Publications

Manly Meals and Mom's Home Cooking: Cookbooks and Gender in Modern America (June 2003)

Housework and Housewives in Modern American Advertising

Married to the Mop

Jessamyn Neuhaus

HOUSEWORK AND HOUSEWIVES IN MODERN AMERICAN ADVERTISING
Copyright © Jessamyn Neuhaus, 2011.

All rights reserved.

First published in hardcover in 2011 by PALGRAVE MACMILLAN® in the United States—a division of St. Martin's Press LLC, 175 Fifth Avenue, New York, NY 10010.

Where this book is distributed in the UK, Europe and the rest of the world, this is by Palgrave Macmillan, a division of Macmillan Publishers Limited, registered in England, company number 785998, of Houndmills, Basingstoke, Hampshire RG21 6XS.

Palgrave Macmillan is the global academic imprint of the above companies and has companies and representatives throughout the world.

Palgrave® and Macmillan® are registered trademarks in the United States, the United Kingdom, Europe and other countries.

ISBN: 978–1–137–34723–7

Library of Congress Cataloging-in-Publication Data

Neuhaus, Jessamyn.
    Housework and housewives in American advertising : married to the mop / Jessamyn Neuhaus.
        p. cm.
    ISBN 978–0–230–11489–0 (hardback)
        1. Sex role in advertising—United States. 2. Stereotypes (Social psychology) in advertising—United States. 3. Women in advertising—United States. 4. Housewives as consumers—United States. I. Title.

HF5827.85.N48 2011
659.1088'640973—dc23   2011018676

A catalogue record of the book is available from the British Library.

This book is printed on paper suitable for recycling and made from fully managed and sustained forest sources. Logging, pulping and manufacturing processes are expected to conform to the environmental regulations of the country of origin.

Design by MPS Limited, A Macmillan Company.

First PALGRAVE MACMILLAN paperback edition: August 2013

10 9 8 7 6 5 4 3 2 1

To Ella, Caroline, Natalie, Jacob, Manny, and Solomon

Contents

Figures

Acknowledgments

I am indebted to the State University of New York Plattsburgh for a Presidential Research Grant and to New York State / United University Professionals for a Professional Development Individual Award, both of which allowed me to pursue the research for this book. In addition, a NYS/UUP Dr. Nuala McGann Drescher Leave allowed me to take a semester's leave from teaching in order to focus on writing. A fellowship at the Institute for Ethics in Public Life at SUNY Plattsburgh, under the leadership of Dr. Tom Moran, helped me devote the necessary time to clarifying this project in its early stages. Thanks also to research assistants Victoria Boccassini and Dylan Brown for tracking down magazine advertisements.

Female Faculty Advancing our Research (FFAR) on the SUNY Plattsburgh campus provided both practical and emotional support during the research for and the writing of *Married to the Mop*. Thank you to all the members: Drs. Monica Corbineau, Lauren Eastwood, Elizabeth Ketner, Martha Lance, Connie Oxford, Robin Riley, Susan Stewart, and Connie Shemo. I am also truly grateful for the support of my colleagues in the History Department at SUNY Plattsburgh: Drs. Sylvie Beaudreau, Vincent Carey, Wendy Gordon, Jeff Hornibrook, Gary Kroll, Jim Lindgren, Jim Rice, Richard Schafer, Doug Skopp, Connie Shemo, and Stuart Voss. A special thanks to Dr. Hornibrook for his suggestion to just take it chapter by chapter.

A fellowship with the Advertising Educational Foundation's Visiting Professor Program in New York City provided me with invaluable insights into the business of ad making. Thanks to all the agency employees who took time out of their busy days to speak with me. I am especially grateful to Sharon Hudson at the AEF, John Bowman and Heather Murphy at Saatchi & Saatchi, and Dr. Katherine Parkin for alerting me to this opportunity and sharing her insights.

A research grant from the John W. Hartman Center for Sales, Advertising & Marketing History at Duke University allowed me to complete a major portion of my research. A special thank you to Lynne Eaton and all the staff and archivists at the Duke University Rare Book, Manuscript, and Special Collections Library for their knowledgeable and friendly assistance.

Thank you also to Dr. Jennifer Scanlon who generously took time to talk with me about different research and writing strategies at an early point in my work; Ed Wilson, reference librarian at the Manchester Public Library in Manchester, Connecticut, who efficiently and cheerfully made available the *Beunhogar* magazines I needed; and Katherine French-Fuller at the Hartman Center and Marisa Kritikson at the Archive Center for their assistance procuring illustrations. Finally, thank you to Chris Chappell and the anonymous reader at Palgrave Macmillan, and Dr. Pamela Walker Laird, for their excellent revision suggestions.

I am extraordinarily fortunate to have the friends and family that I do: thank you all for the many ways you cheered me on during this work. Dr. Kelly Austin opened her home to me during my research trip to Los Angeles. Dr. Michelle Ladd drove me around, helped me brainstorm ideas, and read portions of this book offering both her rigorous critique and her loving encouragement. Dr. Kelly Douglass, supermom and avowed housework hater, gave me courage at several important junctures. I am especially beholden to my parents, Dr. John Neuhaus and A. Lori Neuhaus, for always being my biggest fans. My sister Alison Neuhaus regularly boosted my confidence as a mother and a scholar. My aunt, Dana T. Payne, and grandmother, Alison Merriam Payne, offered hospitality and expressed a flattering interest in this project during my research trips to Washington, D.C.

Most importantly, I am thankful beyond words for the abiding love and support of my significant other, Douglas Butdorf. Navigating our marital boat together through the sometimes treacherous waters of a shared domestic life has been and will continue to be the best ride of my life. For being my partner in all things and because he can always make me laugh, Doug is the one to whom I owe the most.

This book is dedicated to the next generation: Our awesome and amazing son, Solomon William Neuhaus; our Buckeye nephews Jacob and Emmanuel Butdorf; and especially our beautiful and beloved nieces, Ella, Caroline, and Natalie Neuhaus, with all my love. When you grow up and make homes of your own, remember that no matter what you see in the commercials, *real* men do housework.

Introduction

The rejected suitor continues to pursue the woman, sending her flowers and candy, dedicating songs to her on the radio, calling her, and emailing her. As his obsession grows, he follows her to the grocery store, lurks outside her house as she goes about her daily chores, and even watches her dust the living room via a webcam. A soundtrack plays in his mind, articulating his pain: "Baby, come back" and "Don't you want me baby? Don't you want me, oooh . . ." In one of the most memorable advertising campaigns of recent years, mops, brooms, and feather dusters pine for the women who have abandoned them after purchasing new Swiffer cleaning products like the Swiffer Wet Jet. The commercials end with the tagline "Swiffer gives cleaning a whole new meaning."[1]

On the contrary, there's very little that is new about the meaning of cleaning in these television commercials, particularly the person who's doing the cleaning. She's casually but neatly dressed, thin and attractive but not overtly sexy, and working in what is implicitly her nuclear family's huge, clutter-free, and well-appointed living room or kitchen. The person doing the cleaning in most commercials for such products looks a lot like her. She's doing the laundry, she's cleaning the toilet, and she's running the dishwasher. She's often—but not always—white. Like the Swiffer actresses, these women are all gazing with pleasure at their houses, and the products they're using are quickly, easily, even magically removing the hard labor from cleaning. Most significantly, all these women are transforming housework into homemaking.

'Twas ever thus. Beginning in the last decades of the 1800s with the emergence of the modern advertising industry, advertisements for housework products targeted one type of consumer, identified by both marketers and ordinary Americans as "the housewife." In turn, advertising portrayed the housewife as one particular kind of woman doing one particular kind of labor in one particular kind of home, and as *Married to the Mop* demonstrates, continued to do so for a remarkably long time. I show that although Second Wave feminism and other social changes in the 1970s and 1980s finally forced the most blatantly stereotypical depictions of housewives out of ads and commercials, domesticity remained an exclusively female activity throughout modern American advertising. Today advertising continues to signify housework as gendered caring for the home not with images of apron-wearing housewives in heels but with what I've termed "the housewife mom." The housewife mom in advertising—our most significant twenty-first century public representation of housework—continues to perform the same function as the housewife did in all modern advertising: she defines domestic life, turning labor into homemaking and helping maintain normative ideals of femininity.

In order to fully understand the significance of housework advertising, we need to understand the history of housework, the emergence of the cultural figure of the housewife, and the evolution of modern advertising. Americans began to define household labor as "housework" at the end of the 1800s, when the second industrial revolution dramatically altered the U.S. economy and daily life. Beginning in the mid-1800s, as the United States' industrial economy replaced an agricultural one, individual homes and families transformed as well, from sites of subsistence and production into private spaces of individual consumption. While certain kinds of labor associated with family life had long been perceived as either men's work or women's work, industrialization dramatically altered both the physical tasks and the cultural meanings of tasks undertaken in the home. These tasks, newly distinguished from paid wage work, became "housework," thereby defining all domestic labor and care as the responsibility of wives and mothers.

A number of critical technological developments shaped the evolution of modern (gendered) housework. First, the removal of a wide variety of productive tasks from the family dwelling: buying clothes instead of making them; buying meat and vegetables instead of raising and growing them, and so on. Buying rather than producing household necessities evolved unevenly over the course of the nineteenth century, but by the beginning of the 1900s, the lion's share of the labor previously done as productive subsistence family work in domestic dwellings now consisted of purchases made outside the home. Second, the availability of utilities and household technologies changed the nature of work done in the home. Although again unevenly distributed and developed (electricity took far longer to reach wide swathes of rural America, for instance), by 1920 most Americans believed wholeheartedly that even the poorest homes should be equipped with electricity, municipal water supplies (and a bathroom), and a host of household appliances, most significantly an electric or gas stove and a refrigerator.[2] In the next decade, as prices fell, credit buying became popular and more Americans had access to utilities.

Changing home and factory technologies eased certain aspects of household labor in terms of sheer physical effort, but created new higher standards for household cleaning, and multiple new types of household labor. To cite a well-known example, when household cooking moved from the open hearth to the cookstove, one type of labor (the difficulty and danger of cooking over an open flame) disappeared, but another (the dirty and time-consuming job of cleaning and blacking the stove) quickly took its place. Food standards rose as well, with Americans now expecting more elaborate meals than the one-dish stews most common to fireplace cookery. Moreover, as technology changed the nature of housework, it fell more and more directly to the female head of household—the housewife—to do the labor alone.[3] For instance, vacuum cleaners made the filthy work of taking up carpets, hauling them outside, and beating them clean obsolete. However, carpet cleaning formerly had been an infrequent (twice-yearly) task, and Americans commonly saw it as appropriate labor for children or even husbands. But now the housewife could, and everyone seemed to expect she would, vacuum at least once a week, possibly even once a day. So vacuum cleaners brought relief of some labor, but replaced it with a far more gender-specific labor and far higher standards of what constituted "clean."

Concurrently, the housewife became a more clearly middle-class ideal. As industrialization drew greater distinctions between home and work and as a growing middle class of white-collar worker families found an increasing number of ways to display their new economic status via domestic objects and living arrangements, the housewife became newly invested with a middle-class identity and assumed new prominence as a cultural figure. In fact, only in contrast to working-class women and servant women could the housewife embody the ideal of American womanhood. The majority of pre-industrialized homes in the 1600s and 1700s relied on some type of hired household "help" and in some states, indentured servants and slaves, but as opportunities for wage labor in the new factory-driven economy increased and slavery became illegal, the number of women (especially the most desirable servants—young English, Irish, or German immigrant women) available and willing to undertake the role of household servant decreased. Ironically, just as a rapidly growing middle class of white-collar workers sought to hire household help, the pool of servant labor diminished.

By the early 1900s, millions of servants, now consisting primarily of older African American women, still worked cleaning and cooking in American homes, but the pool of available labor never met the (perceived) need. Training schools and cookery classes aimed at producing more servants for middle- and upper-class homes had little success. In some ways, modern housewifery in the 1920s and 1930s seemed to demand the presence of a servant who would do the dirty work while the dainty modern housewife managed her home, maintained her looks and her marriage, and devoted herself to her children. But in reality, by 1920 the majority of Americans began to give up on solving the so-called servant problem and accepted a definition of housework that no longer involved servant labor.[4]

Changing definitions of cleanliness also shaped the evolution of modern housework. The issues of health—both public and private—and the growing acceptance of germ theory from the early to late 1800s clearly influenced the priorities assigned to certain types of cleaning, the methods used to achieve a clean home, and the definition of "clean" itself. But Americans consistently and thoroughly rejected any possible alternative—such as the short-lived efforts of reformers at the turn of the twentieth century who advocated cooperative housekeeping—to the postindustrial structures of home and work. Thus, American values deeply rooted in capitalism and individualism also played a key role in the emergence of modern housework.[5]

Advertising, too, dramatically changed during this period. In the last decades of the 1800s, and definitely by 1900, all the necessary components of our contemporary consumer society were firmly in place: mechanized mass production that revolutionized manufacturing; a truly national market, with Americans all over the country newly linked by improving transportation (particularly the railroads); and new methods of communication such as the telegraph. The venues for advertising also proliferated in the last decades of the 1800s. Daily newspapers became increasingly available, as did other forums for advertising: handbills, posters, pamphlets, illustrated trading cards, the walking billboard "sandwich man," and ads on railway cars. When magazines became standard reading material for millions of Americans, they drew on increasingly sophisticated technologies of printing and photography to create arresting visual advertising. Broadcast commercials became ubiquitous as radio evolved, and advertising went on to play an instrumental role in the creation of the earliest television programming during the post–World War II era.[6]

This is not to say that advertising in and of itself never existed before the nineteenth century. Throughout history we find evidence of people publicly informing other people of goods, services, and events.[7] However, as manufacturing increased exponentially and the number of products available for purchase exceeded the basic needs of Americans, advertising took on the task of creating consumer desire. The new consumerism meant most Americans would be engaged not in subsistence but, to varying degrees, in shopping. Along came a new phalanx of advertising professionals (a change from the previous eras, when manufacturers or retailers themselves created their own advertising) to help move the plethora of new products out of the factory and into consumers' shopping baskets.[8]

The new industry devoted to creating advertising advanced and implemented a whole host of techniques under the umbrella of what we now call "marketing." From the creation of branding and brands—the linking of very specific images and emotions, an "image," with one specific product in order to differentiate it from essentially identical products—to the concept of market research and developing advertising based on quantifiable consumer predictors, modern advertising established ways and means for connecting the individual consumer to vast networks of manufacturing and selling. In the first decades of the 1900s, advertising agencies began to perfect the idea of an "appeal," carefully researching, choosing, and then implementing strategies for selling products based not on the measurable quality of a product but on some less tangible, more emotional or psychological reward—the basis of modern advertising.[9] Agencies also began to specialize within their own field, and today copywriters, creative directors, art directors, account managers, and assorted research and media specialists make up an advertising agency.

From its emergence as a professional stand-alone industry, advertising (and the companies who hired ad agencies) believed that the white middle- to upper-class married woman should be the primary target for many products, particularly those associated with cleaning, cooking, and childcare, and that the figure of the housewife should often appear in advertising aimed at these consumers; in short, that an image of a housewife would help sell housework products. But advertising was only one of many public discourses and discussions that shaped the cultural figure of "the housewife" in the modern era. Indeed, from our first years as a sovereign nation, advisors and experts urged Americans to strive toward certain gendered domestic ideals embodied in the figure of the housewife.[10] During the Progressive Era and the emergence of "scientific housekeeping" and home economics in the early 1900s and 1920s, educated white women dictated a highly idealized, unobtainable domestic ideal of "efficiency" to other American women, especially immigrants. Home economists changed from the earnest founders of a movement that sought to apply rigorous science education to the work of the home in the early 1900s into shills for home-appliance and food-processing corporations by the 1930s, employing the cultural figure of the housewife to set an impossibly high standard of domesticity. In the 1940s, World War II U.S. home-front propaganda campaigns drew heavily on the figure of the housewife, investing her domestic responsibilities with new patriotic import. In the postwar era, the figure of the housewife resided at the heart of what Betty Friedan famously identified as the feminine mystique—rigid gender norms, bolstered by popular media (including advertising) and psychology, that strictly limited women's lives to motherhood and the domestic sphere.[11]

To what extent was the housewife a lived reality and to what extent was she an idealized symbol? While the housewife as a domestic ideal and a signifier of separate gendered spheres undoubtedly flourished throughout the nineteenth and twentieth century, "separate spheres" headed by wage-earning husbands and domestic care-giving wives only partially described the diverse experiences of real Americans. Obviously no wage-earning woman experienced such a sharply divided world, particularly considering how many such women were self-employed or did paid work at home.[12] As a racialized figure, the housewife ideal excluded women of color for much of our history. Even middle- to upper-class white married women who might have appeared to embody the housewife ideal at times exploited, circumvented, or reworked it in order to enact public, political change. Historian Glenna Matthews argues that "when the cult of domesticity [around 1830] reached its height, middle-class women began to organize for exerting influence in the world as never before in such a way that public and private values were genuinely intermingled rather than being dichotomized." Moreover, "domestic feminism would survive into the twentieth century when it surface[d] as the 'municipal housekeeping' argument for woman suffrage."[13]

Women who self-identified as housewives protested that the 1878 U.S. census did not include homemakers in the category of "gainful workers"; planned and implemented boycotts to protest high food prices in the early 1900s; lobbied for food and rent price controls during the Great Depression; and worked for improved residential neighborhood life in the 1950s. The shared identity of "housewife" was one necessary precursor to the emergence of the Second Wave feminist movement in the 1960s and 1970s, and the extensive popular discussion and debate about the very term "housewife" in 1960s women's magazines indicates that ordinary women perceived it as a real but mutable and fluctuating identity.[14] But while history shows complex and varied ways in which real women negotiated domestic gender norms and identity, the cultural *ideal* of the housewife remained fixed and severely limited. Defined and imagined again and again—by household advisors, by cultural commentators, by home economics instructors, by women's magazines, by television shows, by the popular press—as middle- to upper-class, slim, pretty, and until the 1970s, white, the heterosexual and child-bearing housewife figure gendered domesticity, family, home, and the work of the home as female in public discourse. This is particularly evident in modern advertising.

A range of factors shaped the assumption that housework advertising should be aimed at and utilize certain images of housewives, including demonstrable evidence about Americans' purchasing habits, but at the core was the way gender norms dictated the "common sense" belief that men make money and women spend money.[15] From the beginning of modern advertising, the majority of creators and consumers of advertising assumed that women had more interest in, more time for, and a larger emotional investment in consumerism than did men. Moreover, the professional class who created and worked in the advertising industry (and, in fact, all Americans) never defined those potential "women" consumers without also making certain assumptions about race and class. Well into the 1960s, the major advertising agencies and their clients saw little need to consider other potential markets, assuming that advertising created with white, middle-class women in mind had the best chance of success. Historian Roland Marchland asserts that as it emerged full force in the 1920s, modern advertising drew primarily on fantasy images of upper-class luxury when depicting domestic life—*as it ought to be*.[16] That domestic ideal, with a female consumer at its heart, shaped to a large extent how advertisers envisioned to whom and in what way they should market a wide range of commodities.

The 1920s and 1930s saw both ad agencies and the companies that hired them insisting ever more firmly that much of their efforts needed to be aimed at women. But it wasn't only them. At this time, a host of experts espoused a similar definition of woman's social role as consumer. In the new consumer society, smart shopping now defined clever housekeeping. Like the professionals at the advertising agencies, home economists, women's magazine writers, and household-manual authors made a set of interlocking assumptions about the housewife/consumer: they could not define the ideal domestic and consumer role for a woman without also drawing on beliefs about race and class. Advertising agencies and their clients rarely, if ever, said so explicitly, but "Mrs. Consumer," the object of such concerted marketing efforts and the subject of household efficiency expert Christine Frederick's influential 1929 book by the same name, actually meant "Mrs. White Middle Class Housewife Consumer."[17] Ad makers' focus on housewives only increased in the following decades, especially in the post–World War II era when marketing experts explicitly urged advertisers to craft appeals based on the presumed psychology of the average housewife. They asserted that the fundamental role of housework advertising should be convincing her "to see housework as a way of expressing her individual creativity and affirming her femininity."[18]

It should not be surprising that in the 1920s, advertising agencies, their clients, and other advertisers made certain assumptions about housewives in the United States, and that subsequent advertising reflected those assumptions. What's more surprising is how long-lived those assumptions—and the images of housewives in advertising that they fueled—proved to be. In large part, the history of housewives in advertising from the late 1800s to the late 1900s simply illustrates a long-lived stereotype of the domesticated female in advertising.[19] Importantly, it cannot definitively measure the real-life impact and influence of that stereotype.[20] At any point in time, consumers undoubtedly experienced a wide range of individual responses to any single housework ad or commercial, from indifference to dislike to pleasure, and advertising had a range of influences on actual consumer purchasing. But recorded individual interpretations by ordinary American consumers in any truly significant number (unmediated by any marketing or media source) of specific housework advertising such as ads, commercials, coupons, or other types of marketing campaigns, do not exist. In answer to this problem, scholars offer a wide range of analytical approaches when it comes to understanding the complexities of advertising, from reader-response theory to purely textual analysis.[21] Feminist criticism of advertising examines both the content of advertising as well as its potentially negative impact on women and girls.[22]

Advertising industry experts also vary widely in their conclusions about how well or to what extent advertising even achieves its principal goal of selling products. Marketing research offers significant insights into consumer habits, yet the most sophisticated contemporary marketing studies have yet to find a failsafe formula that measures an ad or commercial or other promotion's ability to ensure that at the point of purchase, a consumer will reach for the advertised product.[23]

I draw on two types of sources to explore the meaning and influence of housework advertising from the late 1800s to today. First, I examine ads, commercials, and other marketing materials themselves. Advertisements and commercials from the past do not offer a realistic depiction of American domestic lives but rather evidence of what images of housework and domesticity dominated the marketplace. They offer important clues about the nature and power of the culturally constructed housewife figure. *Married to the Mop* analyzes these sources closely because we cannot let the images and copy from ads and commercials be relegated to the realms of forgotten ephemera. Thoroughly tracing the history of those images is essential because when it comes to housework—to the actual scrubbing of the sink or the mopping of the floor—advertising is by far the most widespread, the most visible, and the most important discourse in the twentieth and the early twenty-first century United States. As such, the images and rhetoric in advertising play a disproportionately significant role in the maintenance of domestic gender norms, and can be more directly linked to reinforcing dominant ideology in real life than other types of advertising.

Advertising is our only truly widespread—that is, regularly viewed by men, women, and children of all races and classes—popular cultural expression about housework. Although real-life experiences and family structures often contradict stereotypes in the media, today the only person most of us will ever *see* doing household cleaning outside of our immediate family/home setting is the woman we see in advertisements and commercials. (In fact, it would be downright weird and vaguely shameful to be "caught" doing housework, even by our closest friends.) We therefore cannot underestimate the power of advertising's monopoly on public representations of housework. Advertising is central to establishing "the meaning of cleaning" in our society and has been since at least the late 1800s. *Married to the Mop* looks closely at the depictions of housewives in ads and commercials to show that up to the present moment, the cultural meaning of cleaning in our most important discourse about cleaning has always been feminine homemaking and care, even as gender norms underwent dramatic changes in many other ways.

We must not only trace the representation of the housewife in advertising, but also ask *why* advertising agencies and the companies that hired them believed so adamantly and for so long that household products should be marketed with images of the housewife. To that end, I also analyze advertising agency documents and trade journals, particularly from the pivotal era of the late 1960s and 1970s. Although ad agencies and the corporations that hire them, past and present, keep most of their specific creative and legal processes a closely guarded secret, scholars can access some sources such as market studies, in-house memos, and articles in trade publications. Such sources illuminate to a certain extent both consumer attitudes toward housework advertising and the decision-making processes of ad makers and their housework product clients. The longevity of feminine domesticity in advertising resulted not only from advertisers' unassailable belief that women are the sole market for housework products, but also because ad makers found at least some measurable evidence that American consumers widely accepted the symbolic function of the housewife in housework product advertising.

Like all of us, the makers of advertising work within a particular social historical context, in which certain cultural norms and ideals prevail and "just make sense." In some part, then, their depictions of housewives in advertising merely reflect the dominant discourse about gender and domesticity. But advertisements and commercials do not transpire casually. They are products of purposeful investigation and interrogation. Advertising does not emerge from flippant assumptions about any aspect of the potential consumer, but rather after careful and often insightful research and discussion about and testing of consumers. To succeed in any way, advertising must have some basis in reality. To assert that advertisements and commercials are *only* expressions of the dominant ideology does not sufficiently acknowledge that those creating ads and commercials are in fact extremely conscious of the dominant ideology and how it might shape the buying habits of the average consumer. It's their business to identify it and to deliberately deploy it in ways that will appeal to consumers. Advertising agencies have done their homework and they have a good idea of what combination of images, music, and representations in a commercial has at least some chance of achieving its goal of selling the advertised product.

From its inception, the business of modern advertising attracted very bright and creative people, including significantly more women than most white-collar professions. Though women (with a few significant exceptions) faced a glass ceiling when it came to executive positions, they played important roles at some of the most influential early agencies.[24] And while it's clear that some of these women imagined the housewife figure in certain stereotypical ways, it's also clear that advertising as an industry actually has little vested interest in simply acting to maintain the status quo. Rather, ad makers' best bet for success was and is clearly identifying when social change makes certain appeals more or less effective. Though the glass ceiling hasn't entirely disappeared, women today make up a majority of advertising professionals, many of whom are specifically dedicated to successfully marketing to other women. Granted, the vast majority of women and indeed all personnel in advertising were, and to large extent still are, white.[25] But nonetheless, advertising is not a monolith, an entity unto itself, hell-bent on proliferating only the most degrading stereotypes of women.

Certainly, there is ample evidence that over the years many of the people creating housework advertising used stereotypical images of "the housewife" because they were sexist pigs. Blatantly demeaning assumptions about women in general and housewives specifically abound in the history of housework advertising. For some ad makers the housewife was a figure of scorn, easily exploitable and effortlessly lured into buying any couponed schlock on the shelf. Patronizing and belittling depictions of female domesticity in ads and commercials themselves, and similar notions articulated in market research and trade publications, demonstrate that for many in the advertising world all women were housewives and all housewives were kind of dumb. Well into the 1970s, many ad makers appeared to picture a typical Mrs. Housewife Consumer as so desperate for any attention, so feeble-minded from raising children and doing housework, that she stood ready and willing to be manipulated into buying any new fabric softener that would make her family at long last notice how Mom always made the towels smell spring-time fresh.

But the persistent presence of the housewife in advertisements and commercials for housework products cannot be completely attributed to the inability of a bunch of misogynistic ad men to accept women's lib. Highly informed men and women employing a variety of sophisticated tools of market and media analysis create advertising, and the longevity of the slim, well-groomed, attractive but not sexy, married mother standing in her nuclear family's nicely appointed middle-class home is not due simply to an obstinate desire on the part of advertisers to maintain hegemonic gender ideals and ignore the realities of Americans' lives. By the late 1970s, study after study cautioned those in the industry against using stereotypical representations of housewives in their ads and commercials, and today's established marketing wisdom advocates carefully taking into account the multiplicity of women's backgrounds and experiences.[26]

Housework advertising does reflect increased attention to diversity in one crucial way: beginning in the 1970s, the depiction of the housewife in advertising included representations of African American, and to a lesser extent, Latina and Asian American women. This was particularly true for targeted media, but as the twentieth century drew to a close, nonwhite housewife moms began making regular appearances in mainstream advertising as well. As a 2004 study comparing 1990s ads in *Essence* and *Ladies Home Journal* concluded: "Advertisers make little distinction between Black and White women in regard to product purchase decision making behavior. . . . Gender identity appears to be more influential than race."[27] Contemporary housework advertising very much bears out this conclusion, vividly illustrating that while ad makers easily incorporated changing attitudes about race and ethnicity into their representations of housework, domestic gender norms remained untouched. Women—not men—no matter what their race or ethnicity, continued to perform all household labor in advertising.

The persistence of the housewife in advertising throughout the late nineteenth and entire twentieth century, and her reconfigured twenty-first representation as the housewife mom, speaks to ad makers' unshakable belief that while domesticity may be depicted with racial diversity in mind, it must always be represented as middle-class gendered homemaking. It also indicates an unshakable conviction among American consumers themselves that domesticity is best symbolically represented as middle-class gendered homemaking. Those who create advertising have been guilty at different times of sexism and stereotyping and the history of the housewife in advertising proves that. But we cannot explain the longevity of the housewife in advertising by trying to prove how advertising agencies either deliberately or even unconsciously set out to demean and oppress women. The documented if uneven efforts of advertising agencies to respond to the changes wrought by 1970s feminism, and particularly the increased representation of non-white women in housework advertising, demonstrates a fundamental truth about ad making: there's no profit in beating a dead horse. Outdated and widely offensive stereotypes cannot move products off the shelves. In the persistence of the housewife in advertising we find evidence of how astonishingly little American attitudes—on the part of both ad makers *and* their target audiences—changed regarding images and ideals about gender and home. Although we cannot draw any simple correlation between advertising and real life, when ad makers use a very particular, clearly identifiable image to define the domestic in housework advertising for over a century, as evidenced by both the advertising itself and internal agency documentation, we can indeed conclude that this representation resonated with consumers and translated into financial success for housework product manufacturers.

Unlike many other types of representations in adverting, the depiction of housework in modern advertising does not demonstrate markedly different historical influences on ads and commercials throughout the modern era, but rather a fixed and virtually unchanging understanding of how to signify housework when marketing housework products. It reveals to what extent U.S. ad makers and consumers in modern America *gender* housework, "framing" it as a female activity. As defined by media scholar Todd Gitlin, frames are

> Principles of selection, emphasis, and presentation composed of little tacit theories about what exists, what happens, and what matters. . . . Media frames are persistent patterns of cognition, perception and presentation, of selection, emphasis and exclusion, by which symbol-handlers routinely organize discourse, whether verbal or visual.[28]

Ad makers are the most important "symbol-handlers" of discourse (both verbal and visual) about household labor in our culture. For all its limitations as a site for historical analysis, housework advertising offers an important way of understanding what "tacit theories" about the representation of housework Americans embrace. The "emphasis and exclusion" in housework advertising presents compelling evidence that for many American consumers, "what happens and what matters" when it comes to household labor can only be "perceived and presented" in advertising through the frame of the housewife, and when the stereotype of the housewife became unpalatable, the housewife mom.

In advertising, the fundamental meaning of household cleaning has always been rooted in images and copy that define "home" as a space created and cared for by good wives and mothers, linking housework products with love and care for the family.[29] Beginning at the end of the 1800s, housework advertising evoked images of maternal, feminine caring, and love, often seeking to evoke anxieties and insecurities while offering solutions (specifically, a product to purchase) to allay those fears, urging consumers to guard the health and happiness of the family.[30] However, other themes, such as women protecting their own beauty with the right housework product, appeared in housework advertising as well. Most significantly, ads and commercials regularly and consistently acknowledged the laborious, repetitive aspects of housework. Many ads and commercials depicted and continue to depict housework as so foul, difficult, and dull that every woman chained to a sink or imprisoned behind a dirty bucket of mop water would gladly welcome the magical assistance of a miracle product to liberate her from drudgery. In some memorable instances, that product even took the form of an actual magic creature.

But whether ecstatic over a clean shirt or miserably bent double over a mop, the most overtly stereotypical images of housewives came under serious attack by the 1970s, when Second Wave feminism began to call into question many aspects of mainstream gender norms. Within just a few decades Americans saw a dramatic shift in laws, politics, and cultural attitudes: as journalist Gail Collins asserts, after the 1960s "everything changed" regarding women's role in society.[31] Overall, ads and commercials improved their depictions of women, with a notable decrease in advertisements that seemed to convey the message that all women were either sex kittens or housewives.[32] Women of color also appeared more frequently in all types of advertising. But housework product ad makers floundered during this transitional period. They began to recognize that certain stereotypical images of the housewife were becoming outdated, even offensive, yet no good alternative presented itself. Ad agencies and their clients recognized only one counterpoint: "the career woman" or "working woman," positioned in direct opposition to "the housewife." As the twentieth century drew to a close, the advertising industry realized that these two sharply limited categories had not found widespread acceptance among consumers and proved an unsatisfactory response to the problem of how to successfully market housework products without the stereotypical image of the housewife.[33]

A far more successful reworking of the housewife figure was the housewife mom, a twenty-first century image of female homemaking deeply rooted in twentieth-century advertising representations of housework as the housewife's care of home and family—care that transforms domestic labor into a labor of (a middle-class mom's) love. The women in today's commercials and ads disinfecting the kitchen counter or spraying air freshener in the living room usually have a child or two hanging around as they demonstrate the products. Many times the children even appear by themselves, with no parent in sight. These kids are not actually participating in any way with the care of the home; they serve no ostensible purpose except perhaps to be served lunch on a sparkling kitchen counter, toweled dry in a germ-free bathroom, or occasionally to make a mess that needs to be cleaned. But as offspring, they define the woman or the targeted viewer as a "mom," and thereby the one caring for the home and, presumably, purchasing the product.[34]

The emergence of the housewife mom in housework advertising reflects two important socioeconomic trends in the late twentieth and early twenty-first century. Firstly, the identification of the "mom market." Today, a wide variety of corporations and ad makers seek to tap into what marketing and demographic experts define as a huge number of female consumers with disposable income who are mothers and who will respond to marketing aimed at mothers.[35] Secondly, both ad makers and consumers readily embrace the housewife mom in contemporary advertising because a new emphasis on motherhood, termed "the mommy mystique" by cultural commentator Judith Warner, powerfully shapes popular representations of women today.[36] Cultural scholars Susan J. Douglas and Meredith W. Michaels label this the "new momism," redefining the term first used in 1942 by author Philip Wylie to censure what he viewed as overprotective, emasculating mothering. Douglas and Michaels describe "the new momism" as

> the insistence that no woman is truly complete or fulfilled unless she has kids, that women remain the best primary caretakers of children, and to be a remotely decent mother, a woman has to devote her entire physical, psychological, emotional, and intellectual being 24/7, to her children. The new momism is a highly romanticized and yet demanding view of motherhood in which the standards for success are impossible to meet.[37]

Douglas and Michaels also point out that the term "mom" itself, rather than "mother," reiterates this normative proscription of women's social roles: "a term previously used only by children [it] doesn't have the authority of 'mother,' because it addresses us from a child's-eye view. It assumes a familiarity, an approachability, to mothers that is, frankly, patronizing." "The rise of it," they conclude, "keeps us in our place, reminding us that we are defined by our relationships to kids, not adults."[38] Part and parcel of the new momism, the housewife mom in housework advertising reiterates and reinforces limiting domestic gender norms. I demonstrate that because she echoes in so many essential ways the *housewife* in all previous modern housework advertising, and because she has changed in so few ways, the female figure in contemporary housework advertising represents not just a "mom" but, more accurately, a *housewife mom*.

The most obviously stereotypical images of housewives are gone from contemporary advertising. The housewife moms in twenty-first century advertising don't agonize over ring-around-the-collar or simple-mindedly obsess over wax build-up. But like the housewives in ads and commercials past, they embody domesticity itself, making a (clean) house into a home. We don't use the term "housewife" anymore (except in an ironical way, as in the popular *Real Housewives* reality television franchise), but American ad makers and consumers accept Mom in advertising because we continue to count on a female figure to frame household labor in our most significant public representations of housework. For both creators and consumers of advertising, she—and only she—is the single truly instantly decipherable representation of domestic life; the only one who can render housework into a recognized activity. It encompasses certain unavoidable drudgery, but drudgery that can be magically resolved and can accomplish important, rewarding domestic work, such as keeping one's family safe. In short, the one who can transform "housework" into "homemaking."

And what of our real domestic lives? Ads and commercials for household products are still far more likely to show women rather than men engaged in caring for the home and children but as in previous eras, we must ask to what degree this reflects the division of household labor in real homes.[39] Although statistics vary quite a bit, much of the available evidence suggests that in fact women still do more housework than anyone else living in their homes. Even more tellingly, 2009 research indicated that young girls do more household chores than young boys and that all children perceive housework as a female responsibility.[40] As gay and lesbian couples and parents report, and as a recent study of female partners of transgendered men demonstrated, housework appears to remain a highly gendered activity, even in families that in other ways directly challenge domestic gender norms.[41]

On the other hand, some studies paint a more hopeful picture of a diminishing "second shift" for women at home (although fewer hours spent doing housework may or may not be made up by increased hours of work done by a woman's partner) and an increasing number of couples who are satisfied with the division of household chores and seem to be enjoying an equitable relationship overall. In addition, many individual and unique factors such as family origin and personal standards of cleanliness shape an individual's experience of, and attitudes toward, housework.[42] Housework is by no means a uniformly unpleasant, oppressive experience for women, or for that matter, men and children, and it has been "reclaimed" by female cultural commentators across the political spectrum.[43] In point of fact, my interest in housework advertising began when I realized how much personal satisfaction I get from keeping my own home clean and clutter-free. But no matter what the variety of individual attitudes about housework, there remains in our society a widespread assumption about the gendered nature of homemaking.

The depiction of housework in advertising both reflects and contributes to this. Without overstating the real-life impact of viewed images, and while acknowledging the difficulties of distinguishing ideology from experience, for over 100 years the representation of housework that the majority of Americans have most often read, heard, and seen is advertising. Nothing else—household manuals and home economics classes, for example—comes close to the sheer quantity of advertisements and commercials for household products that bombarded American men, women, and children from all economic and ethnic backgrounds. That representation remains remarkably unchanged. The most important human actor in these representations evolved at the end of the twentieth century in response to shifting assumptions about women's role in the workplace, but on the surface only. She is no longer the befuddled apron-wearing housewife lamenting her dirty floors and dingy dishes in advertisements and commercials from the early 1900s well into the 1970s. Now an attractive but "realistic" mom dusts, mops, freshens, and scrubs in funny commercials such as those in the Swiffer campaign that draw us in, acknowledging our sophisticated ways of viewing visual texts in the twenty-first century.[44] She even makes regular appearances on the newest mediums of the 2000s, such as brand websites and social media.

But the housewife mom links women to domesticity in the same way as advertisers did a century ago via the housewife. As advertisers now seek to sell household products without relying on the condescending images of housewives in commercials past, they have redeployed the well-groomed, apron-wearing housewife prevalent in most twentieth-century advertising who's rescued from drudgery by miracle products. Today's she's the well-groomed khakis-wearing soccer mom of the twenty-first century rescued from drudgery by miracle products. She is far more palatable and far less obtrusive, but we must recognize her, name her, and examine the cultural work she performs. Because as the history of housework advertising shows, the housewife mom wields real power as the sole signifier of home care.

There are other important themes in twenty-first century housework product advertising, but most of them intersect in some way with the housewife mom. For example, concerns about the environment feed an enormous new "green" cleaning product market, but ads and commercials often couch those concerns in images of mothers caring for their home and family: she's keeping both Junior and the planet healthy and safe. Another notable aspect of 2000s housework product advertising is the theme of pampering oneself, indulging in relaxing home perfumes, for instance. But usually it is the housewife mom who needs to get away from it all with the luxurious new room refresher.

Going from room to room—laundry room, bathroom, kitchen, and living room—in the following chapters I examine the images and copy in print advertising that appeared in newspapers and magazines from the late 1800s to today, and radio advertising that aired from the 1930s through the 1950s and 1960s. I pay particular attention to the especially vivid representations of the housewife in television commercials beginning in the early 1950s. Whenever possible, I look to the archival sources and trade journals that help illuminate how the men and women working in advertising agencies imagined, researched, and figured first the housewife and then the housewife mom, evidence of both their assumptions about and their real knowledge of consumer attitudes. By examining the advertising history of a few key types of products associated with each room, I outline the evolution of the housewife mom, showing that as it became less and less allowable to suggest in word or deed that the woman in the commercial was just a housewife, it remained perfectly allowable to represent housework as gendered labor. Because both the creators and consumers of advertising cannot imagine it any other way, the unpaid work of the home is always, and solely, women's work, and it is her loving care that makes a house a home.

1

The Laundry Room

This chapter traces the reframing of laundry work as gendered housework and homemaking via the figure of the housewife and the housewife mom in ads and commercials for laundry products beginning during the emergence of modern advertising in the late 1800s. Early soap ads and the first detergent marketing depicted housewives eagerly embracing these products as a way to reduce the hard work of doing laundry but also as an aid to good homemaking and care for the family. Advertising from the 1890s through the 1950s emphasized not only the almost magical ability of a soap product to thoroughly clean clothes and linens with ease, but also its ability to help wives and mothers keep their families safe and healthy. Agency documents indicate that although a variety of marketing strategies shaped laundry advertising, ad makers returned again and again to images and copy linking laundry soaps with good homemaking.

In the 1960s, laundry advertising continued to reinforce strictly defined domestic gender norms. Seeking to market household products without stereotypical images but also without alienating their target consumer, the housewife mom began to replace the stereotypical housewife in ads and commercials. Advertising continued to emphasize, and with renewed vigor, how products like detergents and fabric softeners could help wives and mothers care for their families, making husbands and children clean, comfortable, and safe with the right products. In a particularly convoluted attempt to address growing criticism of the housewife stereotype in advertising, housewives in 1970s laundry product advertising also enjoyed some recognition for their loving laundry work, namely in the form of husbands and children suddenly noticing how soft and fresh Mom made their socks and shirts.

Laundry advertising and corresponding commentary from ad agency and product manager executives in the last decades of the 1900s reveals a renewed emphasis on images of mothers caring for their families and their homes, drawing on and expanding the longstanding marketing history of housewives transforming the labor of laundry into a labor of mother's love and tapping into the expanding twenty-first century "mom market." The housewife mom does benefit from a number of twenty-first century emotional rewards for doing laundry, such as a sense of being pampered, the ability to provide special care for special clothes, and the satisfaction of doing good for the environment and the planet. But without a doubt, contemporary laundry product advertising genders homemaking in general and clothing care specifically as female; the almost sole province of the housewife mom.

Today we take laundry detergent for granted, but no such thing even existed until the twentieth century.[1] The entire process of keeping clothes and linens clean has evolved radically since the mid-1800s. Hauling the necessary water and heating it presented the first step in the arduous task of doing laundry in pre-industrialized America. Rubbing and scrubbing the clothes clean, rinsing, wringing, and hanging to dry, then ironing virtually every laundered article all required a massive amount of energy and effort. The cleaning agents available—lye, sal soda, borax—were harsh and unpleasant, and bars and early powders were inconvenient and often not very effective. It's no wonder, as cultural historian Susan Strasser writes, that "women jettisoned laundry, their most hated task, whenever they had any discretionary money at all. . . . Even women of limited means sought relief in the form of washerwomen, commercial laundries, and mechanical aids."[2] Americans took advantage of commercial laundries in significant numbers between 1860 and 1900, and such businesses flourished during the 1920s even as the washerwoman became practically extinct.

Meanwhile, manufacturers experimented with a variety of mechanical washing machines. Maytag marketed its first powered wringer washer in 1909 as "The Hired Girl" (a clear nod to the popularity of paying for laundry work to be done), and its patented rotating drum design soon dominated the market. By the post–World War II era, when the first truly automatic washing machines started to become available, alternatives to home laundering had all but disappeared, although much of the hard work of laundering remained for the millions of women still using wringer washers or scrubbing by hand. By the 1950s, a task that might have been permanently removed from the home became instead "housework."[3] The soap industry kept pace. Lever Brothers' Lux soap flakes, the first non-bar soap specifically marketed for washing clothes (initially, just for woolens, and by the next year, all "fine laundering") migrated from England to the United States in 1916. Lever Brothers followed up with Rinso granulated soap in 1919. Proctor & Gamble (P&G) marketed an early type of detergent in 1933, Dreft, but although more convenient than soap flakes, Dreft did not clean very well. The company remedied that problem in 1946, when it introduced the first synthetic detergent, Tide. Meanwhile, Colgate-Palmolive-Peet Company introduced Super Suds in the late 1930s.[4] The first ads that depicted soap being used for washing clothes or linens, then, featured soaps intended for general household use. Historians of advertising and housework argue that after commonly using servants to advertise housework-related products in the late 1800s, depictions of servants in ads decreased significantly after World War I. When a servant did appear in 1920s and 1930s advertising, she was often a young, pretty, "French maid," indistinguishable from her employer except for her smart uniform—a representation of servant labor with virtually no basis in reality since older African American women with children were by far the most likely to be employed as household servants.[5] Servants in ads finally completely disappeared after World War II. Advertising for laundry products in some ways affirms this account, but such depictions began to appear significantly earlier: when modern marketing began emerging in the late 1800s, advertising invested these products with meanings linked very clearly to the representation of the *housewife* doing the housework. From the earliest days of modern advertising, agencies and manufacturers branded their soap products by redefining laundry work, transforming it from grueling labor ideally done by a hired laundress or a maid, into housework, that is, the responsibility of the housewife.

Ivory, an all-purpose bar soap, began advertising its potential usage as laundry soap at the end of the 1800s. These magazine advertisements demonstrate that some early modern advertising still depicted laundry as servant labor. For instance, an 1898 ad in *Scribner's Magazine* relays a dialogue between Mistress and her servant "Mary," standing next to a rack of drying clothes: "Mary, how do you find the Ivory Soap does?" "Best we ever had, Ma'am." A maid appeared in another ad that same year, also in *Scribner's Magazine*. Wearing a neat uniform, she stands at attention while her young mistress, dressed to go out, admires herself in the glass.[6] Another cleaning product, Borax, utilized the popular trading card format to advertise its product in the late 1800s and one such card depicts a nicely dressed white housewife admiring a clean sheet held aloft by a black laundress in a head scarf and work dress. In the background, another black laundress immerses her hands in the washtubs.[7]

But if such examples illustrate the presence of a maid or laundress in soap advertising, other early ads for soaps in the laundry room very specifically linked these products and the work of laundering with housework and the housewife. A 1901 *McClure's* magazine ad for Ivory as a laundry soap made the process itself almost luxurious and certainly appropriate for a housewife: a prettily dressed housewife, little daughter at her side, washes out a lacy bit of clothing at the pedestal sink in her nicely appointed bathroom. Through the open door we can see the living room of her lovely Craftsman home.[8] A lengthy Borax ad leaflet published in the late 1800s was packed with tips on how "you"—wife, mother, and homemaker—can use Borax in the nursery, laundry, kitchen, and bath. It made it very clear that the housewife really should do the laundry herself: "Table linen can be hopelessly ruined by an incompetent laundress."

The first advertisements for Lux, a flaked soap made by Lever Brothers and introduced in the United States in 1916, also emphasized a brand image of a soap that could transform grueling laundry labor into a pleasant part of homemaking and caring for the family's linens. Even the name emphasized luxury rather than labor. Like Ivory, Lux utilized dual images of laundering in order to convey that image. On the one hand, uniformed maids tending to milady appeared regularly in Lux ads from 1916 well into the 1920s. But on the other hand, numerous ads published during the same time period depicted the pretty, dainty, well dressed housewife herself washing her delicates in her gleaming bathroom sink. The meaning of the product assigned to this essentially meaningless product—its brand—depended heavily upon the representation of laundry work as the work of white, middle-class housewives, not maids or laundry workers.

As documentation from the U.S. Lever Brothers' advertising agency, J. Walter Thompson (JWT), makes clear, even the earliest advertising for Lux intended to represent the *housewife*. In a 1932 creative staff meeting, a JWT executive gave a presentation on the history of the Lux account, beginning with a description of the first 1916 newspaper ads for Lux:

> They are just bursting with news for the homemaking woman. They tell her about a wonderful new soap product, a wonderful new washing method. They are directed at her pride and interest in housekeeping. They tell her of a better, quicker, easier way to wash not only her own fine things but [also] her household linens and blankets and the children's frocks and woolies. . . . They make you feel that Luxing one's own nice things is one of the most enchanting of indoor sports. . . . That women caught the spirit of this copy has been shown again and again in house to house investigations.

He also explained the concurrent use of maids in Lux ads to bolster Lux's brand image as luxurious and "enchanting." His report went on to note: "1919 brought the first universal introduction of the French maid to assist in the laundering of fine fabrics."[9] The JWT agency did not haphazardly depict housewives "Luxing." They investigated, through interviews with women, the efficacy of their brand message, that is, the magical transformation of drudgery, as conveyed by a particular representation—the housewife. A French maid might be pictured to additionally convey the luxury of the product, but the brand's essential message remained linked to the housewife and "her pride and interest in housekeeping," offering her "a better, quicker, easier way" to do her laundry.

Both the housewife figure and, less frequently, maids appeared in 1916 newspaper ads for Lux. For example, in one ad a maid stands at a laundry tub, a frilly blouse drying nearby; in another, a maid holds up a dainty shirtwaist for a lady sitting at her dressing table to admire.[10] Similarly, a 1920 *Ladies Home Journal* ad depicted the pretty young French maid "Marie" helping her lounging mistress look over a collection of stockings, as the copy explains how Marie, "three-quarters angel that she is—saved to you your lace and ribbon happiness, showed you how to make your silk things live and live." Now every night "Marie just whisks up a wonderful bowl of Lux suds." This little fable sought to brand Lux as an elite product in an elite (imaginary) world. Few, if any, *Ladies Home Journal* readers in 1920 lay back in their boudoirs to be attended by a French maid.

The Lux brand far more frequently urged consumers to envision the housewife doing the "Luxing." Newspaper ads in 1916 depicted housewives "Luxing" lacy garments and stockings at their pedestal bathroom sinks or housewives standing in the sunshine hanging blankets on the line. A 1918 ad's *copy* completely belied the *picture* in the ad of a mistress in a silky robe handing off the laundry to her maid by describing how "you, yourself" could easily launder your most delicate garments:

> Don't hate the laundress! Don't squander your energy feeling murderous towards her! She has no grudge against your filmy things. She doesn't want to ruin them. She's simply keeping on washing them in the only way she knows.... You, yourself, with a fraction of the energy you once spent hating the laundress, can now gently rinse the dirt out of your filmiest things—take them from the pure Lux suds soft and gleaming and *new*!

This ad makes clear that laundry, the modern Lux way, need not be hired out. In fact, it would be far better and even more easily undertaken by the housewife. And the housewife could count on the wondrous ability of this particular brand of soap to practically render old garments new. The modern branding of Lux did not simply convey luxury: these early ads, the first ads for the first soap manufactured and marketed specifically for laundry use, consistently addressed its copy to "you"—the housewife—and consistently depicted "Luxing" as a magical transformation of arduous labor into a pleasant part of housework and homemaking, specifically caring for special clothes and household linens.

In addition, some early Lux ads explicitly focused on how the product would aid middle-class white mothers. Although a 1917 Lux ad published in the *New York World* newspaper depicted a slim young maid in uniform getting the family's young children dressed, many other ads focused on how Lux helped Mother care for her children. In an ad published that same year in the *Washington Star*, a pretty young mother admires her pretty young children, under the headline: "Just what you need for the children's clothes." Another 1917 newspaper ad began "You couldn't bear to wash baby's woolens." Not because baby's woolens might be difficult to wash, but because shrinking the garment might cause discomfort to baby, and a loving mother would carefully ensure her baby's comfort. Keeping baby's garments soft and comfortable meant housework, done by the housewife, the mother of the home, not the laundress or maid. Early on, Lux utilized a brand image of good mothering linked to good laundering, defined by product choice.

A similar 1917 ad in the *New York Times* vividly illustrated how Lux branded itself as a mother's helper. The picture shows a gaggle of pajama-clad youngsters greeting their father, under the headline "Woolly as Little Teddy Bears!" The copy continues:

> How sweet they looked to Father—rosy from their merry tubbings—warm and laughing in their fuzzy soft woolens. You love to have them look cunning in their flannel night things—not to have them in yellowed shrunken garments—that catch them under the arms or at the knees—that scratch and irritate their tender little skins. It is almost like play to wash the children's clothes with Lux. You will be amazed. No rubbing is necessary. Dance the woolens up and down in the rich frothy lather and the dirt dissolves instantly.[11]

Tender little teddy bears skins would be quite safe after Mother did some dancing with the laundry. When Father returned from his white-collar job (as his white shirt, tie, and suit indicated) to the sanctuary of his home, he would find his adorable children and attractive wife relaxed and happy in clean clothes; cleanliness and good homemaking achieved not with hard work (or servant labor) but effortlessly—with the right soap. Such highly idealized images of the housewife caring for her children's clothes, and thus her children, with incredible ease does not offer us any evidence of how real consumers and *New York Times* readers might have responded to this rose-tinted representation of the female domestic sphere. But it does demonstrate how early, and to what extent, laundry soap advertising stressed their products' ability to help housewives transform laundry labor into a labor of love, reinforcing and reiterating domestic gender norms in the modern era. As Lever Brothers and JWT built a brand image for Lux in the new world of modern advertising, they carefully framed the qualities of the product with representations of gendered domestic labor, and linked it specifically with the housewife and to some extent, mothers. This is not to say that Lux didn't offer real advantages. In the early twentieth century a flaked soap did present greater ease in laundering. In the 1920s and 1930s, commercial laundries still did a brisk business, and washing machine technology continued to evolve from basic wringer models to electrically powered machines. Electric machines offered a range of advantages, but only about a quarter of non-farm households owned such machines in the 1920s (rural and farming households numbered even less).[12] For the millions of Americans without extra income for their own machines or without easy access to water and power, laundry remained a wearisome household task, requiring boiling water, hard scrubbing, rinsing, wringing, and line drying until well into the 1950s, when automatic machines first became widely available. No wonder then that when Lever Brothers, building on the success of Lux, introduced a granulated laundry soap in 1919, their first marketing efforts depicted housewives enjoying the wondrous ability of Rinso to transform doing the laundry from old-fashioned hard labor to easy modern housework. Again, such claims had a basis in reality: this first granulated packaged soap did offer an important improvement over all-purpose bars or even flaked soap.[13] Rinso advertising and other laundry product ads in the 1920s, 1930s, and 1940s consistently had to reference the fact that doing laundry could be a dirty, tiring, difficult undertaking. But by this time even the hint of servant labor all but disappeared from laundry advertising. Now laundry advertising insisted that their products offered the housewife magical relief from the hard labor of laundry but it inextricably linked her—and only her—to that work, affirming domestic gender norms that defined housework as an integral part of female care. Other kinds of marketing rhetoric—a soap product's ability to save a housewife money or to safeguard her personal daintiness, for example—came and went, but throughout these decades, laundry advertising promised the housewife, first and foremost, less work in the laundry room. But they also always positioned these soap products as an important means for protecting her family's health and well-being.

Rinso advertising frequently utilized the popular "comic strip" or "ad strip" format for newspaper ads in the 1930s. These visually arresting strips told dramatic stories about their product, often exemplifying the growing presence of psychology-based appeals in advertising for all kinds of products.[14] Sometimes they used a combination of photos and drawings, with word balloons for the dialogue. In Rinso ads, housewives constantly demonstrated how daunting and exhausting doing laundry could be—until the arrival of Rinso. In keeping with the era's widespread emphasis in advertising on the wonders of modernity, often the strips portrayed housewives as plodding along in their old ways until a modern friend, daughter, or the ad's copy itself set them straight. As a 1930 ad in *Woman's Home Companion* explained: "There are several ways to do the family wash. Modern women do it the easiest way—without scrubbing or boiling. And they get whiter, brighter washes than those who scrub for hours! 'It's almost like magic!' say women all over the country."[15] In one 1930 photo and word balloon ad, two women on the phone converse about their mutual friend: "Mildred can't come because it's washday. She's scrubbing her clothes—just imagine!" "How old-fashioned! Let's tell her about our 'no-work' way." Rinso promised "no-work," touting its ability to "soak the dirt out," a claim that must have indeed seemed like magic to real consumers who had to scrub the dirt out on a washboard. "Sensational new product saves you hours of backbreaking rubbing," vowed a 1921 Rinso magazine ad. In a 1919 ad, the copy asked, "At 9:00 a.m.: Are your clothes on the line—or are you just beginning the tiresome task of rubbing—rubbing?"

A soap that removed the work from laundering would be especially appealing given the tremendous exertion laundry still required, as vividly depicted in other 1930s Rinso comic strip ads. A 1935 ad opened with a dramatic panel: a young housewife in housedress and apron comes to on the kitchen floor, a friend kneeling beside her, and they have this exchange: "I must have passed out from the heat." "Who wouldn't faint—scrubbing and boiling clothes in this hot weather," the friend replies. She then quickly enlightens the housewife: "I know it sounds too good to be true—but just try Rinso next washday." A pleased husband embraces his wife in the last panel: "My, the house is nice and cool. Didn't you boil the clothes?" "No! And I didn't scrub either. I just soaked my wash snowy in creamy Rinso suds."

In a similar ad, a daughter pays a call to her mother. You can tell Daughter's paying a call because she's wearing a coat and hat, a commonly utilized rhetorical device in housework advertising. In this ad, Daughter finds Mom sweating over the stove: "Mother, it's simply stifling in here! How can you stand it?" Mother answers meekly: "I know it's hot, but I need this wash—I can't let it wait." Worried Daughter: "But darling, must you boil the clothes? Your kitchen's like an oven." Mother, somewhat tartly: "Think I'd stand over a steaming boiler on a day like this—unless I had to? How else can I get the clothes white?" Setting her mother down in an easy chair and pouring her a glass of lemonade, Daughter gently but firmly chides Mother: "I've told you time and time again, Mother—boiling is out of date. Scrubbing too! Let me get you some Rinso." "That's right. I've been meaning to try it," her chastened mother replies. The copy in the last panel summarizes: "Millions now 'take it easy' on washday! Instead of scrubbing for hours in a sweltering kitchen—instead of torturing themselves still further by boiling those clothes—they just *soak* everything in Rinso suds."

Very occasionally Rinso ads referenced the possibility of hiring someone else to do the laundry, but during the Great Depression ad makers often played up the economy angle. In this way, laundry product advertising built not just on the image of ease and convenience, but also the ability of its product to provide a cost-cutting measure for middle-class housewives. In a 1934 strip, husband Bill has this worried exchange with his young wife. She's slim and pretty and wearing a nice ruffled apron but holding a weary hand to her head: "I'll have lunch ready in ten minutes Bill—I've been scrubbing all morning trying to get these shirts of yours nice and white." "I wish you wouldn't work so hard, Dear. Don't you think it would be better to send the wash to the laundry?" "I save at least $3.00 a week doing it myself. I can buy lots of things with that extra $12.00 a month." In a 1933 strip, the recurring character Friend In Hat scolds one housewife: "You're way behind the times to let washday ruin your hands and health. Nobody does anymore." "I can't afford to hire a laundress to do my wash, if that's what you mean," replies the housewife. No, the answer is Rinso! In another 1934 strip titled "Why Modern Mothers Are Not Afraid of Washday," a thrifty young first-time mother already knows the Rinso secret, pooh-poohing her sister's advice to forgo laundry duty now that Baby's arrived. Concerned Husband asks: "I hate to see you do the wash, Honey. Why don't you send it out?" "Because it's so easy to save that money. Think of all the things we need for the baby." "But your sister says . . ." "Oh, don't mind Gladys. She still washes clothes the old-fashioned way—with a washboard." In the last panel she smugly coos to her baby "And here's how I'm saving Daddy lots of money."

In addition to money-saving qualities, ad makers also tried an appeal asserting that Rinso enabled the housewife to maintain her daintiness—an important wifely responsibility—and the last panel of many a comic strip ad saw the housewife fresh as a daisy again, no longer made haggard by exhausting, hot laundry work and happily enclosed in her loving husband's arms. In a 1934 strip, "One Bride Tells Another—About Washday," Friend In Hat tells a sulking Betty: "Remember when you caught the bouquet at my wedding? Two months later you eloped with Bill." "Yes, and when washday comes around I almost wish I hadn't."[16] The crisis is resolved in the last panel, as a perky Betty perches on Bill's lap, and he says: "No scrubbing? That's fine, Betty! I used to hate to see you work so hard."

While Rinso built its appeal on the very real fact that boiling and scrubbing clothes constituted hot, wearying labor that would probably make you sweat, Lux advertising in the 1930s took the popular "whisper gossip" advertising techniques just emerging and applied them to perspiration and laundry, specifically the laundering of one's "underthings." In the infamous "undie odor" campaign, Lux linked laundering not so explicitly to the housewife but rather to all women who wished to avoid "giving offense." By 1930 ad makers began to draw extensively on increasingly sophisticated marketing techniques, rooted in particular emotional appeals—namely fear and anxiety. Lever Brothers played a key role in the development of this type of advertising, according to historian Suellen Hoy:

> Francis Countway, president of Lever Brothers and the individual most responsible for the "discovery" of body odors and the "stop smelling" ad pitch, was inspired by Listerine's successful advertising campaign against the previously unknown halitosis. Countway and his associates admitted, while Lever Brothers' business boomed, that they cared little "about the opinions of softies who think that the Body and Undie Odor copy is disgusting."[17]

A JWT annual report to Lever Brothers noted that in the 1930s, Lux moved away from branding Lux solely as a housewife's product and instead attempted to tap into the enormous beauty product market by using the theme "Underthings absorb perspiration. Avoid offending by washing them daily with Lux."[18]

In these ads, young women risk severe social ostracism and, the worst fate of all, becoming old maids. "She has 'IT'—but not what you think," warned the headline in a 1933 ad in *Better Homes and Gardens*, above a drawing of a young woman in a ball gown sitting sadly alone while three men in tuxes whisper about her. The copy explains: "After one dance they pass her up. They forget that rose-petal skin, those dreamy eyes, her agreeable manner, her grace on the dance floor. . . . Of course, she doesn't realize she's offending. But we all perspire, even though we don't *feel* sticky. Frequently over a quart a day, doctors say." A similar ad that same year appeared in *True Story* and other movie magazines, describing the gossip you risked with undie odor: "Weren't you shocked at Dorothy?" "My dear, I simply couldn't believe it." As the copy chided: "Why *does* she wear her underthings a second day? Everybody perspires a little—and it's easy to offend! How can she take such chances with *personal daintiness*?"

Just as much as single girls, *wives* had to maintain their *personal daintiness* or risk the sanctity of marriage and home. Luxing, promised a 1929 ad, would help wives "Keep the Trousseau Habit." Accompanying a photograph of a woman wearing a glamorous negligee and robe, the advice from a "Famous Authority on Romance" counseled: "Some wives keep romance in marriage forever—isn't one secret the trousseau habit?" She concluded: "Truly Lux has done more to keep romance in marriage than we shall ever know." A lesser-known brand, Vel, made a similar appeal in

1939 newspaper comic strip ads. For example, a critical husband addresses his wife as they are getting ready for bed: "You're no bargain in that get-up, Friend Wife! Did you pick that up at a rummage sale?" Friend Wife replies tearfully: "Don't be sarcastic. This outfit is practically new but I'll certainly have to find a different way to wash it." Vel does the trick because in the last panel: "Gee, Honey, that's swell looking underwear. When did you buy it?" "Joke's on you! All my old things seemed to come to life, like new since I started washing with VEL, the soap-less suds." Vel promised to "give underwear bride-like luster."[19]

While laundry soap ad makers experimented with campaigns in the 1930s and 1940sthat touted a product's ability to keep husbands happy in the boudoir, they far more frequently emphasized the role of housewife as safeguard of a family's health and comfort. For instance, Lux continued to brand its product as a mother's helper during this period. In 1930s ads, Lux appealed to mothers specifically with advertisements in *Child Life* and *Parents*, featuring photos of adorable babies with captions like "His rose-petal skin is tender and sensitive." The ads caution: "A baby's health and comfort may depend on the way you wash his shirts, bands, and diapers. The gentle Lux suds are wonderfully mild, soothing—they protect your precious baby's health!" Quoting a "very famous baby doctor," another ad warns that clothing washed in soap containing alkali "may cruelly irritate the tender skin and delicate tissues." Surely, "No mother wants to run such a risk!" Another featured a testimonial from a "Mother of 5" who made this remarkable claim: "I've never had a fussy baby" since "I've always used Lux for all the children's things." In 1933, Lux even tried an ad in *American Girl* magazine. A smiling baby in the ad's photograph revealed: "Sister knew what made me fuss." The copy continued:

> It was fortunate that Patsy Mallory had attended the splendid "little moth-ers" class at her school. Because she knew what was making baby brother so fussy and fretful. Patsy had learned how easily a baby's skin is chafed and how important it is to wash his garments with the very gentlest of soap. It wasn't long before baby's painful diaper rash disappeared.[20]

Here the diaper rash connection to laundry kept the housewife, and her caring homemaking and mothering, at the center of these ads for laundry soap, even when published in a magazine aimed at young girls. (And, in passing, suggested that proper mothering required training by experts in a classroom.)

During the 1930s Lux used a number of other types of appeals in addi-tion to the ones depicting laundry work as part of good homemaking. For example, ads emphasized that thrifty women used Lux since it would ensure longer life for expensive stockings and other delicate garments, thus allowing women to save money while still looking fashionable. Grocers displayed advertisements emphasizing that as a cost cutter, Lux helped cut down on stocking runs, as did magazine and radio advertising, including celebrity endorsements.[21] But Lux as well as other brands most frequently returned to the image of a mother taking loving care of her children.

The initial Concentrated Super Suds advertisements in the late 1930s branded the product as both the means to totally erase the labor of laundry work and also as a means for careful mothers to protect their families from germs. Longstanding rituals built around cleaning the middle-class home—marking a clear boundary between the home as inside sanctuary and the rest of the world as outside contaminant—became reinvigorated with mainstream acceptance of germ theory.[22] The positioning of cleansers as products with the ability to maintain the sanctity of the home, specifically to keep it free from dirt in both the physical and symbolic sense, influenced all housework advertising in the late nineteenth and twentieth centuries. Laundry was no exception, as early Concentrated Super Suds made abundantly clear. Newspaper ads for Super Suds in 1937, 1938, and 1939 frequently emphasized the ability of the product to attack and defeat germs, and specifically Mother's role in the war on germs. Many times a medical authority, usually a male doctor in a lab coat, proves to the housewife the necessity of fighting germs in the laundry room. The comic strip style ads usually featured a large drawing of the doctor showing a housewife, through a microscope, the presence of the foreign invaders. Some typical housewifely responses: "Heavens—you found all those germs in my soiled clothes?" "I saw sore throat germs in my own wash!" "Germs in <u>my own wash</u>! What can I do to protect my family against them?"[23] Super Suds offered "hospital-clean" protection to the concerned wife and mother, after raising her anxiety: "In this innocent bundle of wash are millions of dangerous germs!" "No matter *how careful* you are, madam—your family wash may harbor dangerous germs—germs that spread infection."

But, as the ads adamantly emphasized, getting clothes "hospital-clean" could be achieved along with the miraculous ability of Super Suds to remove the labor from laundry. Super Suds made sure to depict the housewife as enjoying the modern ease of the product, effortlessly transforming housework into homemaking. As a happy husband notes in the final panel of a 1938 newspaper ad, as he swoops his smiling wife into his arms: "Washday, and not a bit tired—this **is** a pleasant surprise!" "Concentrated Super Suds does all the hard work for me, Jim! And it protects our family's health, removes most germs as well as the dirt!" "Say goodbye to washday drudgery with this new super soap!" read the headline of a 1939 magazine ad, beneath a large drawing of a housewife who gazes with shiny-eyed love at a clean white button-down oxford men's shirt. A similar ad in the *New York Times* makes it clear who would be doing the laundry—"Housewives hail amazing new laundry soap!"—and another newspaper ad, under a photo of a plump smiling baby in a bonnet, advises housewives of their motherly duties: "Guard baby against germs like these [inset drawing of scary microscope germs] present in all soiled clothes!" A similar comic strip ad cautions: "When you've washed baby clothes are you certain they're hospital-clean?" But Super Suds would enable the housewife to achieve this high standard with almost magical ease. One strip clearly articulated how Super Suds transformed laundry from drudgery into joy, when Daughter helps with the wash: "Ooh, Mummy! This new soap's just like magic!"

Like Lux, Super Suds almost certainly did offer appreciable advantages over earlier cleaning agents. But Super Suds advertising promised not just improvement but the total removal of labor ("This new soap's just like magic!") in an era when the majority of American households did laundry with washtubs and wringers. They acknowledged that in the 1940s, with the decline of commercial laundries and the disappearance of the laundress, women continued to face a daunting task when it came to laundry. One newspaper ad painted an especially vivid picture of the burden of laundry on the housewife. The headline reads: "It seems like a bad dream now!" above a drawing of an exhausted woman bending over a washtub while a devil with a pitchfork stabs the small of her back. Similarly, a 1940 ad depicts a housewife confiding to Friend in Hat: "I just don't know what to do, Peggy! I scrub until I'm worn to a rag, yet my clothes never look as white as yours!" Peggy of course happily shares her secret to white clothes, and sets Mary straight: "You don't need to scrub these days!" As a 1949 ad headline put it: "I Used to Work Like a Dog;" "until I discovered how _easy_ it is to get clothes really white!" continues the copy. Such advertising depicted housework as grueling labor, but (like all housework product advertising) promised that the purchase of the right product would relieve that labor. Even more importantly, these campaigns indicated to what extent the most prominent public discourse about housework—advertising—now represented laundry as solely the work of the housewife, that is, the middle-class white wife and mother, slim and attractive but not sexy, often wearing an apron, and conscientiously caring for her home and family.

They also demonstrate the extent to which this particular representation dominated the market place, reinforcing and reiterating domestic gender norms. The Colgate-Palmolive-Peet Company and their ad agency D'Arcy Masius Benton and Bowles (DMB&B) did not rely solely on print advertising to market Super Suds.[24] They test-marketed the product to 7,000 women, for example, and ran numerous advertisements in grocery trade publications (magazines and other material published for managers and owners in the grocery and supermarket business). So, too, did Lever Brothers for Lux, even offering concrete assistance for in-store marketing: "The Lever Brothers salesman will help you give your window real sales appeal with an attractive Lux display."[25] In one trade journal ad, Super Suds promised grocers that "old customers, new customers will crowd your store to buy the new improved Concentrated Super Suds" after a newspaper and magazine ad campaign was estimated by the company to reach 17,000 people every week. A 1939 grocery trade ad suggested store owners use floor displays, pennants, and banners to coincide with newspaper and radio ads, and then: "THE RUSH IS ON! Women flock in to buy." A grocery trade ad the previous year urged window, counter, and floor displays, promising "Watch your sales climb!" Beginning in the 1930s, coupons and mail-in offers also abounded in laundry soap advertising. Colgate-Palmolive-Peet offered Super Suds consumers incentives such as a mail-in offer for monogrammed trays, and marketed their bar soap Octagon specifically for laundry use with incentives ranging from Cannon dish towels ("to brighten up your kitchen") and mixing bowls to fountain pens and dishes, as well as coupons for money off the purchase of the product. To store owners, they suggested in-store ads emphasizing the ease and convenience of the product: "Cuts washing time in half," "Lathers instantly . . . soaks out dirt," and "Grand for laundry use."[26]

In 1939 Colgate-Palmolive-Peet described to store owners the blitzkrieg of advertising planned for Super Suds, including sponsorship of the radio serial *Myrt and Marge*, which reached 6,200,00 listeners coast to coast, 14,280,00 color impressions in magazine ads; 19,653,000 newspaper impressions; and various mail-in offers.[27] P&G's promotional "motion slide film" (a movie with a mixture of still and action images) for Oxydol described to distributors and retailers a similar advertising onslaught the year before. The voiceover described the vast numbers of four-color full-page magazine ads, ads in 340 daily newspapers, sales displays in stores, and radio advertising planned for a reformulated "High Test" Oxydol. The film explained at length why Oxydol would appeal to "Mrs. Housewife" and how frequently she would be seeing and hearing Oxydol advertising. As the sponsors for two extremely popular radio shows—*Ma Perkins* and *The Goldbergs*—Oxydol planned to reach every member of the radio listening audience: "If they've got a radio, they'll be told about Oxydol."[28]

Radio commercials for laundry products in the 1930s and 1940s built upon and reinforced messages in print advertisements. Indeed, the frequency with which manufacturers utilized radio to market cleaning products, including laundry soap and bath soap, specifically to "the housewife" spawned a whole new genre of programming: the soap opera.[29] P&G,

in an effort to market Oxydol detergent, conceived *Ma Perkins* in 1933. Believing, for both quantifiable (in reality, women at this time *did* buy the majority of household cleaning products) and ideological reasons (those women did not by any means all embody the white middle-class ideal), they invented a new form of daytime serial programming aimed explicitly at housewife listeners.[30]

Even savvy media consumers today are rarely consciously aware that advertising is not tangential to our entertainment but rather the reason most of our popular entertainment even exists. The creators of soap operas did not conceive of them as a way to entertain a listening audience, but rather as a means to get a target consumer—the housewife—to hear advertising for detergents and cleansers. Companies didn't just "sponsor" daytime serials: they *owned* them and considered them first and foremost a vehicle for promotion of their products (a system repeated in the television industry). Many market researchers considered housewives the ideal target of radio commercials not just because of their potential purchase of soap, but because housewives constituted a captive audience: they had hours of housework to do but listening to the radio need not interfere with their household labor. They could listen to the serials—and the advertising—all day long.[31] Octagon for example utilized radio advertising, cashing in on the introduction of soap operas such as *Woman of Courage*. A 1939 Octagon trade journal ad described how their show would lure in consumers: "This all-exciting, human story will give you thrills and heartaches, as Martha Jackson struggles on courageously to eek [*sic*] out a livelihood for her crippled husband and her lovely young daughter."[32] Lux too sought to market its products (both laundry and bath soap) via the radio, first airing Lux-sponsored advice to the lovelorn around 1931, and then with *The Lux Radio Theatre* in 1936.[33]

When Rinso sponsored the popular *Amos and Andy Show* in the 1940s, the commercials continued to emphasize the ease with which housewives could tackle the laundry work. "When you've two active youngsters and a husband who's a garage mechanic, you've a full time job just keeping the family fed and in clean clothes," began the male announcer in one such commercial. He went on to link the product's astounding cleaning properties with the patriotic war work—and good homemaking—of Mrs. DeWitt:

> But Mrs. DeWitt of Kansas City Missouri does that and more. She holds a regular job in a war industry besides. You can see that efficiency methods are a must with Mrs. DeWitt. No wonder she wrote us: [woman's voice] "I've used Rinso for my family wash and kitchen use for over 12 years." And you can bet your best bonnet that Rinso's been a big helping hand to

Mrs. DeWitt. Why, with Rinso's soapy rinse suds on the job, it takes as little as a ten minute soaking to get clothes dazzling clean. Then a few quick finger rubs on extra grimy places and they're ready to rinse. Yes, Mrs. DeWitt has plenty of reasons to be proud of the wash she hangs out, every piece.[34]

In this radio commercial, the housewife enjoys the removal of the hard labor from laundry work because with "just a few quick finger rubs" her husband's grease-soaked coveralls are clean. Moreover, she can take pride in her wash, as she provides the best possible care for her husband and children—she's achieving the highest standards of homemaking.

The housewife in this commercial was also supposedly a real woman praising Rinso. The popular testimonial ad appeared throughout all kinds of advertising, even before the emergence of the modern advertising industry at the turn of the century, and continues to be used for some kinds of products. It's hard to say how many letters from product fans in the 1940s were genuine and how many were composed in the creative departments of ad agencies. But if ad makers based even a fraction of such testimonials on real consumer correspondence, they clearly drew on widespread acceptance of housework advertising appeals among their target consumers. A 1949 newspaper campaign for Surf detergent, for example, utilized photographs and testimonials from presumably real consumers advocating for the product.[35] They all attest, specifically, to the ways Surf saves them time and effort in their homemaking duties.

This particular depiction of housewives stands out in the history of laundry soap advertising, because the housewives in these ads are far more realistic than the slim and pretty housewives beaming over their laundry baskets in other kinds of print ads (see fig. 1.1). They are wearing work clothes such as head scarves and heavy-duty bib aprons and they clutch various cleaning implements like brooms and washrags. They sport drab hairstyles, irregular facial features, and some are even downright homely. Undoubtedly, the manufacturer and the ad makers decided this would reinforce the impression that these were *real* housewives giving real testimonials because such realistically clothed and featured women do not appear in other types of Surf advertising specifically or in other laundry advertising. Ad makers and housework product manufacturers preferred to rely on more aesthetically pleasing visual depictions of housewives in newspaper and magazine advertising, apparently believing that a more idealized image of the housewife would better reinforce the brand message. But although at first glance, the "real" Surf housewives might appear to be a more down-to-earth depiction of women rather than a highly idealized housewife figure, according to these real-looking women, Surf worked washday *miracles* on a regular basis. They spouted the same kind

Figure 1.1   1949 Surf newspaper advertisement

Note: Unusually realistic images of housewives appeared in a series of 1949 newspaper ads for Surf detergent. But in typical copy, the product promised washday miracles that would enable the housewife to not merely clean clothes but achieve the highest standards of homemaking and family care.

Source: 1949 Surf newspaper advertisement copyright ©1949–2011 The Sun Products Corporation, Wilton, CT, all rights reserved. Reprinted by permission of The Sun Products Corporation. From N.W. Ayer Advertising Agency Records, Archives Center, National Museum of American History, Behring Center, Smithsonian Institution.

of over-the-top copy used in all ads. A housewife standing next to a wringer washer enthuses: "It's nothing less than a miracle. Saves half the work of washing." In laundry product advertising, the housewife and mother, even on this rare occasion when pictured as realistically dressed and featured woman, always reinforced the magical removal of labor. Moreover, she often expressed a resulting feeling of satisfaction, assuring the housewife that she would be proud of the wash she hung out and of taking good care of her family, reinforcing and reiterating domestic gender norms.

These same themes shaped the marketing for what would quickly become America's laundry soap juggernaut: P&G's Tide. Artherton W. Hobler, an executive at the DMB&B advertising agency, recalls in his unpublished autobiography that in 1941 four classes of soap made up the laundry market: "pure soaps," namely Ivory and Lux; "built soaps" like Rinso and Oxydol; "semi-built soaps" like Chipso and Duz; and "soap-like but soap-less soaps," Dreft and Vel. Hobler summarized: "The pure soaps were used exclusively for fine fabrics, the built soaps for heavy duty work, the soap-like and semi-built for all-purpose washing."[36] Tide's claim to fame in this market was its formula, a synthetic detergent, which made laundered articles notably cleaner, particularly in hard water.

But as Hobler makes clear, clever advertising and marketing as much or even more than actual cleaning properties shot Tide to the top of the laundry soap category. The ad agency and P&G carefully chose a name with a particular brand image in mind: "It had visual aspect, was short, easy to remember and not reminiscent of the name of any other soap or detergent product." It also evoked the image of a beach washed clean by the sweeping ocean tides, while the package—concentric orange and yellow rings—supposedly suggested suds in a washtub with the bold lettering of the name superimposed. As Hobler noted about Tide packaging: "The phenomenon of impulse-buying had taught us the importance of developing a package design which the shopper could easily identify."[37] They also used to very good effect a marketing technique occasionally used by other brands in the past: advertising the product in conjunction with washing machine manufacturers and dealers. P&G placed free sample boxes of Tide in new washing machines, for instance.[38] Also, consumer research played a strong role in the first Tide advertisements: claiming to "get clothes cleaner than any soap" did not resonate as strongly in consumer testing as did cleanliness claims backed up with the phrase "made by Proctor and Gamble."[39] In other words, the successful new branding of Tide built very much on the previous and longstanding successful branding of P&G itself as a well-known and trusted household products company.

P&G and DMB&B launched a tidal wave of Tide advertising. The first magazine ad copy begins "Out of this world . . . Out of Proctor and

Gamble laboratories." In the first radio ads, catchy ten-second spots featured a musical jingle "Tide's In, Dirt's Out. T-I-D-E Tide!" Importantly, the agency linked radio ads to print ads. According to Hobler: "We used newspapers, which was somewhat unprecedented for Proctor and Gamble, for consumers to see in print what they were hearing on the radio."[40] P&G also introduced product sampling in its first Tide ad campaigns, as well as utilizing previously effective marketing techniques such as direct mail, couponing, and a mail-in incentive for clothespins.[41] The results paid off with instant success for the product—though Hobler reveals that P&G deliberately under-shipped Tide to many parts of the country to bolster claims of how rapidly Tide sold out in various locations.[42]

Hobler must have simply taken it for granted that the housewife figure would appear in these ads: all the Tide marketing strategies relied on a representation of a highly idealized housewife transforming laundry into family care. For example, the very first Tide television commercial sought to create a brand image for Tide that linked the product to an emotionally rewarding day with the kids at the beach. In this first 1952 commercial, a housewife hangs sheets by the oceans and then cuddles her little boy dry after swimming.[43] The commercial explicitly connected washing towels with a mother's loving care for her child with this image and with the voiceover's description of Tide detergent as "the kind of clean you like best next to those you love." Other depictions of housewives in early Tide advertising emphasized how much they adored Tide itself. From the first newspaper ad in 1946 and throughout the 1950s, Tide advertising featured pretty white middle-class housewives in neat housedresses and often, heels and aprons, rendered absolutely ecstatic by Tide. Indeed, the Tide housewives reflect how the most stereotypical depictions of the housewife reached a peak in the postwar era. In newspaper ads, these housewives fawn over boxes of Tide, gazing in rapture at the product and at the clean laundry. They hold the box, with its slogans "New Washing Miracle" and "Oceans of Suds" clearly visible, like a beacon of liberation to oppressed housewives everywhere. "Oh, what a wonderful washday!" proclaimed a 1948 newspaper headline.[44] "Nothing but Tide will do," declared a similar housewife. "Tide's got what women want," emphasized a 1949 ad featuring another besotted housewife clutching her box of Tide. In 1953 newspaper ads, housewives literally clicked their heels with joy or leaped ecstatically aloft, again gazing at the product and at clean laundry.

Magazine advertising in 1951 emphasized how the housewife's love affair with Tide resulted in better care for husband and family. A housewife gazes happily at her husband resplendent in a clean shirt and the copy reads: "He wears the cleanest shirt in town! / There isn't any doubt / That all his shirts are washed with TIDE / 'Cause when TIDE's in . . . dirt's out!"

In a similar ad, Mother's care manifests in her little daughter's clean party dress. "She wears the cleanest clothes in town. / So does her little brother. / Their clothes are always washed with TIDE. /They've got a clever mother!" In another, a newlywed dances with her husband, while the copy explains: "They wear the cleanest clothes in town / At home or at a party. / His bride has learned to wash with TIDE! / She's young . . . but she's a smarty!" These print ads represented the work of the housewife as caretaker of the family's clothing—as measured by all the other clothes (and housewives) in town. They equated laundry with achieving the highest possible domestic standards, reinforcing and underscoring domestic gender norms and continuing to visually and rhetorically transform the labor of the laundry into a labor of love. To convey that message, Tide advertising relied heavily on the highly idealized housewife figure, complete with high heels, apron, and small-minded fixation on household products. Like numerous other kinds of housework products, laundry advertising in the late 1940s and 1950s vividly illustrated what feminists identified as a deliberate strategy on the part of ad makers in the postwar era to portray housework as emotionally fulfilling and an essential part of an ideal feminine identity.[45]

In addition to infusing the product with the feminine mystique, advertising certainly emphasized the cleaning capabilities of Tide. But it did not position the product as a miracle relief from exhausting labor—no housewives fainted from the heat of boiling clothes in Tide ads. As the post–World War II years rapidly brought more and more Americans utilities and automatic washers, laundry soap advertising had to turn away from those kinds of vivid depictions of laundry labor. But to a certain extent, the labor-saving qualities of laundry products continued to shape advertising appeals, such as the first newspaper ads in the late 1940s for Surf detergent, which positioned the product as "No-Rinse Surf." Surf was the Lever Brothers Company's response to the incredible new popularity of P&G's Tide, as the similar name attests. The first campaigns built on comparable depictions of the housewife doing her laundry work as well. "New Surf contains a miracle ingredient that floats dirty away—keeps it from getting back into the clothes," began the copy of a 1949 newspaper ad. "Yes, a clean, clean wash—really sweet-smelling CLEAN—so clean you need not rinse! Women everywhere know that's the miracle that No-Rinse Surf has made true." The washday miracle of Surf promised to completely remove the labor of laundering, along with the dirt and any lingering odors.

Other Surf newspaper ads featured housewives skeptical at first but then convinced of Surf's labor-saving cleaning power: "Frankly, I didn't expect to be satisfied—but I tried No-Rinse Surf because I have a big wash and time is important. It was wonderful—the hours I saved, and all the backbreaking work of rinsing. No more long, hard washdays for me," she concludes. In a similar magazine ad, a housewife in her crisp bib apron describes in detail how she tested out Surf, with accompanying drawings for each step:

> I'll admit I was skeptical about this "no rinse" business, so I really put it to the test! I washed all my bedding—quilts, blankets, even spreads—with No-Rinse Surf. What a difference it made not having to rinse those heavy things! I kept peeking at the wash on the line—to see what would happen. Well, my blankets dried so fluffy and smelled fresher than if they'd been rinsed.... Seeing is believing, but I still can't get over the way No-Rinse Surf got my husband's shirts so white—without a bit of bleach or hard scrubbing! I washed in *half* my usual time—and even ironing seemed to go easier.

This ad clearly referenced the work of laundering, making the typical promise of total relief, extending even to the ironing. And like the Tide ads, it featured a particularly demeaning representation of the housewife ideal rendered ecstatic over a clean blanket. Early television commercials for Surf reinforced the brand message with similar images of housewives. A 1950s black-and-white commercial featured a quartet of attractive housewives doing a kind of laundry chorus wearing their ruffled aprons and standing by washing machines or pushing grocery carts. With large showy smiles on their faces, they sing about the ease of doing laundry with Surf: "Use No Rinse Surf for a really clean wash. / It floats the dirt away. / Gets clothes so clean no need to rinse. / Switch to No-Rinse Surf today." From housewife to housewife, word spreads: "Mrs. Jones tells Mrs. Burke, that's the way it goes. / No-Rinse Surf saved half my work / And you should see my clothes—so clean!"

In addition to its emphasis on the housewife achieving clean laundry with ease, Surf continued to revise and perfect its advertising. Like other brands, it carefully ran consumer tests of different marketing strategies. For instance, DMB&B ran an ad in the *New York Daily* on January 12, 1955, inviting readers to send in their opinion as to which quality they would most like to see in a detergent: "sunshine freshness" when you couldn't hang your wash outside or the ability to keep white nylon from going gray. As DMB&B executive John Caples reported, the large number of women who wrote in—about 3,000—indicated consumers' interest in giving agencies their input, as well as the clear preference (1600 versus 1400) of those who wrote in for the keeping-nylon-white appeal. Other tests indicated that real consumers had little interest in qualities such as "causes less sneezing" (a reference to a short-lived campaign for Rinso) or "makes more suds" but did respond to highly perfumed formulas with the scientific-sounding ingredient "Puralin."[46] Manufacturers also extended detergent advertising into the classroom, obscuring their marketing in "lessons" for future housewives in home economics classes.[47]

Even as more effective machine technology and increased numbers of detergents on the market meant that manufacturers and advertisers had to more creatively brand their products with different kinds of appeals, laundry product advertising continued to depict laundry products wielded by housewives as transforming laundry work into caring homemaking. Increasingly, laundry product advertising drew more heavily on images and copy that emphasized how products allowed housewives to easily care for their family's clothing, particularly their children's clothes, and to achieve the highest standards of homemaking via beautifully clean and good-smelling clothes. Laundry soap advertising clearly reflects the postwar emphasis on proscribing women's social roles solely as wives and mothers, and in addition to Tide and Surf, many laundry products much 1950s depicted white housewives in aprons, neat hairdos, and high heels gleefully doing the laundry with ease. It built on the same kind of appeals used by laundry advertisers since the advent of modern advertising itself: linking laundry work with a mother's duties and promising to ease those duties, helping her transform them into a labor of love.

The promise of easing Mother's duties often suggested almost magical relief. On occasion throughout the twentieth century, the laundry product itself might be represented as having the same kinds of cleaning properties as a personified magical helper, specifically sent to aid the housewife in her efforts to achieve good homemaking and to care for her family.[48] An early example of such a magic helper in the laundry room was the Clorox Man. Magazine ads in the 1930s for Clorox multipurpose bleach featured a large anthropomorphized bottle of Clorox come to assist the housewife in the laundry room. In a 1934 ad, the Clorox Man rolls up his sleeves beside a scrubbing board and washtub while a housewife in an apron gazes adoringly at him. "I get by with the women!" the headline read, because "I do the jobs they dread." The copy continued:

"Blue Monday" never comes when I'm at work. I make the "white wash" snowy white. I brighten color-fast cottons and linens. It doesn't matter whether you use washing machine or tub. When I'm on the job—in soaking suds or first rinse—there's always less rubbing and scrubbing. And boiling is a time-and-effort waster you can forget.

The Clorox Man promised more than an easing of labor, however, in a 1939 ad headlined: "A Clorox-Clean Laundry is an Added Safeguard to Health!" As the copy asked: "Why court the spread of disease through germ-laded handkerchiefs, towels, table and bed linens? They may prove a grave menace to the health of the entire family unless made hygienically clean." Fortunately, the magic Clorox Man was on the job, appearing on top of the advertisement. His image still appeared almost 20 years later, in a 1953 advertisement. He offered amazing assistance to the housewife, promising not simply to ease her household labor but also to help her protect and safeguard her home, transforming housework into homemaking.

Magazine ads for Clorox in the 1950s also emphasized the product's role as protector of children's health. In a 1955 ad, a mother helps a little girl into bed. The word bubble over Mom reads: "I'm always proud of our Clorox-clean linens . . . and they're safer for health!" The copy of the ad, above a large drawing of the Clorox Bottle Man, reads: "Yes, homemakers responsible for family health depend on Clorox to make cottons and linens snowy-white, hygienically clean." The ad also featured a drawing of a housewife in an apron using Clorox around the house, but the magic Clorox Man was still there to help her do the jobs she dreaded and fight the "grave menace" of germs.

In another example of a magic helper come to the aid of the housewife, an animated snowman in a 1952 television commercial for Ivory Snow does her laundry, rinsing out her delicates in the bathroom sink, and then manning the washing machine to tackle the family wash.[49] Television commercials such as this one for laundry products frequently used animation and the suggestion of magical cleaning agents and ingredients, if not actual animated magic creatures, to promote their products. A 1958 Rinso Blue commercial titled "Miracle Molecules," for example, attempted to brand the product as a magical cleaner. It featured animated blue capital M letters (the Miracle Molecules) zooming around a dirty pair of overalls, while the voiceover explained: "They rush right in—get under dirt and carry it away, fast and easy."[50] Another 1958 series of Rinso Blue commercials positioned the miracle product as a particular help to the housewife taking care of a big family and doing multiple washes. In "Up to Your Elbows," the officious male announcer has this exchange with a housewife surrounded her children at play:

Announcer: Up to your elbows in kids?
Housewife: Yes, you might say that.
Announcer: Then you must do laundry 2, 3, 4 times a week.
Housewife [good naturedly]: You guessed it.
Announcer: Well, then! We have something new for you.

The animated Miracle Molecules then attack the housewife's laundry for her, and she's amazed at how Rinso Blue enables her to complete the family's wash more easily than ever before. Another commercial, "My Mommy," featured four children describing their mother's laundry work and how "Winso Bu-oo!" (as the young daughter adorably mispronounces it) assists Mommy: "My mommy does laundry 1, 2, 3, 4 a million times a week! That's why she uses Rinso Blue. It gets baby brother's diapers 'specially soft and white—Mommy likes that—cause she loves baby brother." Older brother Bobby, described in the commercial's script as a "12 yr. old 'quiz kid,'" i.e., a glasses-wearing smarty, demonstrates with a scientific diagram how Rinso Blue's Miracle Molecules "speed directly to the dirt," and "carry it all away so Rinso's sparkling Blue Brighteners can go to work." Rinso Blue was only one of many housework products that featured a pseudoscientific demonstration of the product's cleaning powers—a gambit that continues to the present day. But doing laundry with Rinso Blue promised more than scientific cleaning: the Miracle Molecules did Mommy's work for her, but moreover enabled her to easily do the laundry "a million times a week," if necessary, as a means of expressing her love for her family. She'll be pampering Baby Brother with diapers that are "'specially soft and white."

In a final example of a Rinso Blue commercial entitled "Big Family," an animated housewife contends with chores—ironing, folding clothes, diapering baby, standing at a washing machine—in a series of fast cuts. The announcer asks: "Big family? Trouble keeping up with 'em?" The husband butts in at this point: "Honey, I've only got one clean pair of socks left and no work pants!" The announcer attempts to continue: "Do you . . ." but now Junior needs help: "Hey Mom, where's my western t-shirt?" Announcer tries again: "Do you do laundry . . ." and this time the housewife/mom interrupts him as she mumbles to herself: "Diapers, diapers, diapers." The script carefully noted that although she mumbles to herself she is "not disagreeable." Even when a commercial, as this one did, seemed to point out the large amounts of repetitive housework facing a housewife, she could not actually express any outright anger at her family, especially the baby responsible for "diapers, diapers, diapers." Instead, Mom is freed by the Miracle Molecules of Rinso Blue speeding to the dirt and rendering the laundry duties faster and easier; transforming labor into loving care for her big family.

As the Rinso Blue commercials demonstrate, products might promise an easing of labor or special cleaning properties, but laundry advertising consistently reiterated domestic gender norms, depicting laundry not as labor but as homemaking and family care. That same representation of the housewife in the laundry room continued into the last half of the twentieth century. Laundry product advertising in the 1960s and 1970s continued to emphasize how their detergents and fabric softeners—sometimes with the help of magical creatures—would enable mothers to take good care of their families. But the housewife figure began to trouble ad makers and their clients. As the 1970s progressed, she began to look a bit dated, a bit too stereotyped in an era when Second Wave feminism and changing consumer attitudes meant that sexist images in advertising could not go unnoticed. However, advertising agencies and laundry product manufacturers clearly struggled during this time to find bankable strategies for representing laundry work. Advertising continued to rely heavily on positioning laundry work as mother's care for her family even as the housewife mom in jeans started to supplant the housewife in an apron. Indeed, the era saw some of the most ridiculous representations of housewives in all of housework advertising history.

An infamous series of 1960s commercials suggested that Ajax detergent would provide housewives with their own personal knight in shining armor—literally. In these commercials, an actor in armor, wielding a long lance and mounted on a galloping white charger, speeds across suburban landscapes, helping mothers tackle the family's laundry. One observes her children playing in a sandbox and laments, "If there's any dirt around, kids are sure to find it. I didn't think any detergent could get my wash clean." But as she demonstrates how white and bright her Ajax-washed laundry is, the knight appears along with the tagline "Stronger than dirt." That a housewife needed a knight in shining armor to rescue her begged the question: rescue her from what? Well, the never-ending demands of the family laundry for one thing. Still, even the Ajax housewife mom's work in the laundry room was more than mere labor—the Ajax commercials carefully represented the work as part of a mother's loving care of home and family.

One Ajax commercial from this time even directly contrasted a loving mother taking care of her family with other women. It opens with a slim young fashion model with a bitchy expression on her face being photographed. She says scornfully to the camera "I don't need it." In the next shot, a prissy and frowning spinster, working as an office secretary, avows "I don't need it." But then a smiling housewife mom in a blonde ponytail and button-down shirt says: "Well, I certainly do!" She's then shown in her laundry room with two children and husband, and what she needs is "real cleaning power in her laundry detergent." "With my bunch," she says, gesturing out the window to children romping on a tire swing, "I need all the power I can get." With a blare of trumpets, the Knight appears in the backyard.[51]

This commercial vividly illustrates how ad makers in the 1960s had already begun to consider how to continue to market detergents to their target consumers—married women with children—without depicting her as the stereotypical housewife in heels. This commercial offers a clear example of the emergence of the housewife mom. Like her housewife foremothers, she's white, she's pretty but not sexy, and she's clearly middle class as her nice laundry room and her pleasant backyard attest. But she's casually dressed. She's not clicking her heels over laundry detergent. And she's first and foremost, a "mom." Caring for her family is her job; a job depicted in flattering contrast to the self-centered clearly childless model and the dried up spinster stuck behind a desk. Yes, she's got work to do, but the rewards for her labors are shown swinging picturesquely in the backyard.

But ad makers' imaginations failed them, or perhaps became overactive, after this point in the commercial. A knight in shining armor—a particularly condescending magic housework helper—appears to help the housewife achieve good care of her family. In fact, the 1960s and 1970s saw a number of laundry product campaigns that indicated to what extent ad makers wrestled with how to depict housewives doing laundry in a changing era: along with an increase in the more socially acceptable moms doing laundry, commercials for laundry products during this time featured some of the most demeaning representations of housewives ever. For example, in a 1960s campaign even more absurd than a Lancelot in your laundry, Lever Brothers marketed a revamped Rinso (now called Sunshine Rinso) by suggesting that it contained such brightening power that dazzled housewives would be forced to don sunglasses. In one such television commercial, "Alice" pays a visit to "Mary," who's wearing dark sunglasses in her laundry room. Alice: "What's with the sunglasses?" Mary: "I'm washing with sunshine—new Sunshine Rinso with 'sunshine whiteners.' It makes clothes glow like sunshine." A patronizing announcer appeared to remind the gullible female consumer that of course "you won't really need" sunglasses, but "it's as close as you can get."[52]

Like a Miracle Molecule or a knight in armor springing from your box of soap, the awesome power of the sun poured out of Sunshine Rinso. In a radio spot from this campaign, a woman enters a store to buy a sundial:

Clerk: And how big is your garden?
Housewife: Oh, I want the <u>sundial</u> for my <u>laundry</u>.
Clerk: Your <u>laundry</u>?!
Housewife: I use Sunshine RINSO.
Clerk: Delightful, Madam. We use Sunshine Rinso in our laundry. It makes everything glow. My wife won't go near it without wearing sunglasses. Sunshine RINSO gets things as white and bright as they were when my sainted mother dried everything in the glorious Monday sun. I say, what a magnificent idea to have a sundial in your <u>laundry</u>!
Housewife: Doesn't everyone?

In another radio commercial, an encyclopedia salesman begins his doorstep spiel, but stops bewildered: "Another housewife in sunglasses?"

"Uh-uh. I'm washing with sunshine." Similarly, the radio spot called "Guess the Jingle" depicted a housewife completely entranced by Sunshine Rinso:

> **Announcer:** Hello, Mrs. Nealon? This is Jan Wells of "Guess That Jingle." Can you name that jingle we just played?
> **Mrs. Nealon:** Jan, I'm afraid I haven't been listening. I'm washing with this new sunshine detergent Mother told me about. It's got "sunshine whiteners"—to make clothes glow. You know [laughing], I even had to put on my sunglasses. It's really something this stuff. It really does act new.
> **Announcer:** But the jingle, Mrs . . .
> **Mrs. Nealon:** It's like you dried the clothes outdoors. It's called new Sunshine Rinso!
> **Announcer** [excited]: You're absolutely right! Mrs. Nealon, you've just won a year's supply of new glowing white Sunshine Rinso!
> **Mrs. Nealon:** I have?

The premise of housewives befuddled by laundry detergent so blindingly powerful that using it required protective eye gear probably aimed for a humorous new approach to an old product, but like the Ajex knight the cumulative effect was the same stereotypical housewife figure, besotted by a soap product.

Ad makers at this time were beginning to truly struggle with how best to market laundry products. In 1963, an executive at DMB&B gave a speech to P&G clients, specifically the group managers of laundry product brands Bonus, Cheer, Dash, and Ivory Snow. He described the problem faced by ad makers when it came to household products. In order to "make the product interesting," the creative staff had to "make your product a good guy, give it a personality, a world and a life of its own." However, he went, on: "If your product is a beautiful, high-powered automobile, it's easy to make it a good guy. But what if it's less sexy and alluring, *such as a laundry product*? Or a bathroom tissue? How in the world can you make them winsome, loveable good guys?" [emphasis added][53] Throughout the last decades of the 1900s, agencies seemed to truly struggle with this dilemma. Their answer to this problem drew on a longstanding theme in laundry product advertising: laundry work as mother's love for her family, as represented by a revitalized housewife figure—the housewife mom.

As Ruth Schwartz Cowan points out in her history of housework, modern advertising sought to invest laundry with new housework-related meaning, specifically the emotional love and care of the family: "Laundering had once been just a task to be finished as quickly as possible; now it was an expression of love. The new bride could speak her affection by washing tattle-tale gray out of her husband's shirts."[54] After laundry detergent and automatic washing machines became commonplace, advertising sought to brand laundry products even more clearly as enabling the housewife mom to achieve the highest emotional and stain-busting standards possible. This ongoing theme in laundry product advertising became the most widely accepted strategy when housewife stereotypes became unmarketable for laundry products. A 1960s commercial for Fels laundry detergent, a Purex offshoot, made this particularly clear. The voiceover asks: "What is a woman? Someone who cares. For her family, she wants bright clean clothes. Soft fluffy clothes." In rushes Junior wearing a heavily stained shirt and housewife mom removes the shirt and gets to work. The voiceover promises magic: "Washes dirt out, keeps softness in." Laundry no longer required a scrubbing board (for most Americans, anyway). It did, however, require a mother's special attention because "someone who cares," the only person who could transform laundry work into caring, was Mom. The housewife mom didn't wear heels and an apron, or hug boxes of detergent to her bosom, but like the Tide and Super Suds housewives, she bore sole responsibility for her children's safety and happiness and made laundry a labor of love.

Babies especially required Mother's care in the laundry room. For example, in the 1950s P&G sought to brand their new version of Ivory, a flaked soap called Ivory Snow, as the brand for mothers. Typical Ivory Snow ads published in parenting magazines in the 1950s featured cute babies proclaiming: "My Mommy washes all my things in Ivory Snow." The tagline for such ads always read "Safest possible soap for baby's things . . . for yours too."[55] In a good example of how modern advertising never contented itself with traditional media alone, Ivory Snow advertising might arrive at a woman's hospital bedside alongside her newborn, as DMB&B executive Artherton Hobler described:

> Early in 1950, a small Boston company began to distribute to mothers of new babies an assortment of useful and familiar items relating to baby-care. The average package contained a half dozen products and valuable gift certificates and introductory offers provided by participating merchants. Dominating every Gift-Pax assortment, in size, interest and value was a regular size package of Ivory Snow and a message of congratulations from Proctor and Gamble. Thus, Gift-Pax were channeled against the baby wash diaper usage at the time when Mother's interest was focused on the care of the baby; they carried with them hospital endorsement of the product; and they stimulated genuine gratitude on the part of the Mother for [Ivory] Snow.[56]

The "gifting" of certain products to new mothers as part of a concerted effort to reach that particular consumer group continues to this day, and although the origin of the practice is unclear, DMB&B certainly hit upon an important way to powerfully brand their product—in this case, a laundry soap—as a necessary part of good mothering (endorsed by the hospital) and to inspire consumer loyalty to the product.

The branding of Ivory Snow as gentle enough for a baby continued into the 1960s. A series of ads based on the tagline "The softer the diaper, the safer for your baby's skin" appeared in magazines in 1960. The headline for a 1963 ad with a photo of a newborn reads: "Lucky girl. Mommy's nose, daddy's mouth, and the safest diaper possible!" "Where does the diaper come from?" asks the copy. "From an Ivory Snow wash, that's where!" But more explicitly, an Ivory Snow wash done by Mom: "See why Ivory Snow should be part of a mother's special care?" chided a magazine ad in 1962. A 1961 Clio Award-winning television commercial featured a male announcer in a bow tie wielding a "Baby Language Translator." As the baby babbles away, the man translates for the cameras:

> You say your diapers aren't comfortable? Well, feel this [hands baby a cloth diaper]. This was washed in Ivory Flakes [baby cuddles diaper]. That's a baby's idea of soft, eh? Your mother probably washes your diapers in detergent [pours detergent onto high chair tray and baby feels it]. Feels scratchy, you say? [Pours Ivory Flakes out and baby feels them.] Easy way to remember. Ivory Flakes feel softer. They get diapers softer [baby shrieks enthusiastically, while appearing to admire box of product]. Good idea. Mothers, we both suggest you use Ivory Flakes in the machine. Because Ivory Flakes don't just wash diapers. They wash and soften too.

Even when baby himself wasn't hectoring mothers about diaper softness, Ivory's advertising continued to build on the appeal to mothers. So did other brands, like Dreft in a 1970s television commercial depicting a frazzled mom and a cranky baby. The problem? "Maybe diaper problems you can't see but baby can feel." Bounce fabric softener dryer sheets in a 1978 magazine ad used similar copy: "Your most precious bundle deserves Bounce softness and freshness.[57] Ivory Snow television commercials in the 1960s featured loving mothers diapering their adorable babies, and the tag "The safest possible soap a mother can use."[58] In a 1970s television commercial for Ivory Snow, two craggy farmers hold babies wearing cloth diapers. Are they fathers? Do they perhaps change diapers on a regular basis? No, they are just there to demonstrate that even their calloused, work-roughened hands can feel that the diapers washed in Ivory Snow are softer. A 1975 magazine ad suggested another kind of comparison test, for Mom this time:

> Feeling is believing. If you use a detergent, compare your baby's clothes with someone who washes her baby's clothes with Ivory Snow. Maybe it's your

next-door neighbor. Feel the shirt, the blankets, the bibs, the towels as well as the diapers. You'll be able to feel the difference. Once you take this simple test, we think you'll want to give your baby the comfort of Ivory Snow softness. Not just on his bottom, but all over.

Ivory Snow's brand message was clear: good mothers would care enough about their baby's comfort to do laundry the right way.

Laundry product advertising often linked good laundry with good mothering in this way. But as the century progressed, ad makers clearly felt they could also market products by continuing to promise consumers that a certain detergent would make both laundry and mothering easier. By the 1960s, television commercials couldn't suggest that without their product, women would have to stand over a boiling cauldron of clothes. However they could suggest that the family wash presented a lot of work for Mom—work that with the right product could be rendered an easy part of the emotional care for the family. Laundry products no longer had to promise whitening without scrubbing, but they could promise products that would make a wife and mother's possible resentment about bearing sole responsibility for every clean article of clothing and household linen disappear, transforming housework into loving mothering. For example, a woman's voiceover asked in a 1970s Cheer ad, "Ever wonder how your son gets clothes so dirty? Look at his father and stop wondering!" Then the housewife mom smilingly watches hubby and son making a doghouse—and a big mess—in the backyard. Instead of screaming at them to get out of the mud for God's sake, she just laughs and calls them into lunch. The voiceover continues: "There they are, two dirty boys. Creators of dirty laundry. But you have all temperature Cheer. A really advanced formula." The "advanced formula" promised not just cleaning power, but it rendered the work of laundry—cleaning up the filth of the family—so easy that "you" need not scold or fret about dirty clothes. Rather, "you" could take great care of your "two dirty boys" and keep a smile on your face the whole time.

The rambunctious, clothes-staining son, and mother easily providing emotional care through laundry, appeared often in detergent advertising during this period, such as a series of late 1970s and early 1980s commercials for Bold featuring the jingle "He's a bold one, he's a bold one." In one such commercial, Mom and Grandma smile indulgently as they watch a little boy run around the yard chasing puppies and getting his clothes filthy. As Mom explains to Grandma in the laundry room: "Butch gets things dirtier than anyone in the family. But I still want him to look as nice as the rest of us." Grandma: "Found a way?" Of course: Bold detergent. Similarly, although we don't see her at work, the housewife mom in a late 1970s Gain commercial cleans up after her sons. Two boys make a huge, messy milkshake from a variety of ingredients, each causing a different kind of stain when the blender spills onto the tablecloth: "Now your tablecloth is stained and how!" comments the voiceover. But with the magical ability of Gain to remove every particle of each kind of stain (as demonstrated via pseudoscientific animation), "Now your tablecloth is clean again." "Complex stain, complex Gain," the tag ended. Couched in scientific language, Gain's stain-fighting properties still promised Mom a new kind of magic, enabling "you" to clean up after your children with a minimum of effort and without fussing at your mess-making children. As the Tide jingle for 1974–1975s commercial put it: "Kids seem to keep on getting dirty. / You seem to take it all in stride. / You get a lot of dirt with children. / You get a lot of clean with Tide." The housewife mom explained that kids "grind the dirt in," but "I know Tide'll get 'em clean." "Tide gets out the dirt kids get into," concluded the tag. That is, Tide used by the loving mother who "takes it all in stride." Reflecting and reinforcing domestic gender norms, in this commercial it wasn't enough anymore for Mom to simply guard her family against germs—she also had to calmly and lovingly mother her children with clean clothes; to "take it all in stride."

In a series of early 1970s commercials, Tide referenced Mom's ability to tackle dirt and stains, this time using the hidden-camera interview to document supposedly real housewife moms leaving the grocery store with Tide in their shopping baskets. A man in suit carrying a microphone talks with them. In one, a Mrs. Joyce Windsor of Clinton, Maryland, tells an interviewer she uses Tide because it "Gets my clothes clean." The interviewer holds up a very dirty boy's shirt and they converse about it:

Interviewer: Has Tide helped you with a problem that bad?
Mrs. Windsor [closely examining the shirt]: Yes.
Interviewer [amazed]: Really?
Mrs. Windsor: I . . . this is everyday stuff for me.
Interviewer [amazed again]: Really?
Mrs. Windsor: I have two boys, one of them plays Little League baseball so you can imagine what I have to contend with. My boys play out every day. They're playing out today in the mud. So, I stick with Tide.

In another such commercial, Mrs. Ruth Rogers of Bowie, Maryland, reiterates how Tide helps her care for her rough and tumble boys:

Mrs. Rogers: I've tried others. I've always gone back to Tide.
Interviewer [nodding to little boy standing by the shopping cart]: Does he go out and get himself pretty dirty?
Mrs. Rogers: Yes. So do his brothers. My sons like to go fishing.

Interviewer: Yeah?
Mrs. Rogers: And the dirt around here leaves such a stain. Mud, y'know. Usually what I have to do is take the clothes and hose them off first.

From having to "hose down" her children to laughing off the worst kinds of stains, women in late-1970s laundry product advertising faced a mountain of laundry work, but with the right product had no problem at all shouldering this burden. In this series, Tide is that product, and the commercials all go on to demonstrate the housewife mom's loyalty to Tide by having the interviewer offer her "twice as much of another leading product" in exchange for her box of Tide. The women cling to their boxes, wrenching them out of the interviewer's hands: "Give me back my Tide!" As the amused interviewer concludes, chuckling, in one: "Well, that's the way it is. Some ladies won't swap their Tide for even twice as much of another leading detergent."

It is impossible to know to what extent these "real" women offered unscripted testimonials for Tide. Unlike the housewives in the 1949 Surf newspaper ads, these women conform to certain standards of appearance: pretty but not sexy, casually but neatly dressed. They do not differ significantly from the actresses hired to play housewife moms in other commercials. Demonstrating the growing sensitivity among ad makers to charges of stereotyping, these housewife moms aren't befuddled by sunshine in a box and they don't trip out to the clothesline in an apron and heels. At the same time, however, reflecting this transitional period of laundry advertising the housewife mom in these commercials is so bored and lonely that she'll converse with a stranger about laundry, and then cling pathetically to her box of Tide. The condescending interviewer might have been a stand-in for many ad makers themselves, chortling over the little housewife manipulated by clever brand marketing.

In another cringe-worthy series of Tide commercials in the 1970s, real-life housewives take on a hidden-camera challenge: cleaning a particularly dirty load of clothes and, if successful, receiving a year's worth of free detergent. The camera zooms in as each woman contemplates the stained clothes and then a selection of detergents and cleansers. When she chooses Tide, the interviewer always tries to talk her into trying another brand. Again, they cling comically to their box of Tide. In one, an African American woman identified as Mrs. Ginny Stewart, wearing a neat suit dress and neck scarf, assesses the dirty laundry:

Mrs. Stewart: It looks like one big mess. It looks impossible doesn't it?
Interviewer: Could you get this clean?
Mrs. Stewart [fairly confident]: I feel that I could.

Interviewer: If you get it clean, I'll give you a year's supply of free detergent.

Mrs. Stewart [a little sassy now]: Better be the right detergent!

What Mrs. Stewart considers "the right detergent" becomes immediately clear: she selects Tide do this load of laundry, and when the interviewer attempts to talk her into using "a liquid," she hangs onto the box of Tide laughing nervously and insisting "I'd rather use Tide!" As illustrated by this commercial, by the 1970s ad makers clearly felt they needed to diversity the image of the housewife and began to include African American women in mainstream housework advertising. But in every other way, this more racially diverse representation of housewives and housewife moms conformed to previous housework advertising, and upheld gender norms. An idealized housewife mom figure did not need to be white, but she did need to know which brand of detergent could best handle her family's laundry problems.

Getting Hubby's shirt clean had, of course, been a desirable goal in laundry product advertising since the beginning of modern advertising. But detergents and cleaners began to promise not simply clean shirts, but also husbands who appreciated them. As the housewife mom in laundry advertising increasingly demonstrated the important link between laundry products and good mothering, a number of campaigns utilized the appeal of a husband and/or family inspired to actually notice—for a change— Mom's work in the laundry room. Downey fabric softener commercials in the mid-1970s frequently suggested that the product would result in a more appreciative family. In one, a family (mom, dad, daughter, son) on vacation unpacks in a motel room:

Daughter: Gee, Mom, these are different from our towels at home.
Son: Yeah, ours are softer.
Daughter: And where's that nice smell towels are 'sposed to have?
Mom: Back home. In my bottle of Downy.

Now back at home, mom folds laundry at the kitchen table.

Dad [getting cookies out of a cookie jar]: Glad you're home again, doing your *own* wash?
Mom [with arms full of towels]: Oh, I don't mind. Those kids. Really!
Dad [eating cookie]: What now?
Mom: After all the complaining about the towels at that motel, wouldn't you think they notice what *I* do for their things, rinsing them in Downy?
Daughter [coming in taking towel down from around hair]: Mom, this feels soft. It smells like towels are 'sposed to. [takes a deep sniff] Fresh!

Mom: She noticed!
Dad [laughing]: Like she's supposed to.

The commercial ends with the promise: "A noticeable improvement." Dad's last comment suggested that maybe he had already showered the housewife with appreciation for his spring-fresh towels—had he already "noticed?"

In another Downy commercial the husband does finally take note of his wife's efforts in the laundry room. An African American dad explains math problems to his bewildered young daughter, while Mom somewhat broodingly folds laundry in the next room:

> **Mom:** Ralph really pays attention to Janie's homework. Wish he noticed the homework *I* do! Look how nice I get his clothes, with Downy. So soft—he won't notice that! Or how Downy rinses out static cling. Still . . .
> **Janie** [Cut to Janie sniffing Dad's shirt]: Mmmm! Smell! [Ralph sniffs sleeves]
> **Mom:** Downy's April fresh smell! He oughta notice that!
> **Ralph:** Honey, this shirt smells great.
> **Mom:** [laundry in hand, stunned] You noticed!
> **Janie:** We noticed.

Ad makers appeared to be cognizant of the need to avoid the most overtly stereotypical images, and seemed to want to avoid depicting women in their advertising as "just a housewife." But they also could not afford to offend what they believed was their target consumer. So they shifted to a new emphasis on the role of mothers and heightened standards of good mothering: now it included making sure everyone's clothes smelled good. And, as a bonus, maybe at long last the family would look up and *notice* Mom's special care.

Like the Tide commercial, 1970s commercials like this one for Downy also show how the white, middle-class wife and mother caring for her family underwent a cosmetic change at this time, becoming the usually but *not always* white, middle-class wife and mom caring for her family. Housework advertising seamlessly incorporated images of African American housewives and housewife moms, in both targeted and mainstream ads and commercials, illustrating just how powerfully Americans framed housework as women's homemaking but not necessarily white women's work. Racial stereotypes essentially disappeared from housework advertising by the last decades of the twentieth century but domestic gender norms remained firmly in place. In 1970s housework advertising, housewife moms, black and white (agencies were slower to urge their housework product clients to consider other "ethnic" markets), labored in fairly thankless conditions, but with the help of the right laundry product, received new gratitude for a job well done. Laundry product advertising sought to ensure that consumers viewed doing the laundry as more meaningful than mere drudgery—as part of good mothering and caring for the family.

For instance, other commercials in this Downy series combined the appeal of "a noticeable improvement" among family members with an emphasis on how Downy would enable consumers to achieve the highest possible standards of homemaking—higher than your less fastidious neighbor, or in this case, a less caring mother. When Daughter, star of the school play, borrows a friend's towel backstage, she comments to her mother: "Mom, Cathy's towel isn't soft like ours." Mom: "Oh?" Daughter: "And where's that nice smell?" "At home in our bottle of Downy," Mom smugly replies. Similarly, young Ricky appears in the laundry room wearing a t-shirt he traded with pal Jeff, but as he tells his mother, he's going to trade the shirt back because "it doesn't feel as good as mine" and "my shirts are softer" and "smell better." "Hope Jeff trades back my shirt," worries Ricky. One Downy commercial even put words of appreciation into a child's mouth when he was too young to speak them himself. A mother feeding a young baby in a high chair ties on his bib and delivers the following monologue:

> There, Sweetie-poo. Nice and soft. [baby murmurs] I know, you want lunch. Why should you notice how soft I got your bib with Downy? Downy helps it stay white. Still, you ought to notice the smell. Downy keeps clothes smelling [sniffs laundry from basket nearby] April fresh. [Baby murmurs again, and holds bib to nose.] You noticed! I think. Are you grateful enough to eat spinach for me?

The Downy commercials illustrate two important directions for laundry product advertising in the 1970s: first, new ever-higher standards of homemaking and mothering, including providing every member of the family with baby soft, April fresh laundry at all times; second, addressing the fact that real-life women might be feeling like nobody noticed their labors.

By the mid-1970s, advertising agencies began to take seriously the idea that in order to best market their housework-related products they needed to be aware of the Second Wave feminist movement and the subsequent national debates about women's social, cultural, and economic roles in the United States. Agencies such as Batten, Barton, Durstine, and Osborne conducted their own feminist focus groups, for instance.[59] In 1975, JWT circulated a document entitled "Advertising and Women: A Report on Advertising Portraying or Directed to Women" compiled by the Consultive

Panel of the National Advertising Review Board in New York. In the section entitled "The Portrayal of Women as Housewives," the report read:

> The advertising of household products poses special problems. Housework is an emotionally charged subject. Feminist literature is replete with complaints that housework has been women's special burden. Books of fact and fiction have stressed the lonely, repetitive drudgery of housework as a waste of women's talents. The fact that housekeeping has been made easier by efficient appliances, convenience foods, and other modern practices that advertising has helped bring into common use, does little to alter critical perceptions of the job itself.[60]

In other words, advertising agencies felt keenly that housework itself was perceived most widely as "lonely, repetitive drudgery." And yet they still had to effectively market products related to this "emotionally charged subject." As feminists continued to challenge gender norms in all areas of life, ad makers who relied on representations of housewives to sell their housework-related products had to take into account the "critical perceptions of the job itself." The Downy ads reflected the new housewife mom strategy: branding the product as transforming the drudgery of housework and the maligned role of housewife into an appreciated act with "noticeable" results: rewarding homemaking and mothering, not merely boring housework.

In 1977 Rena Bartos spoke to this subject in a video made by the Canadian Advertising Advisory Board and intended for circulation and viewing within the advertising industry. Bartos, a JWT vice president, urged her colleagues and peers to rethink housework-related advertising. Consumer research, she argued, showed that "every woman we interviewed, from the most traditional housewife to the most sophisticated career woman, really rejected the insulting, demeaning, condescending tone of voice of much of the traditional advertising." The video even singled out laundry detergent ads, in a dramatization of consumer comments at the beginning of the video: "I just can't relate to commercials that make it seem that a detergent is the most important thing in my life. It just doesn't mean that much."[61] But during the transitional 1970s and 1980s, even as ad agencies took up the issue of female stereotypes, commercials that implied that "detergent is the most important thing" in a woman's life enjoyed one last major surge in production, with newly revived emphasis on the housewife mom's loving care for her husband and children.

A number of laundry product campaigns in the 1970s seemed determined to not only continue representing the laundry room as a site where housewife moms transformed laundry labor into loving care for family, but also instill new anxiety and guilt. Most famously, Whisk launched a particularly memorable appeal for its product's ability to fight "ring around the collar." In a typical example from this campaign, a husband and wife toss rings onto pegs at the country fair. They're having a good time, until the smart aleck female carney running the game peers down hubby's neck and snipes: "That's not the only ring you've got. You've got ring around the collar." The camera cuts to the wife's anguished face, as she groans in embarrassment. In the next scene, the wife scrubs at her husband's collar in vain, while the voiceover intones: "Those dirty rings! You try spraying and even scrubbing with powders and still you've got [the carney's nasal voice chimes in] 'ring around the collar.'" Again, the shamed wife moans aloud. But with Whisk, she defeats this dread enemy, and in the last scene, the man emerges from the next room carrying a stuffed bear: "This time you deserve the prize!" "I *do*?" Giving her a kiss, he explains: "No more ring around the collar!"

But Whisk was not the only brand attempting to create new kinds of laundry guilt. Bold 3 ran a series where a male voiceover accosts various housewife moms about their laundry. In one, we hear him say to the mother supervising her twins on the playground:

Voiceover: Your twins' clothes look nice, Mrs. Michaels.
Mrs. Michaels [to camera] Thanks! I work hard to do my wash just right.
Voiceover: Too bad it's only second rate!
Mrs. Michaels [stunned]: Whaaaat?
Voiceover: Second rate! Your detergent doesn't get clothes clean and soft and static control [*sic*]?
Mrs. Michaels[scoffing]: Well, no detergent can do that.

Au contraire, Mrs. Michaels. As the Voice explains, Bold 3, "a milestone in laundry history," does precisely that. Mrs. M. tries it and enthuses in the laundry room: "The twins' dirty playsuits come out Sunday clean. But even more, their terry robes are soft and smell good. My regular fabric softener couldn't do better. These clingy socks slid right apart, because Bold controls static." Appeals based on simple cleaning abilities had lost their power, but now advertising suggested new washing responsibilities. Just getting the clothes clean wasn't enough. What about ring around the collar? What about static control? A mother who let her children suffer in static-y socks clearly wasn't living up to the highest ideals of homemaking.

Around the same time, a commercial for Biz portrayed a woman's failure to *really* remove stains from her husband's shirt. Hubby's eagle eye spots something on his white shirt:

Husband: Joan, what's on this shirt?
Joan: Where?
Husband [pointing]: Right here.

Joan: That's where I got out the blueberry stain.
Husband: Well, maybe you got out the stain but it sure left a shadow.

With the application of the correct laundry product—Biz—Joan is able to rectify the terrible mistake of not thoroughly removing the stains her slob husband left on his shirt. In the last scene, Joan, perhaps seeking some recognition of her work in the laundry room, playfully asks her husband: "Where's the shadow?" Husband: "Shadow? Oh! Hey, how'd you get it out?" The wife, suddenly coy, replies: "That's my Biz." In this commercial, Joan successfully rights her wrong, succeeding with "Biz"—the product—in *her* "biz" of doing the family's laundry.

In a Clorox campaign from the late 1970s, "real" housewives are put on notice in their own laundry rooms of just how they've failed their husbands and children when it comes to clean clothes. Each commercial in this series begins with a female interviewer questioning a housewife mom in the driveway of her home. In one such commercial, the interview begins: "How does your daughter *feel* about the wash?" Mrs. Evelyn Schoepp answers, with a cynical laugh, "She couldn't care less." But in the laundry room, as the daughter examines two piles of laundry, a different picture emerges. "Which blouse would you rather wear?" asks the interviewer. "This one [the one washed with detergent *and* Clorox] is much cleaner than this one. It's a good feeling when you wear something clean." A sheepish Mrs. Schoepp comments, "Well I said you wouldn't care!" In the last shot, Mrs. Schoepp tells the camera: "I see now that she does care." Similarly, Mrs. Sandra Edmondson described her teenage son's feelings about laundry: "I don't think he cares about the wash." But Son picks the Clorox piles of clothes, though he's quick to note his masculine disregard for the feminine world of the laundry room: "Well, I think this pile is cleaner, but you know I'm not into wash at all." However, as he notes in the end shot: "If *I* can tell, anybody can."

Many commercials in this series focused not on offspring but on husbands. An African American woman assured the interviewer that her husband "does not care at all" about laundry. But then he picks out the Clorox-cleaned socks: "They just look cleaner. Who wants to walk around in dull socks?" A stunned wife agrees: "Yes! I'd rather see you in these." "I believe he cares," she concluded. Such scripts underscored the need for a housewife mom to better fulfill her caretaking responsibilities in the laundry room, and they also implied that with the correct product, the previously inattentive husband might start to notice the housewife's labors: "he cares." For instance, a smirking Mrs. Clyde Rizzo states that husband Mike "doesn't care about it. At all." But when Mike, in a serious tone, explains: "I'd rather wear these. They look cleaner. And, I'm very particular about my clothes," Mrs. Rizzo exclaims in amazement: "I see he does care about it even though he's never talked to me about it. A clean wash *is* important to Mike." In another commercial, a soon to be chastened Mrs. Rae Morris has this initial exchange with the interviewer:

> **Mrs. Morris**: My husband takes the laundry for granted.
> **Interviewer** [challengingly]: Do you add Clorox?
> **Mrs. Morris** [suddenly less certain]: No . . . I don't.
> **Interviewer** [superciliously]: Let's see if your husband *really* cares.

Sure enough, as the husband confirms: "I like to look clean and feel clean." Mrs. Morris responds: "I think that he really cares. I can see the difference. So it has to be Clorox. He cares!" Housewife moms in these commercials are directly accused of not taking enough loving care of their offspring and husbands via clean laundry. They assume their families don't care. However, as they discover, laundry does matter. But the final lines—"He cares," "I really didn't realize she cared so much," "I believe he cares"—didn't just highlight the women's failings. They also seemed to suggest some kind of worth and value in laundry work. Not only did it matter what product she used, but also the whole important task of emotional caretaking through laundry fell to her. She was no longer "just a housewife" drudging along in the laundry room. Clorox allowed these housewife moms to render the thankless toil of laundry—long recognized by ad makers—into emotionally significant work; to transform it into homemaking and, in particular, caring for children.

In another such transformation, some of first magazine ads for Bounce dryer fabric softener sheets emphasized how the housewife mom could use this laundry product to care for her family. A 1972 ad in the *Ladies Home Journal*, picturing a housewife mom standing by her open dryer, explained: "The Bounce Touch makes her husband's cotton pajamas really soft."[62] A series of ads in women's magazines in 1974 built on this initial appeal. Members of the nuclear family pose next to written descriptions of how Bounce made their clothes clean and fresh while also eliminating static cling. The ads named the families in bold headlines: "The Healys discover the Bounce Touch," for example. And every ad included a photo of Mom standing next her dryer, with captions such as "The Bounce Touch means it's easy for Mrs. Healy to do something nice for her family." In one such ad, an African American mom in a checked shirt, Mrs. Brooks, stands sorting laundry while her husband watches, feeling his shirt and her son sniffs his shirt. The only difference between Mrs. Brooks and Mrs. Healy is the color of their skin. In housework advertising, as "housewife" gave way to "housewife mom," ad makers increasingly depicted more racially diverse women, but in every other respect—wife (wedding ring usually visible) and mother, middle-class, neatly attired and so on—she remained the same. Gender norms linking domesticity with feminine care and home-making continued to be the single most significant social and cultural influence on housework advertising.

By the 1970s, manufactures and advertising agencies knew that they needed to start rethinking how to market laundry products. Yet they struggled for several decades to find ways to advertise laundry products without resorting to the most clichéd appeals, and the era witnessed the creation of some of the most demeaning representations of housewives. Ad makers remained convinced, even though their own research sometimes suggested otherwise, that they needed to strongly link laundry with women caring for home and family. Still, an important evolution happening throughout housework advertising occurred in laundry product advertising: agencies began to move away from guilt-inducing appeals like ring around the collar or magic helpers in the laundry room and moved instead toward the emotional fulfillment of laundry work for one's family. As a housewife mom in a 1989 Gain commercial summarized: "You know [the family's clothes] are clean 'cause they smell so fresh. And when folks notice, you can feel yourself glowing, you're so proud. The huggable smell of Gain makes a mama proud."[63] But although "ring around the collar" went the way of disco and polyester pantsuits, in the 1980s, 1990s, and well into the twenty-first century, "mom" continues to be practically the sole occupant of the laundry room.

Even as laundry product advertising embraced a newly revitalized link between laundry and a mother's love, manufacturers were alert to expanding markets and the housewife moms pictured in their advertising reflected the shift: by the end of the twentieth century, more racially diverse images of mothers appeared in housework advertising. But advertising continued to reinforce domestic gender norms, and in particular, an idealized representation of mothering: housework in general and laundry work in particular continued to be portrayed as part of feminine care for the family. No matter what her race or ethnicity, the housewife mom had to be alert to how good mothering required using a particular brand of laundry soap. For example, Ivory Snow ads from the 1990s in *Essence*, a monthly magazine aimed explicitly at a female African American demographic, demonstrate how manufacturers and ad agencies continued to emphasize the housewife's laundry work as "mom's" work, specifically safeguarding the comfort of one's baby. An August 1990 ad in *Essence* promoted the newly formulated Ivory Snow Liquid, as "still Ivory Snow mild" but "cleans as well as 'adult' detergents—without a laundry list of chemical additives. And it helps baby clothes retain their flame-retardancy."[64]

The ad not so subtly suggests that a mother who did not want to see her baby burned alive would not wash away the flame-retardant coatings on her baby's clothes with some other harsh laundry detergent. In a nod to increasing consumer environmental consciousness, it also promised that Ivory Snow could do this without "a laundry list of chemical additives." Ivory's 100+ year brand image as pure and gentle came to the aid of this appeal, suggesting to the consumer that the product could clean but could do so "gently."

The equation of a mother's care with a laundry soap continued throughout the 1990s. "Our New Bottle For Your New Baby," reads the headline in one such *Essence* ad, above a wicker laundry basket topped with Ivory Snow. The tagline clearly positioned the product as part a mother's care: "The most caring kind of clean." In a similar ad, a large photo of an adorable (African American) baby in a delicate white-footed garment took up almost the entire page in *Essence*. "Dress your baby head-to-toe in the tender loving clean of Ivory Snow," reads the caption. A 1994 ad featured a photograph of newborn cradled in a mother's arms: "Everything that touches her should be as gentle as you," reads the head-line. "Adult detergents can leave baby clothes rough," cautions the copy. "Ivory Snow is different."

In 1992, another Ivory Snow *Essence* ad pictured both expectant mother and her husband smiling over a crib, with the headline "How do you wel-come your baby home[?]" But despite both mother and father appearing in the photo, only "you" could make the necessary preparations for baby's arrival—via the correct laundry product:

> You're painting his room the color of sunlight. Combing the town for the cuddliest bear. Singing to him while he waits to be born. Now's a good time to wash all his things in Ivory Snow, before he comes home. Ivory Snow cleans baby's things safely, leaving them feeling soft (almost) as he is. Nothing stiff or rough against his tender skin. Because the way home first feels stays with him forever.

"Soft and Secure," reads the tagline. This ad demonstrates that by the early 1990s, the representation of the housewife mom had become ubiquitous, even as her complexion and ethnicity might have varied. Moreover, "mom" remained married, middle class (the preparation of an elaborate nursery as a prerequisite to giving birth, for example), and devoted to the care of home and family. It also demonstrates the same old theme of creating anxiety and offering a purchasable solution: this ad suggests that even a slightly scratchy onesie that touches a baby's skin could emotionally and physically scar him for life, and "stay with him forever."

Over the course of the late twentieth century and into the twenty-first, advertisers continued to market their laundry products with images of the housewife mom transforming laundry into an expression of love. They no longer depicted her in a demeaning, simple-minded showdown with her neighbor over who washed diapers better; nor did women hoist boxes of detergent aloft with maniacal glee. But advertising still depicted the housewife mom as caring for her family via clean, soft laundry. Even when she could no longer be depicted solely as a white woman, a mother's care, as expressed in providing clean clothes and linens, continued to be a theme. As a 1993 ad in *Essence* for Downy fabric softener summarized, beneath a photograph of a stack of towels: "Only Ultra Downey gives you more softness. The fluffiest softness. Just what you want for your family."[65]

Tide ads in *Essence* even more explicitly aimed at creating an image for Tide as the housewife mom's best aid in caring for her family's clothes. Side-by-side comparison photos of a set of clothes, one set dirty and one set clean, in a 1990 *Essence* ad reads: "He turned his new school clothes into play clothes. You turned them back." "If it's got to be clean, it's got to be Tide," concludes the tag. "You" had expanded to include black women, but "you" still clearly meant Mom in the laundry room, ensuring Junior had spanking clean clothes for school. Like much of all laundry product advertising by the 1990s, these ads in *Essence* do not actually depict a woman doing the laundry. Careful to avoid any depictions of women in laundry rooms that might trigger memories of the now socially unacceptable images of the grinning housewife in an apron, by the end of the twentieth century many ads and commercials for laundry products avoided altogether the image of a woman and her washing machine. This may well have been even more important in *Essence*: no agency or manufacturer wanted to be accused of using a "mammy" figure in the laundry room. However, agencies had no problem at all with suggesting, with both copy and images, that Mom would of course continue to be responsible for the laundry. For example, a Tide ad in 1991 compared a man's shirt first stained with barbecue sauce, then stain-free: "Ruined by dad's secret recipe. Saved by mom's secret weapon."[66] Ignoring the possibility that if Dad stained it, Dad should maybe clean it himself, the (unseen) housewife mom in this ad called upon her arsenal of laundry products to ensure loving care for her husband.

Similarly, contemporary advertisements published in *Buenhogar*, the Spanish-language version of *Good Housekeeping*, defined laundry as women's work, even if the ads did not actually depict women working in the laundry room. The magazine acknowledged its Latina consumer base by endorsing laundry brand products specific to a Hispanic market, such as Ensueño fabric softener, but advertisements for well-known brands such as Downey and Clorox appeared as well and they just as clearly depicted laundry as gendered care.[67] For instance, in a 2006 ad for Tide, a soccer player in a brilliantly white shirt sits in a locker room and explains: "Gracias a mi mujer hasta los jugadores contraries envidian cómo luce mi camiseta" ("Thanks to my wife, even the players on the other team envy how my shirt shines"). Echoing the themes of domestic care for family strongly evoked in the ads featuring "mom's secret weapon," this ad demonstrated how easily the housewife transitioned into the twenty-first century, continuing to appear (even when she did not, literally, appear in the ad) as the sole actor in the laundry room; even when she was presumably Latina or at least created to appeal to Latina consumers.

An early example of a Latina housewife mom appeared in a 1973 Tide magazine ad in *Family Circle*. It depicted "Lydia Alcala" next to her new Kelvinator washing machine, holding her toddler son. The headline read: "Should a woman use Tide just because Kelvinator packed a coupon for a free box in her new washer? Lydia Alcala says no." The copy reads:

> That coupon got me to try Tide, but I wasn't going to keep using it if it didn't work. I think a woman should make up her own mind. I work part time and my mother babysits for my two-year-old son. She doesn't have the heart to stop David from playing in the dirt even when he's wearing his good clothes. But Tide gets David's clothes so clean, I don't feel I have reason to complain about how dirty he gets.[68]

This Tide ad vividly illustrates some of the important tensions shaping housework advertising generally and laundry product advertising specifically in the 1970s and 1980s. On the one hand, ad makers felt compelled to at least occasionally make some kind of gesture toward women's changing social roles. In this case, it's Mrs. Alcala's "part time" job. The ad even obliquely hints at some of the childcare issues faced by mothers working outside the home. It sought to give lip service to women's "liberation" while at the same time continuing to depict laundry as part of a housewife mom's housework responsibilities.[69] Manufacturers and ad agencies were also both becoming increasingly aware of marketing to different, specific consumer groups, and Mrs. Alcala's vaguely Latina look, and her geographical location noted as "Sweetwater, Texas," may have been chosen with hopes of appealing to consumers of nonwhite ethnic backgrounds. But the fundamental role of the housewife mom via her laundry remained unchanged: she would continue to do the laundry at home, no matter what her outside responsibilities. And as a mother of a lovable scamp of a son who dirties his clothes, she needed the right brand of soap so she would have no "reason to complain." In fact, reflecting the growing "new momism" of the late twentieth century, the housewife moms in contemporary laundry advertising utilize laundry products as a means for better mothering, which by the 1990s and into the 2000s included being a relaxed and perpetually *fun* mom.

For example, a baby covered in pudding sits himself in a laundry basket in a 2008 ad in *Parents*: "Mom will take care of me. . . . OxiClean will handle the stains!"[70] A similar ad ran in *Good Housekeeping*. In this one, a pigtailed girl covered head-to-toe in mud explains: "OxiClean gets the tough stains out . . . and Mom says I'm the best stain-maker ever!" Mom is not pictured, but her relaxed attitude toward giant messes conveys how well OxiClean allows her to do her most important job: be an ever-attentive but also relaxed mother who puts her children's fun before any petty concerns about additional housework. The OxiClean mom is the envy of other, less fortunate kids. In one ad, a gloomy toddler in a shopping cart appears to comment to another, much more cheerful tot: "You're allowed to have Grape Juice and Chocolate?" "Yep! My Mom just buys OxiClean and doesn't worry about stains!" Like the earlier Tide mom, able to "take it all in stride," the OxiClean mom enjoys the product's transformation of dirt and stains from a pain in the neck into a simple part of good mothering.

In an especially vivid example of this kind of marketing, the Clorox brand linked laundry with a mom's ability to "Let kids be kids," as the headline for a series of magazine ads reads. The copy of a 2008 ad in this series, beside a photo of a young girl gleefully kicking a soccer ball, reads:

> Life's too short to worry about stains. Whether it's soccer, football or playing tag in the park, kids and outdoor games are a natural team. Don't let grass stains and mud dampen the fun. . . . Organized sports encourage teamwork and family fitness, especially if you practice with your child between games. It's a perfect chance to spend one-on-one time with your MVP. NEW! Concentrated Clorox 2 Stain Fighter and Color Booster works as hard as your kids play. It powers out tough dirt—now with more stain-fighting power in every drop.

In the first decades of the 2000s, being a good mom means more than just keeping the kid in clean clothes or even defending the family wash from germs. It means playing with kids, making sure they participate in organized sports, and of course doing it all without fussing about stains. The magical ability of Clorox to "power out tough dirt" promised more than clean: it promised good mothering. The housewife mom doesn't actually appear in the ad but the copy clearly evokes her.

In the late 1990s and early 2000s, agencies seemed to have finally fully digested Reno Bartos' advice that consumers were ready to bid goodbye to the brainless housewife, ecstatic because her husband sniffed his shirt appreciatively. Manufacturers began to focus on different ways of marketing laundry products, such as offering new liquid and concentrated "ultra" detergents, and always, an emphasis on making clothes smell good. Today laundry detergents utilize a variety of appeals, from keeping designer clothes beautiful (such as Tide's premium "Total Care" marketed in conjunction with Ann Taylor Loft and promoted by "fashion icon" Tim Gunn) to marketing products as part of charitable giving (Tide's successful "Loads of Hope" campaign, for instance) to "green" detergents that are less harmful for the planet. Tide Coldwater emphasized the environmental benefits of washing with cold water, for instance, and in a 2009 magazine ad Arm and Hammer pictured its detergent nestled into lush green leaves under the headline "It's nature's secret for spotless laundry," and the tagline "Harnessing the Power of Nature."[71] According to the current marketing wisdom, ads and commercials in today's media-saturated environment have to be clever and have to take advantage of new technologies. The Saatchi & Saatchi advertising agency broke new ground for Tide in 2007 with an interactive online campaign on You Tube to promote the stain-removing stick "Tide to Go." They also created the humorous "Talking Stain" ad that premiered during the 2008 Super Bowl (a first for a laundry product).[72]

Ads and commercials for laundry detergent, in keeping with marketing efforts across the board in the twenty-first century, often give a postmodern wink to viewers, trying to give the impression that "yes, we know it's a commercial, and it's for laundry detergent, so let's just have fun with it." A 2009–2010 Gain commercial, for example, depicts various people in a time-stopped moment sniffing appreciatively at someone's shirt, dreamily lost in the wonderful aroma while "Take My Breath Away" plays in the background. In the last shot, the music stops abruptly and a teenage grocery store clerk holding an open bottle of Gain is surprised by his manager. The voiceover dryly comments: "You realize you're in love . . . with a laundry detergent." In another example, P&G recently experimented with limited-edition, retro packaging in an attempt to give Tide a new cultural cache.[73]

In addition to more sophisticated traditional media and marketing campaigns, laundry product advertising (and housework advertising generally) increasingly seeks to incorporate social media. Ad makers are well aware that social media sites may be especially effective in reaching who they see as their target consumers—real-life mothers.[74] Tide's Facebook page, for example, includes both corporate-created advertising posts touting new products and promotions as well as hundreds of comments from what appear to be real consumers (over 1,400,000 Facebook users identified themselves as "liking" the Tide page in June 2011). Hispanic consumers can post on a Spanish-language Tide Facebook page. Most consumers offer positive testimonials for Tide products on Facebook and provide P&G with valuable consumer feedback. A few critical consumer remarks appear as well, perhaps just reinforcing the veracity of the page as a whole.[75] Gain, too, boasts thousands of Facebook fans and followers on Twitter.

But on the other hand, some advertising techniques remain the same. Detergents such as OxiClean, Clorox, Cheer, and Spray and Wash continue to use the old side-by-side shots of clean vs. stained clothing, for example, and although ads and commercials don't often feature long shots of a housewife mom demonstrating the product, she still appears regularly, folding a towel in her pristine laundry room or removing a perfectly laundered article of clothing from her fancy washing machine. For instance, a 2009 commercial for a new Tide product, a "Stain Release" "booster" packet that consumers add to the wash that promises to "remove stains the first time." "Whoa, that's a first," says the housewife mom admiring her clean shirt in the laundry room. As she climbs the stairs in her nicely appointed home, her blonde teenage daughter happens by and takes the basket out of Mom's hands: "Mom, let me grab that." "Another first!" marvels Mom. The commercial isn't suggesting that the product will actually get Daughter to do her own laundry. It just acknowledges in a kind of funny way that of course Mom's the one who invariably hauls that laundry basket up the stairs, reiterating domestic gender norms under the guise of gentle humor. She's not "just a housewife," but she's certainly a housewife mom, the one who's solely responsible for cleaning the family's clothes, indulgently chuckling over the fact that she's the one left holding the laundry basket.

Anecdotal evidence suggests that consumers do not seem offended by this particular representation of mothering, in contrast to a 2010 Tide commercial in which a mother "borrows" her teen daughter's sweater to go clubbing on a girls' night out and then craftily removes subsequent stains and slips the clean sweater back into Daughter's closet. Consumers posted outraged comments on a corporation contact website, complaining that P&G depicted a mom lying to her daughter about her own recreational activities.[76] Mom shouldering the laundry basket to care for her family appears to be a socially and culturally acceptable representation of housework. But Mom using housework products to enjoy a night out and Mom using detergent to pull the wool over her daughter's eyes? Morally offensive.

In the twenty-first century, manufacturers and agencies are seeking new ways and new mediums to create emotion-based appeals for laundry products, but as in the 1970s, agencies continue to wrestle with how to make laundry detergent into "the good guy" when doing laundry is such a mundane activity. In addition to the contemporary appeals featuring moms who know "life's too short to worry about stains," ad makers are exploring other ways to invest laundry product commodities with particular meanings. For instance, business journalist Robert Berner described a 2006 campaign for Tide based on extensive marketing research done by Saatchi & Saatchi: "In an attempt to cultivate Tide's inner 'lovemark,' new ads now dismiss the notion that laundry detergent is a mere commodity. Instead, they reflect P&G's conviction that the 'relationship' women—they're not bothering with men—have with their laundry goes well beyond grass-stained t-shirts."[77] Berner mentions it as an aside, but the fact that Saatchi & Saatchi didn't "bother with men" yet at the same time applied sophisticated marketing research techniques to the creation of advertising for Tide vividly demonstrates just how intertwined laundry and the housewife mom remain in the world of advertising. Statistics vary, but in the real world the purchase of laundry detergent is not solely the province of moms or even women in general. In a 2008 *Adweek* article about the marked absence of any housework advertising aimed at men, journalist Adam Newman cited a study that found American men and women purchasing laundry products in roughly equal numbers.[78] Moreover, the depiction of a laundry soap as so effective and so easy and so pleasant that it might transform the task of doing laundry into something *anyone* in the family can do on a regular basis has never appeared in any significant way in laundry room advertising, even though today the possibility of shared laundry responsibilities is a very real one. Yet the premise of Saatchi's research itself very specifically identified laundry (and perhaps housework as a whole) as *mom*'s responsibility.

The resulting campaign did as well, notwithstanding P&G's fabric care marketing director's assertion that the aim of contemporary laundry product marketing sought to erase the old stereotypical image of housewives and their laundry: "One of our rallying cries was to get out of the laundry basket and into her life."[79] The commercials thus did not depict mom actually *doing* the laundry, but they certainly built on the idea that Mom and Mom alone had an emotional relationship with and responsibility for the laundry. For example, a commercial set to the Kinks' song "All Day and All Night" depicted a "busy mom" wearing white pants straight from her office job to an outing at the park with her daughter.[80] "The message," summarized an advertising industry journalist, was that "Tide lets women focus on the important things. The new slogan says little about cleaning." But it spoke volumes about the direction of laundry product advertising in the twenty-first century.

Advertisers and ad agencies may have thought that looking for a way "out of the laundry basket and into her life" and emphasizing "women's relationship to laundry" was groundbreaking. But although it utilized new insights into the twenty-first century "mom market," it also built on countless earlier campaigns that featured first housewives, then housewife moms caring for their families by providing them with clean, soft, sweet-smelling laundry. Female domesticity as a frame for depicting laundry work and for selling laundry products remains unchanged. "All Day and All Night" might suggest that now a mom can laugh off grass stains on her own pants, but Tide is working that same old magic, allowing her to be a better mother, which is clearly "the more important thing" in this commercial.[81] Similarly, in 2009 commercials, the multi-branded "OxiClean with Arm and Hammer Baking Soda" called the addition of baking soda to a detergent "Mom's Best Secret (Then and Now)" and depicted a mother in the 1970s and then in a contemporary laundry room, both happily getting junior's stained shirts clean. No commercial more clearly demonstrates that the housewife mom from the 1970s to today is the only one entrusted in laundry room advertising to the care of the family, as demonstrated by fresh, clean clothes.

This kind of appeal continues to invest laundry work with emotional meaning and moms doing laundry as an expression of love and care—not a new strategy in the least. In the 2000s, laundry commercials might not show Mom hanging out her laundry, but just like the 1952 housewife in the first Tide television commercial, they do suggest that their product can offer you "the kind of clean you like best next to those you love." "Feel more," urges the tagline for Downy, after a shot of a mom in a nice t-shirt and slacks (the contemporary version of a shirtdress and apron), gold wedding ring clearly visible, drying her daughter in a big fluffy towel, suggesting that soft towels will allow her to better express her love for her child—or vice versa.[82] A 2008 campaign for Downey sought to brand the product as the right one for "moms who really care about soft clothes." The same year Tide ran commercials of an African American mother sniffing her son's old jersey and then enjoying memories of him growing up in flashback shots. The housewife mom is sometimes a racially diverse representation. But being a good mom always means making the family laundry smell good as an expression of loving care. Laundry remains firmly gendered as women's work.

Even a celebrity spokesperson for Tide is just another housewife mom distributing love in the laundry room. Despite recent indications that many real consumers are actually repelled by images of "supermoms," when using the thin, blonde, pretty, celebrity millionaire spokeswoman Kelly Ripa, P&G positions Tide as part of good mothering and Ripa as a good mom: "She's a hands-on mom who is passionate about caring for her family and their clothing."[83] Ripa's a quintessential celebrity mom who apparently prioritizes the family laundry over her multimillion dollar day job, and like all housewife moms in laundry advertising, she transforms the drudgery of laundry into homemaking.[84]

In addition to laundry products that help you be a better mom, in today's advertising, "those you love" might include the housewife mom herself. The "renewing scent pearls" of Downy promised to transform "your sweater into a sanctuary," for instance. A 2009 Gain ad pictured a woman on her bed buried blissfully under a pile of freshly laundered towels, sniffing deeply: "Sniff Sniff Hooray!" reads the tag. Tide's premium priced "Simple Pleasures" and Gain's "Joyful Expressions" lines endorsed by the editors of *Buenhogar* in 2006 offer highly aromatic detergents marketed as luxurious indulgences. In another example, Downy "Radiance" 2008 magazine ads sought to reframe laundry as a luxurious experience: "Where will the scents take you?" asks the ad, next to a photograph of a pretty woman floating through the air, wrapped in flowing purple dress that seemed to emanate from the bottle of fabric softener. A scratch and sniff photo of the product invites the consumer to interact directly with the ad, and imagine herself floating away on the luxurious cloud of fabric softener scent. In the most overt example, in a 2009 commercial a woman "soaks" in a swirl of laundry in a luxurious hotel bathroom, as the smiling Snuggle spokescritter bear places a "Do Not Disturb" sign on the door. "Indulge your senses," urges the female voiceover in this commercial for Snuggle "Crème" fabric softener.

Ad makers did not invent out of thin air such pleasant associations with laundry, which after all is a vastly easier undertaking today than for past generations. Even the discomforts of a public laundromat can't begin to compare to "Blue Monday" a century ago. Today we can literally toss a basketful of dirty clothes into a machine and within a short time they emerge clean and rinsed. As Glenna Matthews, a historian of housework, noted in a 2003 interview: "There is such an immediate payoff to laundry."[85] And although Americans actually spend more time doing laundry than ever, this might just mean that we like this chore more than others. From high-end "boutique" laundry soaps and ironing spray fragrances to front-loading energy-efficient washer-dryer sets in designer colors, today's laundry products promise consumers that doing the laundry can be a painless, even satisfying and pleasurable experience.[86] But although laundry products are proliferating, the essential message of laundry room advertising remains the same.

Manufacturers and advertisers are continuing a project begun at the beginning of modern advertising itself in the late 1800s: redefining laundry working by transforming it from wearisome drudgery into pleasant, rewarding housework. And they are spending ever-increasing amounts of money to do so. For instance, according to Neilson Co. (which did not include online advertising in its 2010 study), P&G spends a whopping annual $140 million on Tide advertising.[87] Yet, the fundamental roots of laundry advertising remain unchanged. The woman floating in the Downy-induced "amethyst mist" sensual dream may not be standing at a clothesline in an apron or rapturously embracing boxes of detergent. Mother's magic helpers no longer appear in the laundry room as embodied magical creatures (although they do in other rooms, as we shall see). But laundry product advertising continues to promise that doing laundry is no mere drudgery and that with the right product, the housewife mom can take perfect care of her clothes and her family's clothes, be a great mom, and even maybe pamper herself with a sensually pleasing experience in the laundry room, akin to soaking in a swirl bath of fabric softener.

2

The Bathroom

It's a truly groundbreaking moment in the history of housework advertising, but don't blink or you might miss it: for about three seconds in a 2009 commercial for Mr. Clean's Magic Eraser, a husband (you can see his wedding ring) demonstrates the product by wiping soap scum off a bathtub. However, just in case the sight of a man kneeling by a bathtub to clean it comes too close to uncomfortably challenging our ideas about the gendered nature of housework, he quickly tosses the Magic Eraser out the window to another man, who uses it to swab down the patio chairs—a suitably masculine household cleaning task. Then *he* tosses it to another man washing a car, truly male-appropriate cleaning work. Maybe we will continue to see more husbands cleaning the bathroom in ads and commercials, but such an alteration would require a seismic change in housework advertising generally and bathroom cleaning products specifically. From 1900 to today, in print and television advertising for such products, men never, ever clean the toilet, sink, tub, or bathroom floor. The sole exception is if they are in the military and are on "latrine duty."

This chapter show how from the earliest print ads for water closet "trap" and "bowl" cleansers to today's toilet and shower-cleaning product commercials, bathroom advertising featured one and only one person from the household's family cleaning the family's bathroom: first the housewife then the housewife mom, often gazing with adoration at her beautifully appointed, newly sparkling home and clearly reaffirming domestic gender norms that link female care with housework. From the end of the nineteenth century and the beginning of modern advertising up to the present moment, advertisers utilized images of housewives in two particular kinds of appeals in order to market bathroom cleaning products: first, the product's ability to banish dangerous germs, and therefore, the housewife's role as guardian of family health, and second, the product's ability to transform this especially unpleasant and potentially demeaning work—cleaning up the family's most offensive dirt—into an easy, even enjoyable task. The figure of the housewife in bathroom advertising underwent remarkably few changes throughout the 1900s. The housewife mom who began to replace the most overtly stereotypically housewife in earlier ads and commercials in the 1970s and 1980s continued to enjoy new easy-to-use products while carefully guarding the family's health in the bathroom, converting tub and toilet scrubbing into female care.

This chapter also demonstrates that in the bathroom, more clearly than in any other room in the house, advertising called upon magic helpers to relieve the housewife of the most odious aspects of housework. They even continued to suggest that certain products could replace servant labor long after other types of housework advertising largely moved away from such rhetoric. Toilet and bathroom cleaner advertising from the end of the 1800s to today emphasize the way certain brands eliminate the inherently distasteful and possibly degrading work of removing traces of the family's bodily filth left behind in the bathroom, transforming that labor into such a pleasant, easy task that it can barely be counted as "work" at all. While never seriously suggesting that anyone else—maid, cleaning woman, children, husband—might pick up a sponge and wipe the bathroom sink, the regular appearance of elves, sprites, and other magical creatures who clean tub and tile in ads and commercials for bathroom cleansers implied that in real life, *nobody* wanted the job of cleaning the bathroom. But since somebody had to do it, bathroom cleaning products promised they would help Mom transform that job from odious labor into homemaking and good mothering.

Before 1840, only a few extremely wealthy Americans enjoyed indoor bathing and waste facilities equipped with plumbed water. That changed as the century progressed. Bathtubs and toilets remained rare until after the Civil War, but in the 1850s patents for mechanical water closets dramatically increased, and even when piped municipal water was not available, Americans used a variety of home systems with tanks, cisterns, and pumps for their water needs, including some of the earliest water closets. By 1900 new homes more and more often included a bathing room and water closet. However, cost remained a significant factor and not until the post–World War I era could large numbers of working-class and poor Americans expect to have their own bathrooms.

Around the turn of the century, other technological and industrial innovations laid the necessary groundwork for modern home bathrooms: the introduction of the siphon style toilet in the 1880s; the American manufacture of solid porcelain, vitreous china, and chrome-plated brass bathroom fixtures in the 1890s; and the invention and production of built-in bathtubs rather than the earlier portable models. Known most commonly as "water closets" until the 1930s, Americans began building "bathrooms" (which included both a toilet and bathing facilities) around that time for practical plumbing reasons. Concurrently, the permanently installed bathtub won out over the wide variety of other available portable and hand-filled bathing facilities.[1]

The emergence of municipal plumbing, home bathrooms, and modern bathing habits owed as much to fears of epidemics as to industrial innovation. Middle-class social reformers led the sanitation movements of the late 1800s and Progressive Era, largely in response to devastating yellow fever and cholera epidemics. As germ theory gained acceptance, household builders and domestic advisors increasingly recommended bathing and mechanical water closets—but only if those water closets could guarantee perfect sanitation and no offensive and potentially harmful exposure to sewer gas.[2] Not surprisingly, as bathrooms with both a fixed tub and flush toilet became the norm, the new household cleaning duties associated with bathrooms focused on maintaining cleanliness and health. Given the very real danger of disease faced by Americans at the turn of the century, it's no wonder that the earliest cleaners marketed for use in the water closet emphasized the product's ability to guard the family's health. Advertisers chose the theme of protecting the family's health well: it built on the very human desire to protect one's family from disease and the very likely possibility that potentially fatal diseases might threaten a family member at some point.

From today's perspective, the menace of unclean bathrooms seems greatly exaggerated in early bathroom cleanser advertising. But it would not have seemed so to consumers at the beginning of the 1900s, particularly since American culture at the turn of the century saw "the development of the domestic woman [that is, the housewife, not a paid domestic employee] as the primary agent of cleanliness and guardian of the home."[3] More important to the history of housework advertising is the way these ads for cleaning the bathroom explicitly linked the completion of housework— cleaning the bathroom—to the housewife, who tackled this new cleaning duty as part and parcel of her family care. In this way, bathroom advertising vividly demonstrates how intertwined modern advertising and the figure of the housewife have been since the emergence of modern advertising itself, and how ads sought to make cleaning the bathroom an important, meaningful part of a housewife's domestic responsibilities, representing an unpleasant cleaning task as good homemaking.

For example, a 1902 ad for Sanitas all-purpose cleaner raised the specter of health-threatening germs hidden in the households' plumbing and promised to assist the housewife fight this hidden menace. Above a drawing of a sink and twisting pipes, Sanitas promised: "Where disease lurks,

Sanitas removes the cause."[4] Similarly, print advertisements for Platt's Chlorides depicted the housewife vigilantly guarding against disease in the bathroom. A Platt's pamphlet ad printed in the early 1900s and titled "Sanitary Precautions Ordered by Officers of Health" begins with a bold headline above a drawing of pipe plumbing: "Where Great Danger Lurks." The copy elaborates: "Looking down into the cleanly [sic] and innocent appearing bowl, with its harmless pan of water at the bottom, how few people realize the amount of foul and deadly decomposing matter just beneath, in the receiving basin."

The copy goes on to call attention to the possibly lethal failure of the ignorant housewife who might inflict terrible illness on her family through neglect of proper bathroom cleaning. Under the headline "A Common and Fatal Error," the copy explains:

> Strange as it may seem, a great many housekeepers believe that after the heat of mid-summer has passed the use of disinfectants can be dispensed with. As far as the streets and yards go this may be correct; but it is indoors where the poisonous gases do their fatal work, and during the autumn, winter, and spring is the time, as the fearful increased mortality occasioned by Typhoid, Typhus, Malarial and Scarlet Fevers, Diptheria, Measles, Small Pox—all of which rage during the cold weather—will sadly testify. When the houses are heated and the windows closed, the gases from sewers are naturally attracted to the higher temperatures of the rooms, there, unless neutralized, to work insidious but certain troubles.[5]

The pamphlet painted a vivid picture of the "housekeeper's" (this refers to the housewife, not a maid) responsibility in cleaning the bathroom. She must be careful to ensure the elimination of invisible gases that carry fatal germs, because "unless neutralized" they would "work insidious but certain troubles." The list of potentially fatal diseases make explicitly clear what kinds of dangers menaced family health, and branded the cleaning product as an important weapon in the housewife's essential job of protecting her family's health.

In a similar magazine ad that appeared in a 1912 issue of *Town and Country*, Platt's Chlorides again utilized the image of the housewife as guardian to promote their brand. Under a drawing of nicely dressed housewives using the product in the bathroom and the cellar, the copy reads: "Fevers prevail in the Fall, due to germs and noxious gases developed during summer. To destroy these, purify the wastepipes, sinks, closets, and the cellar with Platt's Chlorides." The ad's publication in a popular but relatively upscale periodical, *Town and Country*, demonstrates how early, and how emphatically, advertisers marketed bathroom cleaning products with images of, and rhetoric about, the housewife. In 1912, *Town and Country* readers were perhaps far more likely to have a water closet than readers of publications aimed at a working-class audience. But the ad addressed "you," the trim and nicely dressed housewife depicted in the ad, not a maid or servant. The ad did not imply that ensuring cleanliness in the bathroom—a truly icky job—should fall to an upper-class household's servant. On the contrary, the "housekeeper," the woman in charge of the home, held the important responsibility of fighting the "great dangers" lurking in the water closet. Beginning with these early ads, cleaning the bathroom isn't housework—it's homemaking.

While these early ads emphasized the dangers lurking in the bathroom, other appeals reflected the second significant theme in bathroom advertising: a product's ability to ease the housewife's labors. Advertising depicted bathroom cleaning as part of the housewife's responsibility to care for her family, but it also persistently and nearly universally acknowledged the fact that this aspect of housework could be repellent. Reflecting how all types of advertising in the 1920s and 1930s often linked products with modern ease and convenience, and like laundry product advertising from this period, bathroom cleaning product advertising during these decades often focused on how the product would relieve the housewife of this odious chore with almost magical ease. In fact, such appeals often equated their products with an actual magical helper, sometimes in the form of a fantastical creature who embodied the cleaning properties of the product, and other times equating the product with human servant labor.

Linking products with "spokescharacters" or "spokescritters" first appeared as modern advertising emerged in the late 1800s.[6] At that time, companies quickly learned that personifying their product in some way increased consumer recognition, and in the modern advertising world— where *brands*, not products, had to be sold—this was a potentially valuable and lucrative means of making a brand stand out. Sometimes spokescharacters are literally the advertised product itself, such as Mr. Peanut, the Michelin Man, and the anthropomorphized M&Ms.[7] Although it is an old idea, spokescharacters remain a powerful advertising tool in the twenty-first century. Marketing researchers Judith Garretson and Scot Burton concluded in a 2005 study that "the use of spokescharacters results in more favorable brand attitudes."[8] As Warren Dotz and Jim Morton, historians of popular culture and advertising, write:

> Literal characters show no sign of disappearing. They are as popular now as they were at the turn of the [twentieth] century. We are drawn to their unique looks and cheery personalities. Advertisers like them because they offer the best of both worlds: immediate identification and built-in product endorsement.[9]

Advertising scholar Christine Mierau reiterates the point, asserting that these characters appeal "to the American fondness for folksy, colorful humor" and do not "make Americans feel as if they [are] being tricked into buying products."[10] These characters are more than mascots—they are brand icons, with "an astounding life in the consumer imagination."[11]

Such creatures appeared in the early 1900s in some of the first modern housework advertisements for all-purpose cleaners, which, as the century progressed, included the bathroom. Old Dutch cleanser, trademarked in 1906 as the cleaner that "chases dirt, makes everything spick and span," featured a large silhouette drawing of a "Dutch girl" on the label, wearing wooden shoes and a bonnet that hides her face, brandishing a stick as she "chases dirt." Print ads in the early 1900s built very much on the idea that this girl embodied the product's ability to clean. A 1910 magazine featured a large drawing of the Old Dutch girl—she's the one who "Chases Dirt, Cleans, Scrubs, Scours, Polishes," not the housewife who will actually use the scouring powder. The Dutch girl, multiplied, is also the one who in a 1917 ad "reaches the hard-to-clean places" (a swarm of Dutch girls attack a glass bottle) and "wades right in" (getting ready to attack a pile of dirty dishes).[12]

The Old Dutch Girl was by no means the only magical housewife helper in early 1900s advertising, including ads for products put to use in cleaning the bathroom. Spotless Cleanser newspaper ads featured "Jiffy," an elfish fairy with wings, pointy ears, and a wand.[13] A 1913 ad detailed his capabilities: "'Jiffy,' the sprite of order and cleanliness, is at the beck and call of every woman. You can buy his services at all good grocers for 5¢, he will be found in every can of Spotless Cleanser." In the bathroom specifically, Jiffy waved his wand and promised "a Really CLEAN bath." A 1914 ad pledged that Jiffy would "put strength in a woman's elbow and keep it there," and the headline of another assured consumers that it "Brings Rest Before Noon." As another ad claimed: "Its sole mission in life is to lighten women's labor and make living worthwhile. And it DOES THAT!" Another depicts a woman's manicured hand pouring the product onto a cloth while Jiffy waves his wand. "*There's* all the assistance you need—right in your very hands," states the copy. Spotless even suggested, in a 1917 ad, that a can of their cleanser "Gives Every Woman a Hundred Hands," and surrounded the can with 13 smooth, white, manicured hands. "One shake of this no-acid, no-caustic cleanser sets a hundred hands at work for you," reads the copy. Like the early Ivory ads that utilized the housewife figure to reframe laundry work as housework and homemaking, Jiffy offered magical assistance not to servants but to the lady of the house.

However, like some other housework advertising in the early 1900s, Spotless sometimes depicted its product as a *replacement* for servant labor. A 1913 ad promised: "He is the most marvelous servant you can employ," and a 1917 ad depicting Jiffy cleaning around the house characterized the product in terms of its superiority to human servants: "It never shirks. It scours the dirtiest floors as cheerfully as the finest marble. . . . It has no doubles; no rich or poor relatives." A similar 1917 ad promised that Spotless "never talks back—never felt a lazy moment in its life. It's always in a genial mood. . . . If you want this unwearied servant at your beck and call, you must ask for it by name." Likewise, in an Old Dutch print ad around 1918, a long line of Old Dutch girls troop out of the Employment Bureau. The copy reads: "In the Home generally—but more especially so at Housecleaning time, Old Dutch is your dependable helper." "Housecleaning time" refers to the practice of saving major housecleaning chores for a biannual cleaning, but as twentieth century technology lightened certain aspects of housework, women were expected to make "housecleaning" a regular activity.[14] In fact, the representation of housework products as replacements for servants helped reframe all household labor—including cleaning the bathroom—as housework and therefore women's homemaking. The appeal of "Jiffy" was his magical ability to do the work for "you," the housewife. His presence promised a magical removal of hard labor, but consumers and ad makers knew who needed Jiffy's assistance in the bathroom—the housewife.

The possibility of a servant-in-a-can may have seemed especially marketable when it came to the work of cleaning the bathroom, perhaps more so than any other room in the house. As the twentieth century progressed, bathroom advertising continued to feature the housewife enjoying the modern ease and convenience of bathroom cleaning products while conscientiously maintaining perfect cleanliness in this especially germ-filled room of the house. However, the bathroom itself underwent some significant changes during this time. By 1930, bathrooms assumed their modern place in American homes, one that we would readily recognize today. Although Americans gained access to utilities (including municipal water and plumbing) and indoor bathrooms appeared in private homes at an uneven rate, by the end of the 1920s, home builders, fixture manufacturers and dealers, domestic advisors, and average consumers all held in common the *expectation* that indoor bathing and waste disposal should be a part of not only wealthy but also middle- and working-class homes. Becoming a standard feature in newly constructed single homes by the second decade of the twentieth century, the bathroom even achieved the status of domestic fashion during the 1920s, with a new emphasis on color and style and opulence.[15]

Products for cleaning the bathroom specifically increased during this time, but the appeals in 1920s and 1930s bathroom cleaning product advertising continued to rely heavily upon images and copy of housewives guarding their family's health with shiny clean and fresh-smelling bathrooms. For example, early in the century the all-purpose cleaner Sylpho-Nathol echoed claims made by Platt's Chlorides around the same time. Newspaper ads for the product in 1902 emphasized its ability to make all surfaces in the home "pure and sweet," a clear reference to issues of health.[16] And in the 1920s, Sylpho-Nathol's advertising continued to make claims about its germ-fighting ability. Reads the headline of one ad: "Use for Home Health—Said Our Doctor." In the wake of little "Dot's" scarlet fever, the doctor advises the housewife mother to use the product in order to ensure total safety: "It's an effective sanitary measure that safeguards the family against disease." "Knocks Germs Cold—Says Our Druggist," reads another. "I never felt that our bathroom was completely sanitary," confides the housewife in the ad. "But Sylpho-Nathol disposed of *that* difficulty."

These particular 1920s newspaper ads sought to build a brand image of a cleaner that so effectively rid the home of any disagreeable odor that it must be ridding the home of any unseen threat to the family's health as well. Sylpho-Nathol ads emphasized the importance of fighting germs, and the product's ability to eliminate both germs and odors in plumbing. "Sylpho-Nathol is a sanitary healthguard." "Where the sun can't reach, Sylpho-Nathol is bottled sunlight." "KILL those foul odors. Don't merely cover up foul odors with another smell. Use Sylpho-Nathol! It kills them and their *cause*." "Know it is clean. Your bathtub is not really clean until it is free from germs." Sylpho-Nathol ads made it very clear that the housewife needed to ensure pristine plumbing or risk the sanctity of her home and risk failing to successfully achieve the best standards of homemaking.

One Sylpho-Nathol ad from this time clearly linked the product with odor and elimination and good homemaking. The headline lays out the issue: "Our Bathroom Became a Problem." The copy begins with a confession: "Bob says that I'm the best housekeeper in New England. That's not true, of course—but I am sure there isn't a more *particular one* [sic] in the world. Imagine how I felt when my spic-and-span little bathroom developed an odor which we couldn't get rid of." She tries a variety of other cleaners but: "It didn't do a bit of good. I was miserable." The copy continues:

> Bob came in with a grin one evening. "Trust mere man sometimes," he said—"I think we've found the remedy for the bathroom." We had. Bob had brought home our first bottle of Sylpho-Nathol. I wouldn't have thought it possible that anything as easy to use could make that room fresh and sweet again in such a short time. It was almost miraculous.

To be "fresh and sweet" implied more than simply the removal of an unpleasant odor. Bob's wife, the "best housekeeper in New England," required a particular brand of bathroom cleaner to achieve true cleanliness in the bathroom—cleanliness she could smell and which would fulfill her very "particular" standards of homemaking. A vivid example of the highly idealized middle-class married housewife figure in advertising, this Sylpho-Nathol housewife did not just clean the bathroom, but made it "spic-and-span," "fresh and sweet," transforming the labor of cleaning the plumbing into careful homemaking.

Another Sylpho-Nathol ad discussed the product's use in the kitchen, but its emphasis on odor-removal and plumbing cleanliness strongly echoes Bob's wife's dilemma in the bathroom, and it vividly showed to what degree the housewife needed to concern herself with purchasing the correct brand of cleanser to neutralize the danger lurking in hidden pipes:

Our kitchen sink became positively objectionable. We tried everything— poured in gallons of hot suds, ammonia, lye water. Nothing seemed to help. Finally, John sent for the plumber. He opened up the trap—the curved pipe under the sink. *My dear! That's* where the smell came from! I *never* knew a sink drain could be so dreadful.

After the plumber left, the odor was not so bad for a while, but then it grew worse. I'm so proud of my clean, little kitchen. That sink made me too blue for anything. Last Thursday evening, the Lynns were over and Mrs. Lynne came into the kitchen to help me with the coffee and sandwiches.

"What a *perfect dear* of a kitchen you have," she said, going over to rinse her hands at the sink—and then I saw her smile fade. She is such a model housekeeper. I felt like crying. "Oh, isn't too dreadful!" I managed to say. "And we've done everything." It was then she told me about Sylpho-Nathol.

Just as the Friend in the Hat often set housewives straight on the best way to launder, Mrs. Lynne helped the housewife purchase the most modern and effective plumbing cleanser. The reference to the unseen curves and twists in plumbing, and the accumulation there of "dreadful" and harmful waste material, echoed earlier fears of epidemics and germs, but also made very clear that cleaning the depths of household plumbing constituted an important housewifely responsibility. Such ads sought to make cleaning even unseen parts of the plumbing—particularly in the bathroom—a necessary part of housework and homemaking, reinforcing domestic gender norms.

In addition to ill health, the danger faced by housewives in bathroom cleaner advertisements included the profound social embarrassment experienced by the unnamed Sylpho-Nathol housewife in front of Mrs. Lynne. Like the Lux "undie odor" campaigns, these ads suggested that such failures would incur social condemnation. A 1929 magazine ad for Sani-Flush directly referenced the product's ability to spare the housewife possible social humiliation. "Do You Apologize to Your Guests?" questions the headline.[17] The copy elaborates: "Do you feel ill at ease at guests using your bathroom? You have out dainty towels. The bath and lavatory are spotless. What about the toilet, it is noticeably stained and discolored? Sani-Flush will make that immaculate too."

Sani-Flush often referenced the product's ability to clean the hidden recesses of household plumbing, where both potentially humiliating odors and dangerous germs lay waiting to threaten home and family. "Danger Lurks in the Hidden Trap," warned the headline of a 1923 magazine ad, beneath a drawing of a young, pretty housewife pouring the product into a toilet. "The hidden trap, if unclean, is unhealthful. No brush can reach it. Sani-Flush does! Sani-Flush cleans the trap! Purifies it. Destroys all foul odors." In addition to the germ-killing properties of the product, such ads also emphasize how the product will transform the labor of killing dangerous germs in the hidden trap into an incredibly easy and modern task for the housewife, even doing the work for her. Like the majority of Sani-Flush print ads in the 1920s, this ad depicts the housewife using the product, demonstrating how easy Sani-Flush made the odious job of toilet cleaning. Wearing a ruffled apron, the neatly attired housewife on the Sani-Flush label smilingly pours the product into a toilet (see fig. 2.1).[18]

Another woman appears on the product itself: a white woman with a neat hairdo and wearing a long dress with a white apron. The Sani-Flush label lady could be a maid in uniform, visually depicting Sani-Flush as a servant-in-a-can similar to Jiffy and the Old Dutch Girl. She may be one of the fancy "French maids" who are virtually indistinguishable from their mistress in 1920s advertising, or one of the servant-replacing products that often appeared in all types of housework advertising at this time.[19] But she could also be another housewife. Modern bathroom product advertising consistently and persistently linked housework and the *housewife*—not her servant—and defined her visually in exactly the way the Sani-Flush label marks this woman as a housewife: trimly attired, quietly pretty, hair neatly arranged, and wearing a spotless apron over her dress. Moreover, Sani-Flush explicitly marketed its brand as removing all the odious labor from cleaning the toilet, rendering it a perfectly pleasant job that the most refined housewife could undertake with ease.

Products marketed specifically as toilet cleaners put especially heavy emphasis on how they could make an inherently unpleasant task—cleaning the home's receptacle for human waste—so easy it wouldn't even be work at all. Sani-Flush, one of the first such products, repeated over and over in its print ads that using it meant the complete removal of any

Figure 2.1   1922 Sani-Flush newspaper advertisement from author's collection

Note: 1920s advertisements for toilet cleaning products helped frame even this odious household labor as homemaking with images of the neat, trim housewife in a ruffled apron.

odious aspects of cleaning the toilet. In 1920s magazine advertisements, Sani-Flush repeatedly claimed that the product would make cleaning the toilet perfectly pleasant. "Don't Scrub the Closet Bowl," begins the headline of a 1921 ad. "It is as unnecessary as it unpleasant. Sani-Flush will clean your closet bowl with scarcely any effort on your part," explains the copy. "Sani-Flush does all the hard work for you," read another the same year. "Watch It Clean the Toilet Bowl," promised a 1923 headline, and "IT Does the Cleaning—NOT You!" exclaimed another. Similar headlines and copy made the same claim: "One Task Less," "Don't Do Unnecessary Work." "Cleaner Without Hard Work." "Let Sani-Flush do the disagreeable work of cleaning the toilet for you."

A 1923 ad summarized the product's ability to transform cleaning the toilet from a foul chore into a pleasant, easy homemaking task: "The Only NICE Way to Clean a Toilet." "Banish Drudgery From the Task," read another three years later. "What used to be a disagreeable task is over in a jiffy," explains a 1927 magazine ad. Ads in 1928 also emphasized how Sani-Flush made cleaning the toilet easy and with shining clean results. "What was once the most disagreeable household task—cleaning the toilet—is now the easiest. Sani-Flush leaves the toilet bowl white and sparkling. As clean as if you scrubbed and scalded it." "Was this toilet bowl scoured? No! Then how did it get so clean and sparkling and gleaming? *Sani-Flush did it!*" "Like a Clean Dish," read the headline of one such ad, going on to describe the cleanliness of the toilet: "A glistening, spotlessly white toilet bowl. How difficult it must be to keep it so sparkling. No! Not difficult. Not if you use Sani-Flush." Ads in 1929 continued in the same vein: "*Exit* . . . Bathroom Drudgery!" "This toilet bowl is glistening. Spotless. You might think it had been scoured and scrubbed. It wasn't! Sani-Flush cleaned it . . . in no time at all."

Sani-Flush ads stressed the ease of the product as used by the pretty housewife, but at the same time they also sought to raise anxiety about the potential health risks of not using their product, echoing appeals from previous decades. A 1929 ad begins "*Sickness* . . . or Health?" It continues: "Especially must the toilet be kept clean to safeguard the health of the family." "Danger lurks in unclean toilets! Ills breed fast in hot weather. The toilet must be kept immaculately clean," reads another 1929 ad. "Clean Toilets Safeguard Health," reads the headline of another 1929 ad. "The toilet bowl must be kept sanitary. It is dangerous to neglect it," warned a 1926 ad. Sani-Flush made a particular effort to build a brand image of a product that could go into the unseen plumbing to effectively fight germs there: "Sanitation is *imperative!*" warned a 1929 ad, explaining that Sani-Flush "gets down into the unhealthful trap, where no brush could possibly reach, and banishes all foul odors." "Perfect sanitation demands that the hidden, unhealthful trap be kept clean at all times," reiterated a 1922 ad. That same year another ad suggested that even when a toilet appeared to be clean, germs lingered where you couldn't see them: "The bowl may be gleaming white—but if the trap is unclean, the closet is unhealthful." Sani-Flush built on long-established appeals for the healthfulness of certain bathroom cleansers and the housewife using them to safeguard her family's well-being.

But while housewives in 1920s Sani-Flush advertising continued to be charged with vigilantly guarding the family's health by fighting germs in the bathroom, they did so with ease and with the modern convenience of this splendid new product. This type of appeal continued to appear in bathroom advertising in the form of magical servants arriving to ease the housewife's drudgery in the bathroom and to assist her in the transformation of that labor into homemaking. For instance, a 1921 magazine ad featured multiple miniature Old Dutch girls rushing around the tile wall of a nicely appointed bathroom. "Just see how Old Dutch makes the bathroom sparkle and shine!" began the copy. Old Dutch promised that your tub and sink would not only be clean "but sanitary and hygienic as well. Keeping them so is a small task when you use Old Dutch." In a later magazine ad, the Old Dutch girl even confers with the housewife, who's wearing a waist-tied apron and is bent over the tub. In this 1931 ad in *Ladies Home Journal*, the Old Dutch girl chastises the housewife for using an inferior, scratching cleanser:

Old Dutch Girl: Stop! That gritty cleanser will scratch your tub!
Housewife: Never mind! We only rent this place!
Old Dutch Girl: Whether you rent or own, every scratch makes your tub harder to clean.
Housewife: So that's why my cleaning takes so long!

In this exchange, the Old Dutch girl appears as a magical helper, to educate the housewife on an easier way of cleaning. It reinforced domestic gender norms, pointing out to the housewife that even though she's "only renting," she must still maintain high standards of homemaking but also promising her that with Old Dutch she can do so easily.

In a similar ad that same year in *Ladies Home Journal*, three Little Dutch Girls attack the bathtub, the pedestal sink, and the tile floor of a bathroom. "Quicker cleaning," proclaims the headline. This particular ad included a mail-in offer for Old Dutch "service holders" (a small rack to hold Old Dutch cans that consumers could attach to the bathroom wall) as well as a reference to radio programming sponsored by Old Dutch. Both mail-in offers and radio advertising became common components of all types of housework advertising, including bathroom cleansers, by the 1930s and this ad illustrates the variety of different marketing techniques in widespread use at this time. But in all its 1920s and 1930s advertising, Old Dutch promised that the Girl would help reduce the housewife's work time, allowing the housewife to easily maintain high-quality homemaking, even in the bathroom. "Your best helper for all cleaning is Old Dutch Cleanser because it's so quick and active," explained a 1923 ad. A 1939 ad in *Ladies Home Journal* that included a mail-in offer for costume jewelry featured a housewife in a suit and hat about to leave the house because the product "**Zips** me through my cleaning." A 1939 ad in the *Saturday Evening Post* featured a smiling housewife in an apron, supposedly representing a real customer testimonial, with the caption: "'I just sailed through my housecleaning with the help of Old Dutch Cleanser,' writes a housewife." A 1923 ad depicted a housewife in an apron gazing with adoring eyes at her bathtub—an image commonly used in bathroom cleaner advertising—which Old Dutch has rendered sparkling: "Makes bathtubs bright." "Bathrooms take on a new radiance when Old Dutch does the work," promised a 1924 ad. As late as 1949, the Old Dutch girl appeared alongside housewives to assist them in cleaning the tub (see fig. 2.2).[20]

The potential allure of a product that appeared to provide the consumer with a herd of magical cleaning creatures shaped ads throughout the 1930s. One multipurpose cleaner, Wyandot, regularly visually represented its product as akin to a fleet of miniature uniformed maids. In a clear reference to the growing likelihood that Americans had their own bathrooms with porcelain fixtures, and building on the 1920s trend of depicting the bathroom as a potential home style showcase, Wyandot illustrated its product working as hard as a fleet of maids but gently enough for the new kinds of surfaces in well-appointed, high-fashion American bathrooms. As Marchland writes, in the 1920s, "The lowly bathroom rose to the status of a showplace of style and opulence," a trend clearly reflected in such ads.[21] Wyandot advertising was thus able to build a brand image of a cleaner that could come to the rescue of middle-class housewives who "did their own work." But by linking the cleanser to images of and rhetoric about fashionable modern homes, Wyandot transfigured the menial labor of cleaning the bathroom into highly idealized feminine homemaking and care.

A 1930s newspaper ad asked: "Does the Cleaner You Are Using Mar the Beauty of Your Home?" The copy continues: "Surely all those bright and colorful surfaces that beautify the modern woman's home deserve the best of cleaning materials," as illustrated by the tiny uniformed maids attending to the bathroom sink.[22] A similar ad also depicted the Wyandot maids, again in the bathroom sink, and again the ad emphasized the product's ability to thoroughly clean without marring nice surfaces, as

Figure 2.2 1949 magazine Old Dutch advertisement from author's collection

Note: "The Old Dutch Girl" came to the assistance of a particularly stereotypical housewife in this 1949 magazine advertisement.

the headline summarized: "A *Better* Cleaning Material for the Better Type of Home; Wyandot Cleans Easily and Thoroughly . . . Yet Will Not Harm Even the Finest Surface." The Wyandot maids appear to be cleaning the sink, but of course the housewife does the actual cleaning. As the copy notes: "If you don't care particularly about the appearance of your home, if deep scratches or dirty smudges do not worry you, you probably won't be interested in Wyandot. But frankly, we do not believe you are that kind of housewife." The copy demonstrates that Wyandot advertising relied on the representation of the housewife—"you"—and the housewife achieving the highest standards of housework, transforming it from careless cleaning into careful homemaking, to market its product.

In a 1930 ad Wyandot assured consumers that "using Wyandot is like having a thousand tiny hands to help you with your cleaning." A 1932 ad asserted that it was "almost like having an extra servant to do the cleaning jobs of your home." Long after other household products moved away from appeals referencing servants, bathroom advertising continued to utilize copy that equated cleaning products with helpful servant labor. But while it might be "almost like having an extra servant," it wasn't—since as the drawing for this ad showed, the woman bent over the tub was not a servant but the housewife. The brand emphasized that it was "safe for everything but dirt," especially for the white, middle-class, housewife's pretty hands. (As had Spotless cleanser: Jiffy always promised that Spotless "will not injure the tenderest skin" and is "*so* considerate of your tender hands.") A series of 1931 newspaper ads elaborated on Wyandot's ability to clean thoroughly without harming the tub or the housewife's hands. They explicitly noted that the housewife, not a servant (let alone another member of the family), would be doing the labor. But with the product's magical erasure of labor, the housewife need not reveal that fact. "You'd never know she does her own housework," one headline begins. The copy continues:

> Mrs. Johnson is something of a marvel to her friends. Her home is always spotless and attractive. Her hands are smooth and soft. And yet she has no maid. She does her housework all herself, even to cleaning tubs and washing painted walls. Her friends can't understand how she accomplishes so much, and still keeps fresh and lovely.

Staying "fresh and lovely," even when "cleaning tubs" required a truly wonderful product, which a similar Wyandot ad promised. "Housework every morning, yet lovely hands for dinner," it begins. "She's proud of her pretty home, kept always bright and spotless by careful cleaning. And she's doubly proud of her lovely hands . . . always smooth and soft and attractive, although she does her own housework. Her secret is a simple one: she avoids harsh, gritty cleansers that cause roughness and discolorations, and uses Wyandot alone." In a similar ad, a housewife dressed for an outing in a hat and holding a beaded necklace illustrates how "Housework never leaves its brand upon her hands." As the copy explains: "You'd never guess it, to see her lovely, youthful hands—but this modern housewife does her housework all herself—even to cleaning stoves, bathtubs, tile, painted walls, and woodwork. . . . Her secret can be yours." The charge to conceal all traces of doing housework that might be left on one's body reinforced the general theme in bathroom advertising that not only promised to ease the real labor of bathroom cleaning but also reinforced domestic gender norms for women, charging them with maintaining the loveliness of both home and hands.[23]

Wyandot advertising then emphasized the product's ability to clean tough tubs without harming hands, or the delicate surfaces of your home. By positioning it for use in the "better type of home," specifically the better type of bathroom, Wyandot hoped to capitalize on a booming home fashion trend, and build an image for its brand of luxury rather than drudgery. A variety of brands utilized that strategy in the 1930s. For example, Bab-O combined both magical embodiment (the Bab-O girl pictured on the label) and the depiction of bathrooms as opulent showplaces in a series of ads featuring the Bab-O Girl speaking directly to the consumer. "The Beautician to Millions of Bathrooms now speaks for herself," reads the headline above a two-page spread in a 1930 *Ladies Home Journal* ad packed with photographs of various designer bathrooms. "Bab-O" goes on:

> I am Bab-O. I owe my being to the modern American Bathroom. I was created especially to *beautify* enamel and porcelain. In but a few years I have become the beauty specialist to millions of bathrooms a day, the bathrooms of glorified American housewives. The bathrooms I have seen, North, South, East and West are myriad. Magnificent modernistic bathrooms, colorful bathrooms in charming homes, compact ones in city apartments. I have *conquered* all the perils to their gleaming beauty. I have *lightened* toil throughout the home. Everything I touch, *shines* . . . magically. I bring sun-like *brilliance* to all enamel and porcelain. Beneath my velvety caress tubs and basins become pools of brightness. . . . I have heard the praise of housewives everywhere. They speak of me as a *"treasure."* They tell of dull film, water lines, stubborn stains and rust marks dissolving at my *lightest touch!*

New kinds of bathroom surfaces required new kinds of cleaning, and Bab-O promised to do it while also imparting beauty to the room where the least beautiful human functions took place. This "treasure" to housewives promised that cleaning the bathroom would be so easy with Bab-O that this especially daunting, and dirty, housework task could be as gratifying as a beauty treatment. When used by "glorified American housewives," Bab-O transformed mere cleaning into home beautifying—homemaking. As stated in the copy, the product promised to help housewives achieve the highest ideals of homemaking in the bathroom: a scrubbed tub transformed into a "pool of brightness."

Bon Ami, a long-established brand by the 1930s, sought to give its product new marketability by emphasizing how thoroughly—but gently— it cleaned modern bathrooms. "Hasn't scratched yet," was its memorable tag, beneath a drawing of a downy chick. In ad after ad, housewives gazed at shining tubs or sinks, proclaiming how easy and delightful it was to use Bon Ami to keep their beautiful bathrooms looking beautiful. A 1937 ad in the *Saturday Evening Post* featured a supposedly real-life testimonial about the product:

> "As a bride I was so proud of my tiled bathroom and my modern kitchen with its corn colored sink with black tile. A friend told me never to use anything but Bon Ami. Now, after five years, I'm glad I took her advice, for I was astounded when I saw the bathtub of a friend who had built her home when we did . . . her tub was clean, but oh, pitifully dull and scratched looking, while mine, at home, cleaned with Bon Ami shone with its original beauty and luster." So writes Mrs. Eleanor Tomas of Santa Barbara, California.[24]

In this copy, Mrs. Tomas clearly demonstrates how the product helped her care carefully for her home, in contrast to the unlucky friend who merely cleaned her tub leaving it "pitifully dull and scratched-looking."

In a particularly pointed bid to equate the Bon Ami brand with the increasingly opulent bathrooms depicted in popular periodicals and home decorating manuals in the 1930s, Bon Ami marketed its product in new "deluxe" decorator packages meant for display in the bathroom. The art deco-style cans transformed humdrum bathroom cleanser into a chic accessory: "Set it on your bathroom shelf, or on the edge of the tub—this Bon Ami in the new de luxe [*sic*] package. Then you'll realize how perfectly its rich black and lustrous gold harmonize with everything that makes the modern bathroom beautiful and dainty." Another reads: "Women have been eagerly waiting for just such an announcement as this . . . a bathroom cleanser as good to look at, as it is to use. In this lovely new dress Bon Ami can take its place in the fashionable society of gay bottles and boxes that adorn the modern bathroom."[25] Another ad in the same series began with the headline "No longer need you HIDE your bathroom cleaner," and in another, a housewife removing her apron admires the fashionable effect of the designer can: "The touch that completes (in more ways than one) the modern bathroom ensemble. The touch is the touch of color that the lovely new black and gold Bon Ami de luxe Package contributes to the modern bathroom."[26] One ad even suggested that this fashionable can of Bon Ami would be so attractive that perhaps the housewife could entice others into cleaning the bathroom: "Feel the big, over-size container nestle in your hand. No trouble with dirt rings now—for guests and family will gladly dust a little Bon Ami into tub and basin and keep them glistening clean."[27] However, Bon Ami's proposal that their product could potentially lure other people into housework besides the housewife was unique. In bathroom cleaner advertising, as in all housework advertising, cleaning products and their attendant magical creatures promised to ease the labors of the housewife alone. She, and only she, conversed with and benefited from the presence of Jiffy, the Little Dutch Girl, and the Wyandot maids, and only she could really *care* for the home.

The ability of Bon Ami to clean thoroughly without scratching and thus help the housewife transform bathroom cleaning into homemaking continued to be featured in 1940s advertising. "You can't expect your tub to shine like mine . . . if you use a harsh gritty cleanser!" smugly lectures the housewife in apron to her friend, obviously a less capable homemaker, as they stand admiring the bathtub. Another smart housewife in a 1943 magazine ad told her friend: "Your tub would look as new as mine if you'd always used Bon Ami." Ads in the 1940s also equated using Bon Ami with support for the war effort, since keeping things looking new would help them last for the duration. Smart housewives continued to chastise and educate clueless friends and relations, even husbands, in post–World War II 1940s Bon Ami ads.

For instance, in a 1945 ad in *Ladies Home Journal*, two women help a little boy into his pajamas in the nicely appointed bathroom:

Helen: Sis, *what* are you cleaning that tub with . . . *magic*?
Betty: *Bon Ami* magic! It never leaves dirt-catching scratches!
Helen: But I thought a cleanser *had* to be gritty to do a fast job.
Betty: You couldn't be *wronger*, darling! Every scratch is a *dirt trap* that makes your cleaning twice as hard.
Helen: Sa-ay, I guess scratches *do* take scrubbing.
Betty: Bet your life they do! That why I always use Bon Ami. It *slides* all the dirt off in double-quick time—and *polishes* besides.
Helen: Well, I'll admit your bathroom looks like new. Your porcelain and tile really *sparkle*.
Betty: Thanks to Bon Ami! That satin-smooth finish proves it hasn't . . .
Bobby: I know, Mommy! "It hasn't scratched yet."
Helen: Bobby! You *too*? I give up—I'm getting me some Bon Ami magic *tomorrow*!

Bon Ami supposedly not only kept bathroom surfaces sparkling, but reduced the time housewives would spend cleaning the bathroom, while at the same transforming bathroom cleaning into careful homemaking resulting in the cleanest, shiniest bathroom possible. The "Bon Ami magic" would not only reduce work time but result in a tub that could inspire housewifely pride and be a shining object of admiration among other housewives.

Helen might be going to use Bon Ami herself, but when housewives clued in husbands on the magic of Bon Ami, they clearly did not expect the man of the house to actually start using the product to clean the tub himself. For instance, in a 1946 ad, Bill and Ann discuss the time-saving, beautifying merits of Bon Ami as she kneels to clean the bathtub:

> **Bill:** Great Scott, Ann—why stop to clean <u>now</u>?"
> **Ann:** Why not? It only takes a second when your cleanser never leaves <u>dirt-catching scratches</u>!
> **Bill:** What a woman! Company coming any minute, and she talks about dirt-catching scratches! Anyway, what's *that* got to do with fast cleaning?
> **Ann:** *Everything*, my darling cross-patch! Scratches are dirt-traps that make you *scrub*. If I used a gritty, scratchy cleanser you'd have something worry about!
> **Bill:** Well, I admit you polished up that tub in a hurry. Guess I married a smart girl after all.
> **Ann:** Smart enough to stick to Bon Ami! It just *slides* dirt and grease away in no time, and "hasn't scratched yet."
> **Bill:** O.K., sugar, I may not know much about cleaning, but I *do* know you have the prettiest hands in town!
> **Ann:** You can thank Bon Ami for that, too, pet. Cleans like a breeze—but doesn't mar a manicure!

This Bon Ami ad manages to pack in a number of different appeals. The product enables the housewife to do her work quickly, to not only clean but also polish her beautiful bathtub, and of course maintain her manicure, reinforcing domestic gender norms that charged women with keeping both their bathtubs and their nails gleaming and immaculate.

In a final example from this series, a man in a bathrobe and holding a mystery novel wanders into the bathroom to find his wife kneeling by the tub.

> **Mr. Hawkshaw:** The real mystery is how you clean up so fast!
> **Mrs. Hawkshaw:** Here's the clue, hon—a cleanser that doesn't leave <u>dirt-catching</u> scratches!
> **Mr. Hawkshaw:** Sorry, Mrs. Hawkshaw—I'm still baffled. What have scratches to do with fast cleaning?

Mrs. Hawkshaw: Elementary, my good man! The scratches gritty cleansers leave are *dirt-traps*. They make your cleaning twice as hard. But Bon Ami's pure and fine, and don't you remember—it "hasn't scratched yet!"
Mr. Hawkshaw: Um . . . well, of course, I didn't bring my microscope . . .
Mrs. Hawkshaw: Goof! Your own eyes are plenty good enough to see that this tub and tiling are as smooth as satin! As shiny, too. Because Bon Ami not only slides dirt off in no time—it *polishes*.
Mr. Hawkshaw: Speaking of polishing things off, where's the rest of that apple pie we had at supper? I made an investigation of the icebox, but . . .
Mrs. Hawkshaw: Darling, you'll *never* make a detective! Come along. I'll serve it to you with my own lily-white hands. Observe, sir—Bon Ami is mighty easy on a manicure!

Her beautiful hands and beautiful tub owe it all to the magic of Bon Ami; it "slides off" dirt and polishes the tub with no hard work on the part of Mrs. Hawkshaw, allowing her to easily maintain good homemaking and care for her family's home, as well as her manicure.

Bathroom product advertising in the 1950s continued to promise that maintaining perfect cleanliness and shining surfaces in the bathroom would require no hard work for the housewife. Some even continued to equate their products with magical creatures who would do the cleaning for you. In the 1950s, Ajax cleanser advertising introduced a trio of elves in print ads and radio and television commercials, who sang their infectious jingle as they cleaned. In one of the first commercials from this campaign, the three elves attack the tub and sink, singing:

> Use Ajax
> The foaming cleanser.
> Wash the dirt
> Right down the drain.
> You'll stop paying the elbow tax,
> When you start cleaning with Ajax.[28]

The elves claim that Ajax "cleans your bathroom surfaces up to 50% faster," but as the housewife in an apron on the Ajax can's label attests, the elves aren't *really* going to be wiping down your tub. Still, Ajax barraged consumers with images of the elves at work, especially in the bathroom. Newspaper ads featured the Ajax elves cleaning everywhere, making sinks and tubs shine as housewives gazed at them entranced.[29] Ajax even ran a contest to "Name the 3 Ajax Work Savers," with a grand prize of a Westinghouse modern kitchen. In the case of such magical creatures, it seems the ad agencies had found an easy, and attention-grabbing way to turn a bathroom cleanser into "a good guy."

On the other hand, bathroom advertising also continued to raise anxieties about the dangers of an unclean toilet bowl. "Is Your Bathroom Clean Where it Really Counts? One Special Area The Toilet Bowl needs a cleaner strong enough for this important job," reads a 1959 San-Flush ad published in *Good Housekeeping.* Drawing on the popular pseudo-scientific jargon that appears throughout the history of housework advertising, the ad explains: "Sani-Flush cleans and brightens faster than cleansers; disinfects, whitens, faster than bleaches because only Sani-Flush contains Sodium Binoxalate that dissolves hard-water rust stains." In a similar 1958 newspaper ad, Sani-Flush promised that "its fragrant, active ingredients work deep into crevices no brush can reach and its powerful disinfectant leaves your toilet bowl free of many harmful germs." "Kill germs in a dangerous area and make your toilet bowl the cleanest spot in the home," it concludes.[30] In 1958, danger still lurked in the toilet, including the potential for humiliating failures to fulfill homemaking duties. For example, 1958 magazine advertisements for SnoBol asked: "Does your bathroom pass the GUEST TEST?"[31] In another such 1958 ad, as guests are about to knock on the front door, the copy asserts: "Guests notice . . . and so does your family. They see what a fine housekeeper you are when your bathroom is SNO-BOL sweet and clean." Similarly, "Don't blush . . . use Sani Flush," pithily summarized a newspaper ad the same year.[32] For the conscientious housewife in 1950s bathroom advertising, removing germs and odors meant protecting the family, but also protecting her own homemaking reputation.

However, like the Sani-Flush housewives of the 1920s, housewife figures in 1950s and 1960s bathroom product advertising enjoyed the ease and convenience of products that promised to remove the most loathsome labor from bathroom cleaning. The aproned housewife in a 1958 SnoBol ad smilingly bends to clean the toilet under the headline "Cleans Bathrooms Instantly!" "New Pine-Scented SnoBol contains Miracle Detergent," begins the copy. "Cleans toilet bowls instantly! Swish . . . and it's clean," it concludes.[33] A toilet cleaner innovation in the 1960s—the "automatic" cleaners consumers could hang in the tank—led to especially dramatic claims about a product's ability to "do the work for you." Ty D Bol newspaper and magazine advertisements in 1965 began with headlines like "You'll Never, Never Have to Clean a Toilet Bowl Again" and "Make Next Time the Last Time." Copy promised that "Now you can avoid the most unpleasant job in housecleaning," and "You may never scrub the bowl again." In these ads, cleaning toilets is firmly fixed as part of the housewife's housework and homemaking, but the products also promised the removal of the hardest labor from this task. One headline even stated: "With new Ty D Bol in the tank, every time you flush, the toilet cleans itself."

A 1966 ad painted an especially memorable picture of the housewife converting to using Ty D Bol and the product's wondrous ability to clean the toilet. "It's Automatic—Like Magic! Toilet Bowl Cleans Itself!" enthuses the headline. The copy continues:

> Next time you have to scour and scrub the toilet bowl—think of Ty D Bol—get a bottle of Ty D Bol—and forget the whole messy, disagreeable chore. With Ty D Bol, normal flushing keeps the bowl bright and clean—no scum, no rings—even with the hardest water. Try Ty D Bol now; convince yourself you'll never again have to scrub a toilet.

The ads uniformly depicted toilet cleaning as part of housework, but acknowledged and even emphasized that this particular chore might be especially tiresome for the housewife, and promised to make it magically simple. More clearly than almost any other housework product, toilet cleaner advertising had to admit that this particular cleaning task was unpleasant while simultaneously continuing to link it feminine care and homemaking. Assurances that the product would do the scrubbing for you helped ad makers do just that.

Other "automatic" toilet cleaners, introduced around the same time, made similar claims. A 1966 ad for On Guard was headlined "We Clean Toilet Bowls . . . Automatically [sic]." The ad explains: "Cleaning the toilet bowl isn't a pleasant job. That's why we invented an automatic cleaner to do it for you. It's called On Guard." On Guard added a new element to defining a clean toilet bowl: colored water. "It tints the water a pleasing blue. *That's how you know it's clean.*" The ad ends with an appeal that echoed the Sani-Flush ads of the 1920s: "Why should you clean your toilet bowl, when we can do it for you? And do a better job at that." In a similar ad for Depend-O, the headline reads "Depend-O frees you from constantly scrubbing your bathroom bowl." The copy elaborated: "Do you hate scrubbing you bathroom bowl? You'll love Depend-O. It's a wonderful idea! Depend-O hides in your tank, washes your bowl automatically with every flushing." Again, echoing Sani-Flush's characterization of its product as "the only nice way to clean the toilet," in this ad Depend-O allows you to "Free yourself from constantly scrubbing your toilet bowl. Wash it the nicest way . . . automatically . . . with NEW DEPEND-O." As it had for decades, toilet cleanser advertising positioned products as a way to help housewives transform one of the nastiest housework chores into easy homemaking.

But if the essential nature of bathroom cleaning product appeals remained unchanged in the 1960s, the most stereotypical depictions of housewife figures in advertising came under serious attack. In the wake of Second Wave feminism, political figures, academics, and marketing and advertising experts all brought a new critical eye to such images. In response, advertising industry research urged ad makers to seriously reconsider their depiction of women in advertising for housework-related products. The 1975 report "Advertising and Women" prepared by the Consultive Panel of the National Advertising Review Board" and circulated at the JWT agency addressed this issue in the section entitled "The Portrayal of Women as Housewives:"

> The advertising of household products often involves psychologically unflattering portrayals of women. In some instances, they are depicted as being obsessed with cleanliness, as being embarrassed or feeling inadequate or guilty because of various forms of household dirt. Other advertisements show women being mean or catty to each other, or being envious or boastful about cooking or cleaning accomplishments in the home. In summary, the image of the housewife in advertising appears frequently to be not only a circumscribed one, but also that of a person with a warped sense of values.[34]

As the report made clear, the depiction of housewives in advertising continued into the 1970s with the same kinds of images advertising had always used of the housewife and of housework. This was especially true for bathroom product advertising. Housewives in ads for bathroom cleansers from at least the 1920s had been "boastful" of their clean and shining tubs, and certainly catty about how their cleanser worked better than their neighbor's. When it came to cleaning the bathroom, the "warped sense of values" often appeared in the guise of germ-fighting, as if the housewife believed with all her heart that a clean toilet was the ultimate guardian of her family's health and well-being (long after the very real danger presented by epidemics receded).

As a *Sun Times* journalist pointed out in 1978, ads continued to use an idealized housewife figure, even though she no longer wore aprons and high heels: "Many ads today have a superficial contemporary look. They feature a woman in jeans rather than with bouffant hair. But the implicit attitude toward women is still the same—they are presented as housewives or sex objects rather than serious workers."[35] The switch from bouffant hair to jeans signaled ad makers' desire and willingness to revise the image of the housewife in housework advertising, but "the implicit attitude" toward how to market housework-related products remained the same: the wardrobe changed, but not the assumption that a highly idealized female domestic figure was the only frame that could effectively convey the efficacy and desirability of housework products and, indeed, the act of housework itself. Though the housewife mom in jeans came to replace the aproned housewife in bathroom product advertising by the late

1970s, product appeals continued to build on the same two main themes: mothers guarding against germs to protect their families and doing so with almost magical ease. As part of the increasing marketing efforts focused on mothers and the concurrent renewed emphasis on woman's social role as mothers, bathroom product advertising in the last decades of the twentieth century and up to today regularly relies on images and copy about Mom protecting her family against germs in the bathroom.

Numerous 1970s television commercials continued to depict bathroom cleansers and the woman who wielded them as germ fighters. "Killing germs in the bathroom—that's important to me," earnestly explains the housewife mom in one such commercial from a series for Lysol Basin Tub and Tile Cleaner. The musical jingle plays over the big yellow wiping sponge shot, a popular visual cue in bathroom product advertising:

> When you foam the basin
> It's germs you're chasin'
> With the only foam
> That's Lysol!

Foaming cleansers, once novel, now had to be branded, and Lysol did so by evoking the old image of housewives fighting dangerous germs in the family's bathroom. In another 1970s commercial for Lysol Disinfectant Bathroom Cleaner, a housewife mom in a trench coat, mimicking spy noir films, "shoots" in the bathroom. But when she "pulls the trigger" it's on the bottle of cleanser, and aiming her "gun" at the counter, she "kills germs on surfaces."

Similarly, the toilet cleaner DX3 billed itself as "America's new agent for cleaning toilets," and the commercial showed the product "zapping" ring buildup and germs. In the early 1980s, Depend-O toilet bowl cleaner even depicted the housewife mom as a germ-fighting superhero. In the first shot, she's an ordinary housewife mom in a neat button-down plaid shirt but she then magically transforms into a superhero character. Wearing a shiny costume of tights, pink rubber gloves, pink cape, and a large Depend-O logo on her chest, she proclaims: "Depend-O clobbers odors with every flush!" as an animated lightning bolt zaps stains, odors, and germs in the toilet bowl. "To help keep my family's bathroom fresh, I fight bold stains and odors with Depend-O," she says, demonstrating the product. Meant to be humorous and somewhat tongue-in-cheek, these commercials nonetheless ensure that Mom is the bathroom cleaner secret agent or superhero. Neither her husband nor her children play any role in helping to "keep the family's bathroom fresh"—fresh, germ-free, and *safe* for her family. Ad makers seemed unable to imagine any other way to sell bathroom cleaners, even as they began to hear ever more clearly that many consumers, many of their target consumers even, resented demeaning depictions of the housewife in advertising. The bathroom sponge just could not be depicted in any way except in the hands of a housewife mom. No other frame made sense, to ad makers and presumably the consumers they hoped to reach.

Like 1970s laundry commercials that assured consumers' families would notice Mom's work in the laundry room, some 1970s Lysol commercials marketed the brand by promising that cleaning the bathroom would make a real and important difference in your family's life. For example, it revisited the appeal that "Guests notice . . . and so does your family" when it came to Mom's labors to keep the bathroom healthfully pristine. "My family noticed it!" exclaims the housewife mom in button-down shirt and slacks, demonstrating Lysol Basin Tub and Tile Cleaner by spraying the foam onto the bathtub and wiping it off with a big yellow sponge. "For a bathroom that's noticeably fresh," the voiceover promises. In a similar commercial from the same era, each member of the family explains how Mom made the bathroom "noticeably fresh." "I can see the shine!" claims Grandma, admiring the sink. "I can smell the freshness!" avows Dad in the shower. The gratified housewife mom, in turtleneck and slacks, affirms it: "My family noticed!" Very similar to 1970s laundry product commercials that suggested certain brands could obtain recognition for the housewife mom's labors, these commercials placed front and center the possibility that cleaning the bathroom, a potentially thankless task, might inspire real appreciation from the family—if you used a product that would render your work "noticeable."

And like the 1970s laundry product advertising, bathroom cleanser product advertising in the 1970s reflected ad makers' struggle to adapt the housewife figure to the new post-Second Wave era. They clearly tried to remove the most stereotypical images of housewives from their appeals, but at the same time churned out some pretty demeaning images of women. For example, a 1970s television commercial for Blu-Boy featured an officious male announcer in a suit, one of the last of the most overtly condescending "expert" spokesmen, explaining housework products to apparently clueless real housewives. Again emphasizing how the product will remove the labor of bathroom cleaning, he facetiously explains that the blue water "coats your bowl to prevent stains and sediments from sticking to the porcelain," so "You don't have to brush your bowl as often to keep everything sparkling clean. Everything is swished away easily and quickly." The women appear to listen eagerly to his unctuous lecture on toilet cleanliness.

The same announcer appeared in a number of Blu-Boy commercials, including one meant to portray him in face-to-face conversations with "real" women. In front of a sign that says "Consumer Research," he faces a row of women sitting at a table. They are pleasant but normal looking, in neat but casual clothes—instantly recognizable as the new housewife mom was beginning to appear in housework advertising. The announcer begins: "Ladies, we'd like a consumer's opinion. Do automatic toilet bowl cleaners really work?" One of these women, a slim brunette woman with a sculpted hairdo, answers earnestly, in a speech that seems meant to somehow temper the magical claims of all automatic toilet bowl cleaners: "Well, I never thought they worked. I mean none of them clean completely. You still have to brush. But Blu-Boy is different. It works. It doesn't eliminate brushing but I don't have to brush nearly as often or use any other cleaner and Blu-Boy lasts over two months in my tank." Her voice turns confidential, as she admits: "And I love the blue water." The other women chuckle in agreement. The creators of this commercial clearly attempted to heed the advice of the report "Advertising and Women," trying to portray women in a more realistic manner. Putting them in the "Consumer Research" setting, they depict these housewife moms with a kind of agency, offering somewhat more realistic testimonials about the product—"you still have to brush."

The woman seated next to her, nodding encouragingly and riveted to her every word, is an African American woman in a casual print dress and a neat hairdo. Although she doesn't have a speaking role, the presence of this actress demonstrates how by the 1970s, the housewife mom in advertising was usually—*but not always*—white. By the 1970s, ad agencies and their clients were well aware that they might profitably market housework-related products to African American and other "ethnic" (to use their terminology) groups. By the early 1990s, Vanish toilet cleaner, for example, published ads in *Essence* magazine for "Vanish Clear Drop-Ins."[36] They took care to avoid any depiction of a black woman using the product or scrubbing the toilet: such an image would have too closely touched upon the long and deeply troubling history of African American "domestics" and cleaning ladies in our country—definitely an unappealing image, especially in a magazine devoted to uplifting and celebrating black women.[37] Rather, much like any other ad for automatic toilet cleaners, the 1992 ad for Vanish Clear Drop-Ins emphasized the way it would automatically clean the bowl *for* you: "every flush releases tough detergent." But blue water had gone out of fashion, and one of the selling points for this product was that "it helps your bowl stay clean, fresh and crystal clear." The ad also offered a coupon, encouraging consumers to "Try it now."

In contemporary advertising, the housewife mom can be depicted as an African American woman, as long as she is not engaged in dirty, difficult housework tasks. She might well be cooking dinner for her own children (as I explore in the next chapter) but she won't be cleaning toilets. One notable exception to this portrayal of black women and housework is "the Pine Sol lady." The African American actress Diane Amos, who has portrayed "the Pine Sol lady" in ads and commercials from 1993 to today, asserts that the character—who is sometimes shown cleaning floors or other household surfaces—is a straightforward spokeswoman. Amos states that she is proud to be "one of the few national black spokespeople in the country." However, the representation of a heavy set, folksy black woman wielding a bucket and mop disturbingly echoes earlier stereotypes of black women in advertising, according to at least one scholar.[38] Notwithstanding that particular character, however, advertisers routinely use African American actresses to represent housewife moms in housework-related advertising, and by the 1970s, "your" toilet bowl may have well have referred to women of other racial backgrounds as opposed to the stereotypical white housewife of earlier advertising. By 2005, for instance, *Buenhogar* magazine included ads for Clorox toilet cleaning products aimed at Latina customers.[39]

But in other respects, bathroom advertising remained the same. Even magic creatures continued to make an appearance. For instance, with crude special effects, late-1970s and early 1980s television commercials featured a tiny Ty D Bol sailor man (in a miniaturized live action shot) cleaning the toilet bowl and conversing with the normal-sized housewife. In one such commercial, the Ty D Bol sailor man informs the housewife about new "Ring Guard:"

> **Housewife** [bewildered, gazing down into toilet bowl]: What are you doing in there?
> **Ty D Bol Man:** I'm bringing you new Ty D Bol with Ring Guard! [hands her the product]
> **Housewife:** A new Ty D Bol?
> **Ty D Bol Man:** Yes. It means you'll scrub less often because Ty D Bol has Ring Guard. To help keep your toilet bowl ring free, automatically.
> **Housewife** [considering]: Hmm. I'll scrub less often. Cleans and deodorizes too.

Not only was the magical creature come to assist the housewife in the bathroom a longstanding feature of bathroom cleaning advertising, but so was the tagline, which echoed virtually every claim to ease and convenience made by bathroom cleaners: "Less scrubbing for you!" These ridiculous Ty D Bol ads portraying women conversing with a miniature man in the toilet were hardly a step in the right direction for less stereotypical depictions of women doing housework. Even though they attempted to be somewhat humorous, the image of a woman peering down into a toilet and conversing with a magical creature that apparently no one else could see, about how to keep the toilet fresh and clean, did not exactly indicate rapidly changing notions in the advertising industry about how women should be portrayed in housework advertising.

In fact, in ads and commercials, if you were male and you weren't a miniaturized sailor man (or other magical creature) you would never, ever get anywhere near a toilet bowl. From the first modern bathroom cleaner newspaper ads to the slickest multimedia advertising campaigns of today, the housewife mom is the only person who faces "the most disagreeable task in housecleaning." She's a "busy mom," fighting germs and looking for ways to lighten her load, but it's *her* work that needs lightening, *her* toilet bowl that needs magical cleaning. Possibly the sole exception, the only man in any print ad or televised commercial depicted cleaning a toilet, was in a 1983 commercial for Bully. The ad opens with a shot of a platoon of soldiers relaxing in their barracks. The inspecting officer enters and they start to scramble. At this point, a big, burly solider speaks to the camera:

> Latrine duty used to make me melancholy. So I invented my own automatic toilet bowl cleaner. With every flush its continuous bleaching action keeps the bowl fastidiously clean [shot of his hairy man hand placing the product in the tank] No regular brushing! No tattletale blue water . . . I named it after me: Bully.

In the sole instance of a man cleaning a toilet in more than 100 years of housework advertising, the man is living in a male-only institutional environment—it's not a home bathroom and anyway, there are no women living there to do any of the necessary cleaning. Moreover, he's not even doing routine cleaning, but has in fact *invented* a new cleaning product with a macho name that scorns sissy, "tattletale blue water." Even more telling are the *other* Bully commercials that ran in 1983. These commercials featured a housewife cowering below an enormous toilet bowl; she's a marked contrast to the aggressive "Bully" in the barracks. These commercials ended with the tagline: "Don't be bullied by your bowl."[40] Even in the 1980s, the toilet bowl, "where danger lurks," continued to loom over women as an especially daunting housework task. As marketers tapped into the growing "mom market," they focused even more explicitly on depicting the casually dressed, pretty but not sexy, middle-class mom fighting a war against germs and guarding her family's health. For example, the housewife mom as superhero germ fighter reappeared in 2009. In this commercial, a car suddenly smashes through a bathroom wall. The driver, a housewife mom in a nice t-shirt and slacks, leaps out from behind the steering wheel, and as menacing music plays, approaches a mildewed tile wall, then sprays the product. "Tilex. Hard core clean," intones the voiceover. (A print from the same campaign, published in a 2008 issue of *Good Housekeeping*, likened the product to a SWAT team for your bathroom). But the real star of contemporary commercials for germ-fighting bath and toilet cleaners doesn't wear a cape—she's the ordinary housewife mom who, with the help of certain products, renders the family bathroom safe and healthful. Long after Americans no longer had to worry about typhoid-causing sewer gas, and long after many other aspects of gender roles changed in this nation, advertisements and commercials continued to depict the housewife mom—and only the housewife mom—guarding the family against the incursion of germs through the bathroom plumbing. At a time when household cleaning in real homes might well, and certainly should, be a shared task, in bathroom cleaner advertising only Mom can make sure the bathroom is *really* clean.

A print ad for Mr. Clean in 2006 depicted a close-up photo of a toy train and a stretchy Dachshund-shaped toy set up to encircle the base of a toilet. "Wherever bacteria hide, kids will find them," warned the copy. "Trust Mr. Clean to kill 99.9% of bacteria." In the twenty-first century, guarding the family's health narrowed very specifically to keeping "your kids" safe and, moreover, your bathroom a safe playground. Vividly reflecting the new momism of our culture today, when highly idealized images of mothering widely circulate in our media, it's not enough to just eliminate dirt and germs in the bathroom: a good mom is always *fun*. A Clorox campaign made this connection explicit. The 2007 print ads featured dreamy photographs of adorable little children standing in the bathroom, letting their imaginations run free, such as a little girl in a yellow frock, holding an old fashioned teddy bear, imagining butterflies flitting around the pedestal sink and claw-footed tub.[41] "Because a bathroom can be more than just a bathroom. Clorox helps keep it clean. Even the imaginary parts," reads the copy. Television commercials in 2009 reiterated that idea, with gauzy fantasy shots of kids daydreaming and swinging in a bathtub-swing, then lounging in a bathtub-merry-go-round. The commercials predominantly feature children, and so the possibility exists that this commercial might be representing household cleaning in a gender neutral way. However, in the next shot, a woman's hand, with the requisite manicure and gold wedding ring, demonstrates Clorox bathroom cleaning products, such as drop-in tabs, spray cleaners, and the "Toilet Wand." Like the 2009 Clorox laundry ads that appealed to consumers on the premise that the product allowed mothers to "let kids be kids," the Clorox bathroom cleaner commercials suggest that safeguarding children requires more than just battling germs—it means choosing the product that will make your bathroom so exquisitely clean and safe that your children will thrive emotionally and psychologically. A clean bathtub will apparently provide a conduit for wonderful flights of fancy. This campaign clearly depicts the housewife mom as transforming housework into homemaking, using bathroom cleaning products that help her provide not merely a clean bathroom but good mothering.

Lysol also appeals directly to a mother's desire and responsibility to safeguard her children against germs in the bathroom, with commercials featuring the same female voiceover. In recent years, the predominance of male voiceovers has ended and now the majority of housework commercials feature female voiceovers. In this case, feminist-inspired criticism of advertising in the 1970s did inspire a real change. The 1975 "Advertising and Women" report strongly critiqued the tradition of all-male voiceovers in housework advertising:

> It is especially true that in the advertising of household products, women too often are portrayed as stupid—too dumb to cope with familiar everyday chores, unless instructed by children, or by a man, or assisted by a supernatural male symbol. Even off-camera voice-over announcements are made by predominantly male voices. In many of the commercials the implication is clear that, if carefully told what to do, a woman can use the product. Apparently, however, it takes a man to manufacture the product or to understand its virtues well enough to explain it.[42]

Similar critiques followed, backed by market research that demonstrated that the intended consumers of housework products—women—responded better to female voiceovers in many housework commercials. The change has been almost complete, and a vast majority of housework commercials today feature female voiceovers.[43]

But if the voiceovers have changed, the appeal, based on an image of the housewife mom as bathroom germ fighter, has not. In a 2009 commercial for Lysol 4-in-1 Spray, a housewife mom in a neat shirt and slacks, with vaguely Asian features and long black hair, and wearing a wedding ring, helps her young son get ready for his bath in a fashionable bathroom. It features a fancy bowl and pedestal sink and a blooming orchid on the towel shelf. It certainly looks like a pristine bathroom in an upper-class home, but, as in the early 1900s Sylpho-Nathol ad, "danger lurks." Menacing music plays while shadows flit behind the shower curtain. The female voiceover states: "Fact. Soap scum is easy to see. Bacteria aren't." The camera swoops into the bathtub, revealing an assortment of grotesque animated bacteria creeping and crawling over the tub, roaring threateningly. When Mom feels something is amiss, she whips back the shower curtain, but the crafty bacteria quickly slink down into the drain. Just like the "hidden, unhealthful trap" of the 1920s, in this commercial the bathtub drain contains dangerous menaces to the health of the family, specifically the kids. Mom's hand wipes off the animated germs in the sponge shot, while the voiceover continues: "Fear not. There's Lysol 4-in-1 Disinfecting Spray. It's the best on soap scum and kills 99.9% of germs." The campaign's tagline makes the connection between cleaning the bathroom and good mothering absolutely clear: "Lysol. Disinfect to protect."

Another commercial in this campaign made even more explicit Mom's responsibility, that is, the need to "disinfect to protect" her children in the bathroom. In the 2009 commercial, a housewife mom in a fitted t-shirt and khakis, wearing a gold wedding ring, guides her young daughter into the stall of a public restroom. The filthy toilet stall is littered, sprayed with graffiti, and seems more likely to be the scene of illicit drug use than a mother-and-daughter outing. But there's Mom, gingerly putting toilet paper on the toilet seat as her daughter prepares to sit on it. The female voiceover states the obvious: "Public restrooms are *disgusting*. And can be *infested* with germs." But as Mom, grimacing, flushes the toilet with her foot, the stall fades away and morphs into a nicely appointed home bathroom. "But what about your toilet bowl at home?" cautions the voiceover: "It could be infested with up to three million bacteria per square inch." A shot of worm-like animated bacteria appears, and they squirm repugnantly around the bowl. "With regular cleaners, you're not reaching germs under the rim," explains the voiceover, as a generic cleaner fails to reach the worm germs. Lysol, however, "wipes" them off the toilet, as the woman's wedding ring hand swabs it out. In this way, the claims made by Lysol very much echo the claims of 1920s toilet cleaning ads that emphasized the products' abilities to clean where you can't see what you're cleaning. This mother still has to rigorously police the fragile borderland between the sanctity of the home and the dangerous outside world. In the last shot, germs removed and safety restored, the housewife mom enjoys a hug from her happy daughter. Once again, Lysol reminds consumers to "Disinfect to protect."

Lysol's popular Facebook page (over 430,000 users "Like" it) continues to use the same kinds of appeals in a new medium. A June 15, 2011, comment from Lysol on its wall began, "It's important for new moms to keep the home environment safe. One way is by reducing allergen triggers around the house." A link on the comment took users to the Lysol website and, as of June 16, 152 Facebook users "liked" this comment and 7 consumers added their own comment praising Lysol for its ability to fight germs and discussing other ways to keep allergens at bay.[44]

Today's consumers are also responding to appeals to protect the planet, as the phenomenal growth in sales of "green" and "natural" cleaning products attests.[45] Protecting the planet appeals appeared as early as the 1970s and 1980s. For example, a 1987 advertisement in *National Parks Magazine* for Bon Ami featured a large photo of planet Earth and the headline "We'd like to clean up more than a few bathrooms." As the copy explains: "For over 100 years Bon Ami has been demonstrating that you don't have to be tough on the environment to be tough on dirt."[46] Such ads and commercials proliferated dramatically in the early 2000s as environmentalism became a mainstream cause, and this product category increased exponentially. In a 2009 commercial for instance, Nature's Source brand promotes its bathroom cleanser as environmentally friendly. The woman's voiceover, accompanying a shot of a spray bottle split in two, begins: "Think you'll only get half a cleaner? Either it works or it's natural? But why not both?" The "plant-based," biodegradable Nature's Source Bathroom Cleaner promises both, demonstrating in a sponge shot how well it works, and the final shot depicts a housewife mom in a fitted t-shirt, wedding ring visible, gazing lovingly at her sparkling bathroom as the female voiceover assures viewers that the product "Leaves nothing behind but a fresh scent." As this commercial demonstrates, when it comes to cleaning the bathroom, environmental-based appeals still rely on the figure of the housewife mom, who will still be able to *really* clean up this dirty room and continue to keep the family safe.

In the first decades of the 1900s, as municipal water systems, water closets, and bathtubs began to change domestic life and housework, advertising emphasized how certain toilet and bath cleaning products would fight germs and subsequent disease and infection. Not totally without some basis in reality in the days before universal vaccination and dependable municipal plumbing, these ads sought to raise anxiety about what havoc sewer gas and water closet germs might wreck on family members. "You"—the housewife—and nobody else could ensure the family's safety in the bathroom. In the first decade of the 2000s, the housewife mom remains responsible for fighting the germs infesting the tub and toilet. Ad makers still utilize this theme because it remains marketable. The danger of typhoid may have passed for most Americans, but after all, who *doesn't* want to make their home safer for their children? In the post-9/11 era, and when every disaster—natural, man-made, or health-related—is vividly and relentlessly depicted 24/7 on every news channel and website, who *wouldn't* enjoy the feeling of making their home a little haven of safety?[47] When global warming looms and pollution threatens every species' safety, who *wouldn't* be tempted by products promising that your housework won't contribute to the demise of the polar bear?

Ad agencies know that for some Americans, especially perhaps mothers, making the bathroom tile sparkle and the toilet bowl spotless (with environmentally friendly products) may well offer a real sense of satisfaction and, yes, may make them feel a tiny bit safer in an unsafe world. In the script for a 1992 video, "The Images of Women and Men in Advertising," made by the Advertising Educational Foundation, the narrator explains how housework advertising relies on investing housework with meanings above and beyond mundane cleaning:

> While household products is a category often criticized for stereotyping and demeaning women, in order to be relevant and informative, advertisers must directly address the mundane chores associated with these products while also capturing the attention of the audience. To do this, product benefits are dramatized in the context of an emotion or situation to which the target audience can relate.[48]

As this video attests, at the end of the twentieth century, agencies asked themselves how they could "capture the attention of the audience" without demeaning images of housewives. The figure of the housewife mom provided the answer. The "target audience" in the late 1990s and into the 2000s quickly crystallized into "moms," and the figure of the housewife mom ably replaced overtly stereotypical and demeaning images of women. While consumers might recoil from the suggestion that toilet cleaning was solely "women's work," they seem to readily accept that it's *Mom's* job. In the case of bathroom cleaners, the "emotion or situation to which the target audience can relate," stayed the same from the beginning of the twentieth century right into the twenty-first: keep the dangerous germs out. The resulting advertising speaks to many Americans' inability or unwillingness to consider parenting a truly shared responsibility between fathers and mothers. Don't the fathers of these children in the Lysol commercials care that germs threaten bath time? And the ever-present wedding ring in housework advertising also suggests that single mothers are still not the "target audience" either. But ad makers and their clients are certainly correct in assuming that as far as an emotion which captures the audience, fear of outside contamination entering the home and attacking the most vulnerable members of the family continues to have great resonance with Americans in the 2000s.

Yet contemporary advertising also continues to suggest that bathroom cleaning constitutes an unpleasant chore, and products promise magical assistance for Mom in the bathroom. Perhaps the best known are the Scrubbing Bubbles. Scrubbing Bubbles products include disposable toilet brushes, toilet cleaning gel, sprays, wipes, and aerosols for tub, tile, shower, and toilet. S. C. Johnson's Scrubbing Bubbles website features the bubbles zooming around a shining bathroom telling viewers about different products for each part of the bathroom, The Bubbles have their own Facebook page, packed with coupon offers and customer testimonials, and over 2,000 followers on Twitter. Originally owned by Dow Chemical and called "Dow Bathroom Cleaner," the Scrubbing Bubbles commercial campaign in the 1970s was so successful that the company renamed the product. S. C. Johnson continues to pour millions of dollars into extending the Scrubbing Bubbles brand into different types of bathroom products as well as advertising featuring the Bubbles. It's a worthwhile investment: during the 52 weeks ending October 8, 2008, Scrubbing Bubbles sales totaled $102 million.[49] But the Bubbles are not only "good guys:" they are deployed to explicitly relieve the housewife mom of the tiresome jobs associated with cleaning the bathroom. Their well-known tagline, which appears in the majority of Scrubbing Bubbles advertising including the website, is "We work hard so you don't have to."

In print ads and television commercials, the animated bubbles swoosh up and down the tub or shower or tile, leaving a swath of sparkling fresh cleanliness in their wake. The first commercials, when the product was still called Dow Bathroom Cleaner, featured the voice work of Paul Winchell (best known as the voice of Tigger in the Winnie the Pooh Disney movies) as the Bubbles. In these commercials, the Bubbles shout: "Okay germs, you're all washed up!" and "We work extra hard so you don't have to!" as they swarm around the 1970s avocado green bathtub. They emerge from a large animated spray bottle, held by a woman's manicured hand. "You" in the tag "We work hard so you don't have to" refers to her—the housewife. The "you" remains unchanged, and if anything, the brand insists even more adamantly today that its products will magically relieve the housewife mom of her bathroom cleaning chores.

One such product especially emphasized this claim. The Automatic Shower Cleaner claimed to make "scrubbing virtually obsolete," and all advertising highlighted the product's revolutionary ability to "clean the shower for you." In addition to the image of the bubbles on the packaging—an instantly recognizable symbol of a product that claims to remove the hard labor from cleaning the bathroom—print ads and commercials depicted this product as, literally, a "Maid For Your Shower." In a rare twenty-first century reappearance of the household servant in housework advertising and in an indication of how particularly difficult it is for advertisers to depict the drudgery of bathroom housework as homemaking, ads and commercials for the Automatic Shower Cleaner featured photographs of actual human actors dressed as maids and scrubbing the shower. Kelly Semrau, an S. C. Johnson vice president, stated in promotional materials: "This product acts like a team of maids coming into your home and keeping your shower clean on a daily basis."[50] In a 2006 ad in *Good Housekeeping*, the product sprouted six female arms in rubber gloves wielding brushes and scrubbers. When the "Dual Sprayers" feature of the product appeared in 2008, another *Good Housekeeping* ad featured a large photo of the product and two women's heads adorned with maid's caps, their rubber gloved hands spraying toward the camera. "It's like having a maid times two," reads the ad. *Consumer Reports* testing showed that (not surprisingly!) "The Automatic Shower Cleaner" couldn't *really* clean your shower for you.[51] But the tested falseness of the claim—the "bubbles" can't really do "your" work—hasn't even made a dent in the proliferation of similar Scrubbing Bubbles advertising.

For example, Bubbles show up to help out housewife moms in television commercials for Scrubbing Bubbles Toilet Gel and "Mega Shower Foamer." One Foamer commercial (2009) shows two housewife moms casually dressed in jeans and nicely fitted hoodies, scrubbing a glass shower door side by side. Unlike the "splotchy trigger" used by the one who scrubs and scrubs to no noticeable effect, the "Mega Foamer" allows the other to just wipe and walk away. The "Toilet Cleaning Gel" (which is "stamped" into the bowl with a special tool) commercial features a cute housewife mom in khakis demonstrating the product, her gold wedding ring glinting as she then gazes happily down into her toilet bowl where animated bubbles delightedly scrub and clean her bathroom.

A shower-cleaning product, the Action Scrubber, featured a large drawing of the Bubbles on the package and the slightly modified tag: "We scrub hard so you don't have to." Again, Kelly Semrau sang the product's praises, but this time made very, very clear who needed rescuing from housework by the Scrubbing Bubbles:

> As a busy mom, I understand the importance of a clean home, but like most women, I'm not willing to invest too much precious time or back-breaking effort to scrub the shower. That's why it's important to look for cleaning solutions like Scrubbing Bubbles products—they help you accomplish the maximum with a minimum of energy.[52]

It's hard to believe that a vice president of Global Public Affairs and Communications for a major corporation would be willing to candidly discuss the state of her shower with the American public. It seems far more likely that someone in publicity or advertising wrote this copy. Either way, Semrau's remarks demonstrate that while it was completely socially unacceptable in 2008 to suggest that "housewives" needed relief from their burdensome housework, advertising could without impunity pin all household cleaning responsibility on "busy moms." Semrau makes explicit here what so much bathroom cleaning advertising implies in the twenty-first century: ad agencies and their clients assume that not only can housework be repetitive and wearisome, but the ones who must exert "back-breaking effort" and invest their "precious time" into housework are "busy moms" and *only* moms. They assume, based presumably on their informed interpretations of the consumer market, such as purchase behavior and statistics, that these depictions are the best frame for selling bathroom cleansers and all housework products to American consumers. Why not market "The Action Scrubber" as a tough cleaning tool like a sander that any manly husband would willingly wield? Why not market the Toilet Gel as so easy to snap in that any child over six could pick it up and put it in? What about all the women who live alone or with a mate but no children? Don't *they* have bathrooms to clean? Semrau's statement attests to how cemented and unshakable the link between cleaning the bathroom and the image of a female homemaker remains in twenty-first century advertising and marketing discourse, and apparently for ordinary consumers as well.

In short, almost nothing's changed. She's not wearing an apron, but just like the slim and attractive housewife on the Sani-Flush can and virtually all bathroom cleaning advertising that grew as bathrooms became commonplace features of American homes, today's "busy mom" fights germs in the toilet"; she "disinfects to protect"; she keeps the bathroom safe for her children; gazes at her sparkling clean and well-appointed bathroom; and does so with products that magically—from the "Toilet Wand" to the "Magic Eraser"—remove all possible degradation from this aspect of housework. In bathroom advertising the housewife mom symbolically and rhetorically transforms this household labor into homemaking and feminine care for the family.

3

The Kitchen

Of all the magical housework helpers introduced to the American public in twentieth-century advertising, the most successful was a small white humanoid who sprang to life out of tube of dinner roll dough: Poppin' Fresh, the Pillsbury Doughboy. Assisting women in the kitchen since 1965, P. F. is now a cultural icon in his own right. He continues to appear in almost all Pillsbury television commercials; pops up on most pages of the Pillsbury website; and, of course, he has his own Facebook page.[1] Since their inception, Doughboy ads and commercials consistently and memorably depicted a woman's ability to place hot bread products on the dinner table as the ultimate expression of love and care, simultaneously transforming heavily processed premade dough into Mom's "homemade" cooking, and housework into homemaking and feminine care for the family.

The famous tagline associated with the Doughboy—"Nothing says lovin' like something from the oven"—reflects how advertising depicts the task of cooking as particularly gendered homemaking and family care. As historian Katherine Parkin summarizes, twentieth-century print ads for food products consistently emphasized "that women should shop and cook for others in order to express their love."[2] But in addition, food product advertising also often referenced the potentially wearisome and dreary aspects of daily meal preparation. Like the Sani-Flush ads that marketed the product by depicting its ability to guard the family's health and at the same time relieve the housewife of drudgery, modern food advertising marketed products by depicting the way they would help the housewife express her love and care for husband and children *and* relieve her of the more tedious aspects of home cookery.

This chapter examines food product ads and commercials, particularly recipe advertising, from the early 1900s to today. It demonstrates that such advertising persistently utilizes highly idealized images of housewives and housewife moms enjoying the ease and convenience of modern food products but always still devoting themselves to the well-being of their families, thus powerfully reaffirming domestic gender norms. In reality, cooking arguably offers the greatest potential satisfaction and requires the most skill and creativity of all housework. Cooking and eating together are essential parts of building families and communities, and can be a profound source of pleasure and pride, especially as part of a shared ethnic and cultural heritage.[3] So there is truth to the notion that care and feeding are emotionally intertwined, and that many people—men and women— enjoy expressing love for their families with good cooking. However, like all housework advertising, food advertising framed the work of food preparation *solely* as a female labor of love, and consistently emphasized how food products would transform cooking into caring.

This chapter also examines advertising for dishwashing soaps from the early twentieth century to today. In ads and commercials for dishwashing detergents and other cleansers, the kitchen is definitely a place of drudgery, where the loathsome labor of dishwashing robs the housewife not only of time and good spirits, but her beauty—specifically, the beauty of her hands. No other type of housework advertising built such a consistent history of appeals around the notion that without the right product, a housewife faced unrelenting toil that would actually disfigure her body. Dish soaps promised amazingly easy and fast cleanup without damaging delicate hands and moreover, emphasized the way that shining clean dishes reflected the housewife's care for her home, an expression of the highest standards of homemaking. Even as the most overt housewife stereotypes disappeared from ads and commercials for food and dish cleaning products in the late 1970s and 1980s and the housewife mom took their place, and even as companies expanded their marketing efforts toward nonwhite consumers, many aspects of this advertising remained the same: it continued to promise ease and convenience, and the housewife mom still almost always made dinner and almost always did the dishes, transforming those mundane tasks into loving homemaking.

The food advertising discussed in this chapter focuses on a few key products made by two of the largest and most important food companies in the United States: General Foods and Kraft. For many years, General Foods reigned as the nation's largest manufacturer of packaged convenience foods and other food products. General Foods produced an untold number of ads and commercials for decades, beginning in 1929 when the Postum Company renamed itself General Foods Corporation.[4] Kraft, too, has gradually grown from a small company to a multi-brand international corporation. It began as James L. Kraft's one-man wholesale cheese business in 1903, grew to become the J. L. Kraft and Brothers Company in

1909, merged into the Kraft-Phenix Cheese Corporation in 1928, and finally became the Kraft Foods Company in 1945. Phillip Morris acquired Kraft in 1988.[5] Three years before acquiring Kraft, Philip Morris (now Altria Group) bought General Foods, and in 1989 these two brand giants merged into Kraft-General Foods. In 2007, Altria completed a spin-off of Kraft, which now functions as its own independent company.

The rapid expansion of both these major food companies reflects the national transformation in food preparation and eating in the United States. Changes in how Americans cooked and ate vividly illustrated the evolution of the home from a site of production to a site of consumption at the end of the 1800s: from growing or raising and cooking the majority of their foods, Americans began buying all food products, from basic cooking ingredients to highly processed ready-to-eat foods. The modernization of food and eating occurred far more rapidly in urban areas, where by the post–Civil War years railroads, canning technology, and other industrial advances meant increasing variety and availability of meats, vegetables, and canned goods for sale in cities. By the last decades of the 1800s, Americans could purchase a large number of processed foods, especially cereals and crackers. By the post–World War I era, Americans of all classes had come to depend in large part on factory-made or processed food products.

Similarly, kitchens themselves underwent dramatic changes during this period. First, stoves (patented in 1834) became the standard means for cooking food, and iceboxes improved food storage. The introduction of municipal water and electricity wrought major changes in the basic undertaking of food preparation, as electric refrigerators and gas or electric stoves became desirable and increasingly obtainable consumer purchases. These changes occurred at an uneven rate, with electricity, for example, widely available in urban areas several decades before rural Americans could expect to have access. Also, poor Americans continued to try to produce as much of their own food as possible well into the twentieth century and maintained small kitchen gardens, even in the city.[6] But overall, by 1920 a great deal of the productive labor necessary to cook the daily meals had lessened or disappeared for many Americans. Canned and processed foods—and advertising for those products—proliferated.

Other important factors shaped how modern Americans cooked and ate. At the end of the 1800s, American knowledge about and interest in nutrition grew rapidly. Meals became smaller, and a food's "digestibility" became paramount, in large part due to the efforts of new cookery experts and proponents of scientific cookery working in the field of domestic science (later known as home economics). A few domestic reformers, such as Charlotte Perkins Gilman, urged Americans to try communal cooking, but they met with profound failure. When Progressive Era reformers sought to address urban ills, they included what they considered the shocking dietary habits of poor urban immigrants, who insisted upon radical cooking ingredients such as garlic and fresh tomatoes. In middle-class homes, an assortment of new small electric appliances gained popularity by 1900, including toasters, chafing dishes, and waffle irons. Food processing companies had a vested interest in depicting cooking as a time-consuming chore that could be eased with handy new food products, but at the same time large numbers of consumers eagerly embraced premade foods that cut down on kitchen work.[7] For almost all Americans at the beginning of the twentieth century, cooking increasingly became less and less a hard-earned female skill, passed down through the generations and applied to the production of basic foodstuffs. Rather, Americans increasingly relied on written recipes and new kinds of food products and processed foods. That trend continued rapidly throughout the first decades of the 1900s, as the sharp increase in cookbook publication attests.[8]

In fact, recipes played a central role in modern food advertising. Purveying recipes was perhaps the most effective and regularly used means of marketing food products. At least a century before the internet set the twenty-first century bar for interactive advertising, printed recipes in pamphlets, magazines and newspapers, and promotional cookbooks fostered the holy grail of advertising: recipe ads encouraged *active engagement*—rather than passive viewing with the advertisement. Moreover, recipe ads came to readers and viewers under the guise of "service" to the consumer. One of the oldest and most staid means of advertising—through recipes—remains one of the most effective marketing strategies ever invented, since it creates very positive brand images (as a "helper") at the same time it actively inserts itself directly into the consumer's kitchen, increasing the possibility of a product purchase.

Like the first modern advertisements for laundry soaps and water closet cleaners, the first modern print ads for food products sought to successfully brand certain products with images of and copy addressed to "you," the housewife: the first modern ads for kitchen housework depended upon depictions of the housewife. In the early 1900s, the housewife—neatly dressed, slim, pleasant-looking, married and usually a mother, pictured in her nicely appointed middle-class home—appeared regularly in food product advertising. At this time, white middle- to upper-class Americans still actively sought to employ household servant labor, including cooks. But modern food advertising portrayed food preparation as primarily the work of the housewife. Like the early Lux advertisements, even when some of a product's advertisements occasionally utilized imagery of a maid or cook, others focusing on the housewife's responsibility for the housework appeared simultaneously.

Take, for example, Jell-O, one of General Foods' oldest and most successful brands. In 1895, Pearl B. Wait, a cough medicine maker in Le Roy, New York, adapted a previously patented recipe for a gelatin desert and his wife named it Jell-O. In 1899, they sold the business to the Genesee Pure Foods Company; in 1925, the Postum Company (which would become General Foods in 1929) acquired Jell-O. From its very beginning, Jell-O advertised its products with depictions of the housewife: according to Kraft's website, the first Jell-O ad appeared in a 1902 *Ladies Home Journal* and featured a "smiling, fashionably coifed women in white aprons proclaiming Jell-O gelatin 'America's Most Famous Dessert.'"[9] Early 1900s Jell-O magazine ads emphasized how easily the housewife could make this "famous" dessert. "It saves a vast amount of kitchen work," explained one, but the ad also made clear exactly who was doing the kitchen work: "It is a delicious dessert, easily prepared and makes dainty dishes such as the housewife could make only by a long tedious process of flavoring gelatine with fruit juices. It saves time and trouble, and gives better results."[10] "Affords the housewife a choice of many delicate, delightfully flavored dishes," read another. A fashionable, apron-clad housewife appears in another 1900 ad, tossing down her recipe book. "No recipe book required to prepare Jell-O," read the copy.

The presence of this housewife's "Recipe Book" is telling. The publication of recipe ads and cookbooks soared in the early decades of the 1900s. Even as it promised such ease that no recipes would be required, Genesee marketed Jell-O with recipe collections beginning in 1904.[11] Beginning at the end of the 1800s, virtually every major food processor, appliance maker, grocery chain, and utility company—each with its staff of home economists—produced recipe pamphlets, circulars, and books, which often included instructional photographs and drawings along with prominent photos and pictures of products. Consumers loved them and snapped them up by the millions. Recipes continue to feature prominently in food advertising, including General Foods and Kraft products, although recipe advertising peaked around the mid-twentieth century.[12]

Like their first recipe collections, early magazine ads for Jell-O linked the work of meal preparation with the housewife and emphasized how it would relieve her kitchen labor. One 1919 magazine ad featured a child purchasing a package of Jell-O for his mother, but as he explained to the grocer and the copy emphasized, it was the *ease* of the product that appealed to Mama:

> "Mamma wants a package of Lemon Jell-O and a package of Strawberry Jell-O."
> "I suppose something else wouldn't do would it?"

> "Mamma said be sure to get Jell-O because she's got company and she wants to visit 'stead of working in the kitchen and everyone likes Jell-O." There is the whole thing in a nutshell. There is no kitchen drudgery making up Jell-O and everybody likes Jell-O.[13]

This ad pointed directly to the convenient advantages of Jell-O for the housewife who could "visit 'stead of working in the kitchen" and who wished to minimize "kitchen drudgery." Notably, the ad included a recipe book offer for additional easy, pleasing ways to combine Jell-O with other ingredients, demonstrating the increasing importance of recipe advertising to food products.

In another ad, convenience and ease again played a central role in the appeal: "Keeping Trouble Out of the Kitchen," read the headline in a 1911 ad in *Ladies' Home Journal*. The drawing pictured a housewife with a flustered expression on her face, but with an apron neatly tied around her long dress and her upswept hairdo still tidily in place, bending hurriedly toward the oven while a tea kettle whistles on the stove. The copy explains the situation:

> Her pudding is burnt. When hurried and overworked, the woman in the kitchen is sure to have disasters. Cakes will "fall," pies will bake unevenly, and puddings will burn. Everything that keeps trouble out of the kitchen helps woman's work. Jell-O does that. It **never burns**. It doesn't have to be cooked. It never goes wrong. It saves time as well as trouble.[14]

This ad promoted first and foremost the ease of Jell-O and its convenience: it did not even require cooking! But did the "woman in the kitchen" refer to housewife or cook? She looks like a housewife, as represented in other advertising, but the copy hedges a bit.

In fact, like some of the earliest laundry advertising, Jell-O ads did sometimes depict the presence of servant labor. A 1911 ad featured a large drawing of a housewife demonstrating to a maid how to mix Jell-O under the headline "See how easy it is, Tilly?" The copy continued: "Show the new girl just once what can be done with Jell-O and then you will always be sure of one fine dish for dinner. She may spoil everything else, but she will make a fine dessert of Jell-O for she cannot go wrong there."[15] Here, Jell-O promised not less work for the housewife but more satisfactory results from the cook. In an early 1900s recipe collection, the copy again promised that the product could be of help to the cook: "Jell-O will save nine-tenths of the time the cook now spends preparing desserts and those made from Jell-O will be superior in every way, at much less cost."[16]

But in other ads that mentioned the presence of a maid, the copy belied the image of the maid or went on to depict not the maid but the housewife at work in the kitchen. For instance, a 1909 Jell-O recipe booklet, *Desserts of the World*, included an introduction that left open the possibility that someone besides the housewife might make Jell-O: "all of us like something uncommonly dainty and delicious at the end of the meal. It only remains for the housewife or the cook to provide it." But as the copy continued to praise the product, it seemed more concerned with the comfort of the housewife: "For the woman who spends hours every day over a modern cook stove, there are some delightful moments when she prepares, away from the heat and discomfort, the simple, beautiful and delicious Jell-O desserts."[17]

Perhaps "the woman who spends hours" cooking meant a paid servant but more likely the copy addressed "you"—the housewife looking for a beautiful and delicious but easy to make dessert, during "delightful" moments when Jell-O relieved her from some of the hot and wearisome hours at the cook stove. Similarly, an early Jell-O magazine ad featured a drawing of a maid in white apron and cap holding aloft a molded Jell-O dessert. The headline assured consumers: "Do Not Worry!" "You can always have a good dessert if you use Jell-O—and it only takes *two minutes* to make it," read the copy.[18] While the ad depicted a maid serving the Jell-O, the copy directly addressed the housewifely "you," the one who needed to devote but two minutes to the creation of this attractive, family dessert.

By the 1920s and 1930s, Jell-O advertising featured the housewife alone (except when young children demonstrated the simple preparation of Jell-O), and continued to stress how the product enabled housewives to easily create delicious desserts and dishes for her whole family. A 1933 recipe pamphlet depicted how Mother could enjoy less work as well as feed her family wholesome and delicious gelatin foods. In *What Mrs. Dewey Did with the New Jell-O*, Nancy's mother enjoys the ease of Jell-O while at the same time providing her family with a delightful dessert. When Nancy spies the box of Jell-O in the kitchen, she begins "hopping up and down with impatience in her eagerness," and pleads: "Oh, Mother, will you make some right away—for my supper? Pl-ease?" Mrs. Dewey is skeptical that she can get the Jell-O made before dinner, but she finds to her surprise:

> "Set! Already! Why, I can't believe it." But all the other little molds confirmed the news. Perfectly set—in only a little over an hour. Quivering— tender . . . Two spoons cut into the tender shimmering surface, making new facets of ruby-colored light. Two crimson spoonfuls popped into two eager mouths.
>   "Strawberries—just like jellied strawberries!" Nancy cried. "You must have put strawberry juice in it, Mother, after I left!"

"I never did! It's just the extra fruit flavor in this Jell-O. Let me have one more bite. We'll surprise Daddy."

As the drawing of the whole family smiling around the table over a selection of molded Jell-O desserts attests, Daddy is just as pleased as Nancy, and Jell-O is the main ingredient in "Desserts that delight the Deweys." The copy makes clear that Mother, Mrs. Dewey, makes those desserts herself, easily providing her family with delicious and wholesome food.[19]

Modern Jell-O ads like this often linked the product with a wife and mother's care for her family. The cover of another recipe collection, the 1930 *New Jell-O Book of Surprises*, depicted a pretty housewife in a spotless apron effortlessly unmolding a Jell-O salad. The copy described how Jell-O eased the housewife's work in the kitchen while also allowing her to feed her family well: "Revel in the thought, as you serve your Jell-O surprise to an admiring family that it is a treat for every single one of them, young or old. Jell-O is as good for you as it looks." In addition, the section entitled "Salads" promised to increase the family's health: "How to get your family to eat raw vegetables every day, and want more."[20] And speaking of safeguarding the family's health, the small 1920s recipe pamphlet "Mr. Gourmand's Strange Dreams" assured consumers that the nightmares induced by too many rich foods would stop plaguing "Mr. Gourmand" as soon as his wife began serving more wholesome Jell-O desserts instead.[21] This advertising built on appeals to both ease and convenience but also used depictions of wives and mothers guarding their families' health.

Jell-O was not the only General Foods product to emphasize easy food preparation in early modern print advertising. Baking product ads in particular built brands with images and rhetoric about cooking success. All available evidence—cookbook publication, personal reminiscences, marketing research—suggests that throughout the twentieth century, baking often ranked as the most enjoyable kind of cooking that American women did for sheer pleasure, and the kind of cooking most frequently linked with expressions of love and devotion to the family.[22] Yet baking also demands skill and practice, and in the twentieth century Americans increasingly relied on food corporations to supply them with baking know-how. Bearing in mind both consumers' desire to bake and consumers' fear of baking failure, General Foods produced copious recipe collections and cookery instruction to market their baking products, emphasizing how their brands could ensure perfect desserts and other baked goods every time.

Minute Tapioca, for example, relied heavily on rhetoric about how the product could make cooking easy for the housewife. "The newly-discovered use of Minute Tapioca as a Precision Ingredient has proved a real boon to housewives," began the introduction to the 1931 *A Cook's Tour with Minute Tapioca*. The introduction described the product in similar terms as the Jell-O ads, postulating that Minute Tapioca dishes are "not only good for children but children like them. Many of these desserts are gay as a rainbow, yet they are readily digested and economical to prepare."[23] Another recipe pamphlet in 1934 promised *Easy Triumphs with New Minute Tapioca*. "Sure success at last with 47 difficult dishes," it promised readers.[24] Calumet Baking Powder also promised *Oven Triumphs* as did Swans Down Cake Flour in a 1931 recipe pamphlet: "Perhaps you've longed to try your hand at fine baking, but haven't quite dared. Perhaps you have tried—and failed. Perhaps you've been blaming yourself when the real fault lay with—*flour*! More than one woman has made that joyous discovery!"[25]

In fact, General Foods' baking ingredient brands relied heavily on rhetoric about the almost magical ability of its products to ensure not just easier but *better* cakes and other baked goods. If Jell-O's brand image utilized the image of a convenient way to make a pretty dessert without baking, other General Foods brands assured consumers that with the right brand, cooking in general and baking specifically could be transformed from a tricky enterprise with numerous failures into the pleasant, fail-safe production of family-pleasing dishes. A 1929 pamphlet compiled from recipes consumers sent into General Foods using primarily Minute Tapioca but also other General Foods brands such as Grape Nuts and Baker's Coconut, suggested that since real housewives had created the recipes ("selected from 121,619 sent in by housewives all over the world"), the consumer would be assured of success: "If you follow directions, you will have as great success with these delicious dishes as thousands of other women have had—both in the kitchen and at the dining table!"[26] But far more frequently, the rhetoric in advertising recipes equated the *brand* with the housewife's success. "It's more than luck, your success in baking," explained *The Calumet Baking Book* in 1931. It was the baking powder.[27] "Ingredients—The Inside Story of Baking Success," began the copy in *All About Home Baking*, published by General Foods in 1933. It promised that this section would "open your eyes to some important differences in baking ingredients," namely, of course, the superiority of General Foods brands.[28]

Like General Foods, in the 1920s and 1930s, Kraft relied heavily upon recipe advertising that promised to easily transform cooking tasks into homemaking. Moreover, Kraft played a major role in the proliferation of advertising recipes not only on the page but on the air. In the 1930s, a large portion of all food advertising reached consumers over the radio. Like the first soap operas aimed at housewives, radio cooking and homemaking programs aimed at female consumers appeared up and down the radio dial during the 1930s. For example, the best selling advertising cookbook ever, *The Betty Crocker Picture Cookbook* (1950), had its roots in General Mills radio advertising in the 1930s. In 1927 the Washburn Crosby milling company (which merged with other companies into General Mills the following year), invented a fictional spokeswoman to "speak" for the company's test kitchen home economics department. *The Betty Crocker Show* aired recipes, urged consumers to buy General Mills products, and regularly broadcast mail-in offers for additional recipe collections.[29] General Foods had its own program, *The General Foods Cooking School of the Air*, featuring its own spokesperson Frances Lee Barton, who distributed advice, hawked General Foods products, and penned a number of advertising cookery books.[30]

The Kraft Company made an especially profitable incursion into radio advertising in the 1930s. Kraft, identified as the Kraft Cheese company, first sponsored an NBC show called *Woman's Magazine of the Air*, broadcasting on five stations. With joint sponsors, Kraft also advertised on the "Mrs. A. M. Goudis" food talks from 1929 to 1933.[31] A 1957 account history written for in-house use by Kraft's longtime ad agency, JWT, described the success of these early radio recipe commercials:

> Thousands of women listen in regularly to the talks given by Mrs. A. M. Goudis and those who register in the Forecast Radio School of Cookery receive cards each week showing new ways to use the products of the sponsors of the School. Large numbers of these recipe cards are mailed each week. Two years experience with the Forecast School has demonstrated the great effectiveness of this form of advertising with both the retailer and the consumer.[32]

The "great effectiveness of this form of advertising" built both upon the novel appeal of radio and also on the tried-and-proven method of offering consumers free recipes: the combination of radio and recipes was a gold mine of potential consumer interaction with Kraft advertising.

Kraft made both broadcasting and housework advertising history in June of 1933, when it first aired *The Kraft Program* (renamed *The Kraft Music Hall* in 1934), a music and variety show. Not only was the program itself a major hit, attracting the talents of major stars like Al Jolson and Bing Crosby, but the new product linked to *The Kraft Program* also enjoyed instant success. It was Miracle Whip, and it represented a major advertising investment for Kraft. Prior to its test release in New York, Miracle Whip "teaser" advertising appeared in newspapers and on the radio: JWT intended to "create an aura of mystery and excitement" around Miracle Whip and to "surround the introduction of Miracle Whip with as much excitement as possible so that as nearly all women as possible in the area would learn quickly of the new product and be induced to try it."[33] Kraft had sold its own brand of mayonnaise since 1927, but based on extensive consumer and retailer market research in the first years of the Great Depression, the company believed that "mayonnaise became an expensive luxury item. The housewife either made her own or looked for cheaper brands or turned to boiled dressing."[34] Going on the offensive, Kraft moved to capitalize on this change in market conditions, and invented the new salad dressing Miracle Whip. Along with the teaser ads and the radio commercials, Miracle Whip ads appeared in numerous newspapers and magazines. It soon wiped out the competition, rocketing to the number-one sold salad dressing at the end of its intensive introductory drive.[35]

The initial print appeals emphasized that "distinguished hostesses preferred it."[36] But Miracle Whip advertising mostly drew on images of housewives and emphasized how the product could help them care for their families by using the great taste of Miracle Whip to induce husbands and children to eat fruits and vegetable. In one such 1938 ad in *Ladies Home Journal* and *Woman's Home Companion,* Bill's wife worries about his health.

> He really ought to eat more green things and fruit. But for the past few weeks it had been like pulling teeth to get him to eat salads of any kind. He just wouldn't touch them. . . . Then I had an idea. I phoned Bill's mother. . . . "My dear, you're a little slow to catch on," said my mother-in-law tactfully. "Haven't you heard that men are simply crazy about the flavor of Miracle Whip?" . . . I took the hint. And at dinner that night the miracle happened. Bill started to nibble doubtfully at his salad, as usual, but he didn't *nibble* long. He fairly gobbled it up—and yelled for more. What a surprise! Am I proud! Thank goodness. I've at last found the way to make Bill eat salads.

The newly proud housewife in this ad who has "at last found the way to make Bill eat salads" appeared over and over and over again in 1930s Miracle Whip ads (which also almost always included a blurb about the popular *Kraft Music Hall* radio program in smaller print at the bottom of the ad). She transformed kitchen work into feminine care for the family.

It wasn't always the mother-in-law who let housewives in on the Miracle Whip miracle. Over countless dinner party tables, hostesses explained to guests how to get husbands to eat salads. "Don't spare me, Babs," pleads one luckless housewife in a 1937 ad, "Something funny about my salad?"

> **Babs:** The salad's perfectly all right. But don't you like a <u>dressing</u> with more flavor?
> **Housewife:** Is that what Harry means when he says my salads are tame?

Babs: Well, if Harry's like Jim, he'll be crazy about the flavor of Miracle Whip. It's a new kind of dressing with a "kick" men like.

She takes Babs' advice, and the next evening Harry enthuses: "I didn't know salad could taste so good, dear!" Friends often alerted other friends to Miracle Whip's amazing ability to entice male appetites:

Pam: Go ahead Connie . . . tell me what's wrong with my salads.
Connie: Why—nothing really, Pam. They could have a little more zip, that's all.
Pam: That's exactly what Allen says. But what's the answer?

The answer, Pam, is Miracle Whip, as Allen proves the following evening: "Now this is a salad I could shout about." Even when scarfing down another woman's salad, housewives eagerly accepted salad dressing advice from friends: "I've tried every trick to make Bill eat salad. Now look at him gobbling yours! What's the secret?"

Another 1937 ad even suggested that Miracle Whip's ability to render salads palatable to men put it on par with President Roosevelt's national relief and recovery legislation during the Great Depression. "At last! A new deal in salads!" read the headline. Over the dinner table, Peg and Bob discuss the merits of Miracle Whip:

Peg: Glad you like it, dear. You don't often rave about my salads.
Bob: I will if they're all like this one! Something's different about it. What is it, Peg?
Peg: The dressing, Bob. I had it at Mary's luncheon the other day. It's called Miracle Whip.
Bob: The flavor certainly wins my vote!

This particular appeal—that using Miracle Whip enabled the housewife to better care for and please her husband—continued throughout the 1930s and 1940s, and expanded to include children as well.

For instance, a 1938 ad featured a large photo of smiling children tucking into a banana, peanut butter, Miracle Whip "salad": "My children really go for salads made with MIRACLE WHIP!" proclaimed Mom. In a 1941 ad, Miracle Whip satisfied both husband and son: "Potato salad with Miracle Whip!" they exclaim. During World War II, Miracle Whip could bolster its claim by depicting salads as an essential part of wartime defense—keeping Americans nourished and putting victory gardens produce to good use. "Salads help build strong Americans!" says Uncle Sam in a 1942 Miracle Whip magazine advertisement. "America depends on her homemakers for *nutritious* meals that will keep the home front strong.

So do serve *salads* often. . . . But remember—to benefit from those fine food values, your salads must really be *eaten*," explained another. To that end, ads included recipes and serving suggestions, for dishes ranging from gelatin and fruit concoctions topped with Miracle Whip, to chicken salad-stuffed tomatoes. Wartime Miracle Whip ads promised consumers that the product would ensure a family of salad eaters, from Dad to Daughter, as in a 1943 ad with enthusiastic testimonials from family members. Dad: "Even fellows who call salads 'sissy' change their tune when they taste salads with Miracle Whip." Sis: "Mom was always saying 'Eat your salad, Molly—it's so good for you.' But gosh, she doesn't have to say that anymore. I *go* for salads now."

Food advertising throughout the 1940s continued to emphasize how Mom could guard the health of the family and the security of the nation. As other scholarship demonstrates, World War II government propaganda, popular magazines, and advertising for a wide range of products, especially food, depicted housewives as soldiers on the home front and imbued domesticity with new patriotic import.[37] An exaggerated emphasis on female domesticity continued to powerfully shape gender norms in the postwar era, and food advertising reflects this. The housewives in 1950s food product advertising—like the Tide housewives—exemplified the highly idealized and stereotyped images of the apron-wearing smiling housewife. These representations embodied a deliberate strategy by many in the postwar advertising industry (such as the highly influential consumer researcher Ernest Dichter) to exploit what was believed to be the typical housewife's emotional and psychological needs. Advertisers portrayed all housework, and cooking in particular, as part of a woman's only really important and fulfilling life's work—being a wife and mother.[38]

Miracle Whip, for instance, continued to advertise as a product that would help a housewife ensure her family's health, please her husband and children, avoid dinner time failures, and attain the highest standards of homemaking. As a housewife in a neat apron summarized in another 1949 ad: "You'll keep the whole family happy when you serve Miracle Whip!" A 1950 magazine recipe ad for a red gelatin ring with a Miracle Whip center included this copy: "Jane's salads never seem to get eaten. Judy's get compliments galore! Her secret? The one and only Miracle Whip." Newspaper ads in the 1950s featured smiling family members raving about Mom's cooking: "Now I eat every bit of Mom's salads," says Daughter. "Never thought I'd beg for salads . . . but I do!" and "I used to think salads were sissy . . . but not now!" confesses Father." "Bet you'd like <u>my</u> Mom's salad," boasts Junior. "Lots more compliments on my salads," confirms Mom.

A series of recipe magazine ads in 1951 also featured small cartoons of housewives feeding their families "Before" and "After" Miracle Whip.

"Groans used to greet Peg's salads," read the caption to a drawing of a family turning away in disgust from the dinner table. "Grins from ear to ear is the welcome they get now!" reads the happy caption to the family eating Miracle Whip salads while Peg stands by grinning, jauntily posed with hands in apron straps. "Downright blue: Half-eaten salads had Sally really worried," captions an image of Sally sadly clearing the table as husband and children turn their backs and leave the room. But with "the one and only Miracle Whip," Sally's seated at the table surrounded by a happy family, including daughter giving her a loving hug around the neck: "Tickled pink! Calls for 'seconds' keep her happy now!" Mary's family more overtly rejected her homemaking efforts: "Bored: A week ago Mary's family wasn't even polite about her salads," as Dad holds up his hand in a "Stop!" gesture to Mary's tray of salads. "Beaming! Now they greet them with great big smiles!" Nothing subtle about these appeals: without the product, women risked complete homemaking failure and rejection from husband and children.

In part, such ads simply reflected the power of the postwar feminine mystique—the widespread cultural and political definition of a woman's most important life work as marriage and childrearing. Especially during the 1950s when convenience and ready-made food products proliferated and raised the possibility that anyone in the family might be able to do the cooking, food advertising continued to affirm women's central role as nurturers.[39] However, advertising also emerged from careful research and planned strategies on the part of the ad makers like the JWT agency, who were not simply blindly acting out the dominant ideology about gender but who carefully assessed just how to market the product in a way that would elicit the most positive consumer response, in this case Miracle Whip. A JWT in-house history of Miracle Whip summarized their approach to Miracle Whip marketing in the 1950s:

> We attacked the smaller salad eaters of the family—the husband and children. Men and children still did not have the salad habit in America. We told the American housewife that they would get the habit if she dressed her salads with Miracle Whip. . . . Women were becoming more and more convinced, through advertising, through home economics columns and other propaganda that salads were nutritious healthful economical dishes.[40]

When print ads featured Miracle Whip's ability to convince "the husband and children" that they could get "the salad habit," they not only reflected dominant ideas about gender, but specific strategies created by the agency who set out to deliberately link the product with images of feminine care and homemaking. Moreover, the cited rhetoric of these Miracle Whip print ads constituted only a small part of the advertisement. A recipe and a color photo of the completed dish dominated the magazine page. As the JWT product history made clear, *recipes* remained at the center of Miracle Whip marketing: "Over and over again, research has demonstrated that nothing in food advertising gets such attention from women as recipes. In the words of one expert: 'Recipes advertisements are read avidly.'"[41]

What kinds of recipes did these Miracle Whip ads offer consumers? Like many ad recipes, the Miracle Whip recipes had to walk a fine line between offering tempting suggestions for new ways of serving food—so tempting that the consumer would stop and tear out or copy the recipe and try it out later—and printing recipes that seemed too complicated, with too many ingredients that might not be readily on hand. Many scholars indict food corporations for the rise of bland, frozen, and highly processed foods that seemed to take over America in the postwar years; for "recipes" that reframed "home cooking" as slopping together premade foods and threatened to undercut women's skill and ingenuity in the kitchen and their continuing desire to cook good, fresh food.[42] These scholars have a point: the "Sunny Salad" recipe in one of the above Miracle Whip ads that called only for a combination of orange and grapefruit segments, garnished with maraschino cherries and topped with a spoonful of Miracle Whip is a clear example. But on the other hand, advertising agencies and their clients seized upon "service" ads and commercials that included such recipes because their market research seemed to show a connection between such simple recipes (often just serving suggestions rather than a true recipe) and increased sales.

Kraft, in particular, found that recipe advertising offered a direct link to home kitchens, increasing product purchase and consumer loyalty to Kraft products and Kraft recipes. For decades, Kraft's radio and television advertising prominently featured recipes, to enormous success. As a JWT client history summarized around 1956:

> While late comers to TV have knocked themselves out with animated cartoons, pretty girls, and well tailored announcers, to put over their selling messages, Kraft's TV commercials have become famous for their smooth elegance and down-to-earth predictability. No person, be he ever so handsome or witty, ever distracts your attention. You see only the product and a pair of well groomed hands opening that product and making it into something you'd like to go right out to the kitchen and make for yourself, while the announcer's voice tells you, in a simple straightforward manner, how it is done and what it will do for you. The results in sales, in write-ins for recipe folders, and other indications of active interest, have been all the way from excellent to sensational, according to Kraft.[43]

"From excellent to sensational" measurable consumer response to Kraft's marketing strategies, built around recipe advertising, indicated the success of these strategies. And campaigns for specific new products like Miracle Whip also produced such measurable results linked directly to Kraft radio programming.

Similarly, when the first live *Kraft Television Theater* aired on NBC in 1947, the advertised product, "a low-volume, high priced cheese specialty, MacLarens' Imperial Club Cheddar," flew off the shelves: "Within a few weeks every retailer in the entire New York area was cleaned out of this product."[44] In a famous example of the efficacy of Kraft's television advertising, a recipe for clam dip (canned clams and Philadelphia cream cheese) that aired on the *Kraft Music Hall* (renamed in 1958) caused a major run on canned clams in New York City. A JWT copywriter, Margaret Buchen, the creative force behind the clam dip commercials, recalled the praise of her boss the following day: "Baby! What you did last night was terrific. The canned clam people have been calling Kraft all morning. Every TV town in the country is cleaned out of clams. If we've sold that many clams think how much Philadelphia Cream Cheese has moved."[45] As demonstrated by the success of the clam dip recipe, consumers actively sought out Kraft recipes. They not only copied recipes down during programming, but wrote to the company to request recipes. As a Kraft in-house document on the history of their television commercials recalled:

> Our first experience in offering a cook book on the "TV Theater" [around 1957] was rather staggering. Kraft had a book on cheese cookery which was fast getting out of date. It had been an expensive book to prepare, so it was decided to offer it once on the TV Theatre for 10 cents. The expectation was for about 2,000 replies at most.
>
> The book was displayed before the camera and some of the dishes for which it gave recipes were displayed "live" before the cameras. . . . To our amazement, 40,000 requests were received.
>
> Our next venture was to offer, free, the booklet on "Philly" [Philadelphia Cream Cheese] Frostings and Fudge. The technique described above was used. The offer, which ran a number of times, broke all records for any medium, both for volume of requests and low cost per request.[46]

This substantial, and instantaneous, success of recipe advertising on television had particular import for advertising food products and for the depiction of the housewife in food advertising. The housewife rarely appeared as a character in Kraft television and radio commercials, but the format, script, and visual elements of the commercials all unfailingly referenced "the housewife" and how she transformed cookery, easily, into homemaking and family care with the right food products.

From the beginning, Kraft radio and TV commercials followed a particular formula. As a JWT document noted, the agency and Kraft carefully considered how to portray their product via the new medium of radio. They decided to avoid the gaudy strategies often used at the time, and instead planned to "make people hungry for our cheese and salad products with only words, sounds, and recipes." Thus, "the conversational, straight-forward, tightly-knit (as opposed to 'slap-happy') Kraft electronic sell was 'born.'"[47] That sell was a distinctive one and one that translated easily to TV: as the announcer described the product and the dish, the camera focused tightly on a pair of pretty white female hands (two specially chosen dramatists, known later simply as "the hands") preparing a simple recipe.[48] JWT and Kraft decided upon this formula as the best way to convey a recipe on the air in a way that would entice the target consumer, specifically identified as the housewife, to imagine using the product herself. "The product is the star!" explained a JWT executive in a 1964 presentation. He continued:

> The star performs in preparation, use, and in finished dishes for the housewife with no cluttering unessentials [sic] or distracting trappings. The use of hands working in close-up gives the illusion that it is the housewife, herself, who is preparing an appetizing or convenient dish in her own kitchen. For this reason, a complete kitchen is sparingly shown on the screen. The viewing housewife imagines all the action taking place in the familiar surroundings of her own kitchen which can vary in type from apartment Pullman, to farm, to modern suburbia.

JWT might insist that the product was the star, but the format and script of Kraft television commercials put the housewife squarely at the center of Kraft commercials. The housewife cooking for her family provided the sole lens through which Kraft and JWT viewed the labor of home cooking.

Kraft and JWT deliberately focused on how their products, as marketed via recipes on television, could assist housewives with the more laborious aspects of food preparation. As the agency pointed out in a 1967 in-house document, daytime commercials did this even more explicitly than commercials during the evening variety shows:

> Here we're talking even more directly to the woman who has the problem of feeding a family. In the daytime, when it is possible, we try to inject a bit more immediacy into the commercials: "Here is a different vegetable to serve the family this very evening." "Here is a new trick with spinach to spring on the family tonight." "Here is a splendid snack to give the youngsters when they come home from school this afternoon." When possible, daytime commercials try to relate themselves to the woman's problem of the moment.[49]

For the first decades of Kraft television programming, the script (usually read, with some ad-libbing, by Ed Herlihy, the Kraft television announcer), made such statements explicitly, directly linking the recipe preparation shots with housework and the housewife and urging consumers to use Kraft products to address "the problem of feeding a family." The rhetoric of Kraft commercials represented feeding the family as gendered work, and suggested that cooking expressed a woman's love and care for her family. It also reiterated over and over that Kraft products would allow the housewife to achieve good homemaking with ease and convenience. It emphasized that a wide range of Kraft products offered housewives the opportunity to make a wearisome chore more pleasant.

For example, commercials for Kraft Spaghetti Dinner promised, "It'll take you fifteen minutes," "A quicker way hasn't been invented," "Here's a way to outsmart the clock and still give the family a really good meal on meatless nights," "The spaghetti's quick but it doesn't taste quick." "Try it soon. Maaaaybe . . . tomorrow night?" coaxed Herlihy.[50] Make hamburgers "extra good in a jiffy: Cheeze Whiz 'em," suggested another commercial, adding that with Cheeze Whiz you could enjoy "many a cheese treat fast." According to commercials, Kraft Macaroni and Cheese Dinner was especially helpful for time-strapped housewives: "You have a head start on so many good main dishes with Kraft Macaroni and Cheese Dinner on your shelf" (such as the tuna, mushroom, and cream of celery casserole shown on screen); "A good and easy meal to have when you're due early at the PTA meeting maybe, hm?" (suggested menu: mac and cheese with canned salmon mixed in, sliced tomatoes, peach cobbler). "Wives and mothers," began another commercial, "For a nourishing lunch that the kids will like, have a package of Kraft Macaroni and Cheese Dinner in the house. You can fix a piping hot homemade dish like this, Macaroni and Cheese With Tuna, in ten minutes." "That's all there is to making homemade macaroni and cheese," finished Herlihy, in a clear example of how heating up premade foods became, in advertising, "homemade" cooking.

Radio commercials also continued to emphasize serving suggestions and "recipes" with appeals based on their convenience for the housewife who wanted to please her family. For example, the script for a 1956 commercial went:

> Here's how to fix a salad that's fit for the king of your house! Just open a jar of Miracle Whip Salad Dressing—and spoon luscious, satin-smooth Miracle Whip onto a wedge of lettuce or a simple fruit mold. There's a salad that's tempting and delicious—but easy! Everybody likes Miracle Whip. . . . Housewives know it's smart to keep Miracle Whip on hand. They know it's the dressing their salads need. Take home a jar of Miracle Whip Salad Dressing next time you shop![51]

Other Miracle Whip radio commercials in the 1950s reiterated this message. Wives and mothers: plop on the Miracle Whip and, voila, you've solved the problem of feeding husband and children. One commercial suggested broiling hamburgers smothered in Miracle Whip: "Something your <u>children</u> will like! <u>Beef Patties</u>, fixed a new and delicious way!" "<u>Man alive</u>, that's good eating!" claimed the announcer.[52]

In one indication of how Kraft successfully branded Miracle Whip with these serving suggestion commercials, a would-be actress named Ann Merrill, wife and mother to two young sons, wrote to Kraft in 1958 with a sample Kraft commercial script (describing springtime "salad days") and urged the company to make her the new "face" for Kraft Mayonnaise (a separate product from Miracle Whip). "I want to be the 'Mayonnaise Lady' on television (like Betty Furness is 'The Westinghouse Lady,')" she wrote, pointing out that "although Mr. Herlihy does such a fine job advertising your mayonnaise on Wednesday nights [during *Kraft Music Hall*] I wonder why you don't have a woman talking about this product (I've used it <u>twice</u>—today! Does Mr. Herlihy ever use it???)." JWT account executive Maury Holland's politely patronizing reply to Mrs. Merrill emphasized the current success of Kraft commercials: "The commercial material you attach to your letter is good, and you can doubtless do an excellent selling job, but the present form of commercials and their presentation has been arrived at after much research and experimentation. It is proving successful and will probably be continued for some time."[53]

Holland didn't exaggerate when he used the phrase "much research and experimentation:" Kraft and its ad agency devoted extensive research efforts to mayonnaise and Miracle Whip. Again making clear precisely who the real "star" of Kraft food commercials was, in 1957 JWT circulated a market research report entitled "Mayonnaise as Seen by the Housewife." Among the report's findings: although salads had originally been lauded for nutrition, real housewives also looked upon salads as "the 'something different' to relieve the monotony of a meat and potato dinner" and "salad dressings in general are a food area of change, a way the housewife modifies her meals and gains a sense of growth and stimulation."[54] A 1960 report repeated this conclusion, stating: "Research has shown that a majority of women are already adding touches of their own to mayonnaise—blending in such things as chili sauce or whipped cream. It also indicates that those who are not already doing so are interested in the idea when it is suggested to them."[55] These reports affirmed Kraft and JWT's view of cooking as part of a housewife's home labors and family care as well as Kraft's advertising strategy: if real housewives viewed mayonnaise as a desirable ingredient that could make the "something different" and "relieve the monotony" of home cooking, simple recipe suggestions—like mixing in chili sauce—would surely help sell mayonnaise.

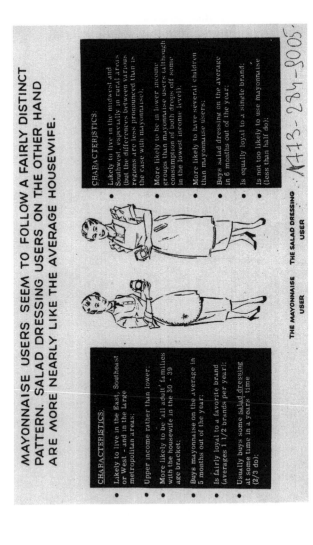

MAYONNAISE USERS SEEM TO FOLLOW A FAIRLY DISTINCT PATTERN. SALAD DRESSING USERS ON THE OTHER HAND ARE MORE NEARLY LIKE THE AVERAGE HOUSEWIFE.

CHARACTERISTICS:

- Likely to live in the East, Southeast or West - and in the large metropolitan areas.

- Upper income rather than lower.

- More likely to be 'all adult' families with the housewife in the 30 - 39 age bracket.

- Buys mayonnaise on the average in 5 months out of the year.

- Is fairly loyal to a favorite brand (averages 1 1/2 brands per year).

- Usually buys some salad dressing at some time in a year's time (2/3 do).

CHARACTERISTICS:

- Likely to live in the midwest and Southwest, especially in rural areas (but the differences between various regions are less pronounced than is the case with mayonnaise).

- More likely to be in lower income groups than mayonnaise users (although consumption of both drops off some in the lowest income level).

- More likely to have several children than mayonnaise users.

- Buys salad dressing on the average in 6 months out of the year.

- Is equally loyal to a single brand.

- Is not too likely to use mayonnaise (less than half do).

THE MAYONNAISE USER

THE SALAD DRESSING USER

Figure 3.1 1960 J. Walter Thompson advertising agency document

Note: This 1960 in-house document from the J. Walter Thompson advertising agency illustrates how ad makers themselves used the housewife figure to frame domesticity generally and food preparation specifically as women's homemaking.

Source: Courtesy of J. Walter Thompson Company. From Kraft Corporation Vertical Files, J. Walter Thompson Collection, The Hartman Center for Sales, Advertising, and Marketing History, Duke University.

One such study included a diagram contrasting the characteristics of "The Mayonnaise User" and "The Salad Dressing User" (see fig. 3.1). Kraft invested considerable time, effort, and marketing research money into trying to understand the business implications of manufacturing two extremely similar products, as well as how to position Miracle Whip in relation to the overall brand image of mayonnaise. This study concluded that "salad dressing users" were "more nearly like the average housewife."[56] As the drawings used to illustrate this report demonstrate, the "housewife" could be very clearly represented among ad makers themselves with the same female figure that appeared in the actual advertising materials: a pleasant-looking woman with a neat hairdo, wearing high heels and a spotless apron. Even though the agency's data suggested economic differences between the salad dressing and mayonnaise user, the housewife images used to represent these two groups of consumers are essentially the same. The salad dressing housewife was older, slightly plumper, "more likely to have several children," and "more likely to be in lower income groups," but she and the mayonnaise user both clearly visually symbolized the gendered meaning of housework for the ad makers working at this agency, framing food preparation with the image of a neat, pleasant-looking woman in an apron.

While this study didn't leave open the possibility that "the salad dressing user" might be employed outside the home, the 1957 "Mayonnaise as Seen by the Housewife" did, noting that their researchers interviewed housewives in four geographical regions who ranged in age, cooking experience, size of family, and significantly, occupation. The study considered all married women, even women pursuing careers or occupations outside the home or who earned a paycheck in any way, "housewives."[57] Like the creators of the JWT report, these researchers just couldn't separate cookery and the housewife figure: the two housewives holding jars of mayo/salad dressing embodied the inescapable "frame" of the housewife that not only appeared in actual advertisements and commercials but in the research and rhetoric articulating their own conception of domesticity that ad agencies used in order to market their food products.

General Foods advertising too depicted the housewife, and only the housewife, cooking/caring for the family—but doing so with the ease, the convenience, the fun, and the magic, of General Foods products. The appeal of convenience increased throughout the 1950s, 1960s, and 1970s, especially in Jell-O advertising. As a 1953 Jell-O cookbook summarized: "Less work in the kitchen, more fun getting and eating meals: that has been the Jell-O promise ever since the century began." A 1961 Jell-O recipe booklet reiterated the promise that "Anyone Can Make Jell-O," continuing: "One of the beauties of Jell-O is that it takes so little kitchen know-how to

turn out a perfect dessert. . . . If you can boil water you can make Jell-O."
So too did the *Jell-O Pudding Ideabook* (1968) assure the housewife that
"because the mixes are so easy to use, everyone can get in on the fun and
ideas—from the new bride to mother of many, from teenager to the most
experienced hostess."

Jell-O television commercials in the 1950s also reinforced the appeal
of Jell-O as an easy and convenient way to make successfully fun and
appetizing desserts for husbands and children. One such Jell-O brand
commercial that combined black-and-white animated shots and live
action footage very explicitly depicted the more wearisome aspects of
housework and positioned Jell-O—the "busy day dessert"—as one type of
relief.[58] In this commercial, a dumpy, downcast cartoon housewife holding
a feather duster trudges on a treadmill while the clock ticks off the tiring
hours. A woman's despairing voice-over chants: "Busy day, busy day, busy,
busy day." The phone rings: "Too busy!" A knock at the door: "Too busy!"
A baby cries: "Oh, Herbert!" Pots and pans clank: "Dinner time, *oh* dinner
time!" The housewife's frown deepens: "Too late . . . to make . . . dessert!"
The announcer's voice-over bursts in: "Wait! It's *not* too late to make dessert! Never too late anymore because now the Jell-O family of famous
desserts brings you new instant pudding that needs no cooking!" A trim
live action housewife in a pretty apron demonstrates how to mix it up,
commenting that that product is a "busy day dessert" ready in minutes, "so
delicious and so quick you can make it just before dessert time while the
children are clearing the table . . . it's that easy!" This commercial vividly
demonstrates how housework advertising suggested that products could
relieve the monotonous, tiring aspects of housework, evocatively depicted
here as a treadmill going nowhere—though the idealized housewife figure, the trim and pretty actress demonstrating the product, escapes that
fate. While no other Jell-O housewives actually plodded on a housework
treadmill in ads and commercials, "Busy Day" (and the accompanying
print ads) did build on the product's longstanding appeal as a convenient,
easy dessert for wives and mothers who wanted to be sure to provide their
families with dessert at the dinner table.[59]

Laying the groundwork for a seamless transition from housewife to
housewife mom in twenty-first century Kraft advertising, ads and commercials for Kraft's Velveeta in the 1950s and early 1960s worked especially
hard to create a brand image of Velveeta as a product that would help
women care for their children, but would also be the main ingredient in
super-easy cooking. For example, in 1960 and 1961, Velveeta television
commercials and print ads positioned the product as a "special help"
to mothers, with the tagline "How Velveeta Helps You in the Big Job of
Being a Mother." A commercial in this campaign marked both an early

appearance of the housewife mom—more casually dressed, focused on her children—and one of the first television commercials to depart from the Kraft "hands" and recipe formula. As the young housewife mom in Capri pants walks through the kitchen picking up toys, the announcer begins:

> And now our good Kraft cooks have a message especially for you young mothers. We know how many times a day some little somebody at your house is thirsty or wants a snack out of that refrigerator. So we'd like to mention what a special help Kraft's famous Velveeta can be to you. When you put just two ounces of this nutritious pasteurized processed cheese spread in a sandwich for your child, you're giving him more milk protein, more calcium, more phosphorous, as much riboflavin, and more vitamin A then there is in a big eight ounce glass of fresh whole milk.

Velveeta advertising commonly linked the product with the nutritional benefits of milk, as part of a concerted effort to market it as an easy way for mothers to ensure good nutrition for the family. As the commercial continued, it offered a "recipe" that would supposedly be especially appealing to children:

> Now here's a way to make these nutritious Velveeta snacks into a real fun thing for the youngsters. Just insert flat wooden skewers into inch square strips of this mellow cheese goodness. And they're Velveeta lollipops, golden and good! [shot of sticks being inserted into cheese strips] Y'see? And the kids love 'em. . . . Just remember: to please your family, and to get more of milk's vital food values into their daily snacks and meals, have Velveeta often.

This commercial vividly illustrated the simple recipes and serving suggestions at the heart of Kraft advertising, as well as the emphasis on Velveeta as a means for mothers to provide good nutrition to children easily.

Foreshadowing the busy moms in twenty-first century advertising, a long series of print ads in this Velveeta campaign that appeared in *Parents* and women's magazines depicted busy mothers juggling children and mealtime preparation. In one, a slim and smiling young mother in Capri pants and a button-down shirt holds a tray of snacks, balancing a baby on her hip and fending off two little children reaching for the tray: "What a fine answer to those 'I-want-a-snack' pleas!" The "recipe" that was such a fine answer? "Happy face" cheese slices on crackers.[60] Other serving suggestions/recipes in this series included rice casserole, deviled egg and noodle casserole, scrambled eggs with Velveeta, and a wide range of sandwiches, such as a "husky Velveeta-Club Sandwich" for Dad. In another ad, a slightly frazzled looking woman in a pleated skirt and baby on her hip, reaches for her toddler, who is about to feed his sandwich to the dog. The sprightly copy suggests that with the help of Velveeta, Mom can navigate such tricky moments with ease: "With a toddler and a new baby, you never know what you'll find when you turn around! Never a dull moment in your BIG JOB of being a mother." In a similar ad, a housewife mom wearing kicky play shorts and a blouse, a baby in her arms, talks on the phone while her toddler daughter eats Velveeta slices: "Doing three or four things at once is a routine part of being a mother, isn't it? See, at the right, three helps Velveeta gives you in this over-all BIG JOB." The included recipes, one of the "helps," consisted of broiled tomatoes on toast with half a pound of melted Velveeta poured on top.

Today these Kraft ads and commercials sound so corny and earnest, the recipes so gag-inducing that it would be easy to ignore their very real impact on food advertising specifically and housework advertising more generally. But JWT and Kraft used recipe advertising reinforced with images of housewives caring for their families because it *worked*. Consumers responded. As a journalist for the trade magazine *Sponsor* summarized in 1952:

> Recipes rank as the No. 1 device for merchandising dairy goods and salad dressings. However, Kraft uses its TV commercials to stimulate viewers to write in for booklets containing recipes for televised dishes. These booklets have developed into a big business with Kraft, and the curiosity excited by TV demonstrations has increased the demand manifold.[61]

The "recipes" often seemed to be little more than serving suggestions, but for good reason, as a 1964 in-house Kraft document explained:

> Recipes on radio and in print had proved their popularity. But a viewing audience could not be expected to get full benefit from the picture while making notes with paper and pencil. Thompson's commercials made no attempt to tell "how to" or to "teach" but aimed at exciting the appetite, while showing the great variety in use of the product and kitchen practically.[62]

As another such document confirmed, "Our major objective must always be to provide a simple service, an interesting idea with definite product advantage in terms of flavor, convenience and so forth, but without the complications of a step-by-step recipe."[63] Or as an account history put it in 1967: "Ideally the recipe material itself is interesting visually, yet simple enough for the viewer to duplicate without a formal recipe at hand."[64] While jabbing popsicle sticks into Velveeta cubes might today seem like a pretty dubious "recipe," easy serving suggestions did in fact hold great consumer appeal.

Dorothy Holland, a Kraft home economist for many years, recalled in a 1992 oral history interview that consumers in the 1950s and 1960s responded in large numbers to the simplicity of the recipes and the emphasis on convenience. "We got mailbags of letters from women," she remembered, including numerous requests to be placed on the Kraft recipe mailing list.[65] Holland's anecdotal evidence was borne out in Gallup research around the time, which concluded that:

> Homemakers viewing the show [*Kraft's Music Hall*] could, the next day, not only remember the commercial but actually "play back" the recipes on shows produced two or three weeks prior to the telephone call. A few home-makers volunteered that they oftentimes viewed the show for the purpose of getting the recipe information only.[66]

The recall of women regarding the Kraft recipe commercials and the huge number of recipe requests indicated just how persuasive many of Kraft's targeted consumers found the recipe advertising—perhaps especially because of the recipe's simplicity and also perhaps because of how effectively Kraft positioned these food products as a means for transforming housework into homemaking.

In a 1980 interview, Dick Courtice, then Vice President and Director of Advertising of the U.S. Retail Food Group at Kraft, explained why the company relied on recipe advertising: "If we depended on the people who nibbled on cheese for our success, we'd be in trouble. We really don't sell cheese, we sell cheese casseroles, sandwiches, and souf-flés." Moreover, "the recipes are also a very efficient advertising vehicle. A single recipe ad can promote several Kraft products, and can bring in smaller-volume items that might not otherwise merit ad budgets, such as mustard or tartar sauce." When Kraft's recipe advertising mailing list grew to 800,000 people in 1972, the company attempted to pare it down, but 79 percent of contacted customers asked to remain on the mailing list. Finally, when the mailing list reached an unmanageable 1.8 million, Kraft discontinued the practice in 1975. Courtice recalled: "We sent a letter saying, 'We're sorry, but we can't afford to send recipes anymore.' That year we got 1,300 Christmas cards, thanking us for the recipes over the years." As the interviewer pointed out, "Christmas cards—1,300 of them—sent to a company by its customers? Sounds like a direct-mail marketers dream come true. It's one indication of the kind of trust and dependence the informative Kraft approach engendered."[67] Kraft purveyed recipes for precisely this reason: millions of consumers read and used them, and appeared to therefore view Kraft products and the company itself favorably.

While Kraft continued to emphasize ease and convenience and recipes throughout the century, General Foods' Jell-O brand floundered a bit in the 1960s and 1970s, as a General Foods dessert division manager admitted in a 1982 interview. He explained that they tried a range of marketing approaches, from the Fifth Dimension standing on a giant box of Jell-O to celebrity spokesman Charles Nelson Reilly "talking to a fruit." According to the General Foods manager, a series of commercials titled "Happy Endings" and "Dessert Dilemmas" actually offended some consumers: "The melodramatic, slice-of-life commercials which were supposed to be funny were not only perceived as not funny, but General Foods even got some angry letters objecting to how dimwitted the women appeared."[68] The "angry letters" offered a concrete example of how, by the early 1980s, ordinary consumers were far more sensitive to housewife stereotypes in housework advertising. Clearly ad makers had to find different ways to visually signify housework in commercials. These particular commercials also reflected what 1970s laundry commercials had shown as well: ad makers and their clients struggled to address the changes wrought by Second Wave feminism, and some of the resulting advertising that strove to be humorous actually offered particularly demeaning representations of housewives.

For example, a Jell-O brand series that appeared in 1969 and 1970 women's magazines featured a large photograph of a housewife holding aloft a dessert (recipe included) made with Jell-O products. The descriptive headlines portray housewives in the most stereotypical way possible. In one, a woman covers her guilty smile with one hand and with the other offers up a slice of Jell-O Pudding Pecan Pie, under the headline: "The 'guess what happened when I backed the car out dear' Pudding." In another, a vapid looking blonde housewife holds aloft "tarts" (premade tart shells filled with a mixture of Cool Whip and Jell-O Vanilla Pudding): "The 'congratulations dear, but exactly what does an assistant vice president do?' Pudding." The housewife swaddled in a $950 fur coat smirks as she bribes Hubby with "The 'notice anything different about me tonight, dear?' Pudding." The last housewife in the series wears a tight smile, a turtleneck, and opens up a can of worms with "The 'dear, don't you think I'd be a more interesting person if I went to work?' Pudding."[69] These particular Jell-O housewives indicated that in the 1970s ad makers continued to work under certain sexist suppositions, including the assumption that ditzy housewives buying fur coats and smoothing it over with their husbands by producing Jell-O desserts would make for humorous, eye-catching advertising.

But at the same time, by the 1970s ad agencies in general and JWT specifically, were well aware that the housewife figure in ads and commercials for food products had to change. Because, as all their research indicated, the target consumer herself was changing. For example, a 1966 JWT slide presentation to Kraft entitled "Women and Food" began by reassuring the food processing company that recipe advertising aimed at female consumers and depicting cooking as care continued to be the most effective way to market food products: "food service advertising has by far the greatest appeal."[70] And for a recipe to succeed, stated the report, "it must be something a woman can make from familiar foods that are usually in the house . . . if it is a recipe for one of the things women buy week after week—eggs, chicken, hamburger, pork chops, fish." In sum: "It will have a better chance of cooking life if it is an easy way to do a familiar dish."[71] As far as the recipes themselves, then, Kraft remained on familiar footing: Kraft recipes had *always* consisted of such simple serving suggestions and assembling of familiar ingredients. The presentation also echoed the 1957 JWT depiction of mayonnaise and salad dressing housewives, with employees of the ad agency itself viewing without question housework and food preparation solely through the lens of the housewife.

However, the presentation also cautioned Kraft executives that housewives "are a new breed—they've grown up in a new products age—they are acquainted with and receptive to product innovation, convenience and ideas." But more than just convenience, the typical young middle-class housewife ("Julie") was "striving for an identity beyond that of just a wife, mother, and chief bottle washer." The presentation did not suggest that "Julie" therefore might be pursuing a career or demanding an equitable split in housework with her partner, but rather that she would use food as her only access to power. Accompanying a slide of Julie being kissed, the presenter explained: "Food is communication. Julie makes it known whether or not she approves of her family's behavior by the kinds of foods she serves. She rewards as well as punishes them with food. The family, in turn, can reward or punish her by praising the meal, refusing to eat it, or by maintaining a deadly silence."[72] In addition to this belittling description of "Julie's" kitchen housework, the presentation mocked her limited repertoire of main dishes:

Julie has an ace in the hole when she really wants to be creative.
[SLIDE: Beef stroganoff]
Beef stroganoff. Other foods she considers "gourmet" are
[slides of Cornish hens and mushrooms, and slides repeat over and over again until slide reading UGH!]

"Julie" then "is constantly looking for menu planning ideas that will help her from falling into a rut."[73] Kraft recipe ads could, of course, do exactly that. A telling example of how ad makers depicted and discussed "house-wives" among themselves, the description of "Julie" illustrates how sexist stereotypes about women and domesticity obviously shaped housework advertising. But simultaneously, on the eve of the Second Wave, ad makers had already begun to grapple with how to market housework products to women who were "striving for an identity beyond that of just a wife, mother, and chief bottle washer." Even as they still freely utilized the highly stereotypical image of a housewife in their own materials, they also seemed to believe that "Julie" would be attempting to break free of domestic confines—even if that only meant avoiding the "rut" of meal planning.

A few years later in 1971, Kraft launched a major advertising campaign in grocery trade publications designed to convince retailers that Kraft was keeping ahead of demographic and social changes when it came to the marketing of food products.[74] "Meet the New Consumer" read the headline of these ads, above large soft-focus photographs of posed women meant to represent the housewife of the late twentieth century. "We're always changing with her," Kraft promised retailers. In the first ad, the copy begins with a summary of the "changes" experienced by the consumer, alongside a photograph of a woman with dark short hairdo, wearing a mock turtleneck with a visible wedding ring who gazes pensively in the distance. The subheadings described this "new consumer:" "1.) She's active in everything from the P.T.A. to a business career. 2.) She has less time for menu planning. 3.) She's as much on the look-out for food serving ideas as she is for bargains." Kraft acknowledged the possibility of "a business career," but did not go so far as to suggest that other members of the family might be doing more cooking. The copy continued: "She may be busy, but she's still interested in keeping her family happily well-fed. And that means varying their meals whenever possible. Kraft helps you help her." After descriptions of storewide promotions, displays, and point of sale advertising that "assists her in her search for something different to serve," the copy promised the retailer that "to her your store becomes an idea stimulator."

The series also depicted the housewife-in-training. Accompanying a photograph of a blonde teenager in a fisherman knit sweater, wearing tweed slacks and a faraway expression, the subheading described this "new consumer:" "1.) She buys more of the family groceries than ever before. 2.) She entertains more. 3.) She's catching up with her mother in food know-how." The copy then explained how Kraft planned to market their products to teenage girls:

> Today's teen-ager is more than a big-spending market. She's an apprentice housewife. And it's important that she gets help in preparing for her future. Kraft talks to her about nutrition, meal planning and proper food

preparation. In magazines like *Seventeen, Ingénue, Coed,* and *American Girl.* With ads that devote more emphasis to service than they do selling. In addition, Kraft offers kits of educational aids to Home Economics teachers throughout the country. These kits include curriculum guides, instructive pamphlets, filmstrips, charts and recipes that help teens become more knowledgeable housewives. And to give teens a better image of themselves, and adults a better understanding of teens, Kraft is one of the sponsors of the America's Junior Miss Pageant. There's an even Newer Consumer waiting in the wings. She's smart. She asks questions. She's not going to be satisfied with ordinary answers.

The "newer consumer" envisioned by Kraft and their advertising agency didn't seem all that new. A pretty young blonde woman taking home economics classes and participating in beauty pageants while buying the family's groceries didn't exactly embody radical feminist change. Still, as these ads demonstrate, Kraft sought to re-envision the housewife, to refigure her as a somewhat more politically correct version of the housewife in housework advertising. They acknowledged "she's smart, she asks questions" and she wasn't wearing a ruffled apron.

One trade advertisement in this series appeared with the same copy but two different illustrations. In one, a white housewife reclines in a wooden rocking chair, magazine in her lap. In the other, an African American mother stands in a nursery, bending over a baby in a wooden crib. The subheadings for both read: "1.) She knows more about nutrition than her mother does. 2.) She's had one or more Home Economics classes at school. 3.) She's the family's nutritionist." This trade ad is one of the most compelling examples of how as early as 1971, ad makers began to use African American and white actresses interchangeably to represent domesticity: the housewife mom who would come to the fore of twenty-first century housework advertising no longer needed to be white. However, she would still be the sole household occupant capable of transforming household labor into homemaking.

Like "the apprentice housewife" ad, the copy of this ad sought to demonstrate to grocers Kraft's ability to change with the times, to leave behind the old, increasingly offensive images of women as apron-wearing housewives and embrace a more up to date, more socially acceptable representation of housework (including, apparently, racial diversity among the actresses and models in ads and commercials). But it also made pointed reference as well to Kraft's long success with recipe advertising:

She wants foods that actually deliver the nutrition they promise. She wants help in planning meals that are well balanced and economical. And she trusts Kraft. For the advice and products she can depend on. Just as her mother did. Just as her grandmother did, beginning all the way back in 1905. . . . Through television and print advertising Kraft provides recipe ideas that are simple, wholesome, inexpensive. And Kraft store promotions aim at helping consumers eat better, more wisely. The New Consumer believes in keeping her family well nourished. She knows what's possible. And she's demanding it be done.

This series of Kraft ads suggested that for food processing companies, the radical changes in social and gender norms espoused by Second Wave feminists all around the nation could be easily co-opted and folded into longstanding marketing techniques like recipe advertising. They continued to view food preparation solely through the lens of feminine care for the home, with the housewife figure continuing to transform the labor of food preparation into homemaking with the ease and convenience of food products advertised with recipes. As shown here, the housewife mom image that would come to replace the housewife made a particularly smooth transition in food advertising (which had long focused on mothers feeding children), and would seamlessly incorporate women of color.

In the late 1960s and throughout the 1970s, advertising industry research and experts cautioned agencies that their target consumers were changing and that marketing for all housework products and food products specifically had to address those changes. But at the same time, the housewife figure remained at the center of all advertising production for food products. For instance, JWT circulated a report compiled by Social Research Inc. in the early 1960s on "The Housewife," with a particular focus on the housewife and food preparation.[75] That the agency chose to use the term "working housewife" in the report to identify any married woman working for a wage outside the home suggests how powerfully "housewife" functioned as the sole lens through which ad agencies and their researchers viewed housework-related marketing. "Housewife" seemed to be the only possible term for a married woman with children— regardless of whether or not she worked for a wage outside the home. Similarly, a marketing trade journal in 1977 suggested the term "workwife" for women who "combined two major societal roles—being a housewife and working outside the home."[76]

These terms indicate that as the frame or lens through which ad agencies saw all married women, "housewife" functioned not simply as another type of female consumer but as the sole human actor in any definition of the domestic. Ad makers could only view food preparation through this lens as well, despite the fact that convenience foods made it entirely possible for almost any other member of the family to easily prepare meals. The link between a mother and wife's care for her family and the preparation of food remained untouched by the increasing numbers of white, middle-class wives and mothers working outside the home, as several comments in "The Working Housewife" report made clear:

> Food can be more important in the home of the working wife than in average homes for several reasons. The meals are an important time for getting together, especially at dinner; the woman feels she can compensate her family for some of the deprivations caused by her absence by indulging their food desires, idiosyncrasies, whims and desire for sweets. . . . And women do realize that food, especially sweets, are a substitute for a lonely child or husband and will comfort them.[77]

As this remark illustrates, the symbolic function of foods—especially baked goods and desserts—as an expression of love and care did not, in the world of ad makers, change just because the wife and mother might be working outside the home. In fact, it assumed new importance, as a means to "compensate" the family for "the deprivations caused by her absence."

Along with being somewhat more lax in allowing the family to eat various snacks and treats to compensate for her inability or unwillingness to be a full-time homemaker, the report continued, ad agencies needed to be aware of some very specific marketing strategies that might be more effective on "the working housewife." For instance, because she would be "less exposed to daytime television watching," in-store displays provided a crucial means of advertising. Working housewives were also "alert to new food and beverage products on the market, especially those that sound quick, easy, or kind of a different main course special that the family will enjoy," and were "especially alert to products that sound kind of luxurious and homemade or especially rich or nice that they would not themselves bother to prepare; but could in a newly available convenience form."[78] These statements summarize, in large part, the strategy that ad makers would put into action in order to market food products in the late twentieth century. The previous emphasis on convenient, easy, "homemade" processed foods only intensified as more and more (white, middle-class) housewives became "working housewives." Notably, the report made only a fleeting reference to the fact that when a woman worked outside the home, her partner probably played a more active role in food preparation:

> If husband and wife get home from work at about dinner time, they become quite expert at methods of having dinner ready "in no time" using "take out" meals, bought from Stop and Shop, Hillman's, Jewel, MacDonald's, pizzerias, Chinese kitchens, etc., or fast dinners of instant and quickly heated products.[79]

But instead of focusing on the intriguing possibility that perhaps convenience food could be profitably marketed to both men and women (and who knows? single folks, teenagers, "empty nesters," senior citizens, etc.), it instead went on at length as to how ad agencies and their food company clients could market to *the housewife*, affirming domestic gender norms. Even when expanding the potential target consumer base for these food products would surely have been a profitable decision, these marketing researchers could only view cooking through the frame of the housewife; could only see housework as feminine care for the family.

A similar 1971 market research report based on surveys conducted by *Better Homes and Gardens* magazine reiterated the emphasis on convenience food products as an aid—or even crutch—of the late-twentieth-century housewife.[80] In a section entitled "Women Demand Change," the report painted a grim picture of women who apparently confounded the researchers by their angry pleas for both equal rights and consumer choice: "The most shocking manifestations of this shift turn up in the aggressiveness and hostility shown by women participating in two movements: consumerism, and women's liberation. These women are demanding change in no uncertain terms." It continued on to describe exactly how those changes impacted food preparation, stating unequivocally that these consumers desired first and foremost ease and convenience, even at the expense of a family's overall nutrition, when discharging their cooking responsibilities:

> researchers found that homemakers are increasingly less preoccupied and less energetic about getting their families to eat certain kinds of diets. Not only are they more permissive, but they indulge in the "negative permissiveness" of not caring very much. The over-riding [*sic*] concern is whether or not the family likes the food and will eat it in a "mood" which is gratifying to the homemaker.
>
> The clear implication is that homemakers today, and perhaps even more those of tomorrow, are attracted by foods which are sure to be accepted. . . .
>
> [H]omemakers are becoming more and more reluctant to spend a lot of time in the kitchen—at least, the time they <u>must</u> spend there. They are looking for "luxury convenience"—distinctly pleasant dishes which can be prepared with minimal time and "mess."
>
> Not only are they reluctant to spend time in food preparation, but they also demand products which can be conveniently and easily handled. According to the study, as the homemaker's sense of rational, significant responsibility for consumed food declines, there is most likely going to be an increase in her vehemence about not working strenuously and arduously.[81]

Ad makers and their market researches clearly struggled to come to terms with the changes in gender norms at the end of the century and this particular study articulated fears that such changes (specifically wives and mothers working outside the home) heralded a generation of slipshod homemaking and slatternly women who didn't "care very much" about nutrition and who instead pursued "luxury convenience."

But whatever critical judgments the authors of "Women Demand Change" hoped to impart in their research about changing gender norms, ad makers and their clients desired only to identify those changes and figure out how to continue to successfully market food products. General Foods and Kraft, leery perhaps of offending their longstanding consumer base, remained wedded to the representation of the housewife and only the housewife as the central figure in their advertising. After all, as one marketing study examining the attitudes of so-called women's libbers toward advertising cautioned in 1977, "attitudes towards such traditional and fundamental roles as motherhood and femininity do not change as rapidly or on as large a scale as many would believe," and so advertisers needed to be careful about too quickly embracing rhetoric or images that might be perceived as belittling those "fundamental roles."[82] Again and again, ad agencies in the 1970s clearly wrestled with how to market house-work-related products when "women's libbers" seemed to be calling into question the very notion of "housewifery," and yet many other consumers continued to respond to advertising that depicted "motherhood and femininity" in "traditional" ways.

In a 1977 videotaped conversation in the "JWT Learning Series," Senior VP Reno Bartos and John Treasure, Vice Chairman, went back and forth about how ad makers should respond to the changing gender norms of the late twentieth century.[83] Their discussion about the term "housewife" is particularly revealing. They agreed that "there are actu-ally more working women than full-time housewives in our population," but as Bartos' following statement indicates, they were clearly not ready to forgo the term entirely: "But the other aspect of it is that many of the so-called working women are also housewives," she said. While Bartos argued that the advertiser who "wishes to reach the housewife is really limiting himself," she went on to explain that ad makers had to reach "the married working woman who is also a housewife." Even as Bartos cautioned other ad makers about the limitations of the term "housewife," her convoluted language—suggesting that the terms "married working woman" and "housewife" must be used simultaneously—demonstrates the unshakable frame of the housewife at ad agencies. As Bartos articu-lated it, for ad agencies—even the most foresighted ones, even the ones who early on questioned a simplistic dichotomy between "housewife" and "career woman"—any woman who somehow "kept house" bore the moniker "housewife."[84]

Yet Bartos also asserted that advertisers needed to change their representations and rhetoric about housewives, linking it to the fundamental aims of the ad business:

> [E]verything we do in advertising starts with defining our target in terms of where we want to place our media and how we want to talk to them. And if we assume our target is [makes hand quotes] quote "any housewife" 18–49 we have a mental picture of a little woman at home in that ruffled apron. Who's a declining species.[85]

Bartos predicted with great accuracy that the "little woman at home in that ruffled apron" would indeed disappear from advertising and that such images of the housewife were absolutely "a declining species" on their way to becoming extinct. But if that was the case, concluded Treasure in the video, ad makers need to find "a new unifying concept"; a new way to market housework products. As contemporary housework advertising demonstrated, and continues to demonstrate again and again, they did: the housewife mom.

What did these changes mean for food advertising? The "new unifying concept" that emerged in the 1980s and 1990s—the housewife mom caring for her family not in a ruffled apron but well pressed khakis—made an easy transition in food advertising. A JWT Research and Planning Department report in 1979 bore out Bartos' statements, concluding that "the traditional role of housewife is diminishing," and suggesting that food ads might emphasize convenience and ease in the kitchen because the 1980s would see more men and children taking responsibility for food preparation.[86] But even as 1970s research indicated changing demographics among their target consumers, even as documents circulated at JWT in the 1980s and early 1990s showed that increasing numbers of men and women shared food shopping and meal preparation responsibilities and that advertising needed to respond, food advertising very rarely used appeals that explicitly described how products could ease the housework chores of women working outside the home. Rather, they continued to promote the housewife mom's "lovin' from the oven," albeit love provided with ease and convenience.[87]

Ads and commercials for General Food products had long utilized appeals that could be readily updated for the late twentieth century: convenience foods that allowed busy moms (no matter whether they were "working" or not) to feed and care for families. The woman in General Foods ads and commercials no longer obsessed over man-pleasing Miracle Whip salads, but she still provided meals for her family using the ad recipes and convenience foods upon which food advertising had long relied. In 1962, a trade journalist described the enormous role that convenience cookery had played in General Foods advertising, including TV commercials (2/3 of General Foods' advertising budget at the time): "The company, the most diversified in the food field, has contributed mightily to one distinctly American phenomenon: the liberated housewife. With its continuing emphasis on convenience foods (TV dinners and the like) it has helped free the housewife from time-consuming, old fashioned cooking."[88] Fortunately for General Foods, while the term "liberated housewife" never became popular, the market for convenience foods continued to grow. Indeed, throughout the 1980s, market research for JWT continued to emphasize that all "housewives"—regardless of their status as wage earners—would respond to advertising that promised "less time in the kitchen." Ad agencies and food companies continued to rely heavily on convenience appeals because their research suggested such marketing would succeed with consumers. For example, 1987 and 1990 research based on *Good Housekeeping* surveys indicated that a majority of the magazine's readers worked full or part-time, relied on frozen and convenience foods, and agreed with the statement "I like to cook but only when I have time."[89]

General Foods promised that with certain products, consumers didn't *need* a lot of time. For instance, Cool Whip advertising since the introduction of the product in 1966 assured consumers that the chemical concoction would replace laboriously hand-whipped cream, as summarized in a 1966 magazine ad: "Yum. That good-old fashioned taste . . . and it all comes whipped. You do nothing but dip it out."[90] Other 1960s print ads emphasized the convenience of the product: "Relax. Nothing could be more foolproof than Cool Whip. You don't have to beat it or mix it or mess with it. It comes already whipped, ready to serve." Another 1968 ad included a coupon and urged consumers to top their Thanksgiving pies with Cool Whip: "Save yourself some pennies and some work. Why bother with a beater when there's Cool Whip? Non-dairy Cool Whip comes already whipped, but tastes like you went to a whole lot of trouble." Another promised "tastes as fresh as homemade."

Advertising recipes and recipe collections reiterated those appeals. In 1979, *The New Joys of Jell-O* depicted a happy family being served by the 1970s housewife mom in short hairdo, turtleneck sweater, and plaid slacks. The copy and photo promised super-easy family-pleasing mealtimes: "Start with a package of Jell-O Gelatin. Then work simple wonders." The recipes in General Foods' 1979 booklet titled *Easy Homemade Desserts* (using General Foods brands like Dream Whip, Post cereals, and Maxwell House) began: "Wouldn't you like to pamper your family with homemade desserts every night? Those great homemade cakes they look forward to, those lavish parfaits and frozen treats they love, their favorite pies? Lovely idea, but you just don't have the time? That's what this book is all about."[91] According to this advertisement, the housewife mom in 1979 could "pamper her family with homemade desserts," but desserts that required virtually no cooking. It was the same promise Jell-O brand products had been making for almost a century.

Appeals that promised to save "a whole lot of trouble" but also assured consumers that the product would taste "as fresh as homemade" made an effortless transition to late-twentieth-century advertising and recipe advertising focusing on easy, convenient cookery. Cool Whip always used such recipes in its advertising. A 1969 ad included an offer for a recipe booklet (send two Cool Whip labels) with "dozens of dessert ideas," for example. "Recipes" that were really just instructions for combining premade ingredients continued to feature prominently in Cool Whip ads. A 1981 ad gave a recipe for "Strawberry Shortcut" (pound cake layered with Cool Whip and strawberries); a 1983 frosting "recipe" combined Jell-O and Cool Whip; 1985 recipes for pies called for filling premade crusts with Cool Whip. "No Bake. No Fuss. No Way to Resist," promised the headline. "Make mouth-watering pies in just 10 minutes with the homemade fresh taste of Cool Whip. . . . These three Cool Whip pies are not only light, creamy, and luscious. They're ridiculously easy to make." This type of recipe advertising continues today. For instance, "Take the shortcut to spectacular," read the headline in a 2008 recipe ad for "Berry Bliss cake" (layers of frozen pound cake, Cool Whip, and Jell-O Pudding).[92] The Cool Whip Facebook page regularly offers similar serving suggestions. The emphasis in Cool Whip advertising on "ridiculously" easy cookery didn't begin in the post–Second Wave era, but the continuing highlighting of convenience cookery throughout twentieth-century advertising suggests how General Foods advertising made the transition to post–Second Wave housework advertising.

One television commercial from the early 1980s positioned Cool Whip as the never-fail dessert option; one that even a fumbling *man in the kitchen* could rely upon. A man wearing an apron in a kitchen strewn with dirty pots and pans has completely failed in his efforts to bake his wife a birthday cake. "Anyone can make a mistake!" begins the friendly voice-over. "A little too much of this, not enough of that and your cooking triumph can turn to tragedy. That's why we make delicious Cool Whip more than delicious. We make it ready to serve." The man piles an entire tub of Cool Whip onto the lopsided cake and takes it happily into the dining room as the voice-over concludes: "If it works for him, it'll work for you." The image of a man/husband/father attempting but failing housework, including food preparation, appeared regularly in popular culture and advertising, up to and including present-day advertising.[93] As this Cool Whip ad demonstrates, while General Foods advertising consistently marketed products with recipes and rhetoric that positioned their products as easy shortcuts to "homemade" cooking, the housewife remained the central figure, the unidentified "you," responsible for the family's food no matter what other social changes shaped family life.

In late-twentieth-century General Foods advertising, however, "you," the housewife, did not necessarily mean a white woman. The Cool Whip cake man was African American, as was the happy bridal couple photographed in front of a table groaning with Jell-O products in the 1975 recipe collection *The New Joys of Jell-O*.[94] As the 1986 General Foods Annual Report concluded, along with a recommendation for increased marketing aimed at the Hispanics, "We're no longer a homogenized society."[95] Cool Whip recipes, for example, appeared in *Essence* magazine throughout the 1990s, as did other General Foods products.[96] In 1990, General Foods ran a two-page ad in *Essence* in the guise of supporting traditionally all-black colleges, suggesting that their "Minute Microwave Dishes" (easily fixed in a dorm room microwave) were part of General Foods' commitment to the advancement of African Americans: "General Foods, the makers of this and many fine family traditions you grew up with, wants to remind you that we've always been there for you . . . and we're still with you. All the way." Another General Foods product, Kool-Aid, very deliberately targeted black consumers in the 1970s and 1980s, with print, radio (on Black radio stations), outdoor, and event advertising created with the objective of "improving the brand image of Kool-Aid in the Black community."[97] Kool-Aid print ads in *Essence* in the 1980s and 1990s featured coupons and large photos of happy family gatherings and an African American celebrity spokesperson, Malcolm Jamal Warner. "Keep everyone in your house smiling," advised Warner.

Indeed, if convenience played a primary role in the marketing of General Foods, appeals to mom's love and care for her family—keep everyone smiling!—still constituted an important aspect of food advertising, whether she was white or African American. Housewife moms feeding and caring for their children with food products appeared regularly in the pages of *Essence* in the 1990s. Quaker Oats promoted itself as a product "For moms who have a lot of love but not a lot of time." "I found a way to be Good Mother and still be a Great Mom," avowed the smiling African American mother pouring Sunny Delight. "Being a good mom just has to feel right. Like starting my family's day with a balanced breakfast that includes Kellogg's Corn Flakes," read the copy for an ad with a large photograph of a smiling black mother and her child. Just like ads aimed at white consumers, very few ads even intimated that women might be working outside the home, and if they did, mothering still took center stage in food ad appeals. General Foods products often equated good mothering with their convenience foods. Jell-O brands in particular emphasized how "fun" food constituted good mothering. In the 1980s and 1990s, Jell-O advertising continued to depict housewives, but featured the late century version of housewife moms. Now General Foods shifted toward appeals based explicitly on the "fun" qualities of the product. As part of a concerted effort to capitalize on Jell-O's image among consumers as a wiggly, jiggly, kind of funny food, General Foods advertising linked it to the modern housewife mom's ability to not simply feed her children but also provide lighthearted fun and playtime.[98] Young and Rubicon (General Foods' ad agency at the time) executive Julie Barnhard summarized in a 1990 videotaped interview that the main positioning message for Jell-O was "a really fun dessert that you can serve to your kids and share their childhood."[99] For example, "Play in the dirt with your kids," read the headline of an early 1990s recipe ad for "Jell-O Pudding Dirt Cups" (with Gummi worms). Other "Snacktivities" recipe ads for Jell-O products emphasized how Mom's Jell-O cookery could provide a bonding experience via the fun of eating Jell-O brand cooking.

Another revealing ad that squarely equated home cookery with Mom's responsibilities to her kids appeared in *Essence* in 1990. A full-page ad that heralded the consolidation of Kraft and General foods—the new Kraft-General Foods, Inc.—depicted a 1960s-era mother in African-print dress and head wrap mixing something with a beater while her smiling daughter watches, and a more contemporary mother in a button-down shirt having a meal with her son. The headline: "The more things change, the more they stay the same." The copy made it clear that home cookery as an expression of loving care remained the job of the housewife mom, even as the twentieth century drew to a close:

> Times have changed. And today, the time you have to cook for your family gets less and less. But, you can count on one thing to stay the same—Kraft's excellent quality. We've made it our business to keep pace with you in these changing times by offering consistently good tasting food products. And convenient new ways to prepare them. And we've been doing it for 75 years. Caring homemakers have come to expect nutritious, high quality foods from Kraft. And that's the one thing we'll never forget.

General Foods advertising made "convenient new ways" to prepare "consistently good tasting food products" the keystone of their advertising, from the beginning of the century when Jell-O ads nodded to the hot and laborious work of daily meal preparation, to the end of the century when acknowledging that "times have changed" and "you" had "less time to cook for your family" became an essential part of transitioning the stereotypical representation of the housewife into the twenty-first century. The "little woman in that ruffled apron" had, as Bartos predicted, become extinct in ads and commercials, but it remained perfectly acceptable, even marketable, to link food products with "caring homemakers," or more commonly, "Mom." As the ad stated, the more things change, the more they stay the same. The merging of Kraft and General Foods into one gargantuan food processing entity meant the merging of advertising as well, but that presented no particular difficulty, as Kraft too had a long history of appeals based on convenient products for "caring homemakers."

In the last decades of the twentieth century, Kraft advertising continued to emphasize the same themes it always had, even when it did not directly depict "the housewife" herself (as in the case of their television advertising): easy recipes and, increasingly, how products allowed moms to express their love and devotion to their children with a minimum of kitchen work. Kraft's ability to market cheese products as easy "helps" for the "big job" of mothering in the mid-century not only continued but proliferated through the 1990s. In fact, appeals based on mother's care would be Kraft's bridge into twentieth-century advertising, especially their forays into "ethnic markets." As Kraft President Jim Kilts mentioned in a 1991 speech, the company expected to use many depictions of Latina housewife moms caring for their children with the right Kraft products in their advertisements: "Advertising portrays the mother as the center of the Hispanic family and shows that just as family members trust her to know what's right, she trusts in Kraft."[100] Subsequent Kraft advertising, for example, included a 2007 product placement for macaroni and cheese in a *Buenhogar* article on organizing your pantry.[101] As the title of a 2005 marketing industry article about Kraft's efforts to expand their Asian American market made clear, the housewife mom continued to star in Kraft's advertising, even if her skin color or ethnicity changed: "Kraft Initiative Woos Asian American Moms."[102]

Similarly, advertisements for Kraft products like Macaroni and Cheese Dinner and Stove Top stuffing in *Essence* often depicted housewife moms providing loving care for their children. In a 1992 *Essence* ad, Stove Top promised that its corn bread stuffing mix could lure children home from the basketball court. Over a photograph of an empty basketball court, a kid's sneakers just disappearing out of the frame, the headline reads: "Mama's making cornbread dressing tonight." The attempt to be culturally relevant, i.e., the use of "Mama," might have indicated a slightly different representation of the (unseen) housewife mom, but in every other respect, here was the same housewife mom who had starred in food advertising since the beginning of the century: providing her children with delicious "homemade" food from a box. By the 1990s, the person representing domesticity in food advertising was not necessarily white, but was always female and she was almost always caring for her home and her children.

Like all its advertising, Kraft utilized coupons and recipes in *Essence* magazine, including a 1994 offer for a cookbook co-produced with the National Council of Negro Women called *Celebrating Our Mothers' Kitchens*. The copy described the contents: "African-Americans share a heritage of good eating passed from generation to generation." Here Kraft was able to simultaneously build an appeal on the very real sense of pride and heritage communities and groups take in a shared culinary past, and at the same time continue to build their brand as part of good mothering, from generation to generation. Kraft recipe collections and print advertisements returned, again and again, to the ways their products enabled "you" to put family-pleasing meals on the table. Utilizing their market research, a 1970 advertising cookbook called *Kraft's Main Dish Cookbook* seemed designed to appeal directly to their old friend "Julie," promising that "each dish has a definite flair or creative touch, a little extra something that doesn't require added time or effort, yet gives you a chance to express yourself."[103] Ad makers did not necessarily imagine "Julie" solely as a white woman in the 1990s, but she was almost always a "mom," the symbolic figure most capable of transforming food preparation into love.

Kraft "Singles"—individually wrapped slices of processed cheese—in particular linked the Kraft brand with good mothering. In a 1976 ad that appeared in women's magazines, a crowd of housewife moms (including African American, Asian, and other vaguely "ethnic" models and older women) each hold aloft a package of Kraft Singles. "Mother knows best," proclaimed the headline. The copy continued: "Mothers want the best for their families—good flavor, good quality, good value. And Mothers find that kind of goodness in delicious KRAFT American Singles pasteurized process cheese food slices." A 1974 ad featuring a large photograph of a grilled cheese sandwich, listed qualities of a good mother for each letter in "Singles," such as "S is for the singles sandwiches you make me," "G because it's the good stuff from Kraft," concluding:

L is for the love that always lingers
E is even when I'm sometimes bad.
Mom, you're the best girl I ever had

"Be a Singles Girl. Make somebody happy with Kraft Singles," concluded the tag.[104] To reinforce the message, the writing appeared in scrawled, crayon-colored "kid" font. That font often appeared in Kraft Singles ads, particularly when emphasizing the "wholesome" qualities of the product. "Please don't put oil in my samwitch. Love David," pleaded a 1988 ad, one in a long campaign to position Kraft processed cheese as superior in ingredients to other sliced processed cheese. "My sister is 10 and she says milk tastes better than oil," sweetly explained a 1989 ad. A 1985 series of magazine ads in this campaign featured large photos of adorable children with copy that directly linked the product with good mothering and guarding children's health. A kid in a bunny suit: "How could I give my little bunny anything but the best?" In a baseball uniform: "How could I shortchange my shortstop?" In a basketball uniform: "How could I let down my guard?" In a football uniform: "How could I hold back from my quarterback?" In typical copy, the mom narrator explained why she wouldn't "hold back:" "Sure I could buy imitation slices. But some use hardly any milk. Kraft Singles are made with five delicious ounces. Plus, my kids get great nutrition like calcium to help their bones grow up strong. Hold back from my quarterback? No way." A 1987 ad in parenting magazines even intimated that a good mother would consume Kraft Singles for her nursing baby, with the tag "Kraft Singles. Because your baby depends on you for calcium."

This equation of the brand with good mothering and good feeding continues to today. A woman's voice-over in a 2009 commercial, for example, describes the benefits of Kraft Singles:

> It's lunch time for the kids. We could throw one of those frozen numbers in the microwave. But wouldn't it be nice to whip up something a little more wholesome? Start with Kraft Singles and create a delicious, melty grilled cheese. And since Singles are made with milk they're not only creamy and yummy. They're actually wholesome! And maybe we'll make an extra one for ourselves. 'Cause our lunch—cold coffee—could be a little more wholesome too. Kraft Singles. Goodness squared.[105]

As often is the case in Kraft advertising, the housewife mom doesn't actually appear in this commercial—just whimsical animated cheese slices forming a clock, a coffee cup, etc., and a live action shot of a smiling little girl taking a large bite of a perfectly browned grilled cheese sandwich. In 2009, as it had for almost 100 years, Kraft advertising continued to build a brand image of a milk-based product that required no major cookery but would nonetheless produce happy, healthy kids—and maybe even better nourished mothers, too.

Today on the Kraft Singles Facebook wall, corporate posts emphasize family activities and promotions, reinforcing the brand image of Kraft

Singles as a mother's helper. Boasting almost 8,400 users who "Like" the page (June 2011), consumers offer positive testimonials about the project and appear to post their own family photos, serving suggestions, and so on, illustrating how social media effectively obscures advertising copy within online "communities." The page also contains numerous links to kid-friendly "recipes." Several such recipes recall the 1960 Velveeta lollipops: Kraft Singles cut into dinosaur shapes and a cracker "lion face" with Kraft Singles "whiskers" for instance. In addition, they reinforce the "new momism" of the twenty-first century: these serving suggestions depict good mothers providing fun as well as food, and promote a highly unrealistic ideal of mother-kid togetherness. The link on the Single's Facebook wall to a "Cheese Butterfly and Caterpillar" recipe, for example, promised, "Your little helpers won't ever want to leave the kitchen!"[106] Similarly, in 2010, Kraft's advertising agency explained that it aimed directly at the "mom market" with the creation of the first official Facebook page devoted exclusively to Kraft Macaroni and Cheese.[107]

Contemporary Kraft Singles advertising also seeks to directly market to kids and young adults with other kinds of promotions. In 2009, for instance, Kraft Singles joined forces with the popular Disney franchise, the Jonas Brothers band. Hoping to entice some of the millions of the band's fans to the Kraft website, Kraft Singles advertised a free download of an ad campaign theme song, "Smiles Under a Single," sung by the Jonas Brothers.[108] But notwithstanding this attempt to lure tweens into Kraft purchases, Kraft recipe advertising remains paramount in Kraft marketing. KraftFoods.com offers literally thousands of recipes, both consumer-generated and those posted by Kraft. Kraft's *Food and Family* magazine has 12 million subscribers, and untold more receive weekly recipe emails and recipe podcasts.[109] Hundred of thousands of Facebook users "Like" the Kraft Facebook pages, including a Spanish language one, and follow Kraft Tweets, both of which are packed with links to other Kraft sites and recipes. This recipe-based and other Kraft advertising almost exclusively directs its appeals to "moms," and focuses specifically on Mom's desire and ability to care for and nurture her family. Industry commentators sometimes even refer to the Kraft brand as "Mother Kraft," a nod to both its enormous presence in food processing and food advertising and its emphasis on Mom's cooking/love. A 1998 tagline summarized how Kraft seeks to position itself as "a company that understands moms" and to market food as an expression of moms' love : "We make it taste good. You make it feel good."[110]

Convenience, too, remains paramount in Kraft advertising. Mary Beth West, CMO of Kraft Foods, explained in a 2008 interview that by tracking hits on their recipe database website, Kraft found that successful marketing had to promise both economy in the midst of the ever-worsening national financial crisis and a clear convenience:

> The cooking thing isn't something people revel in. Eating is something they do revel in. Some of the learning we've done over the past year shows the difference between food recipes from the top of the database to the bottom. "Learn to cook stirfry" is fast to the bottom. "Easy stirfry in 15 minutes" is at the top.
>
> "Cook" implies time and skill they may or may not have. But they know they have to put dinner on the table. They don't reject putting a little of themselves into it, but "cook" sounds like a process, more time. What's a sauté? Framing it more as a food solution and an idea of getting dinner on the table is what it's all about. Despite the economic environment, people don't have any more time than they did a few months ago. But helping them be able to feed a family with food they feel good about is a big idea.[111]

West carefully said "people" and the rest of her statement is gender-neutral as well. But given the long history of Mother Kraft's advertising aimed squarely at easy shortcuts that Mom could use when "feeding a family with food they feel good about," it's hard to imagine that West or anyone at Kraft truly believed that Dad might be scrolling the site as well.

Modern food advertising from 1900 to the 2000s reiterated and reinforced domestic gender norms by linking housewives and housewife moms to food preparation, depicting kitchen labor as relieved with convenience products and transformed into feminine homemaking and family care. Modern kitchen cleaning products linked kitchen labor to the housewife as well, and like food advertising, emphasized how products could lessen the dreariest aspects of housework. Advertising depicted dishwashing in particular as a burdensome part of housework, a notion powerfully reinforced by the inventor of the automatic dishwasher herself. Historians credit Josephine Garis Cochrane for the invention (patented in 1886) and successful industrial marketing (selling two models to hotels by 1888) of the first automatic dishwashing machine. Cochrane later claimed that the impetus for her invention was "the servant problem." As a conscientious upper-class homemaker with a fine family collection of china, she simply could not trust the servants to wash her dishes without chipping them. But in a 1912 interview, Cochrane firmly linked housework (washing dishes) not with paid employees but with housewives: "When it comes to buying something for the kitchen that costs $75 or $100, a woman begins at once to figure out all the other things she could do with the money. She hates dishwashing—what woman does not?—but she has not learned to think of her time and comforts as worth money."[112] Cochran's statement echoed the rhetoric of many a housework advertisement urging women to invest in products that promised to save time and labor. She didn't mention one of the biggest obstacles to home sales of dishwashing machines: early automatic machines were large, clumsy, required an on-tap water source, and the available soap products did not work very well in them. Perhaps most significantly, many consumers did not "hate" dishwashing. In fact, dishwashing had long been one of the few housework tasks often shared with other family members.[113] Yet Cochrane's assumption—that the housewife would be responsible for the family's dishes, and what woman (housewife) doesn't hate dishwashing?—succinctly summarized how soap and detergent manufacturers marketed their soaps for use in the dishpan throughout much of the twentieth century. Even as they linked the product to high ideals of homemaking, kitchen cleaning products routinely emphasized that housewives weary of this chore could turn to their products for relief.

As modern advertising took shape in the early 1900s, so too did the representation of doing dishes as a particularly onerous housework task, one which the housewife might well want to hand off to a magical helper. Soaps made specifically for dishwashing did not appear on the market until after World War II with the invention of the first synthetic soaps, so the first dishwashing advertisements in modern advertising history made up just one part of all-purpose soap advertising. The magic helpers that appeared in early modern advertising to assist housewives in cleaning the bathroom appeared again to help them in the kitchen. For instance, in 1918 the Old Dutch Cleanser girl approached a pile of dishes with her stick at the ready: "Wades Right In," claimed the headline. Jiffy, the Spotless Cleanser elf, took his turn at the kitchen sink as well. In a 1916 ad he applied his wand to a shining frying pan, as the copy described: "Yes, <u>Ma'am</u>; this sprightly cleanser digs right into dirt and grease and makes it vamoose in short order" (see fig. 3.2) Gold Dust's now infamously racist magic helpers, the naked "darkies" known as the Gold Dust Twins, helped the housewife with all kinds of housework, including the dishes. The Gold Dust tag, "Let the Gold Dust Twins Do Your Work," appeared in an early 1900s ad depicting the twins washing dishes, for example. In a 1917 *Good Housekeeping* Gold Dust ad, the Twins appeared but were not doing the work. Rather, in a vivid early illustration of how modern housework advertising depicted dishwashing as a truly laborious task, an enormous, scowling dishpan ropes the pretty, serene housewife in her work dress. She holds aloft a box of Gold Dust, and as her calm expression attests: "You can't scare <u>me</u>!" The copy continues: "I am only a plain little woman, I know—and you are the big old dishpan. You try to tie me down three times a day—but I know how to make short work of you. . . . My Gold Dust takes right hold of the grease and the grease fairly slips off the dishes. The rest is easy."[114]

Figure 3.2 1916 Spotless cleanser print advertisement

Note: "Jiffy" was an early example of the magical helpers that still sometimes appear in housework advertising. In this 1916 ad he promised to make dirt and grease "vamoose" but without "injuring the tenderest skin" of the housewife.

Source: From N. W. Ayer Advertising Agency Records, Archives Center, National Museum of American History, Behring Center, Smithsonian Institution.

The emphasis on wrangling a dirty dishpan into submission with soap that magically removed grease continued into the rest of the century. And magic helpers like the Ajax elves occasionally appeared to wash dishes into the mid-century. But advertisements and commercials for dishwashing detergent especially emphasized, to an enormous degree, a very specific way that dishwashing might "scare" housewives: its effect on their hands. Beginning in the 1920s, when soap manufacturers began to advertise their laundry soaps for use in the dishpan as well, no other appeal appeared so frequently. An account history of Lux Flakes by Lever Brother's advertising agency, JWT, noted that the very first appeal used for Lux as a dishwashing soap in 1922 was "Won't redden or roughen hands." By the 1930s, such rhetoric in ads and radio commercials exemplified the new psychology-based market research, specifically hoping to raise personal anxiety that would lead consumers to make purchases. Like the Lux "undie odor" campaigns from the same era, campaigns for Lux dishes "featured brides and the social embarrassment of dishpan hands" often in the photograph/comic strip style ads so popular during this time.[115]

In one such magazine ad, a housewife confides to her friend as they listen to the radio play "Pale hands I love. . . ."

> **Housewife**: Oh, Mabel, that's the song Jim sang to me so much after we were married. He was so proud of my hands! But he doesn't sing it now—I don't blame him. Dishwashing has certainly ruined my hands—rough, red old things!
> **Mabel**: Why you poor lamb! Don't you know Lux in the dishpan will keep them soft and white?[116]

In a similar ad, a young wife frets about the impact of dishwashing on her marriage. The copy explained beneath a photo of the bridal couple, followed by the comic strip style drawings: "Her hands were softly young and white on her wedding. 'How feminine they are,' her proud husband thought. But soon those lovely hands plunged into dishwater every day. They aged *years*—their rough redness embarrassed her. 'These hands make me look too horribly like a drudge.'" But the story ends happily: "Thanks to Lux, her hands are flower-like, snow-white—as exquisite as a bride's." Lux's promise of beautiful hands in the 1920s and 1930s often referenced the fact that the product would save housewives from looking "too horribly like a drudge." Indeed, in a clear example of housework advertising appeals asserting that the product would magically remove the need for servant labor, Lux and other soaps ran a number of ads in the 1920s and 1930s assuring consumers that their brand would hide all signs of dishwashing on the housewife's body, even if she had to "do her own work."

"Need your hands say . . . 'I have no maid?'" queried the headline of a 1929 newspaper ad. Of course not! Not with Lux, "so rich and cleansing that dishes seem almost to wash themselves!"[117] "Beauty shop experts" in a 1933 magazine ad avowed: "We actually can't tell the difference between the hands of the woman who uses Lux in the dishpan and those of a woman with maids to do all her work." Another 1930s ad depicted the Lux brand as "beauty care," easily erasing all signs of housework:

> Don't imagine that women with exquisite hands always have maids to do their work. Nowadays it's *much* more likely that they're cooking and washing dishes themselves. But they give their hands a very inexpensive, marvelous kind of beauty care. . . . While the tiny Lux diamonds work speedily to leave dishes shining, they soothe and treasure your hands.

Ivory also proclaimed its ability to ensure beautiful hands for women who had no maid—and *needed* no maid!—as in a 1931 magazine ad:

> Last night, as my birthday treat, my husband and I dressed up and dined at a smart little restaurant. At the very next table to ours, two women were discussing an acquaintance of theirs. One of them said in a high-hat way, "Oh, she's *poor*. She hasn't a maid." That remark made me want to make a speech. Poor! Why, nine out of ten of us don't have maids, and we don't feel poor. Lots of us feel *proud* that we don't need the help of maids. In fact—no, I'm not being catty—I took a careful squint at Mrs. High Hat's hands. They weren't a bit prettier or smoother than the hands of any of us who do our work with gentle Ivory.
>
> I'm willing to wager that we're putting the money that could go into a maid's wages into something worthwhile—helping to buy a home, or a car, or good schooling for our children.
>
> And we're not sacrificing the good looks of our hands either—*if* we're cleaning and washing with gentle Ivory. Why, dishwashing three times a day is just the same as putting our hands into three Ivory baths.

Ivory promised not only pretty hands that made hiring a maid unnecessary and but also, as described here, a modern way to be a better wife and mother, contributing to "something worthwhile" with the money saved by using Ivory.

Doing one's own dishes was not merely an inconvenience or even drudgery in these ads: the resulting "dishpan hands" risked the housewife deep social shame and ostracism. For instance, in a 1933 ad, a worried woman overhears unwelcome gossip about herself: "Charming—except for her red dishpan hands!" In another example, a wife in a 1929 ad failed at an important dinner party:

> My dinner table, set with all my best china, for our dinner for Jim's new friends, had *never* looked prettier. But it made my poor hands looked dreadfully coarse by comparison. They simply broadcasted "Dishpan!"
>
> And because I know it's just such little things that others judge us by, I became *self-conscious* . . . ill at ease . . . at my own dinner table.

Of course it was foolish of me. With Lux always in the house I was still using just any ordinary soap for the dishes. Until that night I had not realized just how pitifully rough and red it made my hands look.

Again and again, women in Lux ads were shamed by "pitifully rough and red" hands, hands that "broadcast dishpan," and subsequently incurred the harsh judgments of others. In a 1933 ad, a middle-aged mother fears embarrassing her son: "Dinner with your stylish friends next week? Mercy me, no—I'd be too ashamed of my dishpan hands." In the next panel, a friend gives Mums some good advice: "Of course you must go, Jane! Your hands—start using Lux for dishes—it's that harsh soap that's making your trouble." In the last panel, the housewife gussied up in an evening gown prepares to hit the town with her son:

> **Son:** Ready, Mums? Gee you look wonderful! And your hands as smooth and white as any queen's—I'm proud of you!
> **Mums:** Well, son, I've learned that even a busy woman can have lovely hands.

Transformed from a drudge into a queen, the housewife in this advertisement needed only to buy the right dish soap in order to trade an apron for a ball gown, and to earn the admiration of her son.

Lux was far from alone in suggesting that dishpan-ravaged hands marked a housewife indelibly as a social outcast. A 1936 ad for Super Suds depicted a forlorn woman in an evening dress sitting alone, because, as the headline explained "Dishpan redness ruins party" and in a 1937 ad, a housewife is ashamed to play cards because "Her hands fairly shrieked 'dishwater!'"[118] In a 1935 Ivory ad, teenage daughter Ann bluntly informs her mother of the terrible social faux pas of housework hands. Headlined "No Longer Ashamed of Mother's Hands!" the comic strip depicted a mother and daughter:

> **Mother:** Oh, there's Mrs. Simms! I'd love to meet Jerry's mother, Ann.
> **Ann:** Oh—well—then put on your gloves, Mother. Your hands look terrible!

Ann quickly changes her tune when Mother starts using Ivory in the dishpan, as the last panel depicting Ann in confidential conversation with her fiancé reveals:

> **Jerry:** I was wondering, Ann—when we get married, can you keep your hands soft and pretty?
> **Ann:** Oh, Mother's told me how! I'll keep a supply of large size Ivory.[119]

It's hard to believe that copywriters could, in all seriousness, depict a young man on the eve of his honeymoon wondering about his wife's *hands*. Yet over and over, ads asserted that men judged women's attractiveness by the beauty of their hands. "I've Found **Romance!**" read the headline for a Vel soap ad: "I've found out that men adore soft-smooth hands."[120] As a little girl explained to her dolls in a 1933 ad: "You see, darlings, it's most 'portant for young ladies not to have horrid dishpan hands—or else nobody will love them." Super Suds ads in 1937 asked: "Hands across the table—do yours speak of love or dishwashing?" In a 1932 presentation, a JWT executive summarized the history of Lux dishwashing advertising, beginning in 1927: "Men appeared in many of the pictures, and emphasis was placed upon the romantic value of white hands free from any trace of that dishpan look. . . . [Currently] the message is based entirely on beautiful hands—the same story that has been used since we began exploiting this dishwashing use in 1922."[121] As a 1937 Lux campaign ad asserted: "Romance dies at the touch of dishpan hands."[122]

Advertisers didn't hesitate to equate "dishpan hands" with romantic rejection throughout the 1930s and into the 1940s. A 1941 Lux ad suggested that a husband's roving eye might be caught by another woman's hands. "Tom, why are you looking at the woman over there?" asks Wife in the fashionable restaurant. Flustered Tom answers: "Why, I was admiring her hands. They're beautiful—so feminine." "Yes, and mine would be, too, if I didn't **wash dishes** every day for **you**, Tom Langley." Mrs. Langley's righteous anger, however, is soothed by the purchase of Lux, and in the last panel she cuddles with Tom on the couch. He presents her with jewelry, cooing, "The bracelet's not half nice enough for your pretty hands, darling." In Ivory ads too, dishwashing often caused marital friction. "Was He Cruel or Kind? Let Wives Judge" headlined a comic strip advertisement. Tom comments to his wife, who is tying his tuxedo tie: "Darling, your hands feel as rough as my chin before shaving." Throwing herself on the bed in tears, "Darling" protests: "You liked my hands well enough before we were married. They wouldn't be rough if I didn't have to wash dishes for you!" In a later panel, back in her kitchen with her apron on, the housewife uses Ivory for her dishes: "Glory Be! I can almost feel my hands getting soft and smooth in these creamy white Ivory suds." In the last panel, she plays "Guess Who?" with Tom, who cheerfully scolds her: "Don't flirt with me, woman! You know I'm partial to pretty, soft hands."

In other Ivory ads as well, various brutally honest comments set housewives straight. A 1935 comic strip titled "Child's Frankness Saves Jane's Hands" begins with an awkward social moment:

Alice: Now, say goodbye Junior. Shake hands with Auntie Jane.
Junior: Oh, I don't want to, Mother! Her hands feel funny—just like sandpaper.

Mother: Why Junior! Pay no attention to him, Jane. Some silly childish notion.

Jane: No, Alice. He's right! My hands are coarse and rough! Dishwashing simply ruins them.

Hubby [ruefully]: I wish we could afford a maid, dear.

But, like Lux, Ivory promised that with the right product, having a maid was not necessary for housewives to have alluring hands that showed no signs of housework: "Use Ivory for 'Lady-of-Leisure' hands," reads the copy in the above ad. In the last panel Hubby's swooning over Jane's hand: "It's such a nice smooth little hand." In a 1941 Lux ad, a snide remark from another woman leads to a similar improvement in the housewife's self care—and marriage. An angry young housewife shouts into the phone: "Kitty Gordon, stop criticizing my husband for not hiring a maid. I don't **want** him to, and I don't care if my **hands** do shout **dishpan**." However, as she reveals to her sister later: "Oh, Sis, that cat, Kitty Gordon criticizes Tom because my hands look **red**." "But hon, you could save Tom that criticism . . ." With Lux, of course. In the last panel, Tom's admiring his wife's hands: "Darling, such pretty little hands. I love them!"

The happy endings in dishwashing ads, however, contained a distinct subtext: of all modern housework ads and commercials, no type of product (even laundry soaps) so consistently pointed out that the daily tasks of housework faced by women in the home could create such a burden as to leave them physically damaged. Soap manufacturers and advertising agencies in the 1920s and 1930s used romantic, social status appeals but they also routinely pointed out that the dishpan posed a certain amount of drudgery. As historian Kathy Newman writes, radio commercials for soaps in the 1930s promised freedom from drudgery and at the same time they "were surprisingly frank in their repetition of the negative qualities of housework." She cites as an example a commercial for P&G's White Naptha soap (sponsor of the *Guiding Light* radio serial):

> Maybe only last night you were sitting at the supper table having a good time, and then all of a sudden you remembered that when supper was over it was up to you to do that big pile of dishes. It sort of took the fun out of things, didn't it? You know, if you mind dish washing that much I'll just bet you're using a lazy soap. The kind of soap that just lies down and lets you do all the work. When you want to clean up a pile of dishes in a hurry, want to get grease and caked-on food off of plates, pots and pans, you don't need a nambypamby soap, what you need is a go-getting business-like soap.

While the commercial painted a happy picture of a "go-getting" soap that would make dishwashing easy, it also pointed out that at the end of every good meal, there would be dishes for "you" to do. Newman quotes another dish soap ad that promised in the name itself to do the work for you: "Duz." "Duz" didn't go so far as to promise a magic helper, but it did suggest to radio listeners new ease in the dishpan: "Of course we aren't saying that with Duz, you don't even have to hold the dishcloth, but we do say there will be no more hard scouring to get rid of grease on those sticky baking dishes and fry pans." Newman concludes: "At the same time this ad promises freedom from work, the ad itself is filled with reminders of how much work is involved in housework and of the consequences of that work for the houseworker."[123]

Such copy and images occurred again and again in both print and radio commercials in the 1930s, and they undoubtedly sought to create anxiety where there well may have been none. Like "halitosis," advertising invented "dishpan hands" in order to market different brands of soap while simultaneously exaggerating the drudgery of dishwashing. However, like all housework advertising, such rhetoric and copy did have a basis in reality as well. Immersing one's hands in soap and water on a regular basis could of course cause dry, chapped hands. As Newman points out, ad makers were not wrong to acknowledge "how much work is involved in housework and the consequences of that work" for women in the home. A 1923 JWT market research survey demonstrated that the reason women gave most often for using Ivory and Lux in the dishpan was "Does not hurt hands."[124] (This research also bore out the assumption that by this time women would be doing the dishes: 72% of the survey respondents marked "Self" in answer to the question "Who usually washes the dishes?") Ad agencies and soap manufacturers were surely elated when research confirmed the common sense assumption that immersion in soap and water caused chapping. As a Lux account history for JWT noted, in 1940 "the existence of 'Dishpan Hands was authenticated by a series of tests and case histories."[125] Advertising imagery and copy depicted dry hands as far more than a minor inconvenience, and sometimes even referred to the justifiable frustration of real housewives tackling real housework day after day.

In such ads, housewives forlornly or angrily express their weariness, sometimes, as in the case of Mrs. Langley and her hand-ogling husband, confronting her husband directly. Several newspaper ads for Super Suds illustrated this aspect of dishwashing advertising. In a 1937 ad, a scowling housewife in an apron actually throws a dish to the floor, shattering it, while her husband looks on askance: "I'm all washed up with washing dishes!" shouts the housewife's dialogue balloon, going on to complain: "Look at my hands! All rough and red! That's what all this dishwashing does!" Hubby (bravely, I think—there is still a sink full of dishes she could throw) chides her: "My sister washes more dishes than you—and her hands are o.k. You'd better chat with her!" Of course, Super Suds restores marital harmony: "Darling, how lovely your hands are now—just as smooth and white as ever!" Another Super Suds newspaper ad the previous year depicted a crying wife and an angry husband under the headline: "Dishwashing almost broke up their marriage, until . . ." Standing at the dishpan, the distraught housewife confronts her husband with the evidence of her labors: "But Phil, you don't realize what hard work dishwashing is! And look at my hands!" Phil takes a hard line: "Now see here! You know we can't afford a maid. And that's <u>that</u>." But no maid is necessary, after the housewife realizes that, in Phil's words, "Super Suds is keeping your hands as soft and white as a movie star's!" In a less confrontational depiction of husband and wife, but one that nonetheless still suggests that dishwashing imperils marital bliss, a 1936 Super Suds newspaper ad began with the headline: "Still in love . . . but that dishwashing!" "I must love you a lot, Don," bluntly states the housewife, "or I'd never put up with this dishwashing! I hate it!" In an even more pointed ad, "Dishwashing was ruining Rita's Romance," a young unmarried couple's future together is threatened:

Rita: You haven't said a single nice thing to me in weeks!
Boyfriend: Aw, all I said was you ought to take better care of your hands! Look how red and rough they are!
Rita [to friend in the next panel]: I just wish he had to wash dishes! Then he'd find out!

One spirited young lady even proclaimed: "Nix on Marriage and Dishwashing!" "It ruins your hands." But that was before she heard about Super Suds.

None of these ads suggested that saving a wife's hands might be a good reason for a husband to do the dishes himself. As Rita pointed out, he didn't *have* to do dishes, did he? Although "helping" to dry dishes might be a suitably masculine task (and men wearing dishcloth aprons and drying dishes alongside their wives did appear occasionally in dishwashing ads), dishwashing advertising never depicted the possibility that men might assume more responsibility. The choice was always a maid (although that was never depicted as a realistic possibility) or dishpan hands or the correct brand of soap. Yet the ads did depict, however fleetingly and however easily resolved with a particular brand of soap, the never-ending nature of housework—there were always dishes, every day. They did so to an exaggerated degree, like the 1937 Super Suds ads depicting a woman lying terrified in her bed as enormous bright red claws reach for her. "Dishwashing Hands a Nightmare—Until . . ." read the headline. The next day, Friend in Hat appears and listens sympathetically to the housewife in her apron: "No wonder I have nightmares about dishwashing! Just look how red and rough my hands are!" In a similar ad, a vicious cartoon dishpan reddens the manacled hands of the housewife. But dishwashing advertising in the 1930s and 1940s touched on an element of truth about housework, even if they exaggerated it in order to bolster emotionally charged appeals about sexual and romantic attractiveness.

Advertising had to change when, in the early 1950s, synthetic soaps specifically formulated for dishwashing such as Joy and Glim appeared on the market. But the 1940s saw one last major campaign for laundry and all-purpose soap to be used for dishes: during World War II, Ivory Snow aggressively marketed its soap for dishwashing in women's magazines. As DMB&B advertising agency executive Artherton W. Hobler recollected in his reflections on landing the Ivory Snow account: "There was a large and tempting volume to be obtained in the dishwashing field. The amount of soap used for this purpose was nearly six times as much for wash-bowl laundry work." And the company soon capitalized on it with new kinds of advertising, as Hobler wrote in the 1970s about Ivory Snow: "A change in the advertising alone has made a spectacular contribution to the success of a product."[126] World War II Ivory Snow dishwashing ads included a series of striking, full-page ads with lots of colorful eye-catching drawings, rhyming copy, and appeals to consumers' patriotism. The Ivory Snow ads promised that the product would (1) lather quickly (making it ideal for housewives busy with home, family, and war work) and (2) protect the housewife's hands.[127]

For example, a housewife in headscarf and coveralls starred in a 1944 ad headlined, "I'm on the swing shift . . . *and* the kitchen shift!" "No wonder dishwashing got me down . . . until Ivory Snow came into my life!" The ad then depicts her slaving over a dishpan while an irate husband holding a dishtowel (drying dishes appeared to be an acceptable housework task for husbands in a small number of ads) and a clock both pointed out how long the inferior soap was taking to suds up. But a different sudsy soap was too harsh, and left her hands red and rough, causing her husband to scowl furiously at the other brand. Ivory Snow, of course, could produce suds quickly and leave the housewife's hands soft. A similar 1943 ad featured copy written from the husband's point of view. Headlined, "I thought I married an angel but dishwashing cracked her halo," it depicts a sweet blonde aproned housewife frowning at the sudsless dishpan, her halo all in pieces: "Not that I blame her. Doing dishes three times a day is a real chore. But it wasn't the job itself that tried her so. It was the mild bar soap she was using . . . easy on hands, all right—but mighty slow to make suds. And since she's extra busy with her war work these days—no wonder she got mad." But the fast-sudsing soap leaves her hands bright red: "'How can I appear at my Civilian Defense Office,' she wails, 'with these awful red hands!'" In the last two panels, her halo is restored. "For speedier dishwashing, for snow-white hands," reads the tag, concluding "Aren't your hands as precious as your stockings?" As one of last multipurpose appeals, these Ivory Snow ads often drew a parallel between the product's gentle but superior use for delicates and for dishes, as in the case of a 1943 ad written from a baby's point of view. The baby watches Mother in dismay, as Mother struggles with slow suds and dishpan hands. But then he sets her straight: "One day I got hold of the Ivory Snow that Mother uses for my wooly blankets and her nice underthings. I scootered over to her with it—and pointed to the dishpan." In another ad, the Ivory Snow housewife also received dishwashing soap suggestions from a rather pompous professor husband: "I seem to remember some woman praising the soap she used for stockings as being fast, yet gentle. Wasn't that *you*, my love?"

Ivory Snow ads ran with similar appeals after the war, promising quick suds and pretty hands ("Kindness to hands! Speed in the dishpan!"). The clueless housewife in a 1946 ad using a slow bar soap wore a dunce cap and did dishes from the confines of the stocks:

> There was a young woman named Pritchen
> Whose hands were in lovely condition
> So soft and so white
> It didn't seem right
> That she never got out of the kitchen.

Like earlier ads, Ivory Snow regularly depicted dishwashing as laborious drudgery—unless the housewife purchased the correct soap. However, by the 1950s, soap manufactures could no longer afford to market soap for multiple purposes including dishes when superior synthetic dishwashing detergents dramatically changed the market. In 1947, for example, JWT urged their client the Lever Brothers company to "take steps toward developing a liquid synthetic detergent."[128]

As a JWT report on the product explained, in response to the "aggressively marketed" dishwashing detergent Joy, Lever launched Lux Liquid in 1953. It noted that the first Lux Liquid campaigns drew heavily on the oft-used depiction of dishwashing as Sisyphean labor, with visually arresting new images:

> From the start, copy and layout thinking turned to an effort to make a sympathetic contact with the housewife—an instantly believable approach in which she could identify herself and respond. The result evolved as a

dramatic pictorial presentation of the size of the dishwashing job. Artwork showed a woman literally banked on all sides by dishes—1,000 dishes a week was her task (if she had a family of four).

Like the Duz radio commercial cited by Newman, the Lux Liquid campaign did not promise a magic helper, but it did suggest that it would significantly decrease the housewife's expended time and energy: "It was made clear in the copy that this product was not going to end dishwashing itself. This was no magic eliminator of work, but definitely was a real help that would make the work involved a lot easier. In short, a believable statement with a promise of help."[129] Appearing in women's periodicals like *Ladies Home Journal, Woman's Home Companion,* and *Family Circle,* the ads featured large drawings of housewives in aprons hemmed in by stacks of dirty dishes. "Lux helps you out with the dishes," promised a 1955 ad depicting a housewife behind bars.[130] The copy continued: "You're kept in the kitchen with 3,500 dishes a month. . . . You're always having to do the dishes, when you'd rather be doing something else." Lux promised a speedy escape, and mildness for hands. A smaller drawing of a woman holding up a clean plate and a key suggests that the product will unlock the dishes-trapped housewife. In similar ads, housewives faced down dishes in a boxing ring ("It's a constant battle to keep the sink clear of dishes!") and struggled in a neck-deep sea of dirty dishes ("If you've ever felt you were up to your neck in dishes, then Lux Liquid is for you!"). One Lux Liquid housewife in an apron gazes with horror at dishes stacked in the sink, on the counter, and on the floor as a huge clock looms above her. The copy reads: "If you had a time clock in your kitchen, you'd 'punch in' about 5 ½ hours a week 'work time' for just one dull chore—doing dishes. Stop putting in overtime," it chided.

Echoing the copy in print ads, television commercials for Lux Liquid vividly depicted both the onerous labor of dishwashing and the housewife who would be stuck with this "dull chore," "up to her neck in dishes." The script for a 1955 commercial described the action on the screen:

> Mom patting dog; zoom into dog; pop on dish which he empties, licks clean and sets in dish drainer; pan up to mom's face, which grows dour on cue; pan to dad at table. He turns to see dishes build up stop motion; boy's other hand pushes dishes out of kilter as they build up; baby tosses his dish over as camera pans with it to; pile of baby dishes; pan to show mom looking on; she is taken aback by her pile's growth.

The voice-over accompanying these images acknowledges the drudgery of this housework (and incidentally portrays the family dog as more considerate than Dad) and promised assistance: "Mom likes Rover because he cleans his own dish. Dad, on the other hand, uses 570 dishes every month. Junior uses 770. Even baby uses 250. And Mom does them all, <u>plus</u> her own 720. Mom needs Lux Liquid Detergent."[131] Other Lux Liquid commercials built on this depiction of dishpan drudgery faced by Mom. "Mom has 3,500 good reasons for wanting to eat out—the 3,500 dishes she washes every month!" began the voice-over for one commercial. But they also promised assistance: "There's no liquid like Lux Liquid for making dishes Dish-appear!" Or, as many of the ads and commercials' taglines suggested: "It's the next best thing to a dishwashing machine."

As this copy suggests, dishwashing machines remained out of reach for most consumers until well into the 1970s.[132] So throughout the 1960s and 1970s, dishwasher detergents continued to emphasize the drudgery of dishwashing and a product's ability to lighten the load. Dawn promised that "Dawn Dishwashing Liquid takes grease out of your way," for example. Dawn positioned itself as superior to other dishwashing soaps with this special new ability, and in one 1976 magazine ad enumerated all the ways Dawn provided better, easier cleaning than older dishwashing soaps: "Forget all those things your mother told you about washing greasy dishes," read the headline, as the copy went on to list examples of how wrong Mom was: "Mom said, 'Remember, always do glasses and silver first.' Sometimes we forget, Mom. But Dawn handles grease so well you can actually do a glass after a greasy roaster." "Mom said, 'Rinse with really hot water to get grease off.' That could be hard on your hands, Mom. And with Dawn, you don't have to rinse in really hot water." "Mom said, 'Clean up that gooey sink ring.' Uh-uh, Mom. With Dawn you don't have to worry so much about ring. Dawn takes grease out of your way."[133]

As the reference to hot water and hands illustrated, dishwashing advertising also continued to focus on the effects of dishwashing on housewives' hands, perhaps most famously in the case of Palmolive. Ads in women's magazines in 1966 featured large photos of the product with copy that described it as "the beauty prescription for hands that do dishes," but also an effective detergent: "You never saw more beautiful suds (suds galore!) for fastest dishwashing ever."[134] The product's label (pictured in the ad) repeated the claims, and featured a large photograph of a beautifully manicured white hand. That manicured hand came to play a starring role in Palmolive advertising. Or rather, an actress depicting a manicurist herself became the face of Palmolive. Appearing in television commercials and in print ads, the reoccurring theme depicted the humorously sassy "Madge the manicurist" recommending Palmolive to her customers, to the extent that she even soaked her customer's hand in the soap. "Don't be surprised when your manicurist softens your hands in this new <u>dishwashing</u> liquid!" read the headline in a 1966 advertisement in *Woman's Day*. Under a small inset photo of Madge, the copy continued: "Madge, the manicurist knows. . . . So different (so mild!) it can even be used to soften hands before a manicure."

Palmolive television commercials showed Madge chastising women for their unbecoming hands and startling her customers by soaking their hands in the product. In one, a shamefaced woman with rough hands asks, "Anything I can do?" Madge replies: "Do everything but start with Palmolive liquid. I use it here to soften hands. You're soaking in it." Then Madge reassuringly pats the alarmed ("Dishwashing liquid!?") customer's hand back into the clear bowl: "It's Palmolive!" "Softens hands while you do dishes," became Palmolive's tag, and as Madge always commented, it cleaned dishes well, too. In one commercial, after the great secret is revealed ("You're soaking in it"), a customer angrily tries to remove her hand: "Madge! Dishwashing ruins my hands!" But Madge promises that "Palmolive is more than mild:" "At home you'll love how it suds up, how fast it cuts through grease." In a 1975 magazine ad, Madge scolds one careless woman: "I'm a manicurist, not a magician," but Palmolive gives the customer hope: "And you get more than mildness. Those Palmolive suds are still cleaning right up to the last greasy casserole." Other feisty judgments Madge passed on customers' hands in television commercials included: "Sorry I'm late Madge. I ran all the way here." "On your hands?" and "Madge, I just got engaged!" "Who'd ask for this hand?"

Although none quite as memorably linked hand care with dishwashing in the second half of the twentieth century, other brands certainly did not abandon the appeal. As ad agency documents demonstrate, in the early 1960s the makers of Lux actively sought a marketing strategy centered on hand care. In 1964, DMB&B executives explored how the addition of a scientific-sounding ingredient, "Dermasil," to Lux should be utilized in advertisements and the legal ramifications if such advertising claimed actual improvement in hands' appearance. One memo even suggested that consumers would be deeply thrilled by this promise of more beautiful hands (despite the fact that virtually all soaps had made that promise from the beginning of the century):

> The advertising should have a mood of <u>high excitement</u> reflected by women who have discovered new Lux Liquid with Dermasil. They have tried this miraculous new product and it <u>really</u> works; it actually improves their hands. They are ecstatic and happy. They want everyone to know how really wonderful new Lux Liquid is. . . . Nothing so exciting has ever happened to them before.[135]

Like the hand-besotted husbands copy in 1930s advertising, it's hard to believe that the writers, creative staff, and executives at DMB&B truly thought that dishwashing soap could be marketed as the most exciting thing that ever happened to a housewife. In addition to illustrating a particularly condescending attitude toward real-life housewives, the memo also articulated the longstanding depiction in advertising of dishes as an especially burdensome housework task that ravaged the poor housewife's hands. As it indicates, both within agencies and in the actual advertising, dishwashing seemed especially likely to be represented as the most unrelenting, boring, and beauty-robbing of all housework.

Ivory also equated its brand with young-looking hands, as in 1970s commercials that featured demure, supposedly real housewives giving testimonials about how Ivory dish soap preserved the beauty of female hands. In one such commercial, an interviewer compliments the housewife: "You look young. Your hands look young too." "I hope it doesn't sound conceited," she answers modestly, "but I do get compliments on them." Shots of the housewife buying the product, then with hands immersed in bubbles and holding a big yellow sponge accompanied the dialogue. In another, two women are seated in a newsroom, and the announcer speaks to the camera: "Think you're seeing two young newspaper cubs? Look again. One is a cub reporter. She's 22 and single. But the other's a housewife who's been married for ten years and has two children. Now who's who? Can you tell from their hands?" Of course the viewer can't tell the difference, and after the big reveal, the announcer interviews "Mrs. Sterns:"

Announcer: Were you ever on the paper, Mrs. Sterns?
Mrs. Sterns: Yes, in school, but that was sixteen years ago.
Announcer: How old are you?
Mrs. Sterns: [modestly] I'm 33.
Announcer: You look so young! Even your hands.
Mrs. Sterns: Thank you. I try to take care of them. And Ivory really helps.

The tagline drove home the point: "It helps hands stay young looking." Whose hands? Not the unmarried 22 year old, but the housewife with kids who clearly has to contend with dishwashing in a way that a young non-housewife does not. While the ad nodded to the possibility that in the 1970s a white, middle-class, young woman might well be working for a wage, it clearly demarcated dishwashing (and all housework) as the sole province of the housewife.

As in the case of food preparation advertising, from the beginning of the century it appeared impossible to "frame" kitchen housework as anything but the work of the housewife—the married woman with kids. Like doing the laundry and cleaning the toilet, ad makers seemed unable to consider other markets during the consumer research and creative process or depict anyone doing dishes except housewives. For example, in a print ad from this same Ivory campaign, photographs compared two sets of hands with the headline "Can you match their hands with their age?" The copy went on:

> It's not easy, is it? They both have young looking hands. Nancy MacIntosh, age 20, is a teacher and hardly ever washes a dish. But Mrs. Sherron Sandrini, age 31, does lots of them every day. She says, "I have the same responsibilities most married women have. I make a home for a husband and three children. And that means housework and lots of dishes! That's why I take care of my hands and use mild Ivory Liquid."[136]

For ad makers then, the housewife, and nobody else (with the exception of the occasional dish-drying husband) did the dishes. True, children generate dirty dishes. But a single woman "hardly ever washes a dish?" As a 1956 agency report on Lux made clear, the creators of advertising just could not imagine anyone else doing the dishes. The report identified the market for Lux Liquid detergent: "The market that Lux Liquid was to go after was the young, medium well-to-do housewife who does her own household work. Actually, any young woman who ever does dishes is the market" but the focus point should be the housewife.[137] The report notes just in passing without any real interest or follow-up that "actually, any young woman" might be interested in dishwashing liquid, suggesting that in the minds of ad makers, single women "hardly touched a dish" and bachelors, presumably, ate out until they got married and could be completely disregarded as a potential consumer of dishwashing liquid.

As the 1970s continued, however, agencies had to come to terms with the fact the longstanding depiction of the apron-wearing housewife with her hands in dishwater could no longer effectively represent their product. Yet ad makers still saw dishwashing through the frame of the housewife. Like some of the laundry commercials of the 1970s, Joy dishwashing detergent resolved the tension by suggesting that the product would render the housewife's work noticeable and more appreciated by the family. Joy's particular promise was for shiny dishes—so clean and shiny that they reflected like mirrors and set a new homemaking ideal. In one such commercial, two young teenage girls are having breakfast after a sleepover. The guest admires her face in her breakfast plate:

Guest: Some shine!
Daughter: [holding up product for them to take a sniff] That's Mom's lemon fresh Joy. [girls walk to breakfront and admire display of china]

Guest: No wonder you keep your dishes out like this! Look at 'em sparkle! Gorgeous! Like everything around here.
Mom: Ooo, you are so good for my ego. You'd better stay over more often.

As the tag reiterated, over a final shot of the girls admiring their reflections in a dinner plate: "Lemon fresh Joy cleans down to the shine. What a nice reflection on you." Who "you" was couldn't have been more obvious. Almost as blatant was the product's attempt to sell Joy as an ego booster, which would engender wildly appreciative comments from friends, guests, and family.

In another such commercial, Mom and teenage daughter Jamie eagerly await the arrival of an older daughter, who is coming home for a visit:

Jamie: [worriedly] After two years, think we might seem kind of . . . square?
Mom: Square?
Jamie: Y'know. Like our dishes. Maybe they're not fancy enough anymore.
Mom: [setting table] But they still look so nice!

The older daughter, Penny, concurs with Mom's assessment when she arrives and begins admiring the home:

Penny: Nothing's changed, Mom. Everything looks just like . . . like . . .
Mom: Like home?
Penny: [seeing the set table] Oh and look—flowers. And your pretty dishes. Oooh, look how they shine . . . I can still see myself.
Mom: Still using Joy.
Penny [sniffing]: Mmmm, lemon. You know, Mom? All your little . . . touches. That's what I missed.
Mom: That's what makes a home. A lot of nice little things all put together.
Penny: Yeah, but no one puts it together like you, Mom.

Few housework commercials in the late twentieth century made appeals that so explicitly promised that family members would sit up and take notice of all Mom's "little touches," all the ways she made a comfortable home—if she used the right product. In this commercial, the product very clearly helps transform the mundane labor of dishwashing into the sublime satisfaction of homemaking and feminine care for the family. This mom wasn't wearing an apron and she wasn't shackled to a sink of dirty dishes—such a housewife could no longer effectively market housework-related products. But the housewife mom was coming in to take her place: happily caring for home and children, and receiving well-earned credit for doing so.

In another nod to the times, Joy commercials sometimes featured African American actors. The women in 1970s dishwashing commercials were not always white and in this way housework advertising directly responded to changing markets and social norms. But dishwashing advertising, like all housework advertising continued to unswervingly depict housework as women's work. Whether white or black, by virtue of her feminine care for the family and for the home, the women in 1970s dishwashing advertising transformed housework into a labor of love. In one such commercial, a young black couple has moved into a large new home, and although their dining table hasn't arrived yet, the wife's use of Joy ensures that she's already making a nice home. As they unpack, the husband runs across a box of dishes:

Husband: Hey, look!
Wife: The movers here?
Husband: No, me in this dish! Beautiful and shiny!
Wife: It's a good thing we picked up some lemon fresh Joy. [holds up bottle for him to sniff]
Husband: Mmmmm . . . lemony! Hey, so Joy's how you get the table lookin' so good. Even tonight.

In a flashback scene, they dine on a tablecloth spread on the floor in front of the fireplace. As the wife brings in a salad, the husband compliments her, then gives her a squeeze: "Everything's beautiful, Baby. I'm beginning to feel right at home." Significantly, these appeals emphasized recognition and appreciation for the post–Second Wave housewife—what a nice reflection on you!—without depicting dishwashing as drudgery or its effect on hands but rather its use in good homemaking. A 1971 market research survey for Lux indicated high recognition of Palmolive's hand-saving appeal, "strongly communicated by the antics of 'Madge the Manicurist,'" but also a strong brand image for Joy as the dish detergent for the "young, modern, efficient housekeeper." "Joy has the tangible advantage of Lemon [sic]," continued the report. "Lemon is perceived as a natural cleansing agent."[138] In other words, Joy's advertising seemed to be working to create a brand associated with great cleaning power and not significant concern about hands or about the drudgery of dishes.

In the last decades of the twentieth century, as automatic dishwashers became more common, dish detergents had to revise product lines to include automatic dishwasher detergents and devise a way to advertise them. One product, Palmolive Crystal Clear Automatic Dishwasher Powder, did so with the promise of "lemon" in a 1979 magazine ad: "At last . . . lemon freshness comes to automatic dishwashing," exclaimed the copy beneath a large photo of the product perched on a pile of lemons. But in case there was any doubt that loading the dishwasher was woman's work, the "convenient new packages" with the "easy-open spout" assured consumers: "No broken nails."[139] Such new product features, however, paled in comparison with the newest emphasis in dishwashing advertising: no spots. As historian of advertising Daniel Hill writes, in the age of automatic dishwashers: "'Spotless' and 'sparkling' were the key sell words for package design and copy."[140] Photographs of crystal clear glasses became ubiquitous in both print ads and commercials. Again and again, beginning in the 1970s and continuing to today, dishwasher detergent promised *no spots*. Cascade in particular emphasized the "spotless" claim. A 1973 Cascade dishwasher detergent ad pictures a cake seen through two wine glasses in the foreground of the photograph. The copy asks: "Your cake came out light and lovely. Should the glasses be spotty?"[141] Of course not!

Similar to the dishpan hands copy of the early twentieth century, dishwasher detergent ads and commercials sought to depict spotty glasses as a social faux pas of enormous magnitude. For instance, "Mrs. Sheryl Garbrino" related in a Cascade commercial how close she came to a major social disaster: "My fiancé and some friends were due for dinner. Mom came early to help and found *spots* on my glasses. How embarrassing!" As the voice-over explained, "If you have spot problems, you really should try Cascade." In another Cascade commercial, a couple in a late 1970s commercial relates a domestic crisis centered on glassware:

> **Pat:** I hope I never have another day like that again! [laughs]
> **Dan:** [smiling] Really! We had seventeen people over for dinner, both families.
> **Pat:** And we almost had a disaster!
> **Dan:** I was greeting people at the door . . .
> **Pat:** And then I found spots on my glasses. [flashback shot of couple gazing in dismay at the spotted glasses] Fortunately, none of the people knew what was going on. So I ran into the kitchen and washed them by hand. That got me thinking. [shot of Pat reaching for Cascade in the grocery store; demonstration of Cascade's "sheeting action" in the dishwasher]
> **Dan:** [pulling wine glasses out of the dishwasher] With Cascade, our glasses look fantastic.
> **Pat:** They do. They're practically spotless!

Pat and Dan seem pretty united on the home front, though Pat was the one who rushed into the kitchen to rid "her" glasses of those awful spots. Both agreed that spots on a glass constituted a major housework failure that would completely ruin any social gathering.

In a similar commercial from the late 1970s, a Cascade couple describes the product's magical spotless cleaning powers:

> **Martha:** Holiday entertaining is always hectic. And now that I'm working, it's even more so. But Dick helps.
> **Dick:** Like last Christmas. I was helping get out glasses and I noticed they were spotty. [flashback to Dick and Martha looking at glasses].
> **Martha:** Well, the next time I'll use Cascade.

Martha concludes with an awkward statement that clearly demonstrates the way copywriters struggled during this time to advertise housework products without using demeaning representations of housewives: "With a job, I need products I can count on. That's why I use Cascade." If Dick's "help" consisted of such miniscule acts as getting out glasses, it's easy to see why Martha was looking for a miracle product. Still, although graceless (didn't housewives need to "count on" products before women's lib?), this Cascade ad demonstrates how ad agencies and their clients were searching for a way to market housework products generally and dishwashing detergent specifically in the wake of Second Wave feminism, increasing numbers of women working outside the home, and expanding markets among nonwhite consumers. Cascade, for instance, appeared in ads that demonstrated P&G's marketing efforts to African Americans in the later decades of the twentieth century. A 1990 Cascade ad in *Essence* pictured two black couples at the dinner table, with the copy: "When Lisa made a surprise visit, you didn't have time to worry about spotted glasses. Fortunately, you didn't have to."

But whether black or white, the woman of the home remained the most concerned about clean and super shiny dishes. Like Dick, the husband who apparently believed that finding spots on dishware constituted a significant contribution to the housework, men and husbands didn't actually take on dishwashing duties in late-twentieth-century dishwashing advertising, nor do they do so in current advertising campaigns. In a very rare appearance at the dishpan, a man in his shirtsleeves tackled a sink full of dirty dishes in an early 1950s black-and-white Ajax commercial. Smoking a pipe but wearing a woman's apron, the man was certainly an anomaly in housework advertising, actually demonstrating how Ajax rinsed pots clean and commenting "This foaming action Ajax is terrific." The elves swarmed around the kitchen, showing how "Ajax cleans pots and pans up to twice as easy, twice as fast!" But then the ad concluded in a way that emphasized who would *really* be doing the dishes: "Hey, tell your wife to buy two cans. One for the kitchen and one for the bathroom." In one of the only other commercials ever to show a man doing dishes—an early 1980s Dawn commercial—a man explains the benefits of the product:

> Yeah, I'll do dishes. Especially when Jenny cooks my favorite things, like pork chops. But I hate tackling the greasy dishes—yech! Except for this. [holds up Dawn]. You can't help noticing how Dawn works on greasy gunk. [a manicured female hand demonstrates the product, pouring it into greasy water, then dunking in a plate that comes out clean] Pan came out great. And my hands don't feel greasy. Way to go, Dawn![142]

Jenny's husband might be doing the dishes, but the copy and images take precautions against emasculating him: his wife cooks him suitably masculine foods and the appearance of the pink-nailed woman's hand suggests who the real authority on dishwashing is—the unseen housewife.

Dawn flirted with a somewhat more enlightened view of shared housework in one late 1970s commercial. In a modest kitchen decorated in the popular "colonial" style, a married couple cleans up after a dinner party; a party where the man of the house (in shirt and tie) has shown off his skills in the kitchen. Wife (wearing large ruffled apron and a feathered hairdo) clues him on a better way to do dishes:

> **Husband** [walking into kitchen]: Boy, that was some party.
> **Wife** [appreciatively]: Yeah, that was some dinner you cooked.
> **Husband** [placing arm around wife's waist]: Thanks. But look what I found tucked behind the begonia [holds up a drinking glass].
> **Wife**: Ugh, just when I'm finishing a greasy pan [close-up of pan in sink of suds]. Okay, put it in.
> **Husband**: You're not gonna wash this glass in that greasy dishwater? You told me never to wash a glass after the greasy pots.
> **Wife** [smiling]: Yeah. And before I changed to Dawn Dishwashing Liquid I probably wouldn't have. [shot of product] But Dawn is really effective on grease.
> **Husband** [looks at drying dishes]: Well, everything looks great, but the glass! It will come out greasy!
> **Wife**: Now with Dawn.
> **Husband** [disbelieving]: Hm. Well, *I'll* wash it. Hey, water doesn't feel greasy. My hands don't either. And the glass sure doesn't feel greasy. Honey, you win! Dawn is effective on grease!

Hubby has clearly been on dish duty at least occasionally, because he's gotten lessons from the expert ("You told me never to wash a glass after the greasy pots"), and he's pitching in with the cooking, at least for special occasions. Mitigated in these ways, this commercial still represents a man at the dishpan.

However, this particular commercial was an exception to the rule. Well into the end of the twentieth century, ads and commercials rarely portrayed men washing dishes, and only in certain circumstances. For example, in another 1980s commercial that emphasized cleaning power, a white-aproned dishwasher at a greasy spoon diner demonstrates the grease-fighting qualities of Ajax. But he's washing dishes for a wage: "Professionally speaking, use Ajax for dishes," he states. So if a man were washing dishes, he was doing it for a living—or for purposes of satire, as in a 1989 print ad for Sunlight dishwasher detergent. In a parody of a Roy Lichtenstein pop art painting, a worried man wearing a tie and with beaded sweat on his forehead inspects a glass beer mug. "Oh no . . . SPOTS!" reads his word balloon. "And the guys will be here any minute!" Behind him we can see his friends approaching the front door, a box of pizza in their hands and the TV tuned to a football game.[143] Obviously intended to be humorous, this ad satirizes the depiction of "spots" as a social disaster. At the same time, a man depicted in the role of housewife is supposed to be eye-catching and funny, too. But like the guy washing with Dawn, the ad makes sure to avoid really calling the man's masculinity into question. Even though he's worried about spots, his beer-drinking, pizza-eating, and football-watching activities ensure that he's not *really* a housewife—he's a *guy*. It's a satire: men can't really be housewives, right?

Far more frequently than the occasional ad or commercial that put a man in the vicinity of dirty dishes, dishwashing advertising promised quick cleaning for the housewife, as in a late 1970s commercial for Thrill. The family finishes up a meal of burgers that Dad cooked on the grill, and the housewife compliments him: "Honey, that was delicious!" The kids pull Dad toward a horseshoes game: "C'mon, Dad!" He casts a quick guilty look at his wife, who assures him "Go ahead. These won't take long." Walking into the kitchen, she explains to the camera: "On weekends, Dell loves to cook. But hates to clean up. But cleaning up is easy with Peach Thrill." Similarly, even in contemporary commercials, housewife moms do the dishes. In an example of how the housewife mom is not necessarily white, a 2009 Cascade commercial stars an African American woman wearing what looks like might be corporate casual and headed out the door for work. She unloads the dishwasher while her husband looks into the fridge. As the actress sighs and rinses a not-quite-clean glass pan, the vaguely "black" female voice-over says: "Greasy bits of left on food? Your morning's *not* going to run smoothly." The commercial certainly hints at a busy "working woman's" morning, but like all housework commercials still positions housework as a woman's responsibility. She's the one loading and unloading the dishwasher in today's dishwashing commercials. She's the 2000s version of "the working housewife" first conceived by ad agencies in the 1960s.

Even new kinds of appeals continue to feature the housewife mom. In an effort to capitalize on the growing market for "green" products, the housewife mom in a 2009 print ad for Palmolive "Pure and Clear" smilingly watches her two sons, sitting at the counter in a spotless white kitchen, play with their spoons. "The clean is just one reason to love it. Your family is another," reads the copy. She's not actually up to her elbows in dishwater, but the housewife mom in this ad is still responsible for cleaning and for protecting the kids, i.e., "your family." Clorox Green Works also ran print ads for their "plant-based" detergent, cleverly headlined "Just what the world needs, another dishwashing liquid," suggesting that in fact it is precisely what the environmentally conscious household and world needs.

The twenty-first century female consumer is also still getting beauty treatments in the dishpan. A 2009 campaign for Dawn Plus Hand Renewal detergent promised to "improve the look and feel of your hands in five uses." In some of the ads and commercials, the sponge becomes personified into a man with a vaguely European accent murmuring to himself. In one, he describes himself as a "Hand Man" and as a group of women friends (including an African American woman) laugh together over dinner and then gather in the kitchen to do the dishes, he raves about their hands. In 2009 magazine ad copy signed "The Sponge," the product again promises the end of dishpan hands: "Softer feeling hands in 5 sink loads? Squeeze me, I must be dreaming." More tongue-in-cheek than the earnest 1930s comic ads depicting ravaged dishpan hands, this campaign nonetheless revisited an old theme: a product's ability to erase all visible signs of housework on a woman's body.

But dishwashing advertising no longer emphasizes drudgery, and is far more likely to sell products like Palmolive's Pure and Clear with "green" appeal. Similarly, in the case of a 2009 Dawn campaign (commercials, a guest appearances of spokeswoman Minnie Driver on "The View," and a Facebook page with over 10,000 users who "Like" the page), a dish soap brand utilizes the increasingly common appeals to the consumer's social conscious as well care for the environment. These commercials feature Dawn being used to swab clean birds and marine animals after oil spills have endangered their lives. The message? By buying Dawn with specially marked labeled (with a photo of an adorable seal pup or penguin) consumers can contribute to wildlife conservation, because P&G promises to donate money to the cause if consumers purchase the product and then visit a website. Indeed, according to the company, P&G raised over $100,000 in the fall of 2009 and donated it to the International Bird Rescue

Center and the Marine Mammal Center.[144] But dishwashing detergent advertising also continues to depict dishwashing as a housewife mom's responsibility, continuing to reinforce domestic gender norms. And if your dishwashing also results in clean and healthy marine mammals, achieving the twenty-first century ideals of good homemaking and care not just for your family but the whole planet? Well, what a nice reflection on you.

4

The Living Room

In 1959 the JWT advertising agency put together a furniture polish marketing plan for their client Boyle-Midway. The document summarized extensive consumer research on "the housewife's" attitudes toward dusting:

> While the housewife is convinced that nothing will really keep things from becoming dirty, she sees waxes and polishes as the most helpful in keeping things clean longer. Waxes and polishes contribute also to the housewife's sense of well-being in terms of making the house more attractive. "These waxes and polishes make our home look so nice." The use of waxes and polishes implies doing something extra—increased demands and obligations. Thus the housewife tries to counteract this by choosing products that require the least amount of energy and work.[1]

According to market research then, consumers used furniture polish for both practical reasons—keeping things clean longer—but also for the less tangible result of an increased "sense of well-being." However, the report also indicated that they viewed dusting and polishing furniture as an "increased demand and obligation," so companies who hoped to successfully market furniture polish would have to emphasize that the product required "the least amount of energy and work" possible. Advertising had to promise that the product, not elbow grease, could make the home "look so nice."

Furniture polish advertising had to simultaneously acknowledge the drudgery of housework and assure consumers that the product would eliminate that drudgery. Products for cleaning floors, a far more physically demanding task than dusting, made more dramatic claims about eliminating the hard labor of housework while ensuring the most healthful home environment for the family. But ad makers depicted these products as more than mere cleaning products or even health safeguards. As this chapter demonstrates, from the beginning of modern advertising to today, ads and commercials for floor-cleaning and dusting products portrayed the housewife not simply cleaning up messes but homemaking. As articulated by the JWT marketing plan, many ad makers sought to depict these products as a way to increase the housewife's "sense of well being"; specifically a sense of satisfaction at rendering a house more homelike. The representation of the housewife in such commercials consistently depicted her as the architect of all home comforts, even as the most overtly stereotypical housewife figures disappeared in the late 1970s and early 1980s to be replaced by housewife moms. Both the safety of the family and the pleasures of home and hearth depended upon the housewife's correct purchase and utilization of floor-cleaning and dusting products.

This chapter also examines the history of air freshener advertising. As the twentieth century drew to close, one aspect of making the home pleasant came to the fore of housework advertising: making the home smell good. Eliminating household odors played a role in housework advertising for decades, but in the 2000s the ideal of rendering spring-time fresh every particle of air breathed by the family became an important marketing tool, with advertising depicting it as an essential component of homemaking, transforming the housewife mom's housework labors into loving care of her family.

The living room had long been a significant social and economic domestic locus for precisely that kind of symbolic work. The Victorian parlor, precursor to the living room and family room in modern American homes, was the first domestic space dedicated exclusively to displaying middle-class financial and social status; a place decorated and maintained for exhibiting a family's solidly middle-class consumer values. As architectural styles changed in the early 1900s, and simpler, more open floor plans like the bungalow gained favor, Americans increasingly viewed family living areas in middle-class homes as both a public and private space where family bonds could be maintained and strengthened, particularly through the loving care of a wife and mother. During the post–World War II era, when Cold War fears fostered concerted efforts to bolster "family togetherness," and as television entered and dramatically changed domestic recreational life, Americans increasingly viewed the "family room" as a necessity in middle-class homes, and even the most modest suburban homes proliferating during this time often featured such a room.[2] So from its early figuration as a parlor, the living room and the family room emphasized leisure rather than the necessary domestic labors and routines of laundry work, personal hygiene, or eating. As housework advertising made abundantly clear, these rooms required cleaning but the loving labors of first the housewife and then the housewife mom ensured that this area of the house would be not simply functional but also familial: like the other three rooms I've examined, Mom's cleaning work in the living room makes a house a home.

At the turn of the century before the specialization of cleaning products, many all-purpose soaps and cleansers included a nod to floor, furniture, and woodwork care in their advertising and many pictured living rooms in their ads.[3] For example, in a 1902 magazine ad for Ivory soap, a housewife gazes at her polished floor under the headline: "Give me hardwood floors and rugs, says the woman of today," and "care for them with Ivory," reads the copy. A late 1800s print ad for Gold Dust admitted that "scrubbing floors can never be made a pleasing pastime, but one-half the labor will be saved and the results improved by using Gold Dust Washing Powder." At the end of the 1800s, S. C. Johnson offered a more specialized product: Prepared Wax for polishing floors and woodwork. The earliest prepared wax ads in *The Saturday Evening Post* featured a ring of housewives wielding mops and brooms as they made their floors shine. Ads in 1904 and 1905 included send-away offers for a booklet called "The Proper Treatment for Floors, Woodwork, and Furniture." Pictured on the cover was a housewife in a trim apron polishing the banister of a sweeping staircase. The booklet promised to help "you learn how easily and inexpensively you may beautify your home" and "how you can greatly improve the appearance of old floors." As a 1918 prepared wax ad in *National Geographic* chided: "Any housewife can easily keep her home bright by devoting a little attention to her furniture, woodwork, floors, and linoleum. All they need is an occasional application of Johnson's Prepared Wax." Or as a 1923 Old Dutch ad reminded consumers: "Clean floors make cheerful homes."[4]

As modern advertising took shape and more specialized housework products proliferated in the first decades of the 1900s, appeals for floor and furniture care products continued to emphasize what S. C. Johnson's wax promised in 1905: they would beautify and improve the appearance of a home but without extra effort. A Bon Ami housewife in an apron and cap smiles as she wrings a mop in a 1921 ad under the headline: "When Bon Ami's through—the pattern looks new." She explains in the copy that it's easy for her to achieve this new-looking linoleum: "I've heard so many people say that linoleum is hard to clean. But I'm sure they've never used Bon Ami. Why, it's really no work at all to keep linoleum and Congoleum looking bright and fresh as new with Bon Ami." In a similar ad, the housewife gazes at her shiny floor, Bon Ami in her hand, and boasts: "You'd think it was new linoleum now, wouldn't you?" Another all-purpose cleaner made even more explicit in its very name how the product would eliminate the hard work of keeping furniture and other surfaces shiny. The copy for a 1924 newspaper ad for No-Toil Kleaner promised "No rubbing—no hard work. You just No-Toil on [sic] and wipe it off with a damp sponge."⁵

Bon Ami also worked to keep other household surfaces shiny, according to a 1924 magazine ad. A young mother in an apron and cap wipes down a wall as a smiling little boy opens the door. "Ho there, you young scamp! No more smudgy finger marks! I'm just getting this woodwork nice and clean." But was Mom always the one fighting fingerprints in these early modern ads? Although the vast majority of ads depicted the housewife making the home surfaces shine with ease, a maid appeared every so often to polish a table or two. Like the early ads for laundry soap usage, servant labor makes an occasional appearance alongside the housewife. Several 1924 ads for S. C. Johnson's wax published in *Good Housekeeping* hinted at the presence of household labor. One depicted a maid cleaning the floor, but alongside the maid worked the housewife, scrubbing a wall, and little Daughter polishing the table. In another, a maid cleans the floor, but the housewife polishes a fancy dining room table as well as the curving banister. And the copy spoke to her, the mistress of the home: "You can give every room in your home that delightful air of immaculate cleanliness by using S. C. Polishing Wax."⁶

Similarly, 1924 and 1925 newspaper and magazine ads for the all-purpose cleaner Samoline depicted both housewives and maids applying the product to various household surfaces and the copy promised bright and shiny results, claiming it was "the best thing in the world to clean white woodwork." But while the drawing suggested upper-class housewives might instruct their maids to use it, the copy emphasized the product's ability to lessen "your" laborious work of polishing: "With a damp cloth and little Samoline. . . . It will do the work thoroughly, do it quicker and with less effort than anything you have ever used." As another headline promised: "Samoline will do the hardest job quickly." In short, "One of the finest things about it is, *it lightens housework*."⁷ The appeal of the product—the way it lightened housework—assumed the housewife, not the maid, would be buying and using the product. Magazine ads in the 1920s for No-Toil also pictured a maid and a housewife working together in the home, but as the name made clear and the copy emphasized, the product promised to lighten the housework drudgery faced by housewives. "No-Toil Makes House-Cleaning Easy," summarized one headline. The product even promised to actually do the work for you: "Let No-Toil do your work." "No rubbing. No hard work. Instantly removes grease, dirt, soot, finger-marks and other soil from woodwork, furniture, and tile. Makes white paint like new," pledged the copy.

In contrast, newspaper ads in the 1920s for Sylpho-Nathol, in keeping with their product's main appeal, emphasized the product's ability to protect the family from dangerous germs on the floor. One such ad depicted the housewife policing the boundaries of a safe home via floor cleaning:

> Some housekeepers think that thorough and frequent scrubbing is all that floors ever need. I had that idea, too, before I realized that average soaps and scouring compounds haven't any effect on germs which get into floor cracks and crannies.
>
> Sarah Marsh enlightened me. She popped in one Friday morning while I was mopping up the mud the Harrigan boy always brings into the kitchen when he delivers the meat. I don't believe he knows a doormat when he sees one right under his nose. Sarah watched me fill a fresh pail of scouring suds. "Goodness gracious, Ethel!" she exclaimed. "Why don't you use Sylpho-Nathol in your mop-water? How do you expect to destroy the germs in the dirt that's brought in from the street on people's shoes? Did you ever stop to think of the positive danger that is tracked back and forth across your floors from morning to night?"

At the center of this parable is the housewife, the vigilant guardian of home health and safety, ensuring the elimination of the "positive danger" tracked into the home. Ethel is very clearly policing the boundary—literally at her doorstep—between the safe haven of home and the dangerous outside world that threatens it.[8] However, in most ads, housewives like Ethel achieved that home safety with ease and convenience.

Throughout the 1930s, products continued to promise a bright and shining floor or surface with a minimum of wearisome rubbing or sweating over a mop. "Let's have easier housecleaning—use Old Dutch," began a 1937 ad in *Ladies Home Journal*, accompanied by drawings of a variety of housewives in aprons tackling assorted household tasks. The one mopping her floor remarks to her son, "Now watch this dull looking linoleum perk up!" "Let me try. It looks easy," offers Son, demonstrating how the product so effectively eliminates the hard work of cleaning linoleum that even a child could do it. Newspaper ads for Wilbert's No-Rub Floor Wax in the 1930s made a number of extravagant claims about the product's ability to clean and beautify the housewife's floors. A typical ad began with the headline: "Get rid of the RUB with this new self-polishing floor wax." The copy continued: "You can forget the drudgery of polishing floors when you use Wilbert's No-Rub. It makes the operation as easy as dusting. Simply wipe your floors with No-Rub. *That's all!* By the time the polish dries, your floors will gleam like mirrors. Let No-Rub do the heavy work for you." In other ads, the product claimed to "give dull, scarred floors ballroom beauty" and that the floors would "polish themselves." "Once beautiful floors meant hard work. Now you have No-Rub to do the rubbing and polishing for you." "No modern housewife should be without it," advised one. Another assured consumers that "It sounds like a miracle, but it's true." Radio advertising for this floor wax reinforced the appeal, as did mail-in offers for samples and free mops, and according to marketing materials sent to retailers, this product offered housewives "a sure-fire deal that goes like wild-fire."[9] No-Rub's name itself acknowledged the actual labor required to make a surface shiny. Although it promised to utterly remove that labor so that floors could "polish themselves," and that old battered floors could become as smooth and beautiful as a ballroom floors, it also made abundantly clear that the housewife caring for a home faced a particularly wearisome but also necessary task when it came to keeping the floor shiny and the home beautiful.

S. C. Johnson also continued to aggressively market their furniture and floor waxes, particularly with the radio advertising during the enormously popular *Fibber McGee and Molly* show in the 1930s and 1940s. An image of the radio stars' faces even appeared on the products' cans for a time.[10] Print ads also emphasized the ease and convenience of the product. A 1931 ad in *Ladies Home Journal* for S. C. Johnson's wax and a mechanized polishing machine available for rent from certain retailers made a particularly strong case for the product's ability to significantly lessen the work of the housewife and even totally eliminate what it described as utterly futile and wasted efforts. Illustrated by a drawing of an especially haggard-looking woman on her hands and knees, the headline read: "No woman should be doing work that doesn't do any good!" The copy explained:

> There is no use for any woman to keep on doing work on floors that doesn't do any good. With this special blended wax you make every working minute count—in results! Compare the two methods. Now you scrub a floor clean—and in no time it's dirty again. Isn't that true? Two or three times a week you go over the floor to keep it nice, and what do you see? Here and there a worn spot—that's going to grow—because it's unprotected. Then at last perhaps you try this special blended wax and you find—the wax goes on easily—much more easily than you thought. . . . And your floors are a revelation! The dry smooth wax finish makes your dusting easier. The wax fills every crack and pocket where dust and dirt now collect. Worn spots are things of the past. You never give a thought to them.

This ad combined the appeal of modern ease and convenience with a charge to the housewife about providing the best care possible to her floors. Moreover, the copy painted a pretty picture of a carefree housewife unburdened of "work that doesn't do any good." After using the advertised products, "you" would go on your merry way and "never give a thought" to your floors again while at the same time achieving shiny floors and good homemaking.

Other Johnson wax ads in the 1930s made similar promises. "Wash woodwork? Why? There's a new way to keep it from getting dirty at all," read the headline of one such ad. The copy continued: "It's a joy to see white woodwork gleaming white. But, it's a much more wonderful sensation to see it stay clean for days and days in spite of all the soiled fingers, big and little, that carelessly press against it." In this ad, the wax, not the housewife, fights the fingerprints left by a thoughtless husband and careless children and keeps woodwork gleaming. Similarly, another Johnson wax ad and the mechanical polisher emphasized how it would utterly remove a significant amount of unpleasant labor from the housewife's housework: "One of the nice things about it is what you don't have to do. There is no water-bucket or scrubbing. No getting down on hands and knees. You don't get tired or cross or wet wringing out a mop. You don't even have to get your hands dirty."[11] This copy spoke directly to the housewife, selling not just convenience but well-being: it would save not just labor but your temper as well. Another S. C. Johnson product, Cream Wax, likened the work of polishing furniture to a relaxing beauty treatment in a 1946 magazine advertisement. A housewife in a ruffled apron enthused: "It's no chore at all to give furniture a cleansing facial."[12]

Print ads in the 1930s for another all-purpose cleaning and polishing product, Wyandotte, depicted housewives using the product not merely to save themselves labor but also to safeguard the beauty of the home itself. Copy emphasized how it would not scratch "fine surfaces" and that the conscientious housewife would work to ensure the long-lasting beauty of those surfaces. "Let's take it for granted that you have a charming home," began the copy of a typical print ad, and "your home deserves this better cleaning material." Wyandotte advertising suggested the product was akin to "a thousand tiny hands to help you with your cleaning," and pictured a swarm of miniature maids cleaning mantelpiece, furniture, and woodwork. And the magic didn't stop there when it came to keeping the home bright and shiny: "Many women have found that Wyandotte brings back such freshness and luster that repainting is unnecessary." The Friend in Hat came along in a 1936 Wyandotte ad to confirm this magical ability: "Goodness, Betty, how do you keep your walls and woodwork so clean and new looking?" Two 1937 Wyandotte newspaper ads even suggested that housewives would hail the product with revolutionary fervor. In one, an army of housewives with cans of the product strapped to their backs and shouldering mops march beneath the headline "Women find new ally in war on DIRT!" "Makes the hard jobs easy," guaranteed the copy. In a similar ad, another troop of housewives raise their arms in a salute to an enormous Wyandotte can haloed by the rising sun. "Dawn of a New Day in Household Cleaning," proclaimed the headline.[13]

Legions of mop-wielding housewives celebrating their new ally in housework failed to materialize in the streets of America. But during the 1940s and 1950s a whole slew of new polishing and dusting products did hit the supermarket shelves. By 1960, for example, as described in a JWT advertising agency copy proposal for Boyle-Midway's new floor wax, consumers could choose from a range of brands that all promised long-lasting shine. Glo-Coat ads promised that "all floors love it" and after application "won't spot, stain, scuff." Simonize advertising guaranteed "the brightest floor ever," claiming "it polishes itself." Klear "dries clear as glass;" Six Month "lasts and lasts," saving time and money; Stride promised that "shine comes right back after washing." The proposal reported that marketing research showed that "shine" proved to be the quality most sought after by housewives; however, the similarity in brand claims "has inevitably made brand choice difficult for the housewife. It is understandable if she has developed the feeling that they 'pretty much are all the same.'"[14]

Consumers faced similarly understandable confusion when it came to dusting and polishing furniture, according to the 1959 JWT marketing plan for a new Boyle-Midway furniture polish. Noting that S. C. Johnson and their brand Pledge currently dominated the market, the plan summarized the types of furniture polishes that had become available: oil-based polishing products; water-emulsion cleansing products; cream waxes available beginning in the mid-1940s and requiring buffing; and finally the postwar development of silicone ingredients, which helped wax spread more evenly, made a water repellent barrier on the furniture, and prevented dust from clinging to the furniture. Brands included Johnson's Cream Wax, O'Cedar, Old English, Simonize, and Pledge.[15]

Introduced in 1958 and positioned as the first aerosol furniture wax, a "dusting-polishing wax," Pledge enjoyed instant success. As the DMB&B advertising agency executive Artherton Hobler, who helped develop marketing concepts for Pledge in 1957, remembered, the agency emphasized the convenience of the product: "a new, better, more convenient furniture polish." Hobler recalled a manager at S. C. Johnson describing the appeal of the product as "lets you wax as you dust, without waiting, without changing cloths, without any of the work of waxing."[16] The immediate success of Pledge indicated just how well that appeal worked. According to rival Boyle-Midway in 1959, real consumers sang Pledge's praises during market research interviews: "I think dusting is easy—with Pledge I don't have to polish furniture every time I dust." "My tables look nice and shiny with a minimum of work involved." "With the push button you just spray it on, wipe it off—no waiting for it to dry."[17]

When JWT planned how to market a new Boyle-Midway furniture polish, they considered copy that directly built on the success of Pledge and, as always, the perception that consumers craved shiny, shiny, shiny home surfaces: "a clearer shine because it's a cleaner shine"; "leaves nothing on your furniture but a shine"; "modern 'foam form'"; "Just press . . . poof! . . . wipe off dirt . . . it cleans as it polishes."[18] A 1959 television commercial for the new product—Plus (they had also considered names such as Care, Rave, and Wundru)—focused on a real furniture maker's endorsement of the product, and another highlighted the cleaning shine produced by the Plus. The voiceover enthused:

> It's the new foaming furniture polish Plus. Because it foams, Plus cleans, conditions, then polishes, never just glosses over soil. Watch. [dusting cloth rubbed on furniture, lifted to camera to show dirt on cloth and removal of "haze" on furniture] The cloth proves it. A clearer shine because it's a clean shine![19]

JWT carefully crafted the shot of the dirtied cloth in their marketing plan: "All a woman has to do to prove to herself that the Boyle-Midway product is actually cleaning her furniture is to look at her polishing cloth. No furniture wax has utilized this homey but dramatic device of showing soiled polishing cloths to the camera." But moreover, this particular shot would address another aspect of the marketing designed specifically with "the housewife" in mind: "A woman sometimes feels that if she doesn't work a little to apply the polish that she is not really discharging her responsibilities as a housewife. . . . The fact that the new product is 'worked into the furniture' after it is applied will ease her conscience but still allow us to make a 'no laborious rubbing claim.'"[20] Like the much cited example of cake mixes, when marketers decided housewives needed to add an egg in order to feel they were really baking, these ad makers felt that without some sense of "discharging her [homemaking] responsibilities as a housewife," the product would not succeed. It had to "ease her conscience" while simultaneously assuring it required very little real work.

Moreover, it had to promise shiny, shiny surfaces—not simply clean, but gleaming. When it came to mopping floors and cleaning and polishing the home's surfaces, ads and commercials relied heavily upon appeals that emphasized the product's ability to render the surface clean and shiny although with a minimum of effort. Advertising for waxes, polishes, and cleansers made almost a fetish of a shiny floor or surface, enshrining this unrealistic image as a new ideal of homemaking, symbolically transforming the labor of floor cleaning into feminine homemaking.[21] But that ideal, promised the ads and commercials, need not require long hours with the mop or the dusting cloth. As the Boyle-Midway marketing plan for furniture polish posited in 1959, products for floor care, dusting products, and furniture polish had to promise a pleasingly super-shiny surface without a great deal of effort.

As in the first half of the century, print ads and television commercials for various floor polishes, cleansers, and waxes from 1950 through the early 2000s continued to stress how the product would reduce the workload while at the same make floors gleam and glow. One brand, introduced in 1956, embodied its ability to reduce housework labors such as floor cleaning in one of the most memorable of all magical housework helpers: Mr. Clean. P&G's bald, muscular man in a tight white t-shirt and one large gold hoop earring first appeared on packaging and in ads and commercials for Mr. Clean liquid floor cleaner, and then an all-purpose cleaner. In the 1990s, Mr. Clean became the subject of popular speculation as to his sexual orientation. Today P&G representatives good-naturedly acknowledge the rumors but insist "he was supposed to be a genie."[22] While we might read other meanings into this buff but sexually ambiguous icon, in the context of housework advertising Mr. Clean was just another magical housework helper. And more than any other such helper, Mr. Clean devoted himself to freeing housewives from their toil. Like the Ajax knight riding to the rescue, but in a far wider and more long-lived marketing effort, Mr. Clean appeared in women's kitchens and promised housewives directly that he would be shouldering the burden of housework. The catchy jingle playing in the first animated black and white television commercial in 1958, "Meet Mr. Clean," emphasized this quality: "Mr. Clean gets rid of dirt and grime and grease in just a minute. / Mr. Clean cleans your whole house and everything that's in it." A housewife in heels and an apron follows the genie around the home, singing questions like "Can it clean a kitchen sink?" "Quicker than a wink," answers the narrator.[23]

Other 1950s commercials emphasized how Mr. Clean would assist women in their household labor. In one, a live-action housewife in a dress and a neat upswept hairdo ties on an apron—although she's already wearing one. The voiceover explains: "Now here's a woman who's so tidy she wears an apron over her apron!" Her husband, on the other hand, not so much: he tromps into her spotless kitchen in head to toe muddy fishing gear carrying a string of fish. The voiceover continues: "But she has a husband who likes to hunt and fish. And that's messy!" As the neater than neat housewife gazes unhappily at her muddy floor, the voiceover asks: "Now what cleaner can possibly clean up clean enough for her? Mr. Clean himself!" An animated Mr. Clean then strolls into the kitchen. Another 1950s commercial made an even more pointed reference to the ways that Mr. Clean and *not* Hubby would magically assist with the housework, beginning with the floors. The fully animated commercial begins by showing Mr. Clean, with what looks like a golf bag slung over his shoulder, appearing to be sneaking away from the house. The voiceover begins: "What's this? Mr. Clean departing the scene? After he's cleaned the kitchen floor [shot of immaculate kitchen floor] leaving you to clean the rest of the house?" A housewife in an apron looks wearily at her messy living room, in which two young children have scattered toys everywhere. "Never! Not Mr. Clean!" assured the voiceover. Mr. Clean then appears at the door, shaking his head at the housewife's lack of faith. He removes the cover of his golf bag and instead of golf clubs he's carrying a sponge mop. "He's not just a floor cleaner, not just part-time help. He's your full-time, all-round cleaning man!" The final shot drives home the main point: the kids hold up a drawing of Mr. Clean and Mom surrounded by hearts, captioned "Mom Loves Mr. Clean," while the voiceover concludes: "He's your steady fella for all kinds of cleaning!" "Your steady fella" who would forego a golf outing to help you mop—yes, Mr. Clean promised a special kind of household help.

A series of newspaper ads in 1959 depicted the many uses of Mr. Clean with headlines like "Mothers love Mr. Clean" with an image of a mother washing crayon marks off the wall, and "Any Mrs. Loves Mr. Clean," which showed a housewife doing laundry and cleaning the refrigerator. The series even included "Dads love Mr. Clean," but "Dad" was depicted cleaning the patio furniture, tires, the grill, the garage, and his golf balls.[24] In the late 1950s, in a commercial that was part of a write-in contest to "Name Mr. Clean," a football team in a huddle humorously discussed possible names and the qualities of Mr. Clean ("How about Wyatt Clean, because he cleaned up Dodge City!") but these rugged men weren't depicted actually using the product. Rather, Mr. Clean advertising most often depended on images of the housewife burdened by housework labor being rescued by the magical Mr. Clean.

Numerous other products made explicit mention of how difficult cleaning floors could be, and promised that their product would liberate the burdened housewife. A 1950s animated commercial for Stride floor wax painted an especially vivid picture of the housewife trapped in a never-ending battle to keep her floors beautiful. The exhausted looking, somewhat dumpy, housewife is scolded by the male announcer for her failure to procure the product and free herself. As she tiredly puts her mop away the dialogue begins:

Housewife: I just waxed my floors.
Announcer: But you didn't take our suggestion.
Housewife: [sad confusion pulling her face into a mask of misery] What?
[a crowd of children thunder by leaving black tracks all over the floor]

Well, better re-wax my floors. [near tears, exhaustion bending her over, she reaches for her mop]
Announcer: You wouldn't have to if you'd use that new floor wax from Johnson's.
Housewife: [addled] Johnson's? New wax? [then knowledge dawning] On television! Stride! [cut to live-action demonstration of product, referencing an earlier television commercial for the product] Yes, big splash, breaks into little beads on Stride. That means it won't spot.
Announcer: Stride stays on so you wax less often.

After "Time Passes," the announcer revisits the housewife, who's looking far more chipper and sporting a fluffier, prettier hairdo.

Announcer: Well?
Housewife: Well, now I use Stride Wax.
Announcer: And your family? [children once again charge through, leaving a mess in their wake]
Housewife: Same. But now I'm not rewaxing all the time. [demonstrates the ease of quick touch-up mopping] I just damp mop than shine back the luster again and again. Stride. [proudly] Glad I remembered Stride!
Announcer: [condescendingly] Me too!

Notable for its heavy-handed depiction of the housewife's labors, and a particularly stereotypical depiction of the dopey housewife requiring an authoritative male announcer to figure out how to do housework, this commercial also clearly emphasized how the product would eliminate or greatly lessen the worst of this labor.

Another animated housewife in a 1950s Stride floor wax commercial also enjoyed the convenience of this product: she demonstrated how the "self-polishing" product made floors easy to mop—"Traffic marks buff away in seconds"—and repelled spills like a broken egg or Junior's pogo stick scuffs. As the voiceover explained: "The shine on this floor will bounce back again and again. Because this smart lady has already given it a protective coating with a brand new Johnson's floor wax." The "smart lady" housewife appeared again and again in floor-cleaning product commercials, always beaming at her sparkling floors, made immaculate with a quick swish of her mop. A 1961 Trewax floor wax commercial featured a novel camera angle—up through the floor—to better see how the wax coating kept the floor shining even after spilled coffee and milk. It compared the "dull yellow film left behind by the usual floor wax" with the "crystal clear beauty of Trewax," as demonstrated by the housewife on her hands and knees mopping up the spilled milk. Similarly, a 1966 newspaper ad for Bravo floor wax promised it would "Put a shine on your floor detergents won't wash out! Lets you wash away dirt yet still keep the shine!"[25] The housewife's ability—using the right product of course—to transform dirty floors into gleaming, shining surfaces transfigured mere floor cleaning into feminine homemaking. As in all housework advertising, the housewife in floor-cleaning advertising defined domesticity, framing all household labor not as simple grunt work but satisfying feminine homemaking.

Another floor-cleaning product proposed a new level of good homemaking, stressing how "clear" your floor's shine would be in a 1963 commercial. Crystal Floor Wax invented a new housework problem—the "shattered shine" of inferior waxes—and promised to remedy it. The voiceover, accompanied by a shot of a woman's high heel shattering a piece of acrylic, began: "Walking on a newly waxed floor is something like walking on glass. When your heel hits, the shine shatters." The bemused housewife in a nice blouse and sculpted hairdo holds up the acrylic worriedly then bends it to show how "it breaks into hundreds of tiny cracks that can catch and hold dirt." But "Crystal's shine," on the other hand, "is a shatterproof shine."[26] A floor not only clean but radiantly shiny was by now well established as the housework ideal of the twentieth century. In a similar claim, a 1970s commercial for Future opened with a housewife holding up a bottle of the product and gazing through it, as the male voiceover exclaimed over its clear but tough properties: "If you think it looks good in the bottle, wait'll you see it shine on your floor." Another 1960s Future commercial demonstrated how long that shine would last. When Teenage Son drops a bag of groceries on the floor, the housewife gestures to the still gleaming floor, holds up a bottle of Future and enthuses: "For a shine that can really take it." Floor product commercials insisted that with minimal effort housewives could convert their dingy linoleum into an immaculate expanse of gleaming beauty; a surface that would entrance her as she leaned on her mop and gazed enthralled at her beautiful home, enjoying the fruits not of mere housework but of satisfying homemaking.

In early 1970s commercials, housewives continued to demonstrate how a particular product could withstand the scrapes and scuffs of their family, and continued to pursue blindingly shiny floors. Two such commercials built on the product-demonstration shot with side-by-side comparisons of housewives pushing mops up and down a strip of linoleum. In the Step Saver commercial, a spokesman in a suit discusses the superior lasting shine of the Step Saver side of a divided floor, while two housewives in casual shirts and jeans, each holding a mop and a pail, stand mutely by. According to Mr. Suit, a week ago one of these housewives mopped with Step Saver, the other with an unnamed brand. Now the test: comparing how well each side withstands shoe scuffs, described as "a top floor cleaning problem." Naturally, Step Saver, with "self-stripping action," withstands the abuse better and in its very name promises less labor for the housewife holding the mop.

Similarly, a 1972 Mop and Glo commercial compared the floor-cleaning prowess of two housewives. The opening shot focuses on two identical houses, then cuts to the inside of one, where a tired looking housewife in jeans and an oxford shirt, her hair held back in a head scarf, is on her hands and knees scrubbing the kitchen floor. In the next shot, her neighbor, a pretty housewife in a red turtleneck sweater and slacks, comes strolling into her own kitchen. The voiceover explains: "Five Elms thinks the way to keep a floor beautiful is to scrub and wax. [Mrs. Five Elms raises a weary hand to her head as she kneels among the suds] It's hard work! Seven Elms discovered an easy way to keep her floors looking beautiful and she does it every time she damp mops." The close up of Mrs. Seven Elms shows her pretty long hair and her gold hoop earrings as she enthuses that Mop and Glo "cleans and shines." Directly equating the housewife with her house—"Five Elms" and "Seven Elms"—this commercial clearly linked the housewife with the "hard work" of "keeping her floors beautiful." She's married to the house, Mrs. Seven Elms, and she's fulfilling her housework responsibilities with ease, leaving her home shining with beauty.

It became increasingly unfeasible to represent women with images of "Mrs. House" as the 1970s progressed and the stereotypical image of the housewife came under attack by feminist critics and also became more unpalatable to ordinary consumers. But the particularly laborious nature of floor cleaning continued to shape advertising for these types of products, and many commercials in the 1970s and 1980s focused on how the product would reduce that labor. Drawing on a theme that appeared again and again throughout twentieth-century advertising and briefly seemed to offer one way to contend with changing gender norms in the 1970s, they emphasized the "libratory" qualities of the product. In advertising, of course, "liberation" only ever meant purchasing particular brands in order to expedite housework responsibilities, such as the primly dressed housewives in the 1960s Ajax ad holding aloft protest placards that demanded "Rally Round Ajax for Spring Cleaning!" and "Down with Dirt. Down with prices too." Equating the products with the liberation and protest movements of the time, the headline of the ad offered housewives a "revolution" of their own: "Join the Ajax movement today . . . and save!" According to these ad makers, the housewives' revolution would be couponed.

Floor cleaning product advertising included some especially overt examples of this theme. For instance, a commercial for "new and improved" Klear floor polish airing in 1974–1975 opened with a shot of young housewife on her hands and knees, scrubbing the kitchen floor.

Her mother walks in with a bag of groceries and accosts the housewife: "Up off your knees, Catherine! You don't polish floors like that anymore!" Housewife daughter protests, referencing that ever-elusive shine: "But you always did Mom and I want that great shine you got with Klear." Her mother proffers the product: "But now I get it with this, New Klear." In the final shot, daughter beams ecstatically at the floor, exclaiming: "New Klear shines as well as old Klear! But it's easier!" Her wise mother concludes: "You got to keep up with the times dear! So up off your knees and mop on that clear Klear shine." Drawing on the longstanding theme in advertising of modern products freeing housewives from the hard labor of floor cleaning, these commercials seem to also be attempting to acknowledge changing gender norms but in this case, "keeping up with the times" simply meant purchasing a new product.

Even the old standby image of a magic helper in a product attempted to offer twentieth-century liberation in one 1980s commercial for Mop and Glo. It pictured the housewife as a Cinderella, rescued from her toil by a Mop and Glo fairy godmother. In the commercial, a pretty and petite Cinderella in rags tiredly scrubs the floor. The male voiceover describes this hard housework task: "Scrubbing. Waxing. Once doing the floor was hard work. Then came Mop and Glo. [product magically appears in Cinderella's hand] Mop and Glo cleans and shines at the same time." After swishing the product over the floor, it's transformed into, literally, ballroom beauty and Cinderella also suddenly wears a long formal gown. "The next best thing to a fairy godmother," concludes the voiceover, and in the final shot of the product we see a glass slipper resting beside it.

Still more pointedly, another early 1980s commercial touted the product as an important aspect of women's liberation and promised even more freedom with its new formula. The commercial began with a shot of a large crowd of women, including an African American, scrubbing and scrubbing a floor. They're wearing casual pants and shirts, some stopping to push their sweaty hair off their foreheads or press a hand to their haggard faces. The male voiceover began with a history lesson: "In 1971 millions of women got up off their knees, threw down their brushes, and started doing their floors the easy way. Mop and Glo revolutionized floor cleaning." The women leap to their feet cheering, then smilingly take up mops. The voiceover in this Mop and Glo commercial depicts women in need of freedom from the burdens of housework but continued to view housework as feminine homemaking. The woman of the house would be able to whisk a mop over the floor instead of scrubbing on her hands and knees, but it would still be her pushing that mop. Commercials could no longer depict enslaved housewives, like the bedraggled Stride housewife struggling to keep her floors clean. But the housewife as sole frame for household labor continued. They're wearing more comfortable clothes—not an apron in sight—but they and they alone are cleaning the floors and are subsequently enraptured by the shining expanse of their immaculate floors, clear evidence of their loving homemaking.

Mr. Clean remained the most widely circulated image of a magical helper in floor (and general housework) cleaning advertising during this transitional period, assisting women in the quest for gleaming home surfaces. A slightly suggestive 1965 commercial depicted Mr. Clean as almost menacing—but to dirt, not the housewife. Over a jazzy saxophone soundtrack and in a beat poetry-like chant, two models talk suggestively about the product:

> **Brunette:** [in husky hushed voice] He's mean. [winks]
> **Blonde:** [in breathy little girl voice] Who's mean?
> **Brunette:** He's mean.
> **Blonde:** You mean, Mr. Clean.
> **Brunette:** I mean, the New Mr. Clean. He's meeean.
> **Blonde** [innocently] What made him so mean?
> **Brunette:** [close up of her lips] Dirt. He hates dirt.

As shots of the product cleaning various household surfaces flash by, the blonde gasps and moans in amazement: "Oooh! Ooo!" In case the humorous sexualizing of Mr. Clean wasn't overt enough, over the ending shot of an animated Mr. Clean, a male voiceover says roughly "He hates dirt" and a sultry female voiceover responds "I *love* him." Newspaper ads in the campaign also depicted a "mean" Mr. Clean—with a smiling housewife cuddling up to the product bottle, and the tagline: "You'll love him."[27] Like the Jell-O housewives coaxing and conning their husbands with dessert, this campaign demonstrated certain entrenched sexist ideas about what would be a "funny" and attention-grabbing depiction of women and housework. The models having orgasmic reactions to Mr. Clean's prowess aren't exactly the apron-wearing housewives seen in early advertising, but then again, that housewife in an apron was still appearing in concurrent newspaper advertising for Mr. Clean products.

Throughout the 1970s and 1980s, even when Mr. Clean appeared to work his magic, housewives did the actual housework. Cleaning the kitchen floor in a trippy 1970s commercial, one housewife gazes in awe at her reflection in the shining floor—you can even see her wedding ring. As she jumps for joy, lemons (Mr. Clean's new scent) rain down from the ceiling.[28] Taking a deep sniff of the product, she appears to hallucinate more lemons. An early 1980s commercial pitted Mr. Clean in a boxing ring against "dirt, grease, and grime," but then a woman in a cardigan and slacks wipes down the stove and the bathroom. She crouches by a bucket, holding the product, and sings a love song to the animated Mr. Clean on the label: "He hates a dull and streaky floor . . . He finds the shine and leaves it gleaming," then simpers the tagline, "Love that Mr. Clean."

Hinting that with the right product, the housewife would receive familial recognition for her labors gave ad makers one possible way to transition the housewife figure into the post–Second Wave era. Yes, she'd be the one doing the floor cleaning (or the laundry or the shower scrubbing), but now the product would ensure "noticeable" results. Like the 1970s laundry detergent commercials in which family members notice and appreciate Mom's work, a series in the late 1970s and early 1980s depicted a housewife mom washing kitchen floors with Mr. Clean and, hours later, friends and family members skirting the floor thinking it was still wet. One visiting friend is particularly astonished, when she warns her son to step carefully:

Friend: Jimmy, don't! The floor's waxed!
Housewife: No, it's dry. I washed it hours ago.
Friend: Whaaat? Oh, you're kidding. [kneels down and feels floor] Wow, that shine made me think it was wet!

Husbands and children expressed similar amazement at the housewife's ability to make the kitchen floor shine—with the help of Mr. Clean. Like the Clorox housewives stunned to realize that laundry really did matter to their families, this Mr. Clean housewife enjoys the admiration of friends and family for her careful choice of housework product and the resulting homemaking success.

The Mr. Clean brand has, however, as in the "Dads love Mr. Clean" print ad, occasionally been marketed with images of men using the products. In a 1980s commercial, one of the two or three that starred a real actor as Mr. Clean, the genie wanders into a suburban backyard and talks to a man scrubbing what might be screen doors.

Mr. Clean: Spring cleaning?
Man: Yeah, the whole weekend shot. And with the Yanks playing tomorrow. A double header yet! [scrubs frantically]
Mr. Clean: New improved Mr. Clean would get your work done today.

Just to emphasize the gender diversion of cleaning (if the outdoor cleaning and the reference to professional sports wasn't enough), the commercial also included shots of a woman's hand and a glimpse of her skirt demonstrating the product inside the house.

Inside the house, keeping home surfaces shining remained paramount in housework advertising. In the 1960s and 1970s, advertising for furniture polishes containing lemon oil (or at least lemon scent) assured consumers that this fresh-smelling element would achieve both cleanliness and a shining home surface. Drackett Company's Behold with lemon oil, introduced in 1966, enjoyed high sales, immediately inspiring competitor S. C. Johnson to create Favor, also with lemon oil. They quickly followed with Lemon Pledge in 1967, and a commercial jingle reworking the popular tune "Lemon Tree":

> Lemon Pledge is very pretty
> Puts the shine down lemon good
> Lemon Pledge as you're dusting
> Brings new luster to the wood.
> Lemon Pledge cleans so easy
> Lemon way to make wood glow.
> Lemon Pledge as you're dusting
> Adds protection as you go.[29]

The jingle illustrated the most widely used points in furniture polish appeals: bright shine ("puts the shine down lemon good, brings new luster to the wood"); convenience ("cleans so easy"); and a facilitator of home comforts, of a "pretty" home, where the wood "glows." Even as the housewife mom in casual clothing took the place of housewives in heels in the 1970s and 1980s, these advertisements continued to transform household tasks into homemaking with the frame of female care.

For example, the female-sung jingle for a 1970s Favor commercial described how beautiful "your" home could become: "Favor lets the beauty of the wood shine through." A housewife asked consumers a frank question: "Your furniture ever look a little dull or streaky? Maybe you've got a wax build-up problem. And maybe you should be using Favor?" By this time, dulling "wax build-up" was the enemy in most furniture polish advertising, and many 1970s commercials chastised housewives for their failure to ensure super-shiny wood in the home. In a Liquid Gold furniture polish commercial, a woman's manicured (pink polish) hand gestured to a cracked tabletop while the female voiceover warned: "Look how dry and lifeless this furniture is." The author of *The Furniture Doctor*, who worked in the 1970s as a celebrity spokesman for Old English, asserted that Old English Lemon would "restore old, parched, aging wood," and bring out its "gleam and glow." A Wood Crafter furniture polish commercial compared the "beautiful shine" left by the product with a table "hand rubbed 100 times" and showed no discernable difference: the commercial neatly addressed the important "no laborious rubbing" aspect of polish appeals while also touting the product's ability to assist the housewife in making sure her pretty home remained a gleaming sanctuary of dust-free beauty.

Similarly, a 1970s Pledge commercial promised "Rubbed-in beauty of paste wax . . . instantly." Print ads for other brands also depicted housewives gazing into their gleaming woodwork after minimal effort. Endust, as the name suggested, warned against wax buildup in a 1967 newspaper advertisement. "Clean up dust. Don't spray wax on it," counseled the copy accompanying a large photo of the product and the product's label picturing a woman's hand dusting. Bon Ami Dust 'n Wax could not recommend less waxing per se, but it did suggest in a 1965 print ad that this particular wax would reduce the housewife's labors—even as it bluntly admitted that "nothing makes housework fun" in the headline. In an attempt to negotiate the new demands on ad makers precipitated by Second Wave feminism, this particular campaign sought to more "realistically" depict housework. The copy continued: "Let's face it, housework is no fun. But Bon Ami Dust 'n Wax does make it a little easier. Because Dust 'n Wax gives hard wax protection without hard work. With Dust 'n Wax, there's no need to spend hours cleaning and waxing your furniture. Dust 'n Wax won't make housework fun. But it helps."[30] This copy offers a clear example of how advertising for dusting and polishing products, like all housework products, struggled during the pivotal late 1960s and 1970s to transition the increasingly socially unacceptable housewife figure in housework advertising into the twenty-first century.

Like other housework products, dusting, polishing, and floor-cleaning products learned that the housewife mom offered an effective way to make this transition. For instance, the diligent housewife mom protecting her children by providing the family with immaculate floors made an appearance in a 1970s commercial for Spic and Span. The commercial's script explicitly described how the housewife mom puts her children first and cleans her floors not out of a stereotypical advertising housewife's enslavement to shiny surfaces but rather because she is a caring and loving mother. This commercial opens with a young mother wearing a casual button-down shirt and jeans sitting on the kitchen floor. A feathered blonde hairdo frames her fresh young face, as she gazes lovingly at her toddler sitting near her and her infant cooing on the floor in front of her. Looking directly at the camera, she delivers a housewife mom's manifesto:

> Would you let your little baby crawl on your kitchen floor? Well, I let my little baby. And my big baby. I can let them play to their hearts' content because my kitchen floor is clean. I just washed it with Spic and Span. I trust Spic and Span. [cut to a side-by-side demonstration of mop and product, contrasted against competitor] It cuts through greasy kitchen dirt better

than leading liquid cleaners. [cut back to close up of Mom's pretty face; she speaks earnestly and seriously] These days my mother-in-law is raving about what a great housewife I've become. But that's not why I care about getting my floor really clean. I do it because I care about being a good mother.

The tag concluded: "Spic and Span. For floors clean enough for a baby." Every ounce of this Spic and Span mom's effort and attention is focused on her children. For them and for them alone she mops and cleans. She scorns her old-fashioned mother-in-law's view that she's a great housewife. It's not about keeping the house clean; it's "about being a good mother." This commercial is a vivid early example of how the ad industry and their housework product clients answered the biggest question posed by a post–Second Wave society and marketplace: how can we sell housework products to housewives without using stereotypical depictions of housewives? This commercial exemplifies the "unifying concept" ad makers sought in response to increasing consumer sensitivity about demeaning depictions of women in the media in the clearest, starkest terms: the housewife mom, who's using the product not because she's "just a housewife" but because she "cares about being a good mother."

Housewife moms in 2009 advertising still ensured the safety and well-being of the little ones frolicking on the floor in floor cleaner marketing. In a 2009 commercial for Resolve carpet cleaner, the brand's actor spokes-man stands in a living room looking down at a young girl playing with some blocks. Her mother stands next to him. "Cute kid. Bet you think that carpet's pretty clean," Resolve Man ominously states. The puzzled housewife mom answers: "I just vacuumed a second ago." However, as the spokesman explains, Mom has not *really* cleaned the carpet or safe-guarded her child's well-being: "You only cleaned the surface," he says, as the screen cuts to a shot of scary animated dirt seething in the depths of the carpet. A worried expression creasing her pleasant face, the housewife mom rushes to lift her innocent daughter from the suddenly menacing plush carpet. After applying the product in a demonstration shot, Resolve Man says, satisfied: "That's clean." "*Really* clean!" agrees the housewife mom, the sanctity of her home restored. The image of menacing ani-mated germs, hidden in a carpet's nap and threatening childhood's pre-cious health, and the necessity of certain dust-busting products wielded by the housewife-mom-guardian continues to appear in floor-cleaning product advertising.[31] Even Swiffer utilized this kind of appeal, detouring from its "Mr. Mop" campaign to run an ad in *Good Housekeeping* and *Ladies Home Journal* in 2009 that featured a cute toddler, hands and feet on floor, peering through his legs at the camera, and the headline: "Your floors are their playground."[32]

Such appeals illustrated the advertising industry's answer to the perplexing problem of how to market housework products without depictions of, or rhetoric about, housewives, and not coincidentally also tap into what experts identified as the "mom market." By emphasizing women's role as "mom," the new culturally acceptable mode of speaking about domesticity, ad makers can continue to frame housework as feminine homemaking without using stereotypical images of housewives. As Roger Clayton, then CEO of the Grey advertising agency (United Kingdom branch) explained during a 1988 Grey agency roundtable on the portrayal of women in advertising:

> It isn't that it matters what you show the woman doing, you can show her cooking or washing up or all of those things which people have been worried about showing women doing. What you have to do though is make sure that women you give that portrayal to, you are making it clear that she has that activity in perspective. She isn't any longer the slave, or the drudger [sic]. She is doing it because she wants to, because she chooses to do it and because she's got lots of other things that she does. Things that are just as interesting or more so.[33]

Clayton spoke for many in the advertising world, when he asserted that as long as the woman in the commercial or ad "isn't any longer the slave, or the drudger," housework could remain a gendered labor in ads and commercials. But "lots of other things that she does" quickly narrowed down to "mothering" and the housewife mom became *the* twenty-first century frame for housework in advertising. And when it came to cleaning floors and home surfaces, products promised that she could accomplish these essential homemaking tasks with an ease that would allow her to quickly get to the "lots of other things" she wanted to do.

Similarly, furniture polishing products turned to the housewife mom figure to advertise their products as time saving aids to making home surfaces shine, i.e., good homemaking. A 1984 magazine ad for Favor Lemon depicted a grinning young child leaning on a flawlessly gleaming surface, and the copy spoke directly to the housewife mom intent on maintaining that wood beauty: "Favor resists smears. No kidding. A Favor shine is a tough shine to beat because its unique formula fights off everyday smears, smudges, and fingerprints."[34] Pledge advertising during this time took the ideal of glowing furniture to a new high. By the 1980s, a really shining table had to not simply look shiny but actually reflect the woman's house-loving face as she gazed with smiling adoration at her consumer spouse, the house itself. Some ads compared the Pledge-dusted table with others, contrasting a blurry reflection with a clear one. "I just can't see myself using anything but Pledge," read the headline below a photograph of a grinning woman admiring her reflection in her impossibly gleaming table.[35] "Clearly the more beautiful shine every time you dust," often read the tagline. "How deep is your shine?" questioned a 1984 ad, suggesting that just polishing a surface wasn't enough to really ensure the beauty of the home, specifically, the "beauty of the wood." Print ads in this campaign included testimonials by "furniture care experts" and offers for a promotional videotape entitled "Furniture Care." Another 1984 print ad emphasized the "beauty of the wood" while assuring the consumer no laborious rubbing: "When you spray Pledge on your cloth, you pick up lots of dust quickly and easily. Plus, you get a clear, natural shine no other dusting spray can match. So in the time it takes to dust, you can also bring out the natural beauty of your wood." Just to make clear who exactly wielded that cloth, a 1989 Pledge ad in *Good Housekeeping* featured a woman admiring her wedding portrait— and the dresser it adorned. "16 years. A lot of memories. (And no build-up). And every week I've dusted it with Pledge." The tagline emphasized how the product offered more than simple dust removal: "With Pledge, dusting can be beautiful."[36] With Pledge, "dusting" meant more than removal of dust. It meant the beautifying labor of homemaking.

Similar Pledge ads promised that the product would do more than remove dust: it would make the home shiny and beautiful. In one, a woman's pinkly manicured hand sprays Lemon Pledge on a white cloth; the can reads, "Waxed beauty every time you dust." Dusting need not be simply removing dirt, but enhancing the shining charms of "your" home every time "you dust." "Get more out of dusting with Pledge," promised the tagline. A 1982 ad published in *House Beautiful* and other magazines featured a large photograph of a woman's face reflected in her table with the headline "Now that's what I want from dusting . . . a deep shine." It was not enough to just dust, as she explained in a clear example of how furniture polish appeals linked their products not just to housework but homemaking and a sense of well-being:

> I feel so good about dusting with Pledge. That deep, rich shine tells me my furniture is really clean . . . not blurry like my old polish. Pledge makes my wood shine so clear. I can see more of its natural beauty. And that makes my whole house look great. A deep, clear shine. . . . A more beautiful home . . . I get so much more out of dusting with Pledge!

Like the Joy dish detergent commercials that promised recognition for and satisfaction with housework—"What a nice reflection on you"—Pledge depicted the female domestic figure as seeking not just a clean home but a "more beautiful home" and a sense of well-being: "I get so much more out of dusting."

In contemporary Pledge product campaigns, the idea of housewife moms "getting more" out of dusting continues. The copy and tagline in 2009 print ads for Pledge Multi-Surface—for use on glass, wood, metal, and electronics—summarizes the product's ability to lessen the laborious aspects of housework while also making a home not just clean but beautiful: "Cleaning made simple. With Pledge Multi-Surface, you can clean more faster. That's the beauty of Pledge." The product casts a shadow that reveals Pledge is equivalent to a whole bucket of cleaning products. In a television commercial for this product, the premise, meant to be somewhat tongue-in-cheek, places a housewife mom in a large glass-enclosed room on a sound stage, as the male, British-accented announcer explains this is to demonstrate the product's abilities. The actress enclosed in the room looks Asian American and in her first line defines herself as a housewife mom: "Excuse me, I've gotta get my kids soon. I don't have time to clean all this." Except, of course, with the product, she does, and gazes happily around the room exclaiming, "Wow, I'm done!" Undoubtedly in time to fetch her children.

In fact, a Pledge print ad with a coupon that appeared in a 2008 issue of *Good Housekeeping* directly positioned the product as more than a way to clean. Rather, it promised better homemaking and mothering. The copy explains that though it would not end all housework, it will lighten the load: "Keeps your furniture looking so good, you can dust less often." More significantly, it pictures a nonwhite (her ethnicity is not clearly determined) housewife mom reading a book with her son who smiles up at her happily. "Less time as the maid. More time as the mom," reads the copy. Here the brand's appeal draws on both a longstanding appeal and the new momism, suggesting that, with the right housework product, good mothers can quickly finish up their homemaking duties to focus on their children. But the immaculate, gleaming living room also reinforces the high standard for that homemaking, linking shiny furniture to loving feminine domestic care. In a similar coupon-bearing 2009 ad, a housewife mom in t-shirt, jeans, and a purple fitted cardigan busily trots down the stairs with a basket of laundry, whisks away the dust, and then relaxes on the floor with her kid and some building blocks. "The kids: Home in 20. The cleaning: Done in 15," read the headline. Pledge Multi-Surface Cleaner is, according to the copy, "perfect for multitasking moms." Or, more specifically, multitasking moms who will take care to finish their chores before the kids come home. That is to say, good housewife moms, who frame advertising's depiction of domestic labor, transforming it from a chore into feminine care for the family and for the home.

Housework advertising regularly suggested throughout the twentieth century that good mothers would utilize the latest products and technology in order to devote more time to their children. And certainly it was nothing new for a housework ad to promise reduced drudgery—"less time as the maid." Still, these appeals make abundantly clear how current housework advertising still depicts housework as the labor of women caring for their home—"you can dust less often." But it is labor done by housewife moms who are defined not by their domestic labors but rather by their relationship with their offspring. They seek to beautify their furniture and thus their homes with improbably spotless and gleaming woodwork, using a minimum of effort, not because they are obsessed with home cleaning but because they care about being a good mother and homemaker.

An important exception to the widespread representations of housewife moms dusting and cleaning floors is the female figure in Swiffer product marketing, who although she conforms to the aesthetic of the housewife mom (casually but neatly dressed, pretty but not sexy, slim, cleaning a huge and beautifully furnished home) is rarely shown with children or the signs of children in the home. The P&G brand Swiffer, introduced in 1998, includes lines of floor care and dusting tools with disposable components meant to replace the mop and bucket method of cleaning floors. In recent years, the advertising for the Swiffer products put forth the premise that any woman who tries them (money back guaranteed) will "break up" with her old mop, broom, and feather duster. In these commercials and in the online marketing for Swiffer, the jilted housework tools pursue their former lovers, sending flowers and emails and standing longingly and wistfully outside the women's homes. The tools are not cartoonish or wearing clothes and are, of course, expressionless. But the commercial's clever use of music makes clear the housework tool's emotion. In the original commercials, that music is "Baby Come Back," a popular 1978 song by the rock group Player. Recent commercials in the same vein utilize "Don't You Want Me" the plaintive 1981 song by pop group The Human League. In 2009 commercials, jilted mops and brooms appeared to even more overtly agonize over the cruel rejection they've suffered as the 1980 "Love Stinks" by the J. Geils Band plays.

An advertising industry journalist described this Swiffer campaign in 2008, praising it for its consistent message ("Use Swiffer and you'll never use old-school cleaning tools again") and describing the target consumer for this campaign:

> Life's not fair for the marketers at Proctor and Gamble; they have to leap far higher hurdles than many in advertising's lot. While hawking an already sexy car or stylish pair of leather loafers requires creative energy aplenty, it can't be as tough as establishing the cool factor for toilet tissue, dandruff shampoo or . . . a mop [sic]. Since its introduction in 1998, Swiffer's been

out to convince consumers that the old mop in the hall closet has a date with the dump. And dating, oddly enough is the theme in a new series of ads . . . helped along mightily by a forgotten 1970s rock anthem.[37]

The author of this article reiterates what a marketing executive admitted in a 2003 interview: "Floor care is so boring," said Dave Baker, VP of marketing for Hoover vacuum cleaners.[38] Poor P&G! Their products are fundamentally unsexy. As they had for decades, these marketers wrestled with how to sell "boring" housework products. And as they had since at least the 1970s, they also struggled with how to effectively market to women who did not want to see themselves depicted as hausfraus but also didn't want to see homemaking itself disparaged.

The Swiffer women aren't surrounded by children and might not even be married since unlike most housewife moms in advertising, gold wedding rings aren't prominently featured. However, their gender, their pretty-but-not-sexy appearance, their casual but neat dress so typical of the housewife mom, and their "relationship" with the tools and their houses, are what make the Swiffer women another incarnation of the housewife figure in advertising, the feminine symbol of domesticity who's still married to the mop. The Swiffer premise sets up women as being in love with or at least romantically linked to housework products—and the house. In these commercials, the actress almost always applies the product and gazes with adoration at the results: an absolutely immaculate, shining surface in a nicely appointed, expansive home. They are the "you" in housework advertising that always views the labor of keeping a home clean as gendered work, as feminine care that transforms housework into feminine homemaking.

Swiffer marketing is by no means limited to television commercials. In the first six months of 2002, for example, P&G spent $25 million on marketing a motorized version of Swiffer, the Wet Jet, including paid product placement on "The View." More recently, 2008 advertising included a YouTube contest in which consumers sent in humorous videos of how they've "broken up" with their old mops. In another bid to encourage consumer interaction with the advertising, at the Swiffer website viewers can play an online game called "Do You Match?" It pits "The Mopey Mops" (the viewer's avatar and a mop wearing a droopy necktie) against "The Wet Jets" (a stylish woman and her sparkling Swiffer product), answering questions highlighting the marital accord of the woman and her Wet Jet, the sad inadequacy of the mop, and the trials of the poor woman stuck with this inadequate mate. The Swiffer Facebook page has been especially successful at eliciting consumer interaction, with hundreds of users responding to promotions and commenting on Swiffer postings. For instance, over

1,100 people commented on the June 9 post "Fill in the blank. My floors would be BLANK without my Swiffer." The product line recently underwent rapid expansion, including in 2008 a whole new line of co-branded products with Febreze air freshener. Advertising for those products included a blitz—with samples and print ads—on the Grand Central Station to Times Square shuttle subway in New York City, an example of "ER/PR" (external relations and public relations) marketing.[39] The Swiffer brand will probably continue to depict forlorn housework tools pining for clean-cut housewives Swiffering immaculately clean and shiny home surfaces for the next few years. Its widespread recognition ensures a longer life than most advertising campaigns.

Another brand that depicts lovelorn housework products in contemporary campaigns is Mr. Clean. Mr. Clean has reached the status of advertising icon, and associated advertising might seem to suggest Mr. Clean has become more enlightened over the years, and will be helping a wide range of people with their cleaning tasks rather than just housewives or housewife moms. He celebrated his fiftieth anniversary in 2008 with personal appearances at NASCAR events, P. Diddy's "White Party," and the New Orleans Superdome—all places with (presumably) numerous men in attendance. In the early 2000s, with a new line of products, P&G again sought to market Mr. Clean as a suitably masculine cleaner for suitably masculine cleaning tasks with a line of auto care products.[40] And his Magic Eraser product (which has a fan club on Facebook) advertising does depict men doing housework, albeit fleetingly and balanced by images of women doing housework.

But Mr. Clean's official website features only images of housewife moms. In the kitchen, a slim blonde mom in a sundress holds her young daughter in front of a gleaming counter and stovetop. To illustrate bathroom-cleaning products, a mom offers a rubber duck to an adorable baby in the tub surrounded by bubbles. For the section on multipurpose and floor cleaners, a mom in jeans sitting on a shiny wood floor reads to her young daughter on her lap. "Because so much of life happens on the floor," reads the headline.[41] Moreover, the brand still capitalizes on its image as the almost romantic rescuer of women doing housework. Commercials in 2009–2011, including part of the successful co-branding of Mr. Clean and Febreze air freshener, featured rejected multipurpose cleaners in the cupboard wistfully watching the housewife mom cleaning the house with Mr. Clean products.[42] Like the rejected brooms and mops in the Swiffer campaigns, these products bemoan their failure to perform well enough to retain a place in her heart. Unlike the mute Swiffer brooms and mops, though, these products feature voiceover work by two male actors, expressing their feelings of rejection. In commercials for multipurpose Mr. Clean with Febreze, the two forlorn bottles watch as a housewife mom—her wedding ring glints and evidence of children in the house appears in a number of shots—uses the product to mop the kitchen floor. Their dialogue acknowledges Mr. Clean's superiority. For instance, in a commercial for Mr. Clean with Febreze (an all-purpose cleaner) in a spray bottle, the product is wielded by a woman in a sweater and a wedding ring who cleans the kitchen counter:

> **First Product:** What's that say?
> **Second Product:** Mr. Clean *with* Febreze Fresh Scent?
> **First Product:** [worriedly] Oooooh boy.
> **Second Product:** [sarcastically, desperately] Oh, Mr. "Has It All" comes in here . . .
> **First Product:** [similarly desperate and sarcastic] Hey World, he cleans great. He helps eliminate odors too.
> **Second Product:** [wistfully] Wow . . .
> **First Product:** [sighing] Yeah.
> **Second Product:** He's like a guy that's like a good actor but he's also a musician too. And then sometimes he'll do some modeling.
> **First Product:** [resignedly] I can't compete with this guy.

The housewife mom in this commercial no longer swooned at an animated Mr. Clean coming in with his golf bag full of mops, but the humorous depiction of two rejected cleansers pining for the housewife mom definitely played on the longstanding image of magical Mr. Clean coming to the aid of women who need to get the housework done. In this commercial, she smiles happily as she gazes at her clean counters, sniffing appreciatively. She's not wearing heels and an apron, but she's definitely enamored of her house and with the Mr. Clean product.

In a similar commercial for the Mr. Clean Magic Eraser, the housewife mom's rejection of the slacker products is even more pointed.

> **First Product:** [laughing derisively] Oh, hey, there's that Mr. Clean Magic Eraser thing again.
> **Second Product:** [dismissively] Pssh . . . clean freak.
> **First Product:** [noticing efficacy of product] Whoa . . . is he better than us?
> **Second Product:** [suddenly uncertain] Uh, I mean . . . I mean I feel like it took you three times longer to do whatever . . .
> **First Product:** [interrupting excitedly] Dude! Dude! Microscrubbers! [woman scrubs microwave]
> **Second Product:** [glumly] Yeah, I guess.
> **First Product:** [in awe] Magic Man.
> **Second Product:** What?
> **First Product:** He's a magic man.

Second Product: [a "tear" rolling down the spray bottle] I just want be squeezed.

Giving voice to the sad rejection visually depicted in the Swiffer ads, these inferior cleaning projects are forced to bow to the Magic Man— Mr. Clean—and his ability to win over the woman doing housework. Significantly, by the 2000s, the Mr. Clean brand needed the boost of the Febreze brand as a range of housework products promised ever more "fresh" results. Similarly, the linking of Swiffer and Febreze signals the twenty-first century direction of the Swiffer brand. Air fresheners and fragrance dispensers constitute one of the newest but most profitable categories for housework products. Advertising for air fresheners offers a remarkably revealing example of how persistently manufacturers, ad makers, and consumers (at least in the minds of marketing experts) continue to view caring for the home solely through the lens of the housewife mom guarding her family's well-being and transforming housework into homemaking.

As historian Suellen Hoy notes in her historical analysis of hygiene and cleaning in the United States, products that claimed to "clean the air" in the home began to multiply in the 1950s:

> Growing sensitivity to smells also prompted homemakers to enlist themselves in a "clean fight" against "indoor odors"—household foes that seemed nearly as disturbing and pervasive as germs. Magazine advertisements and television commercials illustrated how unpleasant aromas presented "so many chances to offend." Cooking, bathroom, perspiration, smoking, and refrigerator odors were only a few of many that might embarrass or disgust family and friends. Thus "smart" housewives bought an excess of "freshening" products, tackled all those jobs nobody liked, and killed unwanted odors.[43]

Indeed, almost every type of housework-related product had at one time or another highlighted the elimination of offensive household odors. Recall the 1922 newspaper ads for Sylpho-Nathol that promised to make the bathroom "sweet, clean and healthy smelling."[44] In the second half of the century, a variety of multipurpose cleaners promised good-smelling results. For instance, a series of late 1970s commercials for Mr. Clean positioned the product as "sunshine fresh." Smiling housewives with feathered hair opened bottles of Mr. Clean and enthused about the odor-fighting power. In one, a housewife standing beside a laundry line hung with spanking clean linens and clothing begins: "Nothing like the smell of sunshine on clean laundry. Wouldn't it be nice to get the same freshness with your household cleaning? Well, get ready!" Donning sunglasses, she opens the product as the voiceover promises: "Mr. Clean has captured the sun." "He's sunshine fresh Mr. Clean! Mmmmm!" exclaims the housewife. Another commercial in this series pictures the housewife who uses the product bringing blinding freshness to her home, in contrast to her more slovenly neighbors: the opening shot depicts "Mrs. Anderson's" house basking in radiant sunshine while the neighbor's houses huddle beneath gloomy clouds. The commercial then cuts to Mrs. Anderson herself, wearing a button-down plaid shirt kneeling on her shining kitchen floor and sniffing the product delightedly.

Another longstanding brand, Lysol, made especially concerted efforts to tout its odor-eliminating power throughout the late 1900s to today. Lysol television commercials in the 1960s and 1970s peddled the product's ability to freshen all areas of house—bathroom, kitchen, nursery, living room, closets. "Leaves my kitchen smelling like a breath of fresh air!" enthused a one such commercial. At this time, the housewife mom guarding the safety and comfort of her family began to appear regularly in Lysol advertising as well. The voiceover for another commercial in the early 1970s asked: "Have you used your Lysol Spray today?" Answered the casually but neatly dressed housewife mom: "With three kids? I use it every day." In another 1970s commercial the housewife mom lives up to her daughter's high standards with Lysol spray:

> **Daughter:** [coming into kitchen] Mom, can Charley come to supper?
> **Housewife mom:** [mixing something in a bowl and wearing a full apron] No problem.
> **Daughter:** [sniffing critically and making a face] But do we have to eat in the kitchen? It doesn't smell clean!
> **Housewife mom:** [nodding sadly] I know.
> **Daughter:** But the odors!
> **Housewife mom:** That's why I got this. [holds up product]

The male voiceover intones: "Another kitchen goes Lysol," and in the last shot Daughter sniffs happily: "Boy, now the kitchen smells as clean as it looks!" The housewife mom making sure the house smells clean, *really* clean, in Lysol advertising was married and middle class, but she wasn't always white. In a 1972 ad in *Essence* for example, an African American housewife demonstrated a host of ways that Lysol "makes your nice clean home even nicer."[45] She sprays it in her garbage can, kitchen sink, her kids' sneakers, even totes it to a hotel room to render it more homelike. By 1972, the representation of domesticity in housework advertising— transforming mere cleaning into careful feminine care for home and family—had clearly diversified in terms of race. Housework product ad makers easily incorporated women of color into their advertising: they appeared in both targeted and mainstream publications and commercials. But housework advertising generally and air freshener marketing specifically never swerved from gendering homemaking as female.

For several decades, Lysol spray and its ilk—other all-purpose cleaners and disinfectants that also "cleaned the air"—made up the majority of air freshening products available on the market. However, beginning in the late 1970s and rapidly growing in the 1980s and 1990s, the number and variety of air fresheners expanded to today's vast assortment of both disinfecting and "boutique" style products. But advertising for these products remained consistently focused on how the housewife or housewife mom wielding the product could improve not just the air but the home itself. For example, a series of Twice as Fresh Deodorizer commercials in the 1970s depicted a woman eliminating odors in a variety of rooms, thus making them more pleasantly homey for the members of her family. In one such commercial, a man arrives home to find his wife frying fish:

> **Husband:** Whoa, that smell!
> **Wife:** You love fish!
> **Husband:** Yeah, but I hate the smell.
> **Wife:** I can fix that!

With a wave of the product, she clears the air in the kitchen. Similarly, a housewife mom tackled the nursery. In this commercial, Daddy has apparently changed the baby's diaper because although Baby is in Mom's arms, the dialogue begins with her complimenting him:

> **Housewife mom:** Nice work, Daddy!
> **Daddy:** Love the baby, hate wet diapers! [waves hand in front of face]
> **Housewife mom:** Oh, no problem [demonstrates product]
> **Daddy:** Twice as Fresh works twice as hard! [kisses her on the cheek] Like you.

In acknowledgement of more equitable parenting, Dad's pitching in, but leaves it to the housewife mom to make sure Baby's air is cleared of all objectionable odors because she's not just cleaning: she's caring for home and for family. And as Daddy points out, she works "twice as hard" as he does, not merely cleaning but homemaking and ensuring that both husband and child enjoy the comforts of home.

In the early 1980s, another caring housewife mom touted the benefits of Air Wick: "I'm a *nut* about the air that my baby breathes. It has to smell fresh and clean and it *does* with Air Wick Solid." Other housewife moms in the commercial explain the benefits for other rooms. In the bathroom: "I used to use a room spray but Air Wick Solid is much easier. And it's better!" The kitchen: "Air Wick Solid really helps keep the air smelling fresh and clean, no matter what I cook." As the voiceover summarizes, "The air is beautiful in every home on their street because every family has switched to Air Wick Solid." As in furniture polish commercials in which a clean table wasn't good enough but had to shine like a mirror in order to achieve real home beauty, it wasn't enough to change diapers, clean the bathroom, and cook dinner every night. The ideal housewife mother ensured that the very air breathed by her family would be "beautiful" because she is a "nut" about the air her family breathes.[46] On infrequent occasions, a man's hand applied the freshener—in a 1970s commercial, for instance, a guy shaving in the bathroom observes: "Hoo! This is a good place for a Stick Up" and then slaps the plastic dispenser on the wall—but air freshening products remained inextricably linked to female homemaking, housewives, and housewife moms. The Stick Up packaging, for example, pictured a nicely manicured woman's hand demonstrating the product.

A recurring theme in air freshener advertising suggested that the problem of household odors menaced not just the comfort and well-being of the family, but also the housewife's reputation, that is, her ability to demonstrate to visitors that she'd fully discharged her responsibilities for maintaining the cleanliness and sanctity of the home. Of course, many housework ads and commercials seemed designed to instill anxiety about the potential for such failures, but air freshener advertising (like the first deodorant commercials or Lux's "undie odor" campaign in the 1930s) suggested that odors would make their way stealthily into the home, without the housewife's noticing them, until—disaster!—they offended an outsider invited into the home. In one particularly vivid example of this theme, a late 1970s Renuzit commercial begins with a shot of three ladies dressed for visiting arriving at a neighbor's doorstep. The male voiceover warns: "Sometimes other people notice stale household odors before you do." The catty attacks then begin: "Fried fish last night, dear?" [guest smiles falsely] "I thought George gave up cigars." [sniffing ostentatiously] As "Jane" hangs her head in shame, the third and kinder guest takes her aside: "Jane, haven't you heard about Renuzit solid air freshener?" The voiceover concludes: "Now you don't have to worry about odors anymore." "Or the neighbors," chimes in Jane. As the tagline promised: "Takes the worry out of odors. Continuously."

A longtime staple of housework advertising, the fear of being discovered as a less than ideal homemaker appeared on regular occasions throughout air freshener advertising. Critical relatives and visitors threatened such a judgment in Air Wick brand's Carpet Fresh 1980s commercials. In one, the voiceover promised: "Brings a smile to some very fussy noses. Your nosy neighbors. Your sister-in-law with her nose in the air." A shot of a woman's legs in slacks sprinkling the product on the carpet and vacuuming it up demonstrated that you needed to use the product "every time you vacuum" in order to make sure you kept those noses happy. Similarly, a Carpet Fresh commercial from the same time warned a worried looking woman that "once these odors [shots of a dog, a diapered baby, fish cooking in a frying pan] get trapped in your carpet, they're in your room." As she tackles them with the product and her vacuum, and sniffs appreciatively, proudly gazing around her, the voiceover reminds her: "And let's not forget the mother-in-law with the sensitive nose." But rest assured: the housewife mom uses Carpet Fresh, and the picky mother-in-law is satisfied. A Lysol housewife in a 1970s commercial faced down another sensitive nose in the shape of a dour-faced spinster in a prissy suit: "One day Snoopy Sniffer came to my house!" And Snoopy Sniffer calls 'em as she sees 'em: "This kitchen looks clean but it doesn't smell clean." The distraught housewife wails: "But why?" "Germs! Germs cause odors!" scolds Snoopy Sniffer. After applying the product, as the tagline reads, "It wipes out odors as it wipes out dirt," and Snoopy is satisfied: "It smells as clean as it looks." Much more recently, a 2009 Febreze commercial featured a hostess welcoming in company when her shag rug suddenly morphs into a dog. The message? Hidden odors could emerge at highly embarrassing times.

As significant as the "embarrassing odor" theme that appeared in air freshener advertising, appeals also often relied on images and copy that linked homemaking—the housewife mom making even the air beautiful in her lovely middle-class home—and the product. Beginning in the 1980s, products made a concerted effort to position themselves as not just disinfectants or overpowering masking perfumes, but *fragrances* that would beautify the home. An early 1980s commercial for Glade air freshener begins with a woman in a nice dress walking into her living room and speaking to the camera: "It used to be when a can of air freshener said, for instance, evergreen . . . [a huge pine tree crashes into the room] you got evergreen. Well, Glade's changed all that. All five Glade scents have been improved. They're lighter, more delicate smelling. And they're in a more attractive package." The "more attractive package" also appeared in Renuzit advertising in the 1980s, specifically in a seashell-shaped dispenser advertised in *Good Housekeeping* and *Essence* with the tagline "Good looking. Hard working." More discreetly, Glade introduced an air freshener toilet paper roll in a 1983 print ad that promised to "freshen with every spin." And expanding into fabric sprays, 1984 Glade print advertising assured consumers: "Now Glade does more than clear the air. . . . Fresher fabrics mean a fresher home."[47]

"A fresher home" indicated that the appeal in this ad lay not simply in a promise to tackle offensive odors but in fact to make the house more homey; not "housecleaning" but "homemaking." An added touch of care-taking of home and family with absolutely no extra work at all! Just spray! Interestingly, the market for these products really began to boom in the late 1980s and 1990s, just as the number of hours American women spent cleaning their homes began to slowly decline. Some research suggests that this reduction is not due to other members of the family taking up the slack or a significant nation-wide increase in paid household cleaners, but rather is the result of an overall decrease in the time anyone spent doing housework.[48] Viewed as a part of the history of housework in the United States, it's possible to see the proliferation of air freshener products at the end of the century as a result of the persistent social and cultural need to continue to link women and housework, to continue to add household tasks to the list of necessary feminine home care, even when employment trends and standards of homemaking are actually reducing the time women spend doing housework. An industry consultant in 2004 posited that as Americans clean less, we turn more often to home fragrances and sprays, "not to mask" odors caused by an unclean house, "but to add something different to a home that gives a feeling of cleaning—that somebody has done something here."[49] Though she didn't allow for the possibility that more Americans reached for a spray in order to "mask" the smells of an unclean house, this statement does seem to reveal a sense that the unidentified real woman in charge of housework would, as suggested in the 1959 marketing plan for furniture polish, feel that she had not sufficiently "discharged her duties" as a homemaker unless there was evidence that "somebody has done something here," i.e., someone is caring for the home and family.

"Somebody," in the world of advertising, means "the housewife mom." She's the one taking on this final frontier of making the house a home and sanctuary for her family, particularly her children: making the home smell *really* clean. For example, an early 1980s commercial for HR Rug and Room Deodorizer begins with the camera panning through the chaotic bedroom of a teenage boy basketball player—we can see his torso in uniform as he bounces a ball. Mom, in a plaid shirt and casual but crisp slacks and discreet earrings, is literally kneeling at his feet as she cleans. Facing the camera, she explains how she ensures the air her boy breathes, even when he's too much of a slob to pick up his own room, is fresh and clean: "Sometimes Bobby's room smells like a gym. Odors get trapped in the rug. So I turned to the people who really know rugs and got HR Rug and Room Deodorizer. HR freshens while I vacuum. . . . Its deodorizing action gets into the carpet and overpowers odors every time I vacuum." After demonstrating, she gazes upward and asks "How's it smell up there, Bobby?" "Terrific!" he replies, seemingly appreciative of his mother's labors, although he's stood by mutely dribbling the basketball as she cleans his room. His mother nods approvingly at the product and concludes: "It works." "It" works because *she* works—applying it to the rug in her son's bedroom as she cleans and vacuums "every time I vacuum." In this commercial and similar ones, air freshening is not merely a finishing touch to housework, but an essential part of good mothering—of caring for every aspect of a child's home environment, even when that child is six feet tall.

In the 2000s, air fresheners and home fragrance advertising falls into two distinct camps. One kind of appeal directly addresses the housewife mom caring for children and guarding the sanctity of the home by combining "freshening" with "germ killing" appeals. In contrast, the other type of appeal positions such products as feminine indulgences, a luxurious pampering of the senses—a new kind of homemaking. Lysol brand products exemplify the first type of appeal, just as they led the way in air freshener products in the 1970s. Today, as the tagline "Disinfect to protect" suggests, the brand emphasizes how the product assists housewife moms in keeping the house not only fresh but safe from germs. In a typical commercial, a little boy opens the front door walking in from the rain. He's outlined in animated viruses and germs because, according to the voiceover, "The one you love could be carrying cold and flu viruses." Accompanied by un-ironic menacing music, the camera zooms in on the boy's hand as he reaches for the phone. In slow motion, his sister innocently reaches for the phone, as the voiceover warns: "Fact: The flu virus can live on surfaces for days. So before your child picks it up, pick up Lysol disinfecting spray." A housewife mom's hand comes into the shot and sprays on the product and the squirming animated home invaders disappear. This campaign also included print ads in *Parenting* magazine.[50] The Oust products, directly challenging the Lysol brand, advertise themselves as both a disinfectant and an air freshener, as in the 2008 magazine ad featuring the product eliminating the hovering toilet bowls in the bathroom and the headline: "Is it a surface disinfectant that sanitizes the air? Or is it an air sanitizer that disinfects surfaces? *Yes.*"

In recent years products that promise to quickly wipe down a surface and leave the home fresher and cleaner have proliferated. Again, no one in the industry would dare assert that the rapidly growing market for such products might indicate a desire to "mask" odors or disguise the fact that consumers are cleaning less and looking for ways to make the house look and smell clean without actually doing housework. But the sales figures at the very least suggest that a significant number of real Americans are sold on the idea of a product that vows to freshen up the surfaces of the home while also "sanitizing" the air—with one swipe or one spray. By one estimate, the "quick clean" category, which includes Swiffer brand products, a Pledge brand dusting cloth called Grab-It, and Clorox brand's Ready Mop among others netted $818 million in sales in 2004 and the category continues to grow.[51] Advertisements and commercials will never suggest that such products might tempt real women who have little time and/or inclination to constantly scrub, mop, and clean in order to ensure "beautiful" air for their families to breathe. But that must surely be part of their massive attraction in the 2000s. The euphemistic phrase "busy women" or "busy moms" is undoubtedly often trotted out at various ad agencies when discussing how to market "quick clean" products, and like all modern housework advertising, even as they promise to eliminate—or cover up the lack of—housework, it remains a gendered activity. As marketing strategies demonstrate, corporations no longer necessarily view their target consumer as white, and are comfortable framing domesticity with images of women of different races and ethnicity. Glade, for example, markets some products with bilingual Spanish-English labels, and the Pledge website homepage includes a clearly marked link to a Spanish language version.[52] But the target consumers are always housewife moms; housework can never be visually, symbolically depicted as anything but feminine homemaking.

In air freshener advertising the housewife mom not only cleans and disinfects and makes the home cozy; she beautifies it, and in the process, pampers herself and her home. Echoing some of the advertising for premium priced laundry detergents, air freshener advertising today often includes images and rhetoric positioning products as personal, sensual indulgences in which the housewife can immerse herself. In the early 2000s, an increasing number of air freshening products utilize appeals that position these products not as housework but as products that pamper the female consumer with luxurious fragrances. Not housework, but home perfume. Beginning in the 1990s, industry watchers noted this change. For instance, a journalist in 1997 reported that as traditional sanitizing and freshening sprays lost ground to increasing numbers of highly scented and highly priced candles on the market, Renuzit brand brought out a new line called Crystal AcScents.[53] Another journalist described new advertising for Glade that repositioned the product not as a germ or odor-fighter (housework) but a pretty perfume for the home:

> Over the years, we've seen the beautiful housewife in the flowing skirt poised like Carol Merril in front of Door No. 3., with a vacant smile and vague glance upwards, spraying deodorizer in wide generous arcs. (You had to study the interior décor carefully to deduce that this spacious room she's in, the one with the heather print wallpaper and the inviting shafts of dusty sunlight, is the crapper. Thereupon little imagination is required to

complete the scenario: Dad has done it again, and the guests will be here in 5 minutes.) . . . But what if, just once, an advertiser [were] sufficiently confident with the intrinsic qualities of its product to direct your attention not to the smells you wish to conceal, but to the fragrance you wish to deliver?

He went on to describe how Glade's commercials, featuring long shots of lavender fields, strawberry patches, and flowering meadows, evoked "not industrial-strength fragrance compound L317 but actual whiffs of nature's own perfume."[54] In 1997, as this quote indicates, such commercials merited industry attention and marked an important aspect of housework advertising in the late twentieth and early twenty-first century: positioning products not as helpmates to the housewife mom as she tackles the shit work ("Dad has done it again") but rather as products promoting sensory pleasure for feminine consumers. By 2009, however, such marketing was standard for brands such as Febreze and Glade. In 2008, for example, a Glade advertisement in *Good Housekeeping*, which also included a coupon, depicted a woman lounging on her couch beneath an open window with a pristine white curtain, cuddling a puppy and admiring the Glade product in the foreground of the photo on the gleaming coffee table. Glass Scents decorative air freshener (in an etched glass square container) ads promise consumers that the product will be "a fragrant thing of beauty in any room." In another ad for Glade spray, a woman stands in front of a clothesline hung with immaculate white sheets, arms folded, eyes closed, and head tipped back as she inhales the fragrance of "Clean Linen" Glade spray.

Febreze brand also positions its products as delectable home fragrances, and reflects P&G's market research not on "air fresheners" but what consumers desire from a home "scent experience."[55] Thousands of loyal consumers on Febreze's Facebook page (and followers on Twitter) appear to confirm that they view Febreze as a way to clean the air of bad odors but also to provide a pleasant, even luxurious, home perfume. In a 2009 commercial that combines both the "avoiding embarrassment of hidden odors" and "a pleasing home fragrance" appeal, a housewife mom spritzes the product on the living room curtains, on the couch, and in the air as her giggling children run by. The doorbell rings and a white-haired woman, in a classic suit jacket, arrives. Grandma rushes past the family gathered expectantly at the door and instead runs to inhale the fresh scent of the couch pillows. "In fabrics and in the air, it's a breath of fresh air," concludes the voiceover. Housewife mom has not only ensured that her important visitor (probably mother-in-law) won't find fault with the air, but she's actually infused her home with such a wonderful freshness that even a loving Grandma will forgo hugs in order to wrap herself into the drapes.

In 2009 Glade products commercials directly positioned their products against "pricey boutique" candles and fragrances. Their spokeswoman, a pleasant but not sexy white woman in her early thirties with long light brown hair, appears regularly in the television commercials for this product. In one, she is visiting a friend as they prepare for what appears to be a wedding shower. The Glade Lady picks up a candle and smells it appreciatively, and the following dialogue ensues:

> **Glade Lady:** Why haven't you lit this candle?
> **Hostess:** Because it costs more than my shoes.
> **Glade Lady:** Seriously?!
> **Hostess:** Um hm. I mean, I love the smell but I can't afford to burn it every day.
> **Glade Lady:** Well, that's why I use Glade. My home smells fresh and I never feel guilty about lighting it.
> **Female Voiceover:** You get boutique quality fragrance at an everyday price.
> **Glade Lady:** And yes, it's Glade. [the campaign's tagline]

In a similar commercial for Glade Scented Oil candles the same actress browses in a cute little boutique and picks up a candle but then sees its price tag and quickly puts it down. "Expect boutique quality fragrance without blowing your budget," promises the female voiceover. In other commercials, the Glade Lady demonstrates various Glade products, such as the Glade Plug In, amazing her yoga buddies with her fresh house. They then catch her when she tries to pass off the Glade Plug In as a "boutiquey fragrance I discovered that helps me plug into my karma," but it's all in good fun. Everyone laughs merrily as she admits "And yes, it's Glade."

The Glade Lady is married although she doesn't appear to have children. In one 2009 commercial, she gazes down at her wedding photo resting on a side table, commenting, "They said it would never last. But it's been two months and you're still going strong." The camera pans back and we see she is talking to her Glade Lasting Impression air freshener dispenser. In another commercial, her befuddled husband tries to figure out how the motion-sensor fragrance dispenser works after noticing how wonderful the air smells in his living room, and she saunters by and demonstrates. It's not rocket science, but it's housework, and so even though all you do is press a button if you want an "extra burst of freshness" between 30-minute motion activated fragrance releases, only a woman's hand can reach in and push that button. Surely ad makers and their clients do not still believe, well into the twentieth century, that even the simplest of housework tasks—spraying something into the air—is really beyond the capability of the typical husband. Perhaps, because agencies believe (and some research backs them up) that women purchase more housework-related products, they also believe their target consumer will get a kick out of the idea that only a woman can be responsible for beautifully perfuming the home.[56] But there is no cabal of misogynistic ad men gathering in secret to plot how their work can ensure the continuing subjugation of American women to a rigid gender division of household labor. Rather, this commercial illustrates how at least to some degree modern housework advertising retains the extremely narrow focus it's always had and the sole lens of understanding household labor as female home care. The twenty-first century version of the housewife continues to star in housework advertising, even for products that position themselves not as housework but as an easy way to beautify the home and indulge the senses.

And even when she's not disinfecting and protecting, even when all the product promises is that it smells good, the housewife mom continues to appear. In an especially weird example of how persistently advertising links housework and housewife moms, a series of animated 2009 Air Wick commercials featured an assortment of anthropomorphized animals transformed into housewife moms accomplishing homemaking in nice middle-class houses. A rabbit housewife mom, for example, explains the benefits of the Air Wick Freshmatic Ultra (a timed spray dispenser) in keeping her house fresh as she contends with a string of visitors, including a skunk: "I simply set the time to spray automatically for bursts of freshness throughout the day. So my home smells great. No matter what." Meanwhile, her bunny children frolic around her. In another, a frog housewife mom appreciates how the aroma of Air Wick Plug In "Aqua Essences" reminds her of her homeland: "You can take the girl out of the rain forest but you can't take the rain forest out of the girl." In the final shot, this housewife mom truly fulfills twenty-first century mothering ideals by foregoing boring household rules and jumping happily on the couch with her froggy kids. The owl housewife mom keeps watch over her owl babies while the product takes care of freshening her home: "I may have eyes in the back of my head but I can't keep my eyes on everything. Thankfully, my air freshener is always watching out." The hardworking ant housewife mom vouches that the Freshmatic Mini is small, but like her (as she lifts the couch to vacuum underneath), it gets the job done. Her ant children embrace her as the campaign's tagline flashes on screen: "Air Wick. It's good to be home." So firmly entrenched is the housewife in advertising as the sole frame for the domestic that even when she's not human, she continues to be the only way advertising depicts household labor and homemaking.

"It's good to be home" neatly summarizes how floor cleaner, furniture polish, and air freshener advertising, from the beginning of the 1900s to today, depicts these products as not merely housework-related commodities but essential homemaking tools. Gleaming floors, mirror-like surfaces, and beautiful fragrances in these ads and commercials represent a housework ideal that goes beyond simple (though laborious) cleaning and extends to homemaking; an ideal in which dedicated house-wife moms make every aspect of home "good" and ensure the comfort and well-being of their children particularly. Even as some air freshener advertising seeks to market their products as relaxing female indulgences, the presence of guests, children, and husbands also benefiting from the beautiful air continues to link this work—even if it's just pressing a button or setting a timer—with the housewife. Even if the housewife mom is not actually a human being, but an owl, ant, or rabbit, she makes sure that "it's good to be home."

Conclusion

In 1952, just as television began to assume a central role in American media and households, a student pursuing a master's degree at Ohio State University interviewed 500 white housewives living in Columbus about their attitudes toward television commercials. The majority expressed no strong feelings about commercials in general or commercials about housework products specifically, although a number mentioned Tide, Oxydol, and Duz as brands with especially repetitive and at times annoying commercials. As their years of education increased so too did the housewives' distaste for commercials, but according to most of those surveyed, advertising did not present particularly objectionable imagery or copy regarding a woman's role in the home or the work of caring for a home. However, one interviewee did register a protest: "I sometimes wonder what kind of a picture of an average housewife the advertisers have in mind. They seem to think we are some of kind of sub-morons."[1] This unnamed observer put it very well: for much of the twentieth century, many housework product ad makers utilized images and copy that seemed to reflect a view of female consumers as simple-minded creatures obsessed with shiny floors and gleaming toilet bowls; who often stood entranced by their clean, germ-free house or with their heads buried in a basket of laundry sniffing ecstatically.

One image that demonstrated just "what kind of picture of an average housewife" at least some agencies still had in mind in 1969 appeared not in general interest or women's service magazines but in grocers' trade publications (created for and read solely by store owners and others in the food industry). The ad, for General Foods' product Cool Whip, urged grocers to stock plenty of Cool Whip in their supermarkets in upcoming weeks because a major advertising campaign for Cool Whip would soon be running in magazines and on television, and Sunday newspapers would distribute 45 million coupons. The large headline claimed: "On Sunday, November 16th, 45 million women will reach for their scissors." On Monday, promised the ad copy, those women "will converge on your store, waving their Cool Whip coupons in their hands." Because, the ad concluded, "No woman can resist a bargain."[2] The ad featured a large drawing of a woman, a housewife, sitting in a flowered armchair carefully cutting a coupon out of the Sunday paper.

But unlike the millions of housewives depicted in print ads and television commercials for food products, detergent, and household cleansers during the twentieth century, *this* housewife is not trimly dressed, with a neat apron on and hairdo in place; she's decidedly not slim and pretty. She's squat and unbecomingly clothed in a shapeless sleeveless garment that reveals her flabby arms. Her feet bulge out of house slippers and her hair is rolled in curlers. Her bulbous nose and rotund cheeks hang heavily as she bends over the newspaper. This image is a rare, but revealing, glimpse into how some advertisers and those who hired them *really* imagined "the housewife," and assumed that their readers in the grocery trade imagined her this way, too. This particular housewife appears to fit the "sub-moron" stereotype: unattractive, obsessed with clipping coupons, and at the mercy of her own consumer desires that compel her to the supermarket to buy reduced-price Cool Whip.

Similarly, consider how an advertising industry journalist characterized the marketing strategies of Proctor and Gamble in 1963:

> P&G is concerned solely, and single-mindedly, with the effect of advertising on the minds of American housewives. When the missus gets up in the morning each day, she faces a number of simple, recurring, vexing problems: "Will my husband complain about the coffee this morning? Will the children eat their oatmeal? Will the damned car start so we can get to the school bus on time? Will the grape juice stains come out of Johnny's shirt? How will we ever pay the dentist's bill this month? Why did my mother-in-law invite herself to lunch today, when my hair looks such a fright?"[3]

This reporter reflected widespread attitudes about the grim monotony of life in the suburbs and the simple-minded, petty concerns of the average Mrs. Housewife ("my hair looks such a fright!"), which nonetheless posed "recurring, vexing problems" that P&G promised to fix with household cleaning and personal care products. You'd be hard-pressed to find a better example not only of the patronizing way the advertising industry viewed the housewife but also the aims of housework advertising for much of the twentieth century.

As the unidentified housewife in 1952 pointed out, there was no mistaking the demeaning representation of the housewife consumer, rooted in such attitudes, that proliferated in advertising. But as the Ohio State study and other similar studies showed, most female consumers viewed housework advertising without particularly noticing such demeaning messages.[4] If housework advertising blatantly depicted housewives as "some kind of sub-morons" for much of the 1900s, not many people seemed to notice or to care. On the contrary, marketing that firmly linked housework (laundry and care of clothing; cleaning bathrooms and toilets; cooking and serving meals; washing dishes; cleaning and polishing home surfaces) and home-making (ensuring the health, safety, and comfort of the family) to the housewife worked very well for many brands for many years.

Cultural norms and assumptions influenced how ad makers perceived real consumers and how they depicted housework in advertising, but ad makers framed housework with representations of the housewife not because they actively sought to impose limiting gender norms on the nation or simply out of an unconscious desire to perpetuate the status quo. They used the housewife—the pretty but not sexy, well-groomed married mother caring for a nice home—to frame housework because that's what worked. For most of the twentieth century, the housewife in advertising was also white, but by the 1970s more racially diverse images began to appear, as the housewife transitioned to the housewife mom. Although in this way the image of the housewife mom in the late twentieth century appeared to be changing with the times, American consumers and viewers continued to widely accept a depiction of domesticity that strictly reinforced gender norms, even as they began to object to the most blatant stereotyping in advertising.

The most important job of ad makers is to recognize and respond to shifting consumer attitudes, so not surprisingly, ad agencies and their housework product clients paid close attention to changing ideas about women's social roles, especially the dramatic changes wrought by Second Wave feminism. In a 1975 report on the portrayal of women in advertising, a national advertising review board summarized how those changing ideas might shape housework advertising:

> One problem about the advertising of household products relates to the matter of cumulative impressions. Any number of individual advertise-ments or commercials may be perfectly acceptable when taken one at a time. There is nothing wrong with showing a woman using a household product in the home. An endless procession of commercials on the same theme, however, all showing women using household products in the home, raises very strong implications that women have no other interests except laundry, dishes, waxing floors, and fighting dirt in any form. Seeing a great many such advertisements in succession reinforces the traditional stereotype that a "woman's place" is only in the home.[5]

Ad makers knew they needed to avoid suggesting that women "had no other interests except laundry, dishes, and waxing floors." They knew that they should somehow better represent the multiplicity of women's social and economic roles. By the late 1970s, they *knew* that the overtly stereo-typical housewife in housework product commercials would be, as the summary of one study put it, "irritating" to consumers.[6]

But they had to walk a fine line, avoiding ads and commercials insinuat-ing that a woman's place was only in the home while at the same time being careful to in no way disparage the ideal of home and domesticity. They knew that while consumers might object to overtly demeaning images of the housewife, framing housework as female love and care for the home remained a perfectly viable marketing strategy. While they needed to avoid "an endless procession" of ads and commercials showing women doing housework, they simply could not vary that theme with depictions of *men* doing housework. All evidence suggests that the very idea never crossed anybody's mind, even when their own marketing studies suggested that in real homes men did housework too.[7] The act of housework and its attendant concept of homemaking was so enmeshed with the image and signifier of feminine care for the home—the housewife—that ad makers could not avoid her and replace her with more diverse images of people doing household labor.

Feminist thinkers, writers, and commentators offered them little guid-ance. The Second Wave quickly and thoroughly discredited the stereotype of the housewife in advertising, but offered no viable, popular alternatives for rethinking housework and domesticity. The National Organization of Women offered a "Bill of Rights for Homemakers" in 1979, but critiquing the unequal division of home labor by characterizing housework as uni-formly degrading shit work, and mired in an academic and inaccessible Marxist debate about wages for housework, feminist activists in the 1970s and early 1980s failed to foster widespread rethinking of domesticity and housework. The language of rights was simply no match for the emotional and symbolic associations with homemaking, especially motherhood.[8] In recent years a third and fourth wave of young feminist thinkers and activ-ists have attempted to negotiate the tricky terrain of parenting and domes-tic pleasures but with limited success, particularly in the face of a new momism that reaffirms domesticity in general and childcare specifically as female labor. As Arlie Russell Hoschild famously summarized in *The Second Shift*, the last decades of the twentieth century witnessed a "stalled revolution."[9] When it came to the home front, feminism faltered and in terms of actual labor being done in the home and in terms of our cultural norms, housework and homemaking never stopped being gendered as female in American society. Architectural scholar Beverly Gordon writes: "The home is still primarily perceived as a female space, and we maintain practices that acknowledge this as our cultural norm."[10] Advertising is one of those practices.

In the pivotal last decades of the 1900s, the creators of advertising and their housework product clients grappled with how to represent the "female space" of the home without using demeaning depictions of the housewife, the recognizable symbol of the home. In a telling article, marketing experts in 1977 urged ad agencies to avoid blatant gender stereotypes, cautioning that a female consumer could be "truly resentful" if "she sees herself portrayed by these role stereotypes." Echoing Rena Bartos' advice, they asserted that ad makers had to stop thinking of women as a monolithic group. Yet like Bartos, they could not discuss domestic labor without gendering it, without evoking the devoted wife and mother caring for her family and making the home comfortable. They wrote: "A working woman may be less interested in, for instance, a floor wax which offers a bright shiny finish as much as one which offers a long lasting, easy to apply finish which allows more time to devote to herself or her family."[11] Even "a working woman" would still, they assumed, be responsible for cleaning the family's floor. But they freely acknowledged that real consumers might not be as interested in "a bright shiny finish" as previous commercials implied.

Goodbye apron-wearing housewife, exclaiming over her reflection in the plates or the whiteness of her husband's shirts! Goodbye weary housewife, slaving over her kitchen floor and then rescued by the latest floor cleaner. But what was the alternative? "Career woman" marketing appeared to alienate most female consumers, no matter what their employment status.[12] But the "busy woman" and housewife mom model that continues to dominate housework advertising today, shaped by the assumption that because she now may have the *additional* responsibilities of being a "working woman" a typical female consumer would desire a floor wax (or any other housework product) that works quickly and easily and "allows more time to devote to herself or her family," appeared to be the answer. The housewife mom would continue to be the one to transform housework like cleaning the floor into homemaking, an inescapably feminine domestic task.

It's tempting to dismiss these researchers' assumptions as outdated. After all, 1977 was a rather long time ago in our rapidly changing media environment. But as I've demonstrated, these researchers were in fact positively clairvoyant: their statement about housework product appeals aimed at so-called working women—fast and easy so women can get their housework done and devote more time "to herself or her family"—accurately predicted advertising appeals for virtually all twenty-first century housework products, from the Scrubbing Bubbles shower cleaner to the online Kraft recipe archive. So entrenched were—and are—Americans' gendered definitions of domesticity itself that even when the apron-wearing housewife in high heels, trapped by the drudgery of housework until she's freed by miracle products, could no longer serve as the representation of housework in advertising, ad makers and consumers readily embraced a twenty-first century version: the housewife mom. She stars in today's ads and commercials virtually uncontested. She appears, seemingly unnoticed by most cultural critics and consumers and tapping into the lucrative "mom market" in commercial after commercial. She's still slim, pretty but not sexy, married with children and obviously middle- to upper-class; she's still gazing happily at her house; and she's still acting as the sole household laborer and provider of home comforts.

She is, however, more racially diverse than in past decades. Housework advertising easily incorporated changing ideas about marketing to African American and Latina consumers, including using nonwhite actresses and models in ads and commercials. Racial stereotypes thus virtually disappeared from housework advertising, but our gendered frame for housework did not. Housework remained a female, and only female, endeavor. Moreover, the majority of consumers apparently accept this stereotyping of domesticity. A 2007 study concluded that the average viewers of television commercials readily identify racial bias in advertising, but that "gender stereotypes are generally not perceived as problematic."[13] The stereotype of the housewife mom remains especially unrecognized. Widely socially acceptable as the twenty-first century frame for the domestic, the housewife mom in advertising today vividly represents our culture's unresolved problems around gender, wage labor, parenting, and the home. She's virtually the only person doing housework in any popular discourse viewed by a range of Americans; it's the only image of anyone cleaning the floor, doing the laundry, and cooking the dinner. She's very nearly the only one that Americans ever see in any form outside their own homes doing the everyday domestic labor that must be done in most households no matter what the head of household's race, ethnic background, sexual orientation, or economic class. On her shoulders rests an enormous burden: how to define home, a "female space," in an age when the majority of females in our society cannot and/or do not wish to devote themselves fulltime to homemaking.

The housewife mom frames and genders the work of the home as severely as the housewife ever did. The housewife mom gazing happily at her clean towels, her shining tub, and her fresh-smelling living room, goes unnoticed in today's advertising and is accepted by marketers, advertisers, and many consumers simply as the representation of domesticity itself. Caitlyn Flanagan, a conservative commentator, recently said in an interview: "I am not a housewife. I am an 'at-home mother' and the difference between the two is vast. A 'housewife' defined herself primarily through her relationship to her house and her husband while an at-home mother feels little obligation to the house itself."[14] Yet if that distinction were so clear and easy to maintain, then housework advertising would reflect that change, and market housework-related products to a range of consumers with a range of images of different kinds of people caring for the home. The domestic, the "house itself," would be a gender-neutral concept.

However, the housewife mom continues to be the only lens through which ads and commercials view housework and the home. The housewife mom and advertising that consistently and uniformly represents her as the only person responsible for housework and homemaking "keeps us in our places"—woman *and* men—as effectively as "housewife" did. Perhaps even more insidiously and pervasively than "housewife" ever did. The "mom" in today's commercials and ads is not inanely hugging detergent or manacled to the kitchen sink; she's not wearing an apron; and she may be African American, Asian American, or Latina. And yet there seems to be no other way to demarcate the domestic than with the housewife mom, no matter what ethnicity she might be. If you need to depict housework, you need to depict the housewife mom: a slim, pretty but not beautiful, married woman taking care of her husband and children and making her middle- to upper-class house a home.

In 2000, Barbara Ehrenreich, scholar of gender and labor history in the United States, wrote that "strangely, or perhaps not so strangely at all, no one talks about the 'politics of housework' anymore."[15] Not so strangely, at least in part, because the housewife mom, the "busy mom," and the "busy woman" have so successfully supplanted the stereotypical housewife in today's advertising—our sole popular representation of housework. We— ad makers, housework product makers, and most consumers—appear to accept her as the solution to the problematic aspects of housework and homemaking in the twenty-first century. The "politics of housework," as articulated by Second Wave feminists in the 1970s fell far short, as had domestic reform efforts earlier in the century, of instigating real social and cultural change when it came to the symbolic sanctity of the home. They were unable to offer a compelling alternative, a true liberation from domestic ideology for both men and women that also acknowledged the real rewards and pleasures of homemaking.

For their part, in the crucial decades of the 1970s and 1980s, ad makers sought to acknowledge the multiplicity of women's roles and to avoid depicting women solely as housewives, but with limited success. Market researchers, ad makers, and their housework product clients continued, even when it contradicted their own research and stated conclusions about the diversity of women's lives, to view the work of the home solely through the frame of "the housewife" and the work of paid labor solely through the lens of "the career woman."[16] As then CEO of the Grey advertising agency (United Kingdom branch) pointed out in 1988, advertisers of many types of products relied on two simplistic stereotypes of women: the "unglamorous housebound housewife, usually located in a spotless kitchen at the sink" and "the very glamorous [working] woman, in a designer suit, with an attaché case."[17] By the end of the century, ad agencies realized that these two diametrically opposed stereotypes had failed to achieve much success with consumers. They were an unsatisfactory answer to the problem of marketing housework products in the late twentieth century.

The housewife mom seemed to be the answer, and appears to be widely accepted by Americans today. Not without exception, however: at least some consumers clearly resent the continuing depiction of housework as women's work. For example, a number of blogs and discussion forums created and monitored by mothers criticize housework product advertising and its depiction of housework solely as female homemaking and family care. Other bloggers, commentators, and online forum posters—male and female—sporadically disparage housework advertisings' highly idealized representation of families, household labor, and domesticity. They scrutinize specific commercials and mock housework advertising for the way it stereotypes women.[18] For instance, "SarahMC" wrote in a 2010 post on her blog, "The Pursuit of Harpyness":

> It never fails. The formula must be set in stone somewhere. *Never appeal to men when selling anything that's used to tidy a house!* And I *get it*, I do.[original emphasis] Men and women are not equal on the home-front. Women do more housework than men, and are still responsible for most domestic chores when they live with a man. It's understandable why a company would market directly to those people who are most likely to use their product in the first place. But it doesn't have to be so fucking insulting.[19]

Comments posted in response to SarahMC strongly agreed with her statement that housework advertising "doesn't have to be so fucking insulting," and pointed out additional ways that housework advertising stereotypes women.

"LMN" wrote that "another thing that annoys the crap out of me about these commercials is the fact that the woman is ALWAYS, always, wearing a wedding ring. It might just be a thin gold band but she's always wearing one. Because single women don't clean. Or no woman would be portrayed with a man and children and GASP! not be MARRIED."[20] LMN's scathing description indicates that a small group of savvy consumers recognize, and are offended by, one of the typical characteristics of the housewife mom in housework advertising. "JennyK" summarized the frustration expressed by a number of posters, suggesting that more gender diversity in housework advertising might result in stronger sales: "I have always said that if there was an ad for any kind of household product that showed a man using it like it was no big deal, I would never buy anything other than that product forever and ever."[21]

If housework product corporations and their advertising agencies in the 2000s seem convinced that housewife moms are the only acceptable frame for housework products, and if most consumers appear to accept this stereotyping of domesticity, at least a few real women have registered a protest in cyberspace. As "Laura33" wrote in 2009 on a *Washington Post* blog:

> I would like to blow up the "perfect mommy who adores even the most menial task with a smile" stereotype. The TV mom who is always turned out in her perfectly-pressed khakis, hair done, makeup on, who smiles ruefully when [her son] comes in with a nasty, stained football uniform, then happily whisks it into the washer, where it re-emerges brand-spanking new white, and everyone gathers around in amazement and gratitude, because mom has come through again. . . . I'm waiting for a commercial—just one—where mom turns to junior and says "washer's over there."[22]

As Laura33's acerbic comment demonstrates, there are real consumers who not only recognize but also despise the contemporary gender stereotypes in housework advertising. Echoing the unnamed housewife almost 60 years earlier who pointed out that much housework advertising depicted housewives as morons, these writers insist that housework advertising "doesn't have to be so fucking insulting." But these occasional critiques have not resulted in widespread outrage or a discernable drop in sales. Nor do they suggest that a large number of Americans have really identified and rejected the figure of the housewife mom in advertising, in contrast to the housewife stereotype that came under extensive attack in the 1970s. Such limited criticism has not resulted in any significant changes to housework advertising itself, which continues to utilize, first and foremost, the housewife mom as a signifier of domesticity. Laura33 is going to be waiting a long time for a commercial in which Mom tells Junior to wash his own clothes. For ad makers, housework product companies, and many consumers, the "TV mom" in "perfectly-pressed khakis" and her "hair done" is still the most important signifier for domesticity itself, and the most marketable frame for housework products; the only representation that can symbolically transform mere household labor into home care.

In fact, if the comments on social media sites like the Tide, Gain, Pledge, Febreze, and Kraft's Facebook pages are to be believed, thousands of mostly female consumers readily embrace this frame or at least see no reason to publicly criticize housework product advertising. Instead they readily offer corporations and (and their ad agencies' copywriters) valuable consumer feedback; they freely give positive testimonials about particular products and provide other online content such as photographs and household hints; and they snap up coupon and promotional offers. While a few Facebook users might complain about Tide's high prices or a hard-to-open package, the vast majority does not express any outrage or even mild offense at current marketing techniques (and such mild complaints just give the corporation a chance to demonstrate their willingness to respond to individual consumers). Though not a perfect mirror of real attitudes, such sites do seem to indicate that overall most consumers appear to have accepted the housewife mom in housework advertising and do not take offense that housework advertising portrays women as the sole providers of home cleaning and comforts. Another significant online barometer of consumer opinions, YouTube, also indicates little dissatisfaction with housework advertising. Posted television commercials for housework products rarely illicit the harsh commentary so common to other types of posts, nor do consumer's own joke commercials offer particularly pointed commentary on advertising generally or gender stereotypes in advertising specifically.

The housewife mom is obviously a more socially acceptable but, I argue, just as limiting representation of home labor. Like the housewife before her since the emergence of modern advertising itself, she's devoting herself to her children; just as spellbound by her pristine (and now environmentally conscious) home; still occasionally assisted by magical housework helpers; and still transforming household cleaning into home-making. She's still tending the hearth and still ensuring the safety and comfort of her family. The housewife mom is still married to the mop, albeit a twenty-first-century version of both the housewife and the mop. As in the Swiffer campaign, she's still embracing new products that free her from housework drudgery and allow her to do *her work*, that is, housework, easily and quickly. In 2008, a P&G representative acknowledged that their own research indicated male consumers liked Swiffer products but, she continued, Swiffer advertising would nonetheless continue to focus on female consumers. The rep stated what all housework advertising reflects: "For the most part we think that women are making—or influencing—purchasing decisions."[23] I believe her. With so many millions at stake, P&G cannot afford major miscalculations about their targeted consumers.

But at the same time, advertising reinforces the feminine frame around housework, re-inscribing the myth that in most families a husband always provides the paycheck and a wife/mother always provides the homemaking. As it has throughout the history of modern advertising, it reinforces our widespread assumption that of course women are the ones buying housework products because in our only popular representation of housework, the housewife mom is the only one responsible for housework and for homemaking. We—marketers, manufacturers, and consumers—cannot seem to contend on a broad cultural scale with the complexities of real-life domesticity in the twenty-first century, and so we rely on the simplistic symbol of the housewife mom. We rely on her ability to disinfect to protect, to provide lovin' from the oven, and to make it good to be home.

Note on Sources

Advertising is by its very nature ephemeral, and a historical study of advertising must acknowledge certain important limitations. First and foremost, archives contain only a small percentage of any type of advertising. (I follow convention by referring to printed ads in magazines and newspapers as "advertisements" and those aired on radio and television as "commercials.") In large part this is due to their role in commerce: although they air or are published for public consumption, in many ways they are considered the intellectual property of ad agencies and their clients. Corporations and their ad agencies keep much of the advertising process confidential. Any saved and catalogued advertising is a closely guarded secret, inaccessible to scholars. However, the collections that are open to scholars do offer a significant sample of print advertising since the advertising created by some of the largest and most influential ad agencies can be taken as a good representative sample of advertising as a whole. *Married to the Mop* is therefore based largely on an examination of the selected records and advertising (especially print advertising) created by the J. Walter Thompson Company, the N. W. Ayer agency, and D'Arcy Masius Benton and Bowles agency. These major collections are archived at the John Hartman Center for Sales, Advertising, and Marketing History, Duke University; The Archives Center, National Museum of American History, Smithsonian Institution; and The D'Arcy Collection, Communications Library, University of Illinois, Urbana-Champagne.

Television commercials are especially difficult to study in any systematic way, as no complete, scholarly archive exists, and, again, although they are aired publicly, any recorded copies of commercials usually exist only within ad agencies and their clients' records, forever inaccessible to academics. In addition, commercials present a unique challenge to scholars because they combine music and pictures to create a text fundamentally different from a print ad. It's possible, as Guy Cook writes, that an academic "analysis cannot adequately cope with music and pictures, because they are different from the mode of analysis itself, which is language."[1] Yet television commercials are such a significant part of modern advertising in general, and the source of some of the most indelible images of housewives specifically, that any study of housework advertising would be incomplete without an analysis of television commercials.

I consulted the commercial compilations held at the Film and Television Archive at the University of California Los Angeles. Most of the archival (before 2009) commercials cited are from these collections. I also examined the reels of 1950s to early 1960s Kraft commercials archived in the Kraft Television Oral History Project collection at the National Museum of American History. Finally, I examined a few television commercials archived at The Moving Image Archive, part of the Internet Archive, founded by Rick Prelinger. The Moving Image Archive, http://www. archive.org/details/prelinger, associated with the Prelinger Library in San Francisco, makes innumerable clips and films open and accessible to all viewers including a portion of the 150,000 cans and reels of ephemeral film that Prelinger donated to the Library of Congress in 2002.[2]

The Internet Archive also includes a considerable collection of 1930s, 1940s, and 1950s radio program recordings. Although *Married to the Mop* does not include extensive analysis of radio commercials, I have supplemented when possible my study of print and television advertising with examples from radio. Some of these commercials I heard as recordings on the Internet Archive. I also read radio commercial scripts as well as other types of agency documents describing radio commercial campaigns in the collections listed above.

While I believe these collections offered a reasonably representative sample of advertising, an important part of my argument is that the housewife figure in advertising, beginning in the late 1960s and early 1970s, has not always been exclusively Caucasian. In today's general media she may appear as African American or vaguely "ethnic" in some other way. However, the general collections listed above offer only limited examples of this aspect of housework advertising. I therefore supplemented my research in the institutional archives with my own research on advertising in two key periodicals, *Essence* and *Buenhogar*. First published in 1970, "*Essence* is the only long-standing magazine that targets Black women and addresses specifically their cultural and emotional needs as African Americans and women," and continues to "boast a monthly readership base of 7.5 million worldwide."[3] Its mission and content are slightly different than general women's service magazines like *Good Housekeeping* but are nonetheless comparable enough to include a notable number of housework product advertisements.[4] *Buenhogar* (literally "good home") caters to an even larger and potentially more profitable consumer group: Hispanic women. In different versions, *Buenhogar*, an offshoot of Hearst Corporation's *Good Housekeeping*, began publication in the 1970s. The U.S. version, which was published containing far fewer advertisements than the English language edition, continued until May 2008. Other editions published in other countries continue publication today in 2011.

Essence and Buenhogar are targeted media, their advertising created to market products specifically to African American and Latina women. It's therefore no surprise that when housework product companies advertised in these magazines, the housewife or housewife mom pictured in the ad was almost always African American or Latina. However, the fact that ad makers and their housework product clients (beginning in earnest in the 1970s) so easily and readily translated "the housewife" into an African American woman, for example, in order to market their housework products, demonstrates that advertisers could and did alter the housewife figure when changing market and social conditions demanded. Yet the representation of housework as feminine homemaking in modern advertising remained virtually unchanged. Including these publications in my study therefore offered essential evidence about the history of housework advertising as a whole.

Full issues, systematically stored by date, of Essence are readily available in online databases and on microfilm. I examined all issues (complete) published from 1988 to 1995, and then a representative sample of all issues published from 1970 to 1973, 1989, 1990, 1995, and 2000. It proved more difficult to find archived copies of Buenhogar, but I was able to examine all issues published from 2004 to 2008 at the Manchester Public Library in Connecticut. To round out the archival ad source sample, I also examined the full issues of Good Housekeeping magazine as published in 1989, 1990, 1995, and 2000.

In order to assess contemporary print housework advertising, I examined full issues as published of Good Housekeeping, 2008–2009, and Parents magazine, 2008–2009. To assess contemporary television commercials, I viewed, as broadcast, the commercials on ABC's program, "The View" for a period of ten months (January 2009–October 2009). This program is aimed at female viewers, specifically mothers, and so regularly solicits housework product sponsors. However, the commercials aired during these programs for housework products are the same commercials aired during other types of programs as well. They are not all different in content but merely in frequency, allowing me to view the maximum number during my test period.

Finally, Married to the Mop focuses on a limited but representative selection of housework products. Although not included here, my analysis of advertising for other housework products, such as household appliances (namely vacuum cleaners and sewing machines), and for infant care products, such as diapers, confirms the argument posited in this study.

Notes

Introduction

1. Vanessa Facenda, "This is One Swiffer Picker-Upper," *Brandweek*, February 11, 2008, 22; Brian Rupp, "Pity Those Loser Mops," *Brandweek*, August 25, 2008, 60.
2. Susan Strasser, *Never Done: A History of American Housework* (New York: Henry Holt, 1982, 2000), 6.
3. Ruth Schwartz Cowan, *More Work for Mother: The Ironies of Household Technology from the Open Hearth to the Microwave* (New York: Basic Books, 1983), 45; Christine Bose, Philip Bereano, and Mary Malloy, "Household Technology and the Social Construction of Housework," *Signs: Journal of Women in Culture and Society* 25, no. 1 (1984): 53–82; Eileen B. Leonard, *Women, Technology, and the Myth of Progress* (Upper Saddle River: Prentice-Hall, 2003); Joel Mokyr, "Why 'More Work for Mother?' Knowledge and Household Behavior, 1870–1945," *Journal of Economic History* 60, no. 1 (2000): 1–41.
4. Alana Erickson Coble, *Cleaning Up: The Transformation of Domestic Service in Twentieth Century New York* (New York: Routledge, 2006), 89; Faye E. Dudden, *Serving Women: Household Service in Nineteenth-Century America* (Middletown: Wesleyan University Press, 1983), 107; Marilyn Irvin Holt, *Linoleum, Better Babies and the Modern Farm Woman, 1890–1930* (Albuquerque, NM: University of New Mexico Press, 1995), 40; Laura Ousely, "The Business of Housekeeping: The Mistress, the Domestic Worker, and the Construction of Class," *Legacy: A Journal of American Women Writers* 23, no. 2 (2006): 132–147; Phyllis Palmer, *Domesticity and Dirt: Housewives and Domestic Servants in the United States, 1920–1945* (Philadelphia: Temple University Press, 1989), 90, 138; Strasser, *Never Done*, 164; Daniel E. Sutherland, *Americans and Their Servants: Domestic Service from 1800 to 1920* (Baton Rouge: Louisiana State University Press, 1981), 10, 18.
5. Suellen Hoy, *Chasing Dirt: The American Pursuit of Cleanliness* (New York: Oxford University Press, 1995), 7; Guliz Ger and Baskin Yeniciglu, "Clean and Dirty: Playing with Boundaries of Consumers' Safe Havens," *Advances in Consumer Research* 31 (2004): 462–467; William Smyth, "Oh! To Be Clean: Domestic Cleanliness in Mid-Nineteenth-Century America," *Lamar Journal of Humanities* 17, no. 2 (1993): 53–73; Juliann Sivulka, *Stronger Than Dirt: A Cultural History*

of Advertising Personal Hygiene in America, 1875 to 1940 (Amherst: Humanity Books, 2001), 63. On germ theory, see Lydia Martens and Sue Scott, "Under the Kitchen Surface: Domestic Products and Conflicting Constructions of Home," *Home Cultures* 3, no. 1 (2006): 42–43. For contemporary views, see Don Fernandez, "Swept Up in Need to Clean: In an Era of High Anxiety, We're Finding Comfort in the Conquest of Grime, Germs, and Untidiness," *Atlanta Journal-Constitution*, November 28, 2004, MS1. On domestic reform, see Dolores Hayden, *Grand Domestic Revolution: A History of Feminist Designs for American Homes, Neighborhoods, and Cities* (Cambridge: MIT Press, 1982); Jennifer Scanlon, "Old Housekeeping, New Housekeeping, or No Housekeeping? The Kitchenless Home Movement and the Women's Service Magazine," *Journalism History* 30, no. 1 (2004): 2–10.

6. On magazines, see Ralph M. Hower, *The History of an Advertising Agency: N. W. Ayer and Son at Work, 1869–1939* (Cambridge: Harvard University Press, 1939). On the impact of photography, see Mandy Schutzman, *The Real Thing: Performance, Hysteria, and Advertising* (Hanover: Wesleyan University Press, 1999), 35. On radio, see Kathy M. Newman, *Radio Active: Advertising and Consumer Activism, 1933–1947* (Berkeley: University of California Press, 2004). On television, see James L. Baughman, *Same Time, Same Station: Creating American Television, 1948–1961* (Baltimore: Johns Hopkins University Press, 2007), 192–218; Lawrence Samuel, *Brought to You By: Postwar Television Advertising and the American Dream* (Austin: University of Texas Press, 2001).

7. Julianne Sivulka, *Soap, Sex, and Cigarettes: A Cultural History of American Advertising* (Belmont: Wadsworth Publishing, 1998), 4.

8. Pamela Walker Laird writes in *Advertising Progress: American Business and the Rise of Consumer Marketing* (Baltimore: Johns Hopkins University Press, 1998), 5: "Prior to the 1890s, the vast majority of advertisements were created by merchants and manufacturers, aided by printers but not by specialized advertising professionals. This is still the case for the legions of small advertisers in all media." However, advertising agencies created the vast majority of the ads and commercials I examined.

9. Regina Blaszczyk, *American Consumer Society, 1865–2005: From Hearth to HDTV* (Wheeling: Harlan Davidson, 2005), 124–125; 130–131.

10. Gail Collins, *America's Women: 400 Years of Dolls, Drudges, Helpmates, and Heroines* (New York: Harper Collins, 2003); Christina Hardyment, *Dream Babies: Three Centuries of Good Advice on Child Care* (New York: Harper Row, 1983); Sarah Leavitt, *From Catherine Beecher to Martha Stewart: A Cultural History of Domestic Advice* (Chapel Hill: University of North Carolina Press, 2002).

11. Megan Elias, *Stir it Up: Home Economics in American Culture* (Philadelphia: University of Pennsylvania Press, 2008); Laurel D. Graham, "Domesticating Efficiency: Lillian Gilbreth's Scientific Management of Homemakers, 1924–1930," *Signs: Journal of Women in Culture and Society* 24, no. 3 (1999): 633–675; Janice Williams Rutherford, *Selling Mrs. Consumer: Christine Frederick and the Rise of Household Efficiency* (Athens: The University of Georgia Press, 2003); Laura Shapiro, *Perfection Salad: Women and Cooking at the Turn of the Century*

(New York: Farrar, Straus, and Giroux, 1983); Sarah Stage and Virginia Vincenti, *Rethinking Home Economics: Women and the History of a Profession* (New York: Cornell University Press, 1997).

12. Eileen Boris, "The Home as Workplace: Deconstructing Dichotomies," *International Review of Social History* 39 (1994): 415–428; Nancy Christie, "Women, the Public Sphere, and Middle class Culture," *Journal of Women's History* 20, no. 1 (2008): 237–246; Judy Giles, *The Parlour and the Suburb: Domestic Identities, Class, Femininity and Modernity* (Oxford: Berg Publishers, 2004); Nona Y. Glazer, "Servants to Capital: Unpaid Domestic Labor and Paid Work," *Review of Radical Political Economics* 16, no. 1 (1984): 61–87; Joan B. Landes, "Further Thoughts on the Public/Private Distinction," *Journal of Women's History* 15, no. 2 (2003): 28–39; Susan Ingalls Lewis, *Unexceptional Women: Female Proprietors in Mid-Nineteenth Century Albany, New York, 1830–1885* (Columbus: Ohio State University Press, 2009); Alison Piepmeir, "Stepping Out: Rethinking the Public and Private Spheres," *Journal of Women's History* 18, no. 3 (2006): 128–137; Joan W. Scott and Debra Keates, eds., *Going Public: Feminism and Shifting Boundaries of the Private Sphere* (Urbana: University of Illinois Press, 2004); Nicole Tonkovich, "Ghosts of Domesticities Past," *Journal of Women's History* 18, no. 3 (2006): 118–127; Kim Warren, "Separate Spheres: Analytical Persistence in United States Women's History," *History Compass* 5, no. 1 (2007): 262–277. On race, see Elizabeth Clark-Lewis, *Living In, Living Out: African-American Domestics in Washington, D.C, 1910–1940* (Washington: Smithsonian Institute Press, 1994); Sarah Deutsch, *Separate Refuge: Culture, Class, and Gender on the Anglo-Hispanic Frontier in the American Southwest, 1880–1940* (New York: Oxford University Press, 1987); Evelyn Nakano Glen, *Issei, Nisei, War Bride: Three Generations of Japanese American Women in Domestic Service* (Philadelphia: Temple University Press, 1990); Diane Hotten-Somers, "Relinquishing and Reclaiming Independence: Irish Domestic Servants, American Middle Class Mistresses, and Assimilation, 1850–1920," *Eire-Ireland* 36, nos. 1–2 (2001): 185–201; Jacqueline Jones, *Labor of Love, Labor of Sorrow: Black Women, Work, and the Family from Slavery to the Present* (New York: Basic Books, 1985); Marilyn Maness Mehaffy, "Advertising Race/Raceing Advertising: The Feminine Consumer (-Nation), 1876–1900," *Signs: The Journal of Women in Culture and Society* 23, no. 1 (1997): 121–174.

13. Glenna Matthew, *Just a Housewife:" The Rise and Fall of Domesticity in America* (New York: Oxford University Press, 1987), 35. See also Linda J. Rynbrandt, *Caroline Bartlett Crane and Progressive Reform: Social Housekeeping as Sociology* (New York: Garland, 1999); Daphne Spain, *How Women Saved the City* (Minneapolis: University of Minnesota Press, 2002).

14. Nancy Flobre, "The Unproductive Housewife: Her Evolution in Nineteenth-Century Economic Thought," *Signs* 16, no. 1 (1991): 463–484; Dana Frank, "Housewives, Socialists, and the Politics of Food: The 1917 New York Cost-of-Living Protests," *Feminist Studies* 11, no. 2 (1985): 255–285; Izola Forrester, "Women Capture the Food Market," *Good Housekeeping*, May 1912, 670–675; Lesley Johnson and Justin Lloyd, *Sentenced to Everyday Life: Feminism and the Housewife* (New York: Berg Publishers, 2004); Sylvie Murray, *The*

Progressive Housewife: Community Activism in Suburban Queens, 1945–1965 (Philadelphia: University of Pennsylvania Press, 2003); Annelise Orleck, "'We are that mythical thing called the public:' Militant Housewives During the Great Depression," *Feminist Studies* 19, no. 1 (1993): 147–172; Lesley Johnson and Justin Lloyd, *Sentenced to Everyday Life: Feminism and the Housewife* (New York: Berg Publishers, 2004). On the 1960s debate, see Norah Lee Alter, "I Won't Apologize for Being a Housewife!" *Ladies Home Journal*, June 1979, 24+; Terry Martin Hekker, "Up With Housewives!" *Good Housekeeping*, May 1978, 250+; "Evelyn Kaye, "Housewife Power!" *Parents Magazine*, August 1979, 40–44; Patricia Kroken, "I'm a Housewife and I Have the Right to Be Proud," *Redbook*, July 1973, 38; Shirley Streshinsky, "Why Housewife is No Longer a Dirty Word," *Redbook*, February 1978, 90+.

15. Assumptions about female consumers continue to shape housework advertising, even when industry studies suggest marketing to men could increase sales. Anthony Astrachan, "Marketing to Men: Magnifying Changes in Masculine Marketplace," *Advertising Age*, October 8, 1984, 11–13; "Large Number of Husbands Buy Household Products, Do Housework," *Marketing News*, October 3, 1980, 1; Lenore Skenazy, "Dads are the New Moms, So It's Time to Start Selling Them Stuff," *Advertising Age*, August 20, 2007, 11; Laura Zinn, "Real Men Buy Paper Towels Too," *Business Week*, November 9, 1992, 75–76. Thanks to Dr. Michelle Ladd for her insights into the "provider myth."

16. Roland Marchland, *Advertising the American Dream: Making Way for Modernity, 1920–1940* (Berkeley: University of California Press, 1985), xvii.

17. Annegret S. Ogden, *The Great American Housewife: From Helpmate to Wage Earner, 1776–1985* (Westport: Greenwood Press, 1985), 158; Rutherford, *Selling Mrs. Consumer*, 128, 146–151.

18. Stephanie Coontz, *A Strange Stirring: The Feminine Mystique and American Women at the Dawn of the 1960s* (New York: Basic Books, 2011), 38. Coontz is paraphrasing Betty Friedan's analysis in *The Feminine Mystique* (New York: Norton, 1963, 2001), 324–325.

19. Marjorie Gail Anderson, "'The Happy Housewife' Stereotype in Contemporary Business Magazine Advertisements," M.A. thesis, Louisiana State University, 1989; Ahmed Belkaoui and Janice M. Belkaoui, "A Comparative Analysis of the Roles Portrayed by Women in Print Advertisements: 1958, 1970, 1972," *Journal of Marketing Research* 13, no. 2 (1976): 168–172; Scott Coltrane and Michele Adams, "Work-Family Imagery and Gender Stereotypes: Television and the Reproduction of Difference," *Journal of Vocational Behavior* 50 (1997): 323–347; Scott Coltrane and Melinda Messineo, "The Perpetuation of Subtle Prejudice: Race and Gender Imagery in 1990s Television Advertising," *Sex Roles* 42, nos. 5–6 (2000): 363–389; Alice E. Courtney and Sarah Wernick Lockeretz, "A Woman's Place: An Analysis of Roles Portrayed by Women in Magazine Advertising, *Journal of Marketing Research* 1 (February 1971): 92–95; Gayle Kaufman, "The Portrayal of Men's Family Roles in Television Commercials," *Sex Roles* 41, nos. 5–6 (1999): 439–458; Carolyn Lin, "Beefcake Versus Cheesecake in the 1990s: Sexist Portrayals of Both Genders in Television Commercials," *Howard Journal of Communications* 8, no. 3 (1997): 237–249; William O'Barr, "Representations of Masculinity and Femininity

in Advertisements," *Advertising and Society Review* 7, no. 2 (2006): http://muse. jhu.edu/journals/asr/v007/7.2unit07.html (accessed October 3, 2010).

20. Beth Hentges, Jo Ann Meier, and Robert Bartsch, "The Effects of Race, Gender, and Bias on Linking of Commercials with Perceived Stereotypes," *Current Research in Social Psychology* 13, no. 6 (2007): 64–78; Sue Lafky, Margaret Duffy, Mary Steinmaus, and Dan Berkowitz, "Looking Through Gendered Lenses: Female Stereotyping and Gender Role Expectations," *Journalism and Mass Communication Quarterly* 73, no. 2 (1996): 379–388.

21. On reader response theory, see Janet Staiger, *Media Reception Studies* (New York: New York University Press, 2005). For a good example of textual based analysis of advertising and gender stereotypes, see Daniel Delis Hill, *Advertising to the American Woman 1900–1999* (Columbus: Ohio State University Press, 2002).

22. See especially Jean Kilbourne, *Deadly Persuasion: Why Women and Girls Must Fight the Addictive Power of Advertising* (New York: Free Press, 1999).

23. Joann Lipman, "Television Ads Ring Up No Sale in Study," *Wall Street Journal,* February 15, 1989, 1; Michael Schudson, *Advertising: The Uneasy Persuasion: Its Dubious Impact on American Society* (New York: Basic Books, 1986), xiii.

24. Blaszczyk, *American Consumer Society,* 121–122; Juliann Sivulka, "The Fabulous Fifties: Selling Mr. And Mrs. Consumer," *Advertising and Society Review* 9, no. 4 (2008): http://muse.jhu.edu/journals/advertising_and_society_review/ v009/9.4.sivulka.html (accessed October 3, 2010).

25. Erin Dejesus, "Mad Women," *Bust,* December/January 2009, 50–54; Dee Gill, "More than Just 'Mad Men,'" *Crain's Chicago Business,* October 6, 2008; Bernice Kanner, "Ad Workplace Change, Via One Woman's Eyes," *Advertising Age,* March 28, 2005, 80–81; Jennifer Scanlon, *Inarticulate Longings: The Ladies Home Journal, Gender, and the Promise of Consumer Culture* (New York: Routledge, 1995), 171–195; Juliann Sivulka, *Ad Women: How They Impact What We Need, Want, and Buy* (Amherst: Prometheus Books, 2008). On race, see Jason Chambers, *Madison Avenue and the Color Line: African Americans in the Advertising Industry* (Philadelphia: University of Pennsylvania Pres, 2007); Andrew McMains, "Diversity Study Takes Ad Biz to Task," *adweek.com,* January 9, 2009; Marissa Miley and Ken Wheaton, "Agencies Not Only Lack Black Workers, They Pay Them Less," *Advertising Age,* January 12, 2009, 1; Stuart Elliot, "A Lawyer's Call for a Greater Black Presence in Agencies," *New York Times,* January 9, 2009, B6.

26. Rena Bartos, *The Moving Target: What Every Marketer Should Know About Women* (New York: The Free Press, 1982); Iain Ellwood and Shelia Shekar, *Wonder Woman: Marketing Secrets for the Trillion Dollar Customer* (New York: Palgrave Macmillan, 2008); Bernice Kanner, *Pocketbook Power* (New York: McGraw Hill, 2004).

27. Teresa Mastin, "Product Purchase Decision-Making Behavior and Gender Role Stereotypes: A Content Analysis of Advertisements in *Essence* and *Ladies' Home Journal,* 1990–1999," *The Howard Journal of Communication* 15 (2004): 241.

28. As quoted by James C. Foust and Katherine Bradshaw, "Something for the Boys: Framing Images of Women in Broadcasting Magazine in the 1950s," *Journalism History* 33, no. 2 (2007): 93.

29. As Mary P. Ryan points out in her literary study of domesticity, *The Empire of the Mother: American Writing About Domesticity 1830–1860* (New York: Haworth Press, 1982), 11–12: "Popular literature as an object of historical inquiry is important, and in some ways more complete and resonant, than raw individual experience. It records the way in which that experience was sorted out, evaluated, assigned relative importance, and given human and social meaning." The same holds true for understanding domestic norms via an analysis of advertising.

30. Pamela Walker Laird, "Progress in Separate Spheres: Selling Nineteenth-Century Technologies," *Knowledge and Society* 10 (1996): 19; Mandy Schutzman, *The Real Thing: Performance, Hysteria, and Advertising* (Hanover: Wesleyan University Press, 1999), 117.

31. Gail Collins, *When Everything Changed: The Amazing Journey of American Women from 1960 to the Present* (New York: Little, Brown, and Company, 2009). See also Ruth Rosen, *The World Split Open* (New York: Penguin Books, 2000).

32. Kenneth Allan and Scott Coltrane, "Gender Displaying Television Commercials: A Comparative Study of Television Commercials in the 1950s and 1980s," *Sex Roles* 35, nos. 3–4 (1996): 185–203; Judith Barnes, "Gender Portrayals in Magazine Advertising: A Comparative Analysis of Three Elements in Gender Imagery in Magazine Ads in 1953, 1979, and 1983: Faces, Places, and Products," Ph.D. diss., Rensselaer Polytechnic Institute, 1984; Adreinne Ward Fawcett, "Friedan Sees Real Progress in Women's Ads," *Advertising Age*, October 4, 1993, 2; Eileen Prescott, "Real Men Do Wear Aprons," *Across the Board*, November 1983, 51–56; Nancy Roberts, "From Pumps, Pearls and Pleats to Pants, Briefcases, and Hardhats: Changes in the Portrayal of Women in Advertising and Fiction in *Ladies Home Journal*, 1960–1962 to 1974–1976," Paper presented at the Annual Meeting of The Association for Education in Journalism (Boston: August 9–13, 1980); Kenneth C. Schneider and Sharon Barich Schneider, "Trends in Sex Roles in Television Commercials," *Journal of Marketing* 43 (1979): 79–84.

33. "Ad Needn't Tell What She's Like (She Knows)" and "Function of Woman in Ad is to Sell Product, Stewart Says," *Marketing News*, April 21, 1978, 13; Barbara Bryant, "Combined Career-Homemaker Lifestyle Grows Ever More Popular Among Women," *Marketing News*, January 18, 1977, 3; Karen Gentleman, "Not All Women Watch TV Soaps or Work as High-Powered Execs," *Marketing News*, September 5, 1980s, 5; Marybeth Laruea, "Consumer: Women Torn Between Two Stereotypes," *Madison Avenue*, August 1983, 28–33; William J. Lundstrom and Donald Sciglimpaglia, "Sex Role Portrayals in Advertising," *Journal of Marketing* 41, no. 3 (July 1977): 72–79; Patricia D. Mamay and Richard L. Simpson, "Three Female Roles in Television Commercials," *Sex Roles* 7, no. 1 (1981): 1224–1232; Louis C. Wagner and Janis B. Banos, "A Woman's Place: A Follow-Up Analysis of the Roles Portrayed by Women in Magazine Advertisements," *Journal of Marketing Research* 10, no. 2 (May 1973): 213–214.

34. Bryan K. Robinson and Erica Hunter, "Is Mom Still Doing It All? Reexamining Depictions of Family Work in Popular Advertising," *Journal of Family Issues* 29 (2008), 482.

35. Maria Bailey, *Mom 3-0: Marketing to Today's Mothers* (Deadwood: Wyatt-McKenzie Publishing, 2008); Becky Ebenkamp, "The Post-Soccer Mom," *Brandweek*, June 23, 2008, 22–26; Emily Foshee, "Navigating the Mommy Blogosphere: Reach the World's Largest Target Market," *Public Relations Tactics*, May 2010, 10–14; Nora Lee, *The Mom Factor: What Really Drives Where We Shop, Eat, and Play* (Washington: Urban Land Institute, 2005); "Marketing to Moms," *Adweek*, September 28, 2009, 1–5.

36. Judith Warner, *Perfect Madness: Motherhood in the Age of Anxiety* (New York: Riverhead Books, 2005), 9.

37. Susan J. Douglas and Meredith W. Michaels, *The Mommy Myth: The Idealization of Motherhood and How It Has Undermined Women* (New York: Free Press, 2004), 4.

38. Ibid., 20–21. See also Ben Yoganda, "My Heart Belongs to Mother," *New York Times*, May 14, 2006, C14.

39. Robert Bartsch, "Gender Representations in Television Commercials: Updating an Update," *Sex Roles* 43, nos. 9–10 (2000): 735–743; Emmanuella Plakoyiannaki, "Images of Women in Online Advertisements of Global Products: Does Sexism Exist?" *Journal of Business Ethics* 83 (2008): 101–112.

40. Edumund Andrews, "Survey Confirms It: Women Outjuggle Men," *New York Times*, September 15, 2004: A23; Gabriella Boston, "Sour Economy Adds to Moms' Tasks," *The Washington Times*, January 28, 2009, http://www. washingtontimes.com/news/2009/jan/28/woe-is-mom (accessed October 3, 2010); Marilyn Gardner, "The Artful Dodge of Housework: More Men Pitch in to Help Around the House These Days; But Women Still Do More," *Christian Science Monitor*, July 6, 2005, 11; Constance Gager, Laura Sanchez, and Alred Emaris, "Whose Time Is It? The Effect of Employment and Work/Family Stress on Children's Housework," *The Journal of Family Issues*, no. 30, no. 11 (2009): 1459–1485; Sharon Jayson, "Married Women, Unite! Husbands Do Far Less Housework; So Says Study of 28 Countries," *USA Today*, August 29, 2007; Amy Joyce, "Household Chores Conform to Stereotypes: In the Work-Family Balance Act, Women Still Do Most of the Juggling," *Washington Post*, September 19, 2004, F5; "Married Women Do Twice as Much Housework as Their Husbands Do," *Marketing to Women*, March 2002, 3; Andrew Singleton and Janemaree Mahar, "The 'New Man' Is in the House: Young Men, Social Change, and Housework," *The Journal of Men's Studies* 12, no. 3 (2004): 227–240.

41. Lisa Gidding, "Political Economy and the Construction of Gender: The Example of Housework Within Same-Sex Households," *Feminist Economics* 4, no. 2 (1998): 97–106; Diana Khor, "'Doing Gender:' A Critical Review and an Exploration of Lesbigay Domestic Arrangements," *Journal of GLBT Family Studies* 3, no. 1 (2007): 35–73; Mignon Moore, "Gendered Power Relations Among Women: A Study of Household Decision Making in Black, Lesbian Stepfamilies," *American Sociological Review* 73, no. 2 (2008): 335–356; Kristin Natlie, "'I'm Not His Wife: Doing Gender and Doing Housework in the Absence of Women," *Journal of Sociology* 39, no. 2 (2003): 253–269; Sarah Oerton, "Reclaiming the 'Housewife?' Lesbians and Household Work," in

Gillian A. Dunne, ed., *Living "Difference:" Lesbian Perspectives on Work and Family Life* (New York: Haworth Press, 1998); Carla A. Pfeffer, "'Women's Work?' Women Partners of Transgender Men Doing Housework and Emotion Work," *Journal of Marriage and Family* 72, no. 1 (2010): 165–183.

42. Suzanne Bianchi, "Is Anyone Doing the Housework? Trends in the Gender Division of Household Labor," *Social Forces* 70, no. 1 (2000): 191–229; Sharon Claffey and Kristin Mickelson, "Division of Household Labor and Distress: The Role of Perceived Fairness for Employed Mothers," *Sex Roles* 60, no. 11/13 (2009): 819–831; "Few Couples Argue Over Housework," *Marketing to Women*, April 2006, 8; Maggie Jackson, "Division of Labor: Gender Gap in Housework Narrows, But Remains," *Boston Globe*, November 7, 2004, G1; Ruth Davis Konigsberg, "Chore Wars," *Time*, August 8, 2011, 44–49; Sue Shellengbarger, "Giving Credit Where Credit is Due: Men Do More Housework Than Women Think," *Wall Street Journal*, May 19, 2005, D1. On how individual experiences of housework, see Sarah Pink, *Home Truths: Gender, Domestic Objects and Everyday Life* (New York: Berg, 2004); Nancy Rollins Ahlander and Kathleen Salugh Bahr, "Beyond Drudgery, Power, and Equity: Toward an Expanded Discourse on the Moral Dimensions of Housework in Families," *Journal of Marriage and the Family* 57, no. 1 (1995): 54–68; Glenna Spitze and Karyn A. Losocco, "The Labor of Sisyphus? Women's and Men's Reactions to Housework," *Social Science Quarterly* 81, no. 4 (2000): 1087–1100; Anne-Rigt Poortman and Tanja Van Der Lippe, "Attitudes Toward Housework and Child Care and the Gendered Division of Labor," *Journal of Marriage and Family* 71, no. 3 (2009): 526–541.

43. Caitlin Flanagan, *To Hell with All That: Loving and Loathing Our Inner Housewife* (Boston: Back Bay Books, 2007); Shannon Hayes, *Radical Homemakers: Reclaiming Domesticity from a Consumer Culture* (Richmondville: Left to Write Press, 2010); Darla Shine, *Happy Housewives: I Was a Whining, Miserable, Desperate Housewife—But I Finally Snapped Out of It . . . You Can Too!* (New York: Avon Books, 2006); Jean Zimmerman, *Made from Scratch: Reclaiming the Pleasures of the American Hearth* (New York: Free Press, 2003).

44. The humor in many contemporary housework product commercials often subtly reinforces gender stereotypes. Erica Scharrer, D. Daniel Kim, Ke-Ming Lin, and Zixu Liu Working Hard or Hardly Working? Gender, Humor, and the Performance of Domestic Chores in Television Commercials," *Mass Communications and Society* 9, no. 2 (2006): 215–238.

Chapter 1

1. On the first soaps specifically made for laundry use, see "The House that Lever Built," *Television Age*, October 30, 1961, 35.

2. Susan Strasser, *Never Done: A History of American Housework* (New York: Henry Holt, 1982, 2000), 109, 105.

3. "Wringer Washers 1907–1983" (U.S.A.: Maytag Corporation, 1983), n.p., Business Ephemera Vertical Files, Warshaw Collection of Business Americana, Archives Center, National Museum of American History, Smithsonian

Institution (hereafter cited as Business Ephemera, Warshaw Collection). On the evolution of laundry work, see Ruth Schwartz Cowan, *More Work for Mother: The Ironies of Household Technology from the Open Hearth to the Microwave* (New York: Basic Books, 1983), 105, 143, 195–196; Strasser, *Never Done*, 122.

4. "The History of Lux Flakes, 1916–1951," Account Files Collection, "Lever Brothers," J. Walter Thompson Company Collection, The John W. Hartman Center for Sales, Advertising, and Marketing History, Duke University (hereafter cited as Lever Brothers Account Files, JWT Collection); Research Department, "Lever Brothers Company Advertising History" (1944), Lever Brothers Account Files, JWT Collection (hereafter cited as Lever Brothers Company Advertising History); Lucy Saddleton, "Tide Rolls On," *Strategy*, October 2008, http://www.strategymag.com.

5. Roland Marchland, *Advertising the American Dream: Making Way for Modernity, 1920–1940* (Berkeley: University of California Press, 1985), 202–203; Jennifer Scanlon, *Inarticulate Longings: The Ladies Home Journal and the Promises of Consumer Culture* (New York: Routledge, 1995), 34. Marilyn Maness Mehaffy, "Advertising Race/Racing Advertising: The Feminine Consumer (-Nation), 1876–1990," *Signs* 23, no. 1(1997): 158, argues that the depiction of white "French" maids in 1920s advertising would not have been possible without the earlier depiction, on ad trade cards, of black female servants.

6. Roy Lightner Collection of Antique Advertisements, John W. Hartman Center for Sales, Advertising, and Marketing History, Duke University (hereafter cited as Lightner Collection).

7. Borax advertisement, Business Ephemera, Warshaw Collection.

8. "Ivory Project: Advertising Soap in America, 1838–1998," Archives Center, National Museum of American History, Smithsonian, http://americanhistory.si.edu/archives/Ivory (accessed May 1, 2009).

9. Creative Staff Meeting, "Mr. Day Presiding," May 25, 1932, Lever Brothers Account Files, JWT Collection.

10. Unless otherwise noted, Lux advertisements from Domestic Advertisements Collection, J. Walter Thompson Company Collection, John W. Hartman Center for Sales, Advertising, and Marketing History, Duke University (hereafter cited as Domestic Ad Collection, JWT Collection).

11. "Emergence of Advertising in Modern America," John W. Hartman Center for Sales, Advertising, and Marketing History, http://library.duke.edu/digitalcollections/eaa (accessed May 1, 2009).

12. Christine Zmroczek, "Women, Class, and Washing Machines, 1920s–1960s," *Women's Studies International Forum* 15, no. 2 (1992): 175.

13. As recalled by my grandmother Alison Merriam Payne (b. 1920).

14. Juliann Sivulka, *Stronger Than Dirt: A Cultural History of Advertising Personal Hygiene in America, 1875 to 1940* (New York: Humanity Books, 2001), 208; Carole Lopate, "Selling to Mrs. Consumer," *College English* 38, no. 8 (1977): 831.

15. Unless otherwise noted, all Rinso advertising from Lightner Collection.

16. On "daintiness," see Phyllis Palmer, *Domesticity and Dirt: Housewives and Domestic Servants in the United States, 1920–1945* (Philadelphia: Temple University Press, 1989), 33.

17. Suellen Hoy, *Chasing Dirt: The American Pursuit of Cleanliness* (New York: Oxford University Press, 1995), 147.
18. "Lever Brothers Company Advertising History," Lever Brothers Account Files, JWT Collection, n.p.
19. D'Arcy Masius Benton and Bowles Archive, John W. Hartman Center for Sales, Advertising, and Marketing History, Duke University (hereafter cited as DMB&B Archive).
20. JWT Domestic Ad Collection, Hartman Center.
21. Ibid.; "History of Lux Flakes, 1916–1951," Lever Brothers Account Files, JWT Collection.
22. Hoy, *Chasing Dirt*, 7; Guliz Ger and Baskin Yeniciglu, "Clean and Dirty: Playing with Boundaries of Consumers' Safe Havens," *Advances in Consumer Research* 31 (2004): 462–467.
23. All Super Suds ads from DMB&B Archive.
24. Founded in 1920 as Benton and Bowles, this large and influential agency merged with D'Arcy and Masius in 1985 but because all archived materials are currently classified as the work of DMB&B, I refer it throughout as DMB&B.
25. Domestic Ad Collection, JWT Collection.
26. Barton Cummings Papers, Archive Center, National Museum of American History, Smithsonian Institution (hereafter cited as Cummings Papers).
27. Ibid.
28. "Oxydol Goes Into High" (1938), Moving Image Archive, Prelinger Archives, Internet Archives, http://www.archive.org/details/oxydol_goes_into_high1938 (accessed June 1, 2009).
29. "It was an [advertising] agency man who was responsible for [Proctor and Gamble's] heavy investment in daytime radio." *Printer's Ink*, January 25, 1963, 8.
30. Morleen Rouse Getz, "Daytime Radio Programming for the Homemaker, 1926–1965," *Journal of Popular Culture* 12, no. 2 (1978): 315–327; Jack Neff, "Marketers of the Century: Proctor and Gamble," *Advertising Age*, December 13, 1999, 24–27; Susan Smulyan, "Radio Advertising to Women in Twenties America: 'A Latchkey to Every Home,'" *Historical Journal of Film, Radio, and Television* 13, no. 3 (1999): 299–314.
31. Marilyn Lavin, "Creating Consumers in the 1930s: Irna Phillips and the Radio Soap Opera," *The Journal of Consumer Research* 22, no. 1 (1995): 75–89; Kathy M. Newman, *Radio Active: Advertising and Consumer Activism, 1933–1947* (Berkeley: University of California Press, 2004), 9. See also Ruth Palter, "Radio's Attraction for Housewives," *Hollywood Quarterly* 3, no. 3 (Spring 1948): 248–257.
32. Advertisement from Cummings Papers.
33. Creative Staff Meeting, "Mr. Day Presiding," May 25, 1932, Lever Brothers Account Files, JWT Collection; "History of Lux Flakes, 1916–1951," Lever Brothers Account Files, JWT Collection.
34. "Amos and Andy" (1944), Audio Archive, Internet Archive, http://www.archive.org/details/AmosandAndy1944 (accessed June 1, 2009).
35. All Surf print ads from Advertising Series, Ayer Records.

36. Artherton W. Hobler, "The Triangle of Marketing Success" Mss. (1970s), 125, DMB&B Archive (hereafter cited as Hobler, "The Triangle of Marketing Success").

37. Ibid., 125–126.

38. Saddleton, "Tide Rolls On;" "Laundry Detergent and Laundry Additive Commercials," Classic TV Collection, Moving Image Archive, Internet Archive http://www.archive.org/details/SomeLaundryDetergentLaundryAdditiveCommercials (all commercials accessed June 1, 2009) (collection hereafter cited as "Laundry Detergent," Classic TV Collection, Internet Archive).

39. Hobler, "The Triangle of Marketing Success," 126.

40. Ibid., 127.

41. Saddleton, "Tide Rolls On."

42. Hobler, "The Triangle of Marketing Success," 128.

43. Unless otherwise noted, all archival commercials from commercial compilations held and viewed at The Film and Television Archive, University of California, Los Angeles.

44. All Tide print ads from DMB&B Archives.

45. Andi Zeiser, *Feminism and Pop Culture* (Berkeley: Seal Press, 2008), 58–59.

46. John Caples to Iris Sturtevent, 7 February 1955, John Caples Papers, Archive Center, National Museum of American History, Smithsonian Institution (hereafter cited as Caples Papers); "Assessment of Effectiveness of Germicidal Claims for a Packaged Detergent," March 25, 1954, Caples Papers. The "no sneeze" campaign Rinso ran in the 1940s was, according to the copywriter who designed it, based on the idea that "an improvement in Rinso eliminated most of the 'soap-dust' that caused sneezing." Perry Schoefield, *100 Top Copy Writers and Their Favorite Ads* (New York: Printer's Ink Publishing Company, 1954), n.p. Similar radio commercials for Rinso suggested that the product allowed housewives to avoid "washday hay fever." As broadcast during World War II, "Big Town," Audio Archive, Internet Archive, http://www.archive.org/details/BigTown (accessed 1 June 2009).

47. Lever Brothers advertised a home economics curriculum in 1953 called "Let's Clean Up the Kitchen" based on Surf. See Advertising Series, Ayer Records. P&G produced a number of home economics curriculum packages, including "Learning About Laundering," published in 1977. The package titled "Consumer Advertising: Its Role in Bringing a Product to the Market" took as its case study Cheer detergent. See Cummings Papers.

48. Throughout the history of housework advertising, but particularly in the 1920s and 1930s, ads sometimes depicted various household products and appliances as reliable, satisfactory replacements for maids, cooks, and servants.

49. Scripts and storyboards for Ivory Snow commercial, DMB&B Archives.

50. Scripts and storyboards for Rinso Blue 1958 commercials, Murray Holland Papers, John W. Thompson Company Collection, Hartman Center for Sales, Marketing, and Advertising History, Duke University (hereafter cited as Holland Papers).

51. "Laundry Detergent," Classic TV Collection, Internet Archive. Another example of laundry magic helpers appeared in a 1960 magazine ad for Arm and Hammer detergent: "Like having a houseful of cleaning women," reads the ad,

as five miniature cleaning women with laundry baskets march up and down the page alongside a large drawing of a housewife in an apron admiring a clean pair of pants. "It conquers dirt while it pampers you." D'Arcy Collection, Communications Library, University of Illinois at Urbana Champagne (hereafter cited as D'Arcy Collection).

52. Scripts and storyboards for Rinso television and radio ads, Lever Brothers Account Files, JWT Collection; commercial in "Laundry Detergent," Classic TV Collection, Internet Archive.

53. "The Agency and the Company: How We Can Live and Prosper Together," Presentation before Al Harris' Group, 8 March 1963, DMB&B Archive.

54. Cowan, *More Work for Mother*, 177.

55. Ivory Snow ads from DMB&B Archives. In another type of appeal, During WWII, Ivory Snow advertising emphasized how its gentle formula made it ideal for extending the life of precious stockings. They ran a short-lived scare campaign about perspiration: "To help guard stockings, remember PERSPIRATION IS ACID . . . it WRECKS stockings!" reads the alarming copy in a 1942 newspaper ad.

56. Hobler, "The Triangle of Marketing Success," 137.

57. All Bounce print ads from DMB&B Archives.

58. "Laundry Detergents," Classic TV Collection, Internet Archive.

59. Steve Craig, "Madison Avenue Versus *The Feminine Mystique*: The Advertising Industry's Response to the Women's Movement," in Sherrie A. Inness, ed., *Disco Divas: Women and Popular Culture in the 1970s* (Philadelphia: University of Pennsylvania Press, 2003), 15.

60. Consultive Panel of the National Advertising Review Board, "Advertising and Women: A Report on Advertising Portraying or Directed to Women" (New York: 1975), 10, Marketing Vertical Files, J. Walter Thompson Company Collection, John W. Hartman Center for Sales, Advertising, and Marketing History, Duke University.

61. Rena Bartos Papers, J. Walter Thompson Company Collection, John Hartman Center for Sales, Advertising, and Marketing History, Duke University (hereafter cited as Bartos Papers).

62. DMB&B Archive.

63. As cited in Barbara Stern, "Literary Analysis of an Advertisement: The Commercial as 'Soap Opera,'" *Advances in Consumer Research* 18 (1991): 167.

64. All ads in *Essence* viewed as published, archived online or microfilm (see Note on Sources).

65. In an early nod to the "greening" laundry product campaigns of the 2000s, a 1991 Downy ad in *Essence* promoted a cardboard refill box, which meant "less waste building up in the environment."

66. Other laundry product brands advertised in *Essence* during this time included Bounce, Cheer, and Clorox.

67. Advertisements in *Buenhogar* viewed as published. See Note on Sources.

68. Nan Findlow Papers, J. Walter Thompson Company Collection, John Hartman Center for Sale, Advertising, and Marketing History, Duke University (hereafter cited as Findlow Papers).

69. See Bonnie Fox, "Selling the Mechanized Household: 70 Years of Ads in *Ladies Home Journal*," *Gender and Society* 4, no. 1 (1990): 29; Scanlon, *Inarticulate Longings*, 108; Denise Warren, "Commercial Liberation: What Does 'She' Mean?" *Journal of Communications* 28, no. 1 (1977–1978): 169–173.

70. Contemporary magazine ads viewed as published (see Note on Sources).

71. Christina Cheddar Berk, "P&G Will Promote 'Green' Detergent, *Wall Street Journal*, January 19, 2005, 1; Laurie Freeman, "P&G Takes the Lead with High Tech Detergents," *Advertising Age*, April 14, 1986, 3–4; Carol Hill, "Lever's Surf Detergent: Winner by a Nose," *Marketing and Media Decisions*, March 1987, 37–41; Walecia Konrad, "Tide's Quest for Liquid Success," *Madison Avenue*, June 1985, 44–47; Jennifer Lawrence, "P&G Tries New Ultra Detergents," *Advertising Age*, February 2, 1992, 1; David Moin, "Ann Taylor Loft and P&G Put Fresh Spin on Laundry," *Women's Wear Daily*, August 22, 2008, 10; Jack Neff, "Tide Coldwater," *Advertising Age*, November 7, 2005, 76.

72. Saddleton, "Tide Rolls On;" Adam Newman, "The Man of the House," *Adweek*, August 11–18, 2008, 18.

73. Anne-Christine Diaze, "The Work," *Advertising Age*, May 23, 2011, 23.

74. On the impact of social media on advertising, see Teressa Iezzi, *The Idea Writers: Copywriting in a New Media and Marketing Era* (New York: Palgrave Macmillan, 2011). Thanks to John Neuhaus for this reference. On social media and marketing to moms, see, for example, Christine Birkner, "Mom's the Word," *Marketing News*, May 15, 2011, 8; Barbra Grondin Francella, "Want to Reach Moms? Find Her on Facebook," *Convenience Store News*, January 11, 2011, 63; Pradnya Joshi, "Harnessing the Power of the Mom Blogger," *New York Times*, March 3, 2011, 3+; "Study: Stay-at-Home Moms Dominate Social Media," *Denver Business Journal*, September 6, 2009, http: www.bizjournals. com/denver/stories/2009/09/14/daily43.html (accessed May 29, 2011).

75. Tide brand's Twitter pages are also popular: Tide, Tide Loads of Hope, and Tide to Go had over 5,000 followers in June 2011. On P&G's use of social media advertising, see, for example, Bob Morris, "Proctor and Gamble Quits Soap Opera Advertising for Social Media," *Politics in the Zeros*, December 12, 2010, http://polizeros.com/2010/12/12/proctor-gamble-quits-soap-opera-advertising-for-social-media/ (accessed June 15, 2011).

76. "Marsha McRoyal," "Comments," October 27, 2010, and "Robin," "Comments," December 8, 2010, *eCorporateOffices*, October 27, 2010, http://ecorporateoffices.com/ProcterandGamble-1174 (accessed February 20, 2011). On the other hand, on a feminist discussion forum web site "Kate" posted a comment on September 23, 2010, praising the commercial: "Of course it still reinforces the idea that women are responsible for cleaning up, but at least it assumes that moms have their own lives outside of housework." Posted in response to "zelle," "Women in Advertisements," *Feminist Legal Theory*, http://femlegaltheory.blogspot.com/2010/09/women-in-advertisements.html (accessed February 20, 2011).

77. Robert Berner, "Detergents Can Be So Much More," *Business Week*, May 1, 2006, 66. Saatchi & Saatchi CEO Kevin Roberts argued that in the twenty-first century, the worn-out concept of "branding" needed to be replaced by

strategies to inspire consumer "loyalty beyond reason" rooted in a deeply personal and satisfying love for certain specific consumer products—"lovemarks." See Kevin Roberts, *Lovemarks: The Future Beyond Brands* (New York, NY: Powerhouse Books, 2004), 66.

78. Newman, "The Man of the House," 17. However, other evidence suggests women do buy more laundry products than men. For instance, the hundreds of consumer commentators on Tide's June 2011 Facebook page appeared to be overwhelmingly female.

79. Berner, "Detergent Can Be So Much More," 66; Gabrille Sandor, "Attention Advertisers: Real Men Do Laundry," *American Demographics*, March 1994, 13–14.

80. Theresa Howard, "Tide Washes Hands of Demonstration Ads and Aims for Fun," *USA Today*, May 8, 2006, B6.

81. Berner, "Detergent Can Be So Much More," S10.

82. In a different version of this commercial, a handsome African American dad comforts his toddler son, who rests his head on Dad's sweet-smelling t-shirted shoulder.

83. Claudia H. Deutsch, "A Fresh Approach to Marketing for Proctor's 'Fresh Approach to Laundry,'" *New York Times*, August 8, 2008, C7; "Kelly Ripa to Appear in New 2x Ultra Tide Advertising Campaign," PR Newswire, October 1, 2007; Elizabeth Custer, "Ad Nauseum," *MomLogic*, http://www.momlogic. com/2009/02/electrolux_kelly_ripa.php (accessed February 20, 2011); Lenore Skenazy, "That Supermom in Your Ad? Real Moms Can't Stand Her," *Advertising Age*, October 29, 2007, 20.

84. Susan J. Douglas and Meredith W. Michaels, *The Mommy Myth: The Idealization of Motherhood and How it Has Undermined Women* (New York: Free Press, 2004), 110–139. See also Susan J. Douglas, *Enlightened Sexism: The Seductive Message that Feminism's Work is Done* (New York: Henry Holt, 2010), 259–261.

85. Joyce Cohen, "Washday Blues Really Are a Thing of the Past," *USA Today*, August 8, 2003, 5D.

86. Denise DiFulco, "Luxe Laundry Rooms are Putting a New Spin on Old Chore," *Washington Post*, November 10, 2005, H1; Cohen, "Washday Blues Really Are a Thing of the Past"; and Patricia Gaylor, "Laundry List," *Kitchen & Bath Business*, January 2009, 3.

87. Elaine Wong, "How P&G Fights the Tide of Private Label," *Adweek*, June 7, 2010, 21–22.

Chapter 2

1. On early water home water systems, see Maureen Ogle, "Domestic Reform and American Household Plumbing, 1840–1870," *Winterthur Portfolio* 28, no. 1 (Spring 1993): 36, 51. On plumbing patents, new home building, and bathrooms in working-class homes, see Jacqueline Wilkie, "Submerged Sensuality: Technology and Perceptions of Bathing," *Journal of Social History* 19, no. 4

(1986): 653–654. On the siphon toilet, see Merritt Ierley, "The Bathroom: An Epic," *American Heritage* 50, no. 3 (1999): 76–82, 84. On porcelain and vitreous china fixtures, see May N. Stone, "The Plumbing Paradox: American Attitudes Towards Late Nineteenth-Century Domestic Sanitary Arrangements," *Winterthur Portfolio* 14, no. 3 (1979): 286. On built-in tubs and chrome fixtures, see Juliann Sivulka, *Stronger Than Dirt: A Cultural History of Advertising Personal Hygiene in America, 1875–1940* (New York: Humanity Books, 2001), 117–118, 169. On different kinds of early bathing receptacles, see Wilkie, "Submerged Sensuality," 650. See also Thomas C. Hubka and Judith Kenny, "Examining the American Dream: Housing Standards and the Emergence of a National Housing Culture, 1900–1930," *Perspectives in Vernacular Architecture* 13, no. 1 (2006): 46–69; Maureen Ogle, *All the Modern Conveniences: American Household Plumbing, 1840–1890* (Baltimore: Johns Hopkins University Press, 1996); Gail Caskey Winkler and Roger Moss, "How the Bathroom Got White Tiles . . . And Other Victorian Tales," *Historic Preservation* 36, no. 1 (1984): 32–35.

2. Suellen Hoy, *Chasing Dirt: The American Pursuit of Cleanliness* (New York: Oxford University Press, 1995), 59–86; Stone, "The Plumbing Paradox," 288–289.

3. Sivulka, *Stronger Than Dirt*, 112. As Lydia Martens and Sue Scott write: "Protecting the members of a domestic circle from harm has been conceived as a primary concern of the domestic practitioner, ingrained in the very meaning of homemaking and housewifery." "Under the Kitchen Surface: Domestic Products and Conflicting Constructions of Home," *Home Cultures* 3, no. 1 (2006): 42. See also Nancy Tomes, *The Gospel of Germs: Men, Women, and the Microbe in American Life* (Cambridge: Harvard University Press, 1998).

4. Advertising Series, N. W. Ayer Advertising Agency Records, Archives Center, National Museum of American History, Smithsonian Institution (hereafter cited as Advertising Series, Ayer Records).

5. All Platt's Chlorides advertisements from Business Ephemera Vertical Files, Warshaw Collection of Business Americana, Archives Center, National Museum of American History, Smithsonian Institution (hereafter cited as Business Ephemera, Warshaw Collection).

6. Warren Dotz and Jim Morton, *What a Character! 20th Century American Advertising Icons* (San Francisco, CA: Chronicle Books, 1996), 9. See also Julie Franz, "Spokescritters Speak Up from Retail Shelves," *Advertising Age*, June 9, 1986, 11–12.

7. Dotz and Morton, *What a Character!* 24.

8. Judith A. Garretson and Scot Burton, "The Role of Spokescharacters as Advertisements and Package Cues in Integrated Marketing Communications," *Journal of Marketing*, no. 4 (October 2005): 118–132.

9. Dotz and Morton, *What a Character!* 30.

10. Christine Mierau, *Accept No Substitutes: The History of American Advertising* (Minneapolis: Lerner, 2000), 76.

11. John Voight, "Mascot Makeover," *Adweek*, July 7, 2003, 20.

12. Roy Lightner Collection of Antique Advertisements, John W. Hartman Center for Sales, Advertising, and Marketing History, Duke University (hereafter cited as Lightner Collection).

13. All Spotless Cleanser ads from Advertising Series, Ayer Records.

14. Unless otherwise noted, all subsequently cited Old Dutch advertisements are from D'Arcy Collection, Communications Library, University of Illinois at Urbana Champagne (hereafter cited as D'Arcy Collection). On "house-cleaning," see Susan Strasser, *Never Done: A History of American Housework* (New York: Henry Holt, 1982, 2000), 61–63.

15. On American expectations regarding the bathroom, see Strasser, *Never Done,* 102. On the bathroom of the 1920s, see Roland Marchand, *Advertising the American Dream: Making Way for Modernity, 1920–1940* (Berkeley: The University of California Press, 1985), 125. See also Sivulka, *Stronger Than Dirt,* 161; Ellen Lupton and J. Abbott Miller, *The Bathroom, The Kitchen, and the Aesthetics of Waste* (Cambridge: MIT List Visual Arts Center, 1992), 26.

16. All Sylpho-Nathol advertisements from Advertising Series, Ayer Records.

17. Unless otherwise noted, all Sani-Flush ads from Advertising Series, Ayer Records.

18. Sani-Flush ad reproduced here from author's personal collection.

19. Marchand, *Advertising the American Dream,* 202–203.

20. Old Dutch ad reproduced here from author's personal collection.

21. Marchand, *Advertising the American Dream,* 125.

22. All Wyandot ads from Advertising Series, Ayer Records.

23. Ann McClintock discusses domestic labor and hands as fetish in Victorian England in *Imperial Leather: Race, Gender and Sexuality in the Colonial Context* (New York: Routledge, 1995), 98–100.

24. Unless otherwise noted, all Bon Ami ads from D'Arcy Collection.

25. Lightner Collection.

26. D'Arcy Collection

27. Lightner Collection.

28. In this chapter, all archival commercials from commercial compilations held and viewed at The Film and Television Archive, University of California, Los Angeles. Contemporary commercials (2009) viewed as broadcast on cable and network television (see Note on Sources).

29. Unless otherwise noted, Ajax newspaper ads from D'Arcy Collection.

30. Account Files Collection, "Boyle-Midway," J. Walter Thompson Company Collection, The John W. Hartman Center for Sales, Advertising, and Marketing History, Duke University (hereafter cited as Boyle-Midway Account Files, JWT Collection).

31. SnoBol print ads from the D'Arcy Collection.

32. D'Arcy Collection.

33. All brands of "automatic" toilet cleaner print ads from D'Arcy Collection.

34. Consultive Panel of the National Advertising Review Board, "Advertising and Women: A Report on Advertising Portraying or Directed to Women," March 1975, 11–12, Marketing Vertical Files, J. Walter Thompson Collection, John

W. Hartman Center for Sales, Advertising, and Marketing History, Duke University. Hereafter cited as "Advertising and Women" (1975).

35. Barbara Lovenhiem, "Admen Woo the Working Woman," *Sun Times*, June 17, 1978, archived in the ***Renos Bartos Papers, John W. Hartman Center for Sales, Advertising, and Marketing History, Duke University (collection hereafter cited as Bartos Papers).

36. All ads in *Essence* viewed as published, archived online or microfilm (see Note on Sources).

37. See, for example, Annie S. Barnes, "White Mistresses and African-American Domestic Workers: Ideals for Change," *Anthropological Quarterly* 66, no. 1 (1993): 22–36; Elizabeth Clark-Lewis, *Living In, Living Out: African American Domestics in Washington, D.C., 1990–1940* (Washington: Smithsonian Institution Press, 1994); Bonnie Dill, *Across the Boundaries of Race and Class: An Exploration of Work and Family Among Black Female Domestic Servants* (New York: Routledge, 1994); Brenda Clegg Grey, *Black Domestics During the Depression in New York City, 1930–1949* (New York: Garland, 1993); Susan Tucker, *Telling Memories among Southern Women: Domestic Workers and Their Employers in the Segregated South* (Baton Rouge: Louisiana State University Press, 1988).

38. David Ford, "Diane Amos: Making a Tidy Living as Pine Sol Lady," *San Francisco Chronicle*, February 15, 2002, WB4; Lorraine Fuller, "Are We Seeing Things? The Pinesol Lady and the Ghost of Aunt Jemima," *Journal of Black Studies* 32, no. 1 (2001): 120–131. On the other hand, a 2009 Pine Sol commercial plays with gender roles a bit. Amos enters a lavishly decorated, romantic bedroom. Reclining in a sultry nightgown, she admires a very handsome and young African American man, who is shirtless and sexily mopping the floor with Pine Sol. "That's the power of Pine Sol, baby," purrs Amos. However, this man is mopping the marble floor of a bedroom suite, not the bathroom.

39. Advertisements in *Buenhogar* viewed as published. See "Note on Sources."

40. Boyle-Midway Account Files, JWT Collection.

41. Author's personal collection.

42. Consultive Panel of the National Advertising Review Board, "Advertising and Women: A Report on Advertising Portraying or Directed to Women" (New York: 1975), 11, Marketing Vertical Files, J. Walter Thompson Company Collection, John W. Hartman Center for Sales, Advertising, and Marketing History, Duke University.

43. R. Stephen Craig, "The Effect of Television Day Part on Gender Portrayals in Television Commercials: A Content Analysis," *Sex Roles* 26, no. 5/6 (1992): 197–211; Thomas W. Whipple and Mary K. McManamon, "Implications of Using Male and Female Voices in Commercials: An Exploratory Study," *Journal of Advertising* 31, no. 2 (summer 2002): 79–91.

44. In a rare example of consumer criticism on Facebook of gender stereotypes in housework advertising, Scott M. Devine commented on June 15, 2011, at 11:16 a.m.: "What about new dads? Guess we don't have to do anything or we don't matter."

45. Michael McCoy, "The Greening Game," *Chemical and Engineering News*, January 26, 2009, 13.

46. Lightner Collection.
47. Garret Condon, "The Assault on Germs: Americans Wary of Unseen Dangers," *San Francisco Chronicle*, July 28, 1993, C3; Don Fernandez, "Swept Up in Need to Clean: In an Era of High Anxiety, We're Finding Comfort in the Conquest of Grime, Germs, and Untidiness," *Atlanta Journal-Constitution*, November 28, 2004, MS1; Becky Ebenkamp, "Sanitized for Your Perfection," *Brandweek*, January 9, 2006, 17; Lydia Martens and Sue Scott, "Under the Kitchen Surface: Domestic Products and Conflicting Constructions of Home," *Home Cultures* 3, no. 1 (2006): 39–82.
48. Script for "Changing Portraits: The Images of Women and Men in Advertising," Advertising Educational Foundation, 1992, Bartos Papers.
49. "Birth of a Megabrand?" *Household and Personal Products Industry*, June 1996, 61+; "Dow Chemical to Sell Unit to S.C. Johnson," *New York Times*, October 29, 1997, B4; Jack Neff, "Scrubbing Bubbles," *Advertising Age*, November 13, 2006, 10.
50. "Americans Stepping Into Dirty Showers to Get Clean," PR Newswire, March 14, 2006.
51. "Scrub the Automatic Shower Cleaner," *Consumer Reports*, November 2006, 7.
52. "Scrub-a-Dub-Dub: Why So Many Avoid Cleaning the Tub," *PR Newswire*, January 7, 2008.

Chapter 3

1. Judith Liesse, "Doughboy Pops Up for Pillsbury Mixes," *Advertising Age*, May 7, 1990, 65; "Pillsbury's Poppin' Fresh Still Piping Hot in Ad World," *U.S.A. Today*, November 6, 1995, B2.
2. Katherine Parkin, *Food is Love: Advertising and Gender Roles in Modern America* (Philadelphia: Temple University Press, 2006), 1. See also Jean Kilbourne, *Can't Buy My Love: How Advertising Changes the Way We Think and Feel* (New York: Simon and Schuster, 1999), 109: "Food has long been advertised as a way for women both to demonstrate our love and to insure its requital."
3. Meredith Abarca, *Voices in the Kitchen: Views of Food and the World from Working-Class Mexican and Mexican American Women* (College Station: Texas A&M University Press, 2006); Arlen Voski Avakian, ed., *Through the Kitchen Window: Women Writers Explore the Meanings of Food And Cooking* (Boston: Beacon Press, 1997); Anne Bower, *African American Foodways: Exploration of History and Culture* (Urbana: University of Illinois Press, 2007); Hasia R. Diner, *Hungering for America: Italian, Irish, and Jewish Foodways in the Age of Migration* (Cambridge: Harvard University Press, 2001); Lela Nargi, *Around the Table: Women on Food, Cooking, Nourishment, Love . . . and the Mothers Who Dished It Up for Them* (New York: Jeremy P. Tarcher, 2005); Psyche A. Williams-Forson, *Building Houses out of Chicken Legs: Black Women, Food, and Power* (Chapel Hill: University of North Carolina Press, 2006).
4. Leon Morse, "General Foods," *Television/Radio Age*, June 10, 1974, 27. General Foods was the second largest advertiser in the United States 1979–1980,

spending a total of $343 million. "General Foods: Multi-Product Advertising," *Magazine Age*, January 1981, 64.

5. "Kraft Timeline," 1977, Corporation Vertical Files, "Kraft," J. Walter Thompson Collection, The Hartman Center for Sales, Advertising, and Marketing History, Duke University (collection hereafter cited as Kraft Corporation Vertical Files, JWT Collection).

6. Priscilla J. Brewer, *From Fireplace to Cookstove: Technology and the Domestic Ideal in America* (Syracuse: Syracuse University Press, 2000); Harvey Levenstein, *Paradox of Plenty: A Social History of Eating in Modern America*, Revised Edition (Berkeley: University of California Press, 2003), 28; Shelley Nickles, "Preserving Women: Refrigerator Design as Social Process in the 1930s," *Technology and Culture* 43, no. 4 (2002): 693–722; Susan Strasser, *Never Done: A History of American Housework* (New York: Henry Holt, 1982, 2000), 28–29; Ann Vileisis, *Kitchen Literacy: How We Lost Knowledge of Where Food Comes From and Why We Need to Get It Back* (Washington: Island Press, 2008), 38, 43.

7. Mary Drake Mcfeely, *Can She Bake a Cherry Pie? American Women and the Kitchen in the Twentieth Century* (Amherst: University of Massachusetts Press, 2000), 98; Katherine Leonard Turner, "Buying, Not Cooking: Ready-to-Eat Food in American Urban Working-Class Neighborhoods, 1880–1930," *Food, Culture and Society* 9, no. 1 (2006): 12–39.

8. Sherrie A. Inness, *Dinner Roles: American Women and Culinary Culture* (Iowa City: University of Iowa Press, 2001), 71–87; Harvey Levenstein, *Revolution at the Table: The Transformation of the American Diet*, Revised Edition (Berkeley: University of California Press, 2003), 103–107, and Harvey Levenstein, "The American Response to Italian Food, 1880–1930," in Carole M. Counihan, ed., *Food in the U.S.A.: A Reader* (New York: Routledge, 2002); Jessamyn Neuhaus, *Manly Meals and Mom's Home Cooking: Cookbooks and Gender in Modern America* (Baltimore: Johns Hopkins University Press, 2003), 21–22; Laura Shapiro, *Perfection Salad: Women and Cooking at the Turn of the Century* (New York: Farrar, Straus, and Giroux, 1986), 72.

9. "Fortunes of a Giant," *Advertising Age*, October 29, 1962, 79+; "The History of the Wiggle," http://brands.kraftfoods.com/jello/explore/history (accessed May 27, 2009).

10. Advertising Series, N. W. Ayer Advertising Agency Records, Archive Center, National Museum of American History, Smithsonian Institute (hereafter cited as Advertising Series, Ayer Records).

11. "The History of the Wiggle," http://brands.kraftfoods.com/jello/explore/history/ (accessed May 27, 2009).

12. Neuhaus, *Manly Meals and Mom's Home Cooking*, 30–32.

13. Roy Lightner Collection of Antique Advertisements, John W. Hartman Center for Sales, Advertising, and Marketing History, Duke University (hereafter cited as Lightner Collection).

14. Domestic Advertisements Collection, J. Walter Thompson Company Collection, John W. Hartman Center for Sales, Advertising, and Marketing History, Duke University (hereafter cited as Domestic Ad Collection, JWT Collection).

15. As cited in Daniel Delis Hill, *Advertising to the American Woman 1900–1999* (Columbus: Ohio State University Press, 2002), 60.
16. *Jell-O: The Dainty Dessert*, n.d., n.p.
17. *Desserts of the World* (Le Roy: Genesee Pure Food Company, 1909), n.p.
18. Domestic Ad Collection, JWT Collection.
19. *What Mrs. Dewey Did with the New Jell-O! 48 Fascinating Recipes* (General Foods, 1933), n.p.
20. "New Jell-O Book of Surprises: Desserts, Salads" (USA: General Foods, 1930), 3, 13, 17.
21. *Mr. Gourmand's Strange Dreams*, n.d., n.p.
22. Neuhaus, *Manly Meals and Mom's Home Cooking*, 172, 293; Parkin, *Food is Love*, 35–37.
23. *A Cook's Tour with Minute Tapioca* (Orange: Minute Tapioca Company and General Foods, 1931), 3.
24. *Easy Triumphs with New Minute Tapioca* (Orange: Minute Tapioca Company and General Foods, 1934), n.p.
25. *The Calumet Book of Oven Triumphs!* (General Foods, 1934), no page; *Home Baked Delicacies Enhance the Fame of the Modern Hostess* (General Foods, 1931), n.p.
26. *30 New Recipes from the $20,000 Cookbook* (Orange: Minute Tapioca Company and General Foods, 1929), n.p.
27. *The Calumet Baking Book* (General Foods, 1931), 3.
28. *All About Home Baking* (General Foods Corporation, 1931), 10.
29. Neuhaus, *Manly Meals and Mom's Home Cooking*, 32, 169–172. See also Jennifer Horner, "Betty Crocker's Picture Cookbook: A Gendered Ritual Response to Social Crises of the Postwar Era," *Journal of Communication Inquiry* 24, no. 3 (2000): 332–345; Bridget Kinsella, "The Checkered Career of a Kitchen Classic," *Publisher's Weekly*, September 2, 1996, 34–36; Susan Marks, *Finding Betty Crocker: The Secret Life of America's First Lady of Food* (New York: Simon and Schuster, 2005); Rosyln Sigel, "After 65 Years in the Kitchen Betty Crocker is Still Strong," *Publishers' Weekly*, July 19, 1991, 23–24.
30. On radio recipe and homemaking shows, see Evelyn Birkby, *Neighboring on the Air: Cooking with the KMA Radio Homemakers* (Iowa City: University of Iowa Press, 1991); Erika Janik, "Good Morning Homemakers!" *Wisconsin Magazine of History* 90, no. 1 (2006): 4–15; Joyce Lamont, Linda Larson, and Sue Zelickson, *Joyce Lamont's Favorite Minnesota Recipes and Radio Memories* (Osceola: Voyageur Press, 2008).
31. NBC Program Information, "Kraft Radio," n.d., 1, Kraft Television Theatre Oral History Project (hereafter cited as "Kraft Radio.")
32. Untitled timeline account history of Kraft's radio broadcasting, 1957, Information Center Vertical Files, J. Walter Thompson Collection, John W. Hartman Center for Sales, Advertising, and Marketing History, Duke University (collection hereafter cited as Information Center Vertical Files, JWT Collection).
33. JWT Research Department, "The History of Miracle Whip," revised 1960, n.p., Kraft Corporation Vertical Files, JWT Collection (hereafter cited as "The History of Miracle Whip," 1960).

34. Ibid.

35. "Kraft Radio," 2.

36. "The History of Miracle Whip," 1960, n.p. Unless otherwise noted, all Miracle Whip ads from Domestic Ad Collection, JWT Collection.

37. Amy Bentley, *Eating for Victory: Food Rationing and the Politics of Domesticity* (Des Moines: University of Illinois Press, 1998); Neuhaus, *Manly Meals and Mom's Home Cooking*, 99–159; Rebecca Bolin Swenson, "Conflict in the Kitchen: Shaping the Identity of Women, Wives and Patriots on the American Home Front," *Media Report to Women* 34, no. 2 (2006): 5–14.

38. As famously identified by Betty Friedan in *The Feminine Mystique* (New York: Norton, 1963, 2001). On Dichter and food advertising, see Parkin, *Food is Love.*

39. Katherine Parkin, "Campbell's Soup and the Long Shelf Life of Traditional Gender Roles," and Erika Endrijonas, "Processed Foods from Scratch: Cooking for a Family in the 1950s," in Sherrie A. Inness, ed., *Kitchen Culture in America: Popular Representations of Food, Gender, and Race* (Philadelphia, PA: University of Pennsylvania Press, 2001).

40. "The History of Miracle Whip," 1960, n.p.

41. Ibid.

42. See Shapiro, *Something from the Oven;* and Vileisis, *Kitchen Literacy.*

43. Untitled client history, dated "about 1956," Kraft Corporation Vertical Files, JWT Collection.

44. "Kraft Commercials Stress Service to Housewife," n.d., 4, Kraft Television Theatre Oral History Project, Archive Center, National Museum of American History, Smithsonian Institute (collection hereafter cited as Kraft Television Theatre Oral History Project, document hereafter cited as "Kraft Commercials Stress Service to Housewife"). General Foods also advertised heavily on television, sponsoring popular show such as "The Goldbergs" (1949); Bob Hope specials; "I Love Lucy" in the early 1950s; and "I've Got a Secret" (1962).

45. On the clam-dip recipe, see Sylvia Lovegren, *Fashionable Food: Seven Decades of Food Fads* (New York: Macmillan, 1995), 208. On Margaret Buchen's memory of the clam dip commercial, see her unpublished manuscript, November 11, 1983, n.p., Kraft Television Theatre Oral History Project.

46. "10 Years of Kraft Television Commercials," 1967, 6–7, Kraft Television Theatre Oral History Project (document hereafter cited as "10 Years of Kraft Television Commercials").

47. "Background material for S. R. Bernstein's story on the Kraft-JWT relationship in the 1930's to 1950's as recalled (and researched) by M. W. B.," Client History, March 1964, Information Center Vertical Files, JWT Collection.

48. "10 Years of Kraft Television Commercials," 5.

49. Ibid., 24.

50. Unless otherwise noted, all Kraft archival television commercials from Kraft Historical reels, Kraft Television Theatre Oral History Project.

51. Unless otherwise noted, All Miracle Whip radio commercial scripts, Kraft Corporation Vertical Files, JWT Collection.

52. "The History of Miracle Whip," 1956, Kraft Corporation Vertical Files, JWT Collection.
53. All Merrill correspondence in Maury Holland Papers, John W. Hartman Center for Sales, Advertising, and Marketing History, Duke University.
54. Social Research Inc. for JWT, "Mayonnaise as Seen by the Housewife," 1957, 3–4, Kraft Corporation Vertical Files, JWT Collection (document hereafter cited as "Mayonnaise as Seen by the Housewife").
55. JWT Research Department, "The History of Mayonnaise," February 1960, n.p., Kraft Corporation Vertical Files, JWT Collection.
56. "The History of Miracle Whip," 1960, n.p.
57. It did point out, in passing, that "the working woman" might be especially interested in Miracle Whip: "Miracle Whip serves an admirable purpose, especially for the upper lower class housewife, the working woman, the more 'modern' (possibly careless) women who enjoy the savings the product represents, and the fact that they need not bother to spice up mayonnaise." "Mayonnaise as Seen by the Housewife," 40.
58. Unless otherwise noted, all archival commercials in the remainder of this chapter are from commercial compilations held and viewed at The Film and Television Archive, University of California, Los Angeles. Contemporary commercials (2009) viewed as broadcast on cable and network television (see Note on Sources).
59. Print ads for "Busy Day Dessert" in Lightner Collection.
60. Unless otherwise noted, all print Velveeta ads are from the Domestic Ad Collection, JWT Collection.
61. "How Kraft Used the Air," *Sponsor*, May 1952, 27.
62. "Kraft TV," 1964, 3, Kraft Television Theatre Oral History Project.
63. Thomas H. Watson, "Philosophy Pertaining to Kraft TV Commercials," May 21, 1958, no page, Kraft Television Theatre Oral History Project.
64. "10 Years of Kraft Television Commercials," 13.
65. Oral History Interview with Dorothy Holland, August 11, 1992, Tom Wiener, Kraft Television Theatre Oral History Project.
66. "For: Food and Advertising Trades," n.d., n.p., Kraft Television Theatre Oral History Project.
67. "The Courtice Recipe," *Marketing and Media Decisions*, November 1980, 60, 62.
68. Barbara Mahlman, "Watch That Wobble, See That Wiggle, Taste That Jiggle," *Madison Avenue*, January 1982, 54.
69. Lightner Collection.
70. "Women and Food," JWT presentation, 1966, 16, Information Center Vertical Files, JWT Collection (hereafter cited as "Women and Food").
71. Ibid. 18.
72. Ibid., 1, 11.
73. Ibid., 14.
74. "1971 Corporate Trade Advertising Series," letter and all cited sample ads sent to Kraft District Sales Mangers, Key Account Representatives and Salesmen, Zone Mangers, Supervisors, 1971, Information Center Vertical Files, JWT Collection.

75. Social Research Inc., "The Working Housewife," n.d., Marketing Vertical Files Collection, J. Walter Thompson Company Collection, John W. Hartman Center for Sales, Advertising, and Marketing History, Duke University (document hereafter cited as "The Working Housewife").

76. Suzanne H. McCall, "Meet the 'Workwife,'" *Journal of Marketing*, July 1977, 55.

77. "The Working Housewife," 53, 61.

78. Ibid., 59, 63.

79. Ibid., 57.

80. "The Seventies: A Marketing View," section entitled "Women Demand Change," February 1, 1971, Corporation Vertical Files, "Standard Brands, Inc.," J. Walter Thompson Company Collection, John. W. Hartman Center for Sales, Advertising, and Marketing History, Duke University (document hereafter cited as "Women Demand Change").

81. Ibid., 1, 17.

82. Jacob Ducker and Lewis Trucker, "'Women's Lib-ers' versus Independent Women: A Study Preference for Women's Roles in Advertisements," *Journal of Marketing Research* 14, no. 1 (November 1977): 474–475. See also "Research Profiles Pragmatic, Unliberated Woman Segment," *Marketing News*, May 15, 1981, 1–3.

83. "JWT Learning Series," DVD, 1977, Rena Bartos Papers, John W. Hartman Center for Sales, Advertising, and Marketing History, Duke University (source hereafter cited as "JWT Learning Series" DVD; collection hereafter cited as Bartos Papers).

84. For example, a 1979 report by the Newspaper Advertising Bureau Project circulated at the JWT agency called "Women, Work, and the Markets of the '80s" consistently labeled female consumers either "working women" or "housewives." Marketing Vertical File, J. Walter Thompson Company Collection, John W. Hartman Center for Sales, Advertising, and Marketing History, Duke University. See also Valerie Free, "The Elusive Female," *Marketing Communications*, September 1985, 33–36.

85. "JWT Learning Series" DVD; Bartos Papers.

86. As quoted by Parkin, *Food is Love*, 73–74.

87. Parkin, *Food is Love*, 21–29; 64–66; Advertising Educational Foundation presentation, "Gender Issues: Changing Roles of Women and Men in Advertising," 1992, Marketing Vertical Files Collection, J. Walter Thompson Collection, John W. Hartman Center for Sales, Advertising, and Marketing History, Duke University.

88. "Fortunes of a Giant," 31.

89. Dorren Mott and Carolyn Craig, Consumer Research Department, "Food: Fast and Easy," Good Housekeeping Institute Report, March 1987, Chicago Office Marketing Vertical File, J. Walter Thompson Company Collection, John W. Hartman Center for Sales, Advertising, and Marketing History, Duke University; Consumer Research Department, "1990 Food Trends," April 1990, Chicago Office Marketing Vertical File, JWT Collection.

90. Unless otherwise noted, all Cool Whip print ads are from the Domestic Ad Collection, JWT Collection.

91. *It's Dessert Time!* (White Plains: General Foods, 1953), 33; *Jell-O Gelatin Recipes Plain or Festive* (General Foods, 1961), 3; *Jell-O Pudding Ideabook* (General Foods, 1968, 1974), 1; *The New Joys of Jell-O* (General Foods, 1979), n.p.; *Easy Home Desserts* (General Foods, 1979), 2.

92. Contemporary Cool Whip ads from *Good Housekeeping* magazine (see Note on Sources).

93. Carla Marinucci, "Male Bashing: Despite Men's Changing Roles, It's Still Politically Chic to Ridicule Them in Ads," *Chicago Tribune*, February 15, 1989, 15; Erica Scharrer, D. Daniel Kim, Ke-Ming Lin, and Zixu Liu, "Working Hard or Hardly Working? Gender, Humor, and the Performance of Domestic Chores in Television Commercials," *Mass Communication and Society* 9, no. 2 (2006): 215–328.

94. *The New Joys of Jell-O* (White Plains: General Foods, 1975), 93.

95. "General Foods Annual Report," 1986, Corporation Vertical Files, "General Foods," J. Walter Thompson Company Collection, John W. Hartman Center for Sales, Advertising, and Marketing History, Duke University.

96. All ads in *Essence* viewed in online archives of the magazine or on microfilm (see Note on Sources).

97. "Kool-Aid Objectives," April 1973, Caroline Jones Papers, Archive Center, National Museum of American History, Smithsonian Institute.

98. Mahlman, "Watch That Wobble," 55.

99. *Behind the Scenes: The Advertising Process at Work*, VHS, directed by Dick Young (New York: The Advertising Educational Foundation, 1990).

100. "Speech for President of Kraft USA," November 1991, Kraft Television Theatre Oral History Project. A 2008 study of Spanish-language commercials bears out his statement that the portrayal of women as mothers is a central component of such advertising. See Marcelo Royo-Vela, "Adaptation of Marketing Activities to Cultural and Social Context: Gender Role Portrayals and Sexism in Spanish Commercials," *Sex Roles* 58, 5/6 (2008): 379–390.

101. *Buenhogar* ads viewed as published (see Note on Sources).

102. Sonia Reyes, "Kraft Initiative Woos Asian American Moms," *Brandweek*, July 25–August 1, 2005, 10.

103. *Kraft's Main Dish Cookbook* (Kraft, 1970), n.p.

104. Unless otherwise cited, all Kraft print ads in remainder of chapter from the Domestic Ad Collection, JWT Collection.

105. Contemporary commercials viewed as aired (see Note on Sources).

106. Kraft Singles, June 7, 2011, 9:04 a.m. post, *Kraft Singles*, https://www.facebook.com/home.php#!/KraftSingles?sk=wall (accessed June 16, 2011).

107. "Case Study: Kraft and PR Heat Up Mac & Cheese Facebook Fan Page for New Product Launch, With Explosive Results," *PR Newswire*, February 7, 2011. For some brands, including Kraft's Oreo brand, Facebook actually attracts more consumers than the brand's website. Jack Neff, "What Happens When Facebook Trumps Your Brand Site?" *Advertising Age*, August 23, 2010, 2.

108. "Kraft Singles Debuts 'Smiles Under a Single' with Jonas Brothers Fans at the World Premiere of 'Jonas Brothers: The 3D Concert Experience,'" press release, www.kraftfoodscompany.com/MediaCenter.

109. Becky Ebenkamp and Todd Wasserman, "Kraft Throws Online Video, Cat Cora into Marketing Mix," *Brandweek*, September 26, 2006, no page.

110. Aaron Bar, "Kraft Giving Moms a Hug," *Adweek*, September 14, 1998, 2. On the nickname "Mother Kraft," see Peter Oberlink, "The New Kraftsmen," *Madison Avenue*, January 1987, 32.

111. Emily Bryson, "Kraft Tests Recipe for Selling in a Recession," *Advertising Age*, November 10, 2008, 20. A 2009 commercial for Velveeta emphasized its economy: a mom in the supermarket slices various products in half with a chainsaw until she gets to the cheese counter and sees the value of a large block of Velveeta, as compared to cheddar.

112. J. M. Fenster, "The Woman Who Invented the Dishwasher," *American Heritage Invention and Technology Magazine* 15, no. 2 (1999), 55.

113. Rachel Dickinson, "A Machine to Wash Dishes—Gently," *Christian Science Monitor*, September 7, 1999, 22; Strasser, *Never Done*, 279.

114. Old Dutch ad from Lightner Collection; Spotless Cleanser ad from Advertising Series, Ayer Records; Gold Dust ad (doing the dishes) from "Ivory Project: Advertising Soap in America, 1838–1998," Archive Center, National Museum of American History, Smithsonian, http://americanhistory.si.edu/archives/ Ivory (accessed 7/26/06); Gold Dust ad, author's private collection.

115. "History of Lux Flakes, 1916–1951," n.d., n.p., Account Files Collection, "Lever Brothers," J. Walter Thompson Company Collection, The John W. Hartman Center for Sales, Advertising, and Marketing History, Duke University (collection hereafter cited as Lever Brothers Account Files, JWT Collection; document hereafter cited as "History of Lux Flakes").

116. All Lux print ads from the Domestic Ad Collection, JWT Collection.

117. "Through coupon tests, the J. Walter Thompson agency discovered that the most effective headlines for Lux dishwashing soap were 'Do Women with Maids Have Lovelier Hands?' and 'Need Your Hands Say 'I Have No Maid?'" Roland Marchland, *Advertising the American Dream: Making Way for Modernity, 1920–1940* (Berkeley: University of California Press, 1985), 205.

118. All Super Suds ads from D'Arcy Masius Benton and Bowles Archive, John W. Hartman Center for Sales, Advertising, and Marketing History, Duke University (hereafter cited as DMB&B Archive).

119. All Ivory ads from Lightner Collection.

120. DMB&B Archive.

121. Creative Staff Meeting, "Mr. Day Presiding," 25 May 1932, Lever Brothers Account Files, JWT Collection.

122. Untitled Lux account history, Lever Brothers Account Files, JWT Collection, n.p. (hereafter cited as "Lux Account History").

123. Kathy M. Newman, *Radio Active: Advertising and Consumer Activism, 1935–1947* (Berkeley: University of California Press, 2004), 33–35.

124. JWT Research Department, "1923 Questionnaire by Mail: Lux for Dishwashing," Lever Brothers Account Files, JWT Collection.

125. "History of Lux Flakes," n.p. See also "Housewives' Hands," *The Science News-Letter*, October 17, 1953, 246. However, the authors of this study recommended using rubber gloves, rather than a particular brand of soap. Naturally this solution was dismissed in the very few dishwashing ads that even mentioned rubber gloves, like the housewife in the 1936 Ivory ad whose bulky rubber gloves cause havoc in the dishpan, as she exclaims to Friend in Hat: "Horrors! There goes another dish . . . these slippery rubber gloves!" In another rare depiction of rubber gloves in the dishpan, a 1965 Ivory Liquid ad depicted gloves as completely unnecessary: "To prove Ivory Liquid's mildness, Mrs. McCausland has washed dishes for 30 days with one wearing gloves. Can you tell which one?" Domestic Ad Collection, JWT Collection.

126. Artherton W. Hobler, "The Triangle of Marketing Success" Mss. (1970s), 135, 133, DMB&B Archive.

127. Unless otherwise noted, all Ivory Snow Ads from the DMB&B Archive.

128. "Case Report on Lux Liquid Detergent," March 29, 1956, n.p., Lever Brothers Account Files, JWT Collection.

129. Ibid.

130. Lux Liquid print ads from Lever Brothers Account Files, JWT Collection.

131. Lux Liquid television commercial scripts from Dan Seymour Papers, J. Walter Thompson Company Collection, John W. Hartman Center for Sales, Advertising, and Marketing History, Duke University (collection hereafter cited as Seymour Papers).

132. Strasser, *Never Done*, 279.

133. Dawn print ads from DMB&B Archive.

134. Palmolive print ads from Lightner Collection.

135. "Call Report Meeting," July 29, 1964, n.p., Seymour Papers; Lever Brothers— Lux Liquid memo, July 24, 1964, n.p., Seymour Papers.

136. Domestic Ad Collection, JWT Collection.

137. "Case Report on Lux Liquid Detergent," around 1956, n.p., Lever Brothers Account Files, JWT Collection.

138. "Lux Dishwashing Telephone Survey," August 19, 1971, Information Center Vertical Files, JWT Collection.

139. Lightner Collection.

140. Hill, *Advertising to the American Woman 1900–1999*, 64.

141. Nan Findlow Papers, J. Walter Thompson Company Collection, John Hartman Center for Sales, Advertising, and Marketing History, Duke University.

142. The following two Dawn commercials from "Ad View," Duke University Special Collections, http://library.duke.edu/digitalcollections/adviews/ (accessed September 1, 2010).

143. 1989 and 1990s *Good Housekeeping* ads viewed as published (see "Note on Sources").

144. "Dawn," http://www.dawn-dish.com/en_US/savingwildlife/home.do (accessed October 4, 2009); Andrew Adam Newman, "Tough on Crude Oil, Soft on Ducklings," *New York Times*, September 25, 2009, B6.

Chapter 4

1. "Marketing Plan," 1959, n.p., Account Files Collection, "Boyle-Midway," J. Walter Thompson Company Collection, John W. Hartman Center for Advertising, Sales, and Marketing History, Duke University (collection hereafter cited as Boyle-Midway Account Files, JWT Collection; document hereafter cited as "Marketing Plan").

2. Regina Blaszczyk, *American Consumer Society, 1865–2005: From Hearth to HDTV* (Wheeling: Harlan Davidson Inc., 2005), 38, 39, 45; Winifred Gallagher, *House Thinking: A Room-By-Room Look At How We Live* (New York: HarperCollins, 2006), 65; Katherine C. Grier, *Culture and Comfort: People, Parlors, and Upholstery, 1850–1930* (Amherst: University of Massachusetts Press, 1988), 24–25; James A. Jacobs, "Social and Spatial Change in the Postwar Family Room," *Perspectives in Vernacular Architecture* 13, no. 1 (2006): 70–72, 79; Robert Lewis, "Domestic Theater: Parlor Entertainment as Spectacle, 1840–1880," *European Contributions to American Studies* 44 (2000): 48–62; Russell Lynes, "The Parlor," *American Heritage* 14, no. 6 (October 1963): 54–101; Annemarie Money, "Material Culture and the Living Room," *Journal of Consumer Culture* 7, no. 3 (2007): 355–377; Talya Rechavi, "A Room for Living: Private and Public Aspects in the Experience of the Living Room," *Journal of Environmental Psychology* 29, no. 1 (2009): 133–143; Cheryl Robertson, "Male and Female Agendas for Domestic Reform: The Middle-Class Bungalow in Gendered Perspectives," *Winterthur Portfolio* 26, no. 2/3 (1991), 124, 129; Lynn Spigel, *Make Room for TV: Television and the Family Ideal in Postwar America* (Chicago: University of Chicago Press, 1992), 39.

3. Space constraints prevent me from discussing carpet sweeper and vacuum cleaner advertising, but my research on such ads and commercials confirmed this chapter's analysis of other types of floor cleaning products.

4. Ivory ad from Roy Lightner Collection of Antique Advertisements, John W. Hartman Center for Sales, Advertising, and Marketing History, Duke University (hereafter cited as Lightner Collection); Gold Dust ad from "Ivory Project: Advertising Soap in America, 1838–1998," Archives Center, National Museum of American History, Smithsonian, http://americanhistory.si.edu/archives/Ivory (accessed May 1, 2009); S. C. Johnson *Saturday Evening Post* ad as cited in Samuel C. Johnson, *The Essence of a Family Enterprise: Doing Business the Johnson Way* (n.p.: Johnson and Johnson, 1988), 44, National Museum of American History Library, Smithsonian Institution (hereafter cited as Johnson, *The Essence of a Family Enterprise*); 1904 and 1905 S. C. Johnson Wax ads from Lightner Collection; 1918 Johnson Wax ad from Domestic Advertisements Collection, J. Walter Thompson Company Collection, John W. Hartman Center for Sales, Advertising, and Marketing History, Duke

University (hereafter cited as Domestic Ad Collection, JWT Collection); Old Dutch ads from D'Arcy Collection, Communications Library, University of Illinois Urbana-Champaign (hereafter cited as D'Arcy Collection).

5. Bon Ami ads from D'Arcy Collection. All No-Toil advertisements from Advertising Series, N. W. Ayer Advertising Agency Records, Archives Center, National Museum of American History, Smithsonian Institution (hereafter cited as Advertising Series, Ayer Records).

6. 1924 S. C. Johnson Wax ads from Lightner Collection.

7. Samoline ads from Advertising Series, Ayer Records.

8. Lydia Martens and Sue Scott, drawing on the work of anthropologist Mary Douglas, write that cleaning is a "magical practice through which consumers define boundaries that juxtapose what is of 'the self' and 'inside' and therefore safe and clean, and what is of 'the other' or 'outside' and therefore dangerous and dirty." "Under the Kitchen Surface: Domestic Products and Conflicting Constructions of Home," *Home Cultures* 3, no. 1 (2006): 43.

9. Advertising Series, Ayer Records.

10. Johnson, *The Essence of a Family Enterprise*, 47, 81. Fibber McGee also appeared in a late 1960s television commercial as a celebrity spokesman for Glo Coat, another Johnson product.

11. Domestic Ad Collection, JWT Collection.

12. Lightner Collection.

13. Wyandotte ads from Advertising Series, Ayer Records.

14. "Boyle-Midway Self-Polishing Hard Finish Floor Wax Copy Proposal," 1960, Boyle-Midway Account Files, JWT Collection.

15. "Marketing Plan," 3, 17.

16. Atherton W. Hobler, "The Triangle of Marketing Success" Mss. (1970s), 7, D'Arcy, Masius, Benton, and Bowles Archive, John W. Hartman Center for Sales, Advertising, and Marketing History, Duke University (document hereafter cited as "The Triangle of Marketing Success").

17. "Marketing Plan," 12.

18. Ibid., 37.

19. Television commercial script, 1959, Nan Findlow Papers, J. Walter Thompson Company Collection, John W. Hartman Center for Sales, Advertising, and Marketing History, Duke University (collection hereafter cited as Findlow Papers).

20. "Marketing Plan," 34, 36.

21. "'By Their Floors Ye Shall Judge Them,' admonished one floor polisher ad. 'It is written that floors are like unto a mirror, reflecting the character of the housewife.'" Roland Marchland, *Advertising the American Dream: Making Way for Modernity, 1920–1940* (Berkeley: University of California Press, 1985), 171.

22. Todd Wasserman, "Where Will the Genie Go Next?" *Brandweek*, October 17, 2005, 23.

23. Unless otherwise noted, all archival commercials from commercial compilations held and viewed at The Film and Television Archive, University of California, Los Angeles. Contemporary commercials viewed as broadcast on cable and network television (see Note on Sources).

24. D'Arcy Collection.
25. Ibid.
26. Television commercial script, Findlow Papers.
27. D'Arcy Collection.
28. This visual device continues to appear in housework advertising: A 2011 Pine Sol Lemon Fresh commercial featured a woman standing a kitchen being buried in lemons.
29. Hobler, "The Triangle of Marketing Success," 11.
30. Endust and Dust 'n Wax advertisements from D'Arcy Collection.
31. Vacuum cleaner advertising has utilized similar appeals throughout its history.
32. Unless otherwise noted, contemporary print advertisements viewed as published (see Note on Sources).
33. "Grey Roundtable," VHS, 1988, Rena Bartos Papers, J. Walter Thompson Company Collection, John Hartman Center for Sales, Advertising, and Marketing History, Duke University.
34. Domestic Ad Collection, JWT Collection.
35. All Pledge print ads, 1980–1990, are from the Domestic Ad Collection, JWT Collection.
36. *Good Housekeeping* ad from supplement sample (see Note on Sources).
37. Brian Rupp, "Pity Those Loser Mops," *Brandweek*, August 25–September 1, 2008, 60.
38. Jura Konicus, "The Seven Deadly Chores: Help is on the Way: New Stick Mops and Sponges," *The Washington Post*, January 30, 2003, H11.
39. Jack Neff, "Mops' Niche Attracting a Crowd," *Advertising Age*, June 24, 2002, 13; "Break Up With Your Old Cleaning Ways and Show Off Your Moves with Swiffer," *PR Newswire*, January 9, 2008; Vanessa Facenda, "This is One Swiffer Picker-Upper," *Brandweek*, February 11, 2008, 22.
40. Mr. Clean Celebrates 50th Anniversary," *PR Newswire*, October 16, 2008; "Mr. Clean Gets $50M Push," *Advertising Age*, August 18, 2003, 3.
41. *Mr. Clean*, http://www.mrclean.com/en_US/home.do (accessed June 17, 2011).
42. Elaine Wong, "Mr. Clean Finds Fresh Smell by Teaming With Febreze," *Brandweek*, August 11–18, 2008, 14.
43. Suellen Hoy, *Chasing Dirt: The American Pursuit of Cleanliness* (New York: Oxford University Press, 1995), 170.
44. Advertising Series, Ayer Records.
45. All ads in *Essence* viewed in online archives of the magazine or on microfilm (see Note on Sources).
46. "As germ consciousness waned during the course of the twentieth century, domestic aesthetics and self-presentation became once more prominent as aspects of cleanliness." Martens and Scott, "Under the Kitchen Surface," 43.
47. Domestic Ad Collection, JWT Collection.
48. Bryan K. Robinson and Erica Hunter, "Is Mom Still Doing it All? Reexamining Depictions of Family Work in Popular Advertising," *Journal of Family Issues* 29 (2008): 472.

49. As quoted in Jack Neff, "High-Tech Lines Refresh Stale Air-Care Segment," *Advertising Age*, June 28, 2004, 12.
50. As Stuart Ewan writes, Lysol advertising beginning in the 1920s "divided the house into an assemblage of minutely defined dangers, so mothers were told that they should be aware that even 'the doorknobs threaten [children] with disease. Indeed, family safety and survival were at stake for the mother who had become the buyer and dispenser of goods." Stuart Ewan, *Captains of Consciousness: Advertising and the Social Roots of the Consumer Culture* (New York: McGraw Hill, 1976), 170.
51. Sarah Ellison, "P&G Campaign to Push Swiffer Vacuum Cleaner," *Wall Street Journal*, September 8, 2004, B3; Kevin O'Rourke, "Three Rules for Cleaning Up in the Household Cleaners Aisle," *Drug Store News*, December 13, 1999, 84.
52. Jack Neff, "With Glade Cleaner, SCJ Eyes Hispanics," *Advertising Age*, May 17, 2004, 10.
53. Sean Mehegan, "Waxing Odiferous," *Brandweek*, March 31, 1997, 18–19. See also Pam Weisz, "Dial Looks to Undercut Boutique Air Fresheners with Upscale Renuzit," *Brandweek*, July 24, 1995, 16.
54. Bob Garfield, "Glade's New Ads Rise Above Usual Stench," *Advertising Age*, May 12, 1997, 89.
55. Deborah Ball Sarah Ellison, and Janet Adam, "Just What You Need! It Takes a Lot of Marketing to Convince Consumers What They're Lacking," *Wall Street Journal*, October 28, 2004, B1.
56. See Eleftheria Parpis, "She's in Charge," *Adweek*, October 6–13, 2008, 38.

Conclusion

1. John Richardson Thayer, "The Attitudes of Columbus Housewives Toward Television Advertising," M.A. thesis, Ohio State University, 1952, 39.
2. D'Arcy Masius Benton and Bowles Archive, John W. Hartman Center for Sales, Advertising, and Marketing History, Duke University.
3. "What It's Like at a P&G Agency: An Insider's Report," *Printer's Ink*, January 25, 1963, 9.
4. In a similar 1960 study, housewives interviewed by a graduate student reported basically favorable views toward advertising especially television commercials and newspaper advertisements. Hamilton Herbert, "An Investigation of Advertising and Interpersonal Sources of Influence Relating to Housewives' Everyday Marketing Changes," M.A. thesis, University of Chicago, 1960, 20. For an earlier study about housewives' individual perceptions of advertising, see Henry C. Link, "A New Method of Testing Advertising Effectiveness," *Harvard Business Review* (January 1933): 165–177.
5. Consultive Panel of the National Advertising Review Board, "Advertising and Women: A Report on Advertising Portraying or Directed to Women" (New York: 1975), 11, Marketing Vertical Files, J. Walter Thompson Company Collection, John W. Hartman Center for Sales, Advertising, and Marketing History, Duke University.

6. Alice Courtney and Thomas Whipple, "Consumer and Practitioner Evaluations of Alternative Role Portrayals in Television Advertising," n.d., n.p., Rena Bartos Papers, J. Walter Thompson Company Collection, John Hartman Center for Sales, Advertising, and Marketing History, Duke University (collection hereafter cited as Bartos Papers). See also Stephen Brown, Adel El-Ansary, and Nancy Darsey, "The Portrayal of Women in Advertising: An Overlooked Area of Societal Marketing," *Academy of Marketing Science Journal*, 4, no. 3 (1976): 577–604; Lois Geraci Ernst, "Advertising to Women: It's Not the Game it Used to Be," *Communiqué* 57, no. 3 (March 1976): 14; William Lundstrom, Donald Sciglimpa, "Women in Advertisements: Retrospect and Prospect," *Journal of Advertising* (Summer 1979): 37; Cyndee Miller, "Liberation for Women in Ads," Marketing News, August 17, 1992, 1; "New Generation's Advent Means Marketing Change," *Marketing News*, May 1978, 8; Thomas Whipple and Alice Courtney, "How to Portray Women in TV Commercials," *Journal of Advertising Research* 20, no. 2 (April 1980): 53.

7. See, for example, a D'Arcy Masius Benton and Bowles 1980 study, as discussed in "Large Numbers of Husbands Buy Household Products, Do Housework," *Marketing News*, October 2, 1980, 1–3.

8. "Challenge to Congress: NOW's Bill of Rights for Homemakers," *Ms.*, October 1979, 83–84. See also "Occupation Homemakers: A Symposium," *Ms.*, May 1977, 91–94. On Second Wave feminist analysis of housework that emphasized the home and housework as, solely, a place of oppression, see, for example, Stacy Gillis and Joanne Hollows, "Introduction," in *Feminism, Domesticity, and Popular Culture*, ed. Stacy Gillis Hollows (New York: Routledge, 2009); Shelley Mallett, "Understanding Home: A Critical Review of the Literature," *The Sociological Review* 52, no. 1 (2004): 75–76; and Lydia Martens, "Feminism and the Critique of Consumer Culture, 1950–1970," in Gillis and Hollows, *Feminism, Domesticity, and Popular Culture*. For examples of this type of Second Wave analysis, see especially Ellen Malos, ed. *The Politics of Housework* (New York: Schocken Books, 1980). See also Jessie Bernard, "The Paradox of the Happy Marriage," in Vivian Gornick and Barbara K. Moran, eds., *Woman in Sexist Society: Studies in Power and Powerlessness* (New York: Basic Books, 1971); Marlene Dixon, "The Rise of Women's Liberation," in Betty Roszak and Theodore Roszak, eds., *Masculine/Feminine: Readings in Sexual Mythology and the Liberation of Women* (New York: Harper and Row, 1969); Linda Gordon, "Functions of the Family," in Leslie B. Tanner, ed., *Voices From Women's Liberation* (New York: Signet, 1971); Jane O'Reilly, "The Housewife's Moment of Truth," in Francine Klagsbrun, ed., *The First Ms. Reader* (New York: Warner Books, 1973). For Betty Friedan's discussion of housework, see *The Feminine Mystique* (New York: Norton, 1963), 237–257. I should note that Friedan's analysis followed Simone de Beauvoir's in *The Second Sex*. See Andrea Veltman, "The Sisyphean Torture of Housework: Simone de Beauvoir and Inequitable Divisions of Domestic Work in Marriage," *Hypatia* 19, no. 3 (2004): 121–143. For a recent and thoughtful discussion of the real-life impact of Friedan's work, see Stephanie Coontz, *A Strange Stirring: The Feminine Mystique and American Women at the Dawn of the 1960s* (New York: Basic Books, 2011).

9. Arlie Russell Hoschild, *The Second Shift* (New York: Penguin, 1989, 2003), 13. For a more recent analysis that reaches some of the same conclusions regarding gender and home life, see for example Kathleen Gerson, *The Unfinished Revolution: How a New Generation is Shaping Family, Work, and Gender in America* (New York: Oxford University Press, 2010).

10. Beverly Gordon, "Woman's Domestic Body: The Conceptual Conflation of Women and Interiors in the Industrial Age," *Winterthur Portfolio* 31, no. 4 (Winter 1996): 281.

11. William J. Lundstrom and Donald Sciglimpaglia, "Sex Role Portrayals in Advertising," *Journal of Marketing* 41, no. 3 (1977): 72, 78.

12. "Ads Glorifying Career 'Superwomen' Can Alienate Full-Time Homemakers," *Marketing News*, May 1981, 1–2; Rena Bartos, "What Women Like and Don't Like in Ads," *Advertising Age*, March 1982, M2–M3; John Ford and Michael LaTour, "Differing Reactions to Female Role Portrayals in Advertising," *Journal of Advertising Research* (September/October, 1993): 42; John Frisbie and Lawrence Wortzel, "Women's Role Portrayal Preferences in Advertisements: An Empirical Study," *Journal of Marketing* (October, 1974): 41–46; Lori Kesler, "Marketing to Women: Behind the Wheel of a Quiet Revolution," *Advertising Age*, July 26, 1982, M; Margaret Maples, "Why Marketers Are Turning Away from the 'Total Woman,'" *Marketing Communications*, June 1982, 13.

13. Beth Hentges, Jo Ann Meier, and Robert Bartsch, "The Effects of Race, Gender, and Bias on Linking of Commercials with Perceived Stereotypes," *Current Research in Social Psychology* 13, no. 6 (2007): 71.

14. As quoted in Lisa Belkin, "You Want it Clean? You Clean It!" *New York Times*, April 9, 2006, S1+.

15. Barbara Ehrenreich, "Maid to Order," *Harper's Magazine*, April 2000, 59–71.

16. In 1961, Betty Jane Stearns responded to ad makers' dualistic thinking, writing in "Five Fallacies About Women," *Journal of Marketing* 25, no. 5 (1961): 52: "Is it not possible that the women who work (some nineteen million of them) have great interest in new recipes and that many of them do not think of themselves in a housedress?"

17. "Grey Roundtable," VHS, 1988, Bartos Papers.

18. See, for example, Kate Allison Granju, "Working Moms," March 17, 2010, *Babble*, http://www.babble.com/CS/blogs/homework/archive/2010/03/17; "A. Jeffry," "Men Do House Cleaning Too!" May 14, 2007, *SocyBerty*, http://socyberty.com/society/men-do-house-cleaning-too/; Gwen Sharpe, "Women Take Joy in Cleaning," March 8, 2008, *Sociological Images*, http://thesocietypages.org/socimages/2008/04/08/home-made-simple-squad-women-take-joy-in-cleaning; "Swiffer, Pine-Sol, and the Brilliant Exploitation of Women's Fantasies about Housework," November 27, 2010, *Posterous*, http://thinkbrandfirst.posterous.com/swiffer-pine-sol-and-the-brilliant-exploitati; Lisa Wade, "If Only Women Spent Less Time Cooking," March 10, 2008, *Sociological Images*, http://thesocietypages.org/socimages/2008/03/10/if-only-women-spent-less-time-cooking; "zelle," "Women in Advertisements," *Feminist Legal Theory*, http://femlegaltheory.blogspot.com/2010/09/women-in-advertisements.html (all sites acc. February 20, 2011).

19. SarahMC, "Mom Will Clean It Up! A Rant," August 25, 2010, *The Pursuit of Harpyness,* http://www.harpyness.com/2010/08/25/mom-will-clean-it-up-a-rant/ (accessed February 20, 2011).

20. "LMN," "Comments," August 26, 2010, *The Pursuit of Harpyness,* http://www.harpyness.com/2010/08/25/mom-will-clean-it-up-a-rant/ (accessed February 20, 2011).

21. "JennyK," "Comments," August 25, 2010, *The Pursuit of Harpyness,* http://www.harpyness.com/2010/08/25/mom-will-clean-it-up-a-rant/ (accessed February 20, 2011).

22. Laura33, "Comments," posted in response to Laura Garfinkle, "Mom the Moron," *Washington Post,* May 11, 2009, http://voices.washingtonpost.com/parenting/2009/05/mom_the_moron.html (accessed February 20, 2011).

23. Adam Newman, "The Man of the House," *Adweek,* August 11–August 18, 2008, 17.

Note on Sources

1. Guy Cook, *The Discourse of Advertising Second Edition* (New York: Routledge, 1992, 2001), 42. On the difficulties of analyzing commercials specifically, see also Alice Courney and Thomas Whipple, *Sex Stereotyping in Advertising* (Lexington: D.C. Heath and Company, 1983), 15.

2. Jason Guerrasio, "Prelinger Archive Finds a New Home," *The Independent Film and Video Monthly* 25, no. 9 (2002): 9–10; Jim Regan, "Ephemeral Films, Resurrected on the Web," *The Christian Science Monitor* (March 15, 2006): 25.

3. Jennifer Bailey Woodard and Teresa Mastin, "*Essence* and its Treatment of Stereotypical Images of Black Women," *Journal of Black Studies* 36, no. 2 (November 2005): 266.

4. Teresa Mastin, "Product Purchase Decision-Making Behavior and Gender Role Stereotypes: A Content Analysis of Advertisements in *Essence* and *Ladies' Home Journal,* 1990–1999," *The Howard Journal of Communication* 15 (2004): 236.

Index